BUYING

RETAIL

IS

STUPID!

D1413943

Second Edition

Published by
Newmark Management Institute
18345 Ventura Boulevard, Suite 314
Tarzana, CA 91356

Printed by O'Neil Data Systems, Inc.
Los Angeles, CA 90025

Cover designed by Steve Gussman

Library of Congress Catalog Number 90-60100

ISBN: 093276701X

Printed in the United States of America

Second Printing

BUYING

RETAIL

IS

STUPID!

By

TRISHA CRUMLEY
DEBORAH NEWMARK
BONNIE CUNNINGHAM

ACKNOWLEDGEMENTS

David, my loving husband and soulmate, I dedicate this book to you and thank you for: understanding my zealotry, rarely complaining about being the chef or having "reservations" for dinner, listening to "computerese" instead of sweet nothings, talking me out of throwing my computer out the window, and your patience on your birthday when you had no hot water for your shower because I forgot to pay the gas bill (Oops!). Your inspiration and sense of humor contributed infinitely to my portion of this endeavor.

Kingsley, I also dedicate this book to you for always being there and for being my support system no matter where life has taken us.

Special thanks go to my partners, friends and family for their insight and patience, especially Tawny, Damon and Mr. Hobbes.

– Trisha Crumley

I dedicate this book to my greatest fans:

My husband, partner and closest friend, Jerry, who encouraged me to become an author and supported me throughout the project.

My mom and dad, Anne and Harry, who taught me it was more important to get along with people than to get A's on my report card.

My older sister, Marcia, who taught me class and how to shop with style.

My younger sister, Gail, who taught me to feel from my heart.

And my younger brother Steve, who taught me that anyone can do anything if they really put their mind to it.

– Deborah Newmark

I dedicate this book to my co-authors, Trisha and Deborah, for their endless enthusiasm and commitment to putting together a quality product. I also dedicate this book to their husbands, David and Jerry, for their vision and support. Last but not least, I dedicate this book to my partner in life, Jim, for his love and sense of humor which kept me going through the hard times.

– BONNIE CUNNINGHAM

TABLE OF CONTENTS

vii

TABLE OF CONTENTS

TABLE OF CONTENTS

FOREWORD

The three intrepid authors of BUYING RETAIL IS STUPID collaborated on this book for reasons which are shared in many ways by the entire buying public. Prices are going up, up, up! And they, like most of us, have felt pressed for time and money. The family budget is being stretched and finding the right thing at the right price can be time consuming, stressful and frequently disappointing.

What started out as three women's attempt to pool information about stores known to each of them for their great bargains, turned into a two year research and writing project. As they became more and more excited by the tremendous savings available through discount shopping, Trisha Crumley (Ph.D. shopper), Deborah Newmark (specialty merchandiser), and Bonnie ("I hate to shop") Cunningham, took to the streets in earnest! The result is the most comprehensive guide to discount shopping in Southern California. The book includes over 1,900 stores and services where you can buy almost EVERYTHING from A to Z—appliances, art work, cars, cellular phones, clothes, furniture, groceries, jewelry, luggage, musical instruments, pets, stereos, travel services, wallpaper, zippers—and at savings from 20 to 80% off retail prices.

The alliance of the professional shopper, the expert merchandiser, and the lady who hates to shop, has resulted in a unique tool, guaranteed to save you time and save you money as you discover the joys of discount shopping. There is no doubt that, when you use BUYING RETAIL IS STUPID, you will marvel at the great buys you find and the ease with which it happens.

Purchasing this book was a smart decision. It is easy to use, and you will get back double (or more) the price of the book with your first purchase or when you use your first BUYING RETAIL IS STUPID discount coupon. And with each subsequent purchase, your savings will grow and grow. As you use the book, write to us and let us know if you, too, agree with the three talented, clever women who wrote it, that BUYING RETAIL IS (Indeed) STUPID.

Gerald Newmark
Publisher
Newmark Management Institute

INTRODUCTION

We agree with everything our Publisher said in his Foreword about how great the book is and how clever and talented we, the authors, are. As you can see, in our group, we prefer "honest arrogance to false humility." Now that you know a little about us, we'd like to introduce you to the content and organization of the book and then suggest how you can realize the maximum benefit from it.

ORGANIZATION AND CONTENT

BUYING RETAIL IS STUPID is devoted to discount shopping in the Southern California area, primarily Los Angeles county, but also with Orange, Riverside, and San Bernardino counties represented. Additional stores are included from many other places such as Palm Springs, Barstow, Oxnard and San Diego. The last section is devoted to <u>discount catalog</u> firms from all over the United States. We decided to include <u>discount catalogs</u> so that you could engage in <u>discount shopping</u> beyond the borders of Southern California and without leaving your home. "Catalog Buying" has become very popular because it is convenient, fun, and cost effective.

In each section of the book, stores are described with enough information to give you a good feel for what each one has to offer and how it operates. All sections include many stores that offer items for sale that you would never find in a shopping mall. Some stores specialize and so offer a tremendous selection with great prices. Others offer additional discounts for volume purchases.

BUYING RETAIL IS STUPID has something for everyone. Sure, the budget conscious can find $300 suits for under $90 and other great buys for less than $25, but you can also find $1600 suits for $600. Some stores offer terrific bargains in very modest, low overhead facilities, but you'll also be pleasantly surprised by the first class surroundings and service in many of the stores. Some stores will even become your favorites that you will visit for years to come.

USING THE BOOK

The Table of Contents and alphabetical Store Index make it easy to locate exactly what you are looking for. The process is basically the same whether you are interested in "catalog shopping" or in finding the best price at the nearest store.

Let's say you are looking for bathroom tile. If you turn to the Table of Contents, you'll find ceramic tiles under the Building and Remodeling section. If you have a specific store in mind, refer to the alphabetical store index to find the page number. We suggest you call the store to verify location, hours, merchandise availability and price before making the trip. These things do change.

Review the catalogs in the Table of Contents for the merchandise that interests you and then write for your free (in most cases) catalogs. You will have a lot of fun going through them when they arrive. And don't miss sending for your free U.S. Government Books publication and the Consumer Services Guide. They are rich in consumer information which will save you time, money, and frustration, and will guide you to a healthier life.

DISCOUNT COUPONS

Don't forget the BUYING RETAIL IS STUPID coupons located in the back of the book. Every store designated with double asterisks will give you an additional percentage off their regular discount prices upon presentation of a BUYING RETAIL IS STUPID discount coupon.

THE IDEAL GIFT

Finally, think about BUYING RETAIL IS STUPID as an ideal gift because it fits everyone and everyone can use it—friend, relative, business associate, student—anyone you want to remember you as they save money and have fun with discount shopping throughout the year.

So, "**Good Shopping** and **Happy Savings**."

Trisha Crumley
Deborah Newmark
Bonnie Cunningham

A NOTE FROM HUSBANDS OF THE AUTHORS

Behind every successful woman, there is a husband at home cheering. When our wives first came up with the idea of joining forces to prepare a new, expanded, computerized BUYING RETAIL IS STUPID, we said, "Wow! Go for it."

Now, several research and writing years later, how do we feel about our initial decision to encourage them?

Notwithstanding that:

- We often eat alone or have a pizza delivered (as an alternative to going hungry).
- Social engagements are often cancelled or not accepted (they are busy writing or meeting).
- Thousands of dollars are spent/saved on bargain shopping (they are practicing what they preach).

We are still excited by their project because:

- They are very enthusiastic and have had much fun writing the book (thus they are more fun to be around, during the limited time we have with them), and
- The book is terrific and will make a real contribution to saving people time and money

All in all, we are not sorry we encouraged them to undertake this project. We are glad they have completed it. We look forward to it becoming a best seller. And, who knows? We may even learn to enjoy the role of "house husbands."

David Crumley
Jerry Newmark
Jim Jollett

Authors' Response to Husbands' Note

Seriously, we wish to acknowledge the contribution by our husbands to the research, writing and editing of this book. Without their help and guidance, there is no question that the book would have been much, much better.

To Our Readers

We want to hear from YOU! If you know of any other great discount businesses not already included in this book, please send us their name, address and telephone number. We'd like to include them in future editions of Buying Retail Is Stupid! And if you have any comments about any of the shops listed in this book, we'd like to hear those, too. This book is for YOU. Please write to us at Buying Retail Is Stupid!, 18345 Ventura Boulevard, Suite 314, Tarzana, CA 91356. Also, you can order additional copies of the book for yourself, friend, family, and for business associates by simply completing the order form in the back of the book. We look forward to hearing from you.

Editorial Note

The information in this book has been compiled to the best of our ability. Although we have visited and/or contacted almost all the stores, we have relied principally on data supplied by the businesses themselves. We are not responsible for any misinformation, or if a store has closed, moved or changed policies since publication. This book is intended solely as a guide and does not imply endorsement of any business.

LEGEND

ADDITIONAL LOCATIONS

Wherever any of the listed stores has from one to five other locations in Southern California, the cities and the telephone numbers have been included following the description of the store. Where any store has six or more additional locations, only the number of locations is indicated. In this case, please consult your local telephone directory for a store located near you.

CREDIT CARD ABBREVIATIONS*

AE =	American Express	MC =	MasterCard
DC =	Diners Club	OPT =	Optima
DISC =	Discover	V =	Visa

* Other forms of payment are also listed if a vendor doesn't accept credit cards.

STORES ACCEPTING COUPONS

Stores that accept BUYING RETAIL IS STUPID discount coupons are designated by double asterisks (**) placed at the end of the store name.

ANTIQUES & COLLECTIBLES

THE ANTIQUE CLOCK SHOP
1060 Hamner Ave.
Norco, CA 91760
714/736-9598
HOURS: MON-FRI: 8:30-5
CREDIT CARDS: CASH OR CHECKS ONLY

At The Antique Clock Shop you will find over 100 elegant antique clocks for sale. The owner, John Cox, has turned his hobby into a business. As antique clocks in working condition are very expensive, Mr. Cox buys old clocks in need of repair. After working his magic, the clock is placed for sale in the store. Because of the low prices paid originally for the clocks, you'll find the prices far below what you would pay in an antique or jewelry store. If you have an antique clock in need of repair, John Cox's repair work is first-rate. So if you are looking for an antique clock, this is the place to start!

ANTIQUE HOUSE
2865 Foothill Blvd.
La Crescenta, CA 91214
818/957-3166
HOURS: TUES-THUR, SAT: 10-6   FRI: 10-9   SUN: 12-5
CREDIT CARDS: DC, DISC, MC, V

You'll save money and be amazed at the buys in antiques here. There are 3,000 square feet filled with lovely turn-of-the-century American Oak pieces, country pine imports from Denmark, elegant mahogany and walnut from 1860 to 1930, European and American period pieces. You'll find prices between 20 to 40% less than you can expect at most antique stores. You can spend hours looking over quality antique furniture, art, sterling, cut glass, primitives, glassware, trunks, quilts, books, jewelry, China, lighting, clocks, mirrors, and more. Delivery and shipping services are available. They offer full service antique restoration and repair, and quality consignments are accepted. Antique House will buy one piece or your entire estate. For your convenience, they have a lay away plan (4 month maximum) and instant financing on approved credit.

COLLECTOR'S EYE
18564 Sherman Way
Reseda, CA 91335
818/996-3100
HOURS: MON-SAT: 10:30-6:30
CREDIT CARDS: AE, MC, V

This is definitely one of our favorites. Walking into the Collector's Eye is like walking through a rainbow and finding the pot of gold. All of their elegantly displayed vintage jewelry is arranged by colors and/or style. You might find an antique vanity draped in pearl necklaces, brooches, earrings, bracelets, chokers and rings. Another display might consist of 75 various styles in shades of blue or perhaps, sterling silver. The antique jewelry, real and costume, is from the early 1800's up through the early 1960's and all at 50–70% below retail. You can literally spend hours browsing through this oasis of jewelry acquired from estate sales, swapmeets and retirement homes. If you can bring yourself to look away from the jewelry (it took us three visits), you will discover a selection of paintings, needlework and prints. The Collector's Eye offers jewelry repair and will also buy your vintage jewelry. A definite stop when in the San Fernando Valley!

ESTATE HOME FURNISHINGS
11901 Holser Walk, Suite 300
Oxnard, CA 93030
805/983-2211
HOURS: 7 DAYS A WEEK: 10-6
CREDIT CARDS: MC, V

Why pay retail when you can take advantage of outstanding values and quality merchandise at Estate Home Furnishings? Browsers and buyers alike will be delighted roaming through 17,000 square feet of momentos and memories. Whether you're looking for furniture, antiques, collectibles, glassware, jewelry, paintings, sterling, clothing, china, lamps or pianos, Estate Home Furnishings has it all. They are also noted for their large collection of antique dolls. With three estates arriving weekly, the selection of merchandise is always changing. So, if you're in the mood for a drive, it would be well worth your while to head up to Estate Home Furnishings. They offer great terms, too.

GRUBB & GRUBB'S GENERAL STORE
18523 Sherman Way
Reseda, CA 91335
818/996-7030
HOURS: MON-SAT: 9:30-5:30
CREDIT CARDS: AE, MC, V

This is a one-stop shop for vintage clothing and antiques. Grubb & Grubb's General Store has an extensive line of clothing for men and women, costume jewelry, vintage shoes, purses and hats. After you have put together the perfect outfit, you can explore their antique furniture, kitchenware, and art.

MELROSE ANTIQUE MALL
7201 Melrose Ave.
Los Angeles, CA 90046
213/965-9424
HOURS: MON-SAT: 11-6   SUN: 12:30-5:30
CREDIT CARDS: MC, V

The Melrose Antique Mall has 66 antique dealers who stock their own merchandise in large showcases. There is a huge assortment of antiques, and their inventory is constantly changing. Each dealer gives their own discount and you can usually save 20 to 25% over most stores and antique shows. If you have your resale card, you can save an additional 10%. You will discover a vast array of antique jewelry, pottery, china, silver, dolls, books, clothing, toys, and other collectibles. Some of the familiar brand names you will spot are Miriam Haskell, Eisenbach, Tiffany, Roseville-Hall, Bauer Limoges, Lalique, Baccarat, and Waterford. All the people are informed and friendly.

RAY FERRA'S IRON & ANTIQUE ACCENTS
342 N. La Brea Ave.
Los Angeles, CA 90036
213/934-3953
HOURS: TUES-FRI: 10-5   SAT: 10-3
CREDIT CARDS: MC, V

If you've been looking for replacement glass for an old antique lamp, then Ray Ferra can come to your rescue. If the problem isn't replacement glass, he also does rewiring for most lamps, ceiling fixtures, and crystal chandeliers. Commercial and residential lighting are two of his specialties. He carries both reproduction and original Tiffany lamps, handles, and many hard to find lighting items. He has been providing excellent service since 1967, and you can save 20% or more off retail prices, even if you could find it elsewhere.

SOMETHING OLD SOMETHING NOUVEAU
1303 Lincoln Blvd.
Santa Monica, CA 90401
213/395-8088
HOURS: TUES-SAT: 11-5
CREDIT CARDS: MC, V

All merchandise is on consignment here. Items are dated upon arrival and discounted 20% after the first two months. Each month thereafter another 10% is taken off. This store is a cozy 1918 bungalow that sells collectibles, antiques, furniture, silver, china, glass and linens. The second Saturday of every month there is a collector's jamboree sale where 35 dealers set up stalls along the house and in the parking area. Shopping at Something Old Something Nouveau can lead to some truly marvelous finds.

WEBSTER'S ANTIQUE IMPORTERS**
27050 Henry Mayo Dr.
Valencia, CA 91355
805/257-4312
HOURS: MON-SAT: 10-5 SUN: 11-4
CREDIT CARDS: MC, V

Webster's is a direct importer from England. They're one of the largest independent retailers of antiques, with the lowest overall prices. You will find wonderful treasures here at savings of 20 to 30% less than other English antique dealers. Items that are usually difficult to locate, such as a complete bedroom set, are not only available at Webster's, you will have a selection from which to choose. If you are a genuine antique buff, you should visit Webster's often. New shipments arrive on a regular basis to their 8,000 square foot store. You can save a few more quid if you make your purchase with your BUYING RETAIL IS STUPID discount coupon, 10% more in fact!

APPLIANCES

ADCO
818/340-9910
HOURS: BY APPOINTMENT ONLY
CREDIT CARDS: CASH OR CHECKS ONLY

Jean Chapman works on an extremely low mark-up which enables you to buy major appliances for less than cost-plus-10%. They work completely from catalogs at ADCO (since 1955) and will even give price quotes over the phone. After you have made a decision regarding the product you want, call them with the manufacturer's name, model number of the item, and any other pertinent information. A 25% deposit is required on all orders and you can pick up the merchandise when it arrives or make arrangements for delivery. Give them a call and schedule a visit.

ALBEE'S DISCOUNT APPLIANCES
6305 Wilshire Blvd.
Los Angeles, CA 90048
213/651-0620
HOURS: MON-SAT: 9:30-7:30 SUN: 11-6
CREDIT CARDS: AE, DISC, MC, V

It would be easier to list what Albee's don't carry. They sell everything and at about 10% above cost. The savings are terrific on television and video sets, stereos, washers, stoves, refrigerators, sewing machines, hair dryers, cameras, vacuum cleaners, fans, computers, fax machines, and hundreds of other items. They have a vast selection from all the top name brands.

BAR'S TV & APPLIANCE, INC.
3619 W. Magnolia Blvd.
Burbank, CA 91505
818/841-2277
HOURS: MON-FRI: 9:30-8:30 SAT: 10-6 SUN: 12-5
CREDIT CARDS: DISC, MC, V

Offering discounts of 10 to 30%, Bar's TV and Appliance also has special sales during the months of March, June, July and Novem-

ber. Both locations have been in existence since 1948 and have always offered such names as MGA, Zenith, RCA, GE, Speed Queen and other outstanding brands. Family owned and operated, factory authorized service is provided on everything they sell. Televisions, TV projectors, a full line of stereos, microwave ovens, refrigerators, washers, dryers, gas and electric ranges, dishwashers and cooktops are some of the items available at Bar's.
Additional Locations: Canoga Park (818/883-6653)

BARRETT'S APPLIANCES
2723 Lincoln Blvd.
Santa Monica, CA 90405
213/392-4108
HOURS: MON-FRI, SUN: 8-6   SAT: 8-5
CREDIT CARDS: MC, V

Since 1946, Barrett's Appliances has been offering low price guarantees on every major appliance for your kitchen and laundry room. Buying their inventory as part of a national buying group, they are able to pass on the huge volume discounts they receive. Brand names include Maytag, Amana, Whirlpool, Speed Queen, Westinghouse, Wolf, Creda, and many more. Their award winning service department and friendly sales people have one thing in mind— making sure their customers are satisfied! While credit cards are accepted, you'll receive an additional 3% discount paying by cash or check. Another reason to shop here is their low price policy. If within 30 days of purchase you see the same item advertised for less by any appliance dealer, Barrett's will gladly refund you the difference upon presentation of the ad. They pride themselves in being involved with their local community activities.

CARLSON'S T.V. & APPLIANCES**
342 Fifth St.
Santa Monica, CA 90401
213/393-0131
HOURS: MON-SAT: 9-6   SUN: 11-4
CREDIT CARDS: AE, MC, V

Carlson's carries a large stock of brand name televisions and appliances, at just 10% above cost. They say their prices are lower, on an overall basis, than their best known competitors. On display are over 100 refrigerators, 20 freezers, 40 washers, 20 air conditioners, 30 ranges and 20 dishwashers. You'll find Westinghouse, Frigidaire, Hot Point, RCA, Gibson, Maytag and others. In the same location since the late 1930's, they're proud of their reputation "built on service." Fast delivery is also available. If you use your BUYING RETAIL IS STUPID coupon, you'll save an additional $10! Deals don't get any better than this.

FATOR'S APPLIANCES & PLUMBING
533 S. Western Ave.
Los Angeles, CA 90015
213/386-1743
HOURS: TUES-SAT: 9-5
CREDIT CARDS: MC, V

Family owned and operated, Fator's offers major appliances for the home at 5–10% above cost. Knowledgeable salespeople are always happy to give useful information and to point customers in the right direction. They also have microwaves and gas barbecues. If you're going to install your new dishwasher yourself, you'll be relieved to know that Fator's carries a complete supply of plumbing materials. There's plenty of parking and free delivery to local areas.

FRIEDMAN'S–THE MICROWAVE SPECIALISTS
5515 Stearns
Long Beach, CA 90815
213/598-7756
HOURS: MON-SAT: 10-6 SUN: 12-4
CREDIT CARDS: MC, V

"I have more time for lovin' since I got my microwave oven," is the motto at Friedman's. And we kid you not, Judy Hatzger is in love! She not only manages the store, she gives free cooking classes in the store every Tuesday 11:30 to 1:00 and 6:30 to 8:00 for anyone who purchases a microwave. And you can come back to the classes as many times as you want. As a regular guest on KIEV radio cooking show, you know she can cook. Friedman's will give you a lifetime price guarantee which means if ever in your lifetime you find your microwave at a lower price, they'll refund the difference. With over 75 microwaves from which to choose, if you can't find what you want, it hasn't been invented yet. If by any chance, even

after knowing about all of the wonderful services Friedman extends, you're still not satisfied, they will give you your money back after 30 days. Now that's what we call real old fashion service!
Additional Locations: Encino (818/501-0794), Montclair (714/625-2361), Pasadena (818/577-2223), Thousand Oaks (805/496-3821)

HERB BEAN SALES CO.
8920 Melrose Ave.
Los Angeles, CA 90069
213/655-5878
HOURS: MON: 9-7 TUES-FRI: 9-6 SAT: 9-5
CREDIT CARDS: MC, V

At Herb Bean Sales Co. you can buy a refrigerator and appliances for your kitchen, stereo for your den, washer and dryer for your laundry room and a bed to sleep on. There are 7,000 square feet filled with a wide variety of merchandise to choose from, namely Calpholon cookware, Sub-Zero refrigerators, Thermador major cooking appliances, Sealy mattresses, Whirlpool, Amana and Maytag washers and dryers. Herb Bean has been offering great deals to his customers since 1964. Stop in and talk with their knowledgeable staff. You'll save 15 to 20% off retail on appliances and 50 to 80% off retail on beds. Financing is also available.

MARTINEL CO.
8151 Beverly Blvd.
Los Angeles, CA 90048
213/651-2800
HOURS: MON-SAT: 9-5:30
CREDIT CARDS: MC, V

This is not your usual whitegoods store. Martinel's carries major appliances, televisions, and housewares at discounts of 20 to 50%. They have 20 experienced salespeople to help you and there is parking in front of the store. Free gift wrapping is available on almost everything. This store is a favorite for those who want to find everything under one roof.

MICRO OVENS WEST COAST
14670 Firestone Blvd., #410
La Mirada, CA 90638
213/921-8933
HOURS: MON-FRI: 11-5   SAT: BY APPOINTMENT ONLY
CREDIT CARDS: CASH OR CHECKS ONLY

Micro Ovens West Coast has been in business over 14 years selling
all major brands of microwaves. They sell their ovens at cost plus
10 to 12% so their prices are really terrific. You can pick up your
microwave, or they will arrange delivery. Other top brand kitchen
appliances are available at huge savings. They also stock a spare
parts inventory for microwave ovens.

NAT DIAMOND EMPIRE FURNITURE**
4431 W. Adams
Los Angeles, CA 90011
213/732-8128
HOURS: MON, FRI: 10-7   TUES-THUR, SAT: 9:30-6
CREDIT CARDS: MC, V

This store has been in business over 50 years selling furniture and
appliances at 20 to 50% below retail prices. They carry a huge
inventory of General Electric appliances which include refrigerators,
freezers, stoves, washers, dryers, and more. Nat Diamond Empire
Furniture also carry the latest furniture trends and styles. You'll
save an additional 10% off their already terrific prices by using your
BUYING RETAIL IS STUPID coupon.

OLYMPIC SALES CO., INC.
134 W. 135th St.
Los Angeles, CA 90061
213/719-9500
HOURS: MON-FRI: 8:30-6   SAT: 9-6
CREDIT CARDS: MC, V

If you have a wine collection or are thinking about creating one, then
you want to see the folks at Olympic Sales Co. They manufacture
the Vinotemp wine cellar. Owner Alvin Patrick says, "Compare
first then come see us. We will not be undersold." Whether you
want your wine cellar built-in or free standing, Olympic can help

you. They will visit your home and give you an estimate on which wine storage device is best for you. You'll save at least 20% or more off the retail price.

PASQUINI
1501 W. Olympic Blvd.
Los Angeles, CA 90015
213/739-8826
HOURS: MON-FRI: 7:30-9 SAT: 9-4
CREDIT CARDS: MC, V

If you like coffee, espresso and cappuccino, visit Pasquini for the finest in home machines. You'll save at least 15% off retail prices on their wonderful selection of machines. They've been in business since 1956 and their secret is personalized service. They will show you how to use your new machine, and you can purchase the cups, saucers, grinding machines, and coffee beans here too. Repairs and service are also available for their machines.

∞ SEWING MACHINES & VACUUM CLEANERS ∞

RAINBOW VACUUM CENTER
634 E. Colorado Blvd.
Glendale, CA 91205
818/247-1943
HOURS: TUES-SAT: 10-6
CREDIT CARDS: AE, MC, V

The last time you were on a nuclear submarine, did you happen to notice how clean and dust free it was? The Rainbow Vacuum is purchased by the U.S. Navy for the super clean environment that must be maintained on their subs. Doctors recommend the same product for their allergy patients needing their homes to be dust free. This is the largest distributor of Rainbow Vacuums along with all types of other vacuums, parts and accessories. They'll beat anybody's price on brand names such as Hoover, Eureka, Electrolux, Panasonic, Royal, Kenmore, Filter Queen, and rebuilt Kirbys. Warranty and repair work is done right on the premises. Their 2,000 square foot showroom always has over 400 vacuum cleaners in stock. They also carry a large commercial vacuum cleaner, called the "Upkeeper," for parking lots. Senior citizens always receive an additional 10% discount on their purchases.

SINGER BURBANK SEWING CENTER
150 N. Golden Mall
Burbank, CA 91502
818/845-8311
HOURS: MON-FRI: 9-5:30 SAT: 9-5
CREDIT CARDS: AE, DISC, MC, V

Not only are sewing machines priced 20 to 50% below retail, when you buy a new Singer sewing machine, free lessons are included. If you've seen what sewing machines can do today, you know how important it is to have lessons. Their machines are guarantied for 25 years against factory defects (2 years on electrical and 3 months on anything else). They also sell Singer vacuum cleaners and cabinets, notions, scissors, and take trade-ins. All repair work is done on the premises. If you inherited your grandmother's old Singer and you would like to restore it, you can find the parts you need here.

U.S. SEW-N-VAC
21430 Sherman Way
Canoga Park, CA 91303
818/348-6014
HOURS: MON-SAT: 9-6
CREDIT CARDS: MC, V

Why not check out U.S. Sew-N-Vac the next time you need a sewing machine, vacuum cleaner or typewriter? You can save 10 to 40% off retail prices. They specialize in Royal, Eureka, Panasonic and Hoover vacuum cleaners and are an authorized Riccar dealer. In addition to sales, they offer same-day repair service on sewing machines and vacuums with free pick-up and delivery. Trade-ins are accepted and financing is available.

VACUUM & SEWING CENTER
21360 Devonshire Blvd.
Chatsworth, CA 91311
818/998-6988
HOURS: MON-FRI: 9:30-5:30 SAT: 9:30-5
CREDIT CARDS: MC, V

New, rebuilt and used vacuum cleaners made by Hoover, Eureka, and Royal, and sewing machines by Riccar and Singer are some of the brands found at the Vacuum & Sewing Center. You can select from over 100 different vacuum cleaners and 10 different models of sewing machines in stock. They guarantee their service and merchandise for one full year. With friendly salespeople and a skilled technician on the premises you can't go wrong. Free pick-up and delivery is also available. Savings run 20–50% below retail.

∞ USED APPLIANCES ∞

A APPLIANCE FACTORY
3851 Pyrite Rd.
Riverside, CA 92509
714/681-5300
HOURS: FRI-MON: 9-7 TUES-THUR: BY APPOINTMENT ONLY
CREDIT CARDS: MC, V

Washers, dryers, refrigerators, stoves, freezers or dishwashers, this is truly an appliance recycling factory with 10,000 square feet of showroom and 5,000 square feet of factory. Save at least 50% off what the same item would cost brand new! There are always at least 300 reconditioned units for sale and at least 3,000 units on hand. (Reconditioned means they replace all worn parts.) You won't find any plastic appliances, only metal, because appliances made out of metal last much longer than the ones made of plastic. If you see a unit not yet reconditioned, you can "stake your claim", and it will be moved up to the front of the line for reconditioning. Included in the sale price is a 30 day warranty, and you can purchase their service warranty for six months or one year ($35 every six months) which includes parts and labor service in home. If the unit can't be fixed, you'll receive a replacement. Also, if your service agreement is renewed every year, the price stays the same as the original contract price. There is usually something on special; if they are overstocked on some items, those units can be on special for 30% below what they charge normally. They will also paint the appliances for you should you desire a different color.

ART & ARTIFACTS

∞ ART DEALERS ∞

EDWARD WESTON FINE ARTS
19355 Business Center Dr.
Northridge, CA 91324
818/885-1044
HOURS: MON-FRI: 8-6
CREDIT CARDS: AE, MC, V

This is a showroom of wholesale art that generally deals with gallery owners. If you are an art connoisseur this is your kind of place. They have posters, limited edition graphics, original oil paintings and sculptures, pottery, photography, southwest art and artifacts all at 20% to 50% off retail prices. You can find Picasso, Miro, Chagall, Dali, Bragg, Bert Stern, George Barris and hundreds of other artists here. If your schedule during the week doesn't fit into their posted hours, call to arrange an evening appointment, and don't forget your credit cards.

H. LEWIS REX FINE ART**
6701 Variel Ave., #D47 (Valley Swap Meet)
Canoga Park, CA 91303
818/715-9980
HOURS: SAT & SUN: 10-6
CREDIT CARDS: MC, V

Choose from over 200 pieces of fine original oil paintings with savings of 25 to 40%. They carry artists such as Domina, Parnel, Millet, Perry and Mario, and also have a large selection of Southwestern art. Get on their mailing list to be notified about special sales during summer and Christmas. They sell to the public only at the Valley Swap Meet in Canoga Park. You can paint yourself an

additional 10% discount when you use your BUYING RETAIL IS
STUPID discount coupon when shopping here!

∞ FRAMES & FRAMING SERVICES ∞

ACTA FAST FRAME**
16054 Sherman Way
Van Nuys, CA 91406
818/786-9336
HOURS: MON-SAT: 9-6
CREDIT CARDS: AE, MC, V

Look no further for a store that specializes in museum quality
custom framing at competitive prices. They also sell art, limited
editions, posters and ready-made frames. Acta Fast Frame carries a
large variety of over 1,000 different frames from which to choose.
Discounts range from 10 to 45% off retail prices. They have year-
round specials on framed art posters, some as low as $29.95.
When you take your signed lithograph, painting or other artwork to
Acta Fast Frame for framing, be sure to have your BUYING RETAIL
IS STUPID discount coupon handy because you can save an
additional 10% on nonsale items!
Additional Locations: Redondo Beach (213/316-2881)

DISCOUNT FRAMES
12811 Victory Blvd.
N. Hollywood, CA 91606
818/763-6868
HOURS: MON-SAT: 9:30-5:30
CREDIT CARDS: MC, V

This is the solution you've been searching for if you need to have
your paintings reframed to match your new decor. Discount Frames
has one of the biggest selections of picture frames in Los Angeles,
and you can take advantage of the tremendous savings they offer on
every size, color, style and shape. They also provide excellent

custom framing for your favorite photographs, paintings, etchings, or whatever else you want to have framed.
Additional Locations: Tarzana (818/343-5566), Woodland Hills (818/884-0500)

DISCOUNT PICTURE FRAMES
102 S. Manchester
Anaheim, CA 92802
714/956-0121
HOURS: MON-FRI: 10-6   SAT: 10-5
CREDIT CARDS: MC, V

Do you have an unframed painting that has been sitting in the back of your closed for a while? All ready-made frames are discounted 10 to 20% off retail prices, and they stock over 15,000 picture frames at Discount Picture Frames! Now that's what we call a selection! Their customers drive a long distance to get their custom framing service, too. Owner Mike Neben has been in business at this location since 1970, and his courteous staff will take care of everything for you. No seconds or close-outs here, just first quality merchandise and service.

FRAMING OUTLET**
8301 W. 3rd St.
Los Angeles, CA 90048
213/655-1296
HOURS: MON-SAT: 10-6
CREDIT CARDS: MC, V

In business for more than five years, Framing Outlet provides professional custom framing and has ready-made frames as well. You can also purchase posters at bargain savings of 50% off retail. This is great place to shop for special frames to adorn your desk or credenza. With their wide variety in brass, silver, porcelain and marble, they have the largest selection of picture frames in Los Angeles. Their trained staff will help you design a framing layout that will fit perfectly in any room of your home. You will regularly save 10 to 20% on your custom framing at Framing Outlet, and you will save an additional 10% when you present your BUYING RETAIL IS STUPID discount coupon.

GREY GOOSE
111 N. La Brea Ave.
Los Angeles, CA 90036
213/931-8087
HOURS: MON-FRI: 9-5   SAT: 10-6
CREDIT CARDS: MC, V

Everything you want in custom framing at competitive prices can be found at the Grey Goose. A metal frame measuring 24" x 36", including dry mounting and glass of your choice, is runs just $39.50 and is available in 25 different colors. Shoppers will generally save 50% on what others charge for metal frames. Check out all their other varieties of frames, too.
Additional Locations: Los Angeles (213/652-0273)

ARTS, CRAFTS & HOBBIES

∞ ART SUPPLIES ∞

THE ART STORE
11450 S. Ventura Blvd.
Studio City, CA 91604
818/505-1383
HOURS: MON-FRI: 9-7 SAT: 9:30-5:30 SUN: 11-4
CREDIT CARDS: DISC, MC, V

Here's the place to go for a complete selection of artist materials, graphic supplies, fine art, furniture, custom framing and much more. You will be gratified to find their salespeople very knowledgeable about their products. Whether you are into art as a hobby, or you are a seasoned professional, The Art Store offers terrific discounts of 20 to 40% off suggested retail prices. Make sure you get on their mailing list for notification of special sales and general information.
Additional Locations: 6 other stores throughout S. CA

CLINTON ART SUPPLIES
160 S. La Brea Ave.
Los Angeles, CA 90036
213/936-8166
HOURS: MON-FRI: 8:30-5:30 SAT: 9-6
CREDIT CARDS: MC, V

You will encounter two floors with 10,000 square feet filled with a variety of supplies and equipment necessary for fine art, illustration art and production art. Experienced salespeople at Clinton Art Supplies will assist you in solving any problem you might have with graphic layout and design work. Make sure you check out their special retail prices. They have been serving the art community in the Los Angeles area since the late 1960's.

∞ BEADS, RHINESTONES & CRYSTALS ∞

BOHEMIAN CRYSTAL
812 S. Maple
Los Angeles, CA 90014
213/627-9554
HOURS: MON-SAT: 9-5:30
CREDIT CARDS: MC, V

Bohemian Crystal has one of the largest selection of beads, rhinestones, pearls, metal parts, trimmings, apparel embroidery products, appliques, and all the accessories needed to make custom jewelry. Crystal accessories and chandeliers are also available. At Bohemian Crystal you can save 10 to 40% off retail prices. They have been in business since 1944 and occupy 5,000 square feet of property. You can purchase quality items made of Bohemian crystal from Czechoslovakia or Austria. Whether you're buying a set of crystal stemware for yourself, or a crystal ball for your favorite fortune teller, you can't go wrong shopping here for price and selection.

KLEIN'S BEAD BOX**
309 N. Kings Rd.
Los Angeles, CA 90048
213/651-3595
HOURS: MON-FRI: 10-4 SAT: 10-3
CREDIT CARDS: AE, MC, V

Put together your own designs with wholesale merchandise from Klein's Bead Box. You can be as creative as you want with beads, Swarovski crystals, rhinestones, glass jewels, pearls, sequins and appliques. A professional skater we know from Orange County tells us that Klein's is the only place that carries what she needs for her costumes. Make earrings and necklaces or spice up that basic black dress hanging in the back of your closet! Get free advice from the designers that shop at Klein's and don't forget to check out the close-out table for even better buys. Call them for a catalogue and for information on classes they offer. Take your BUYING RETAIL IS STUPID coupon with you for an additional 5% discount.

∞ CRAFT & FLORAL SUPPLIES ∞

H & H CRAFT & FLORAL SUPPLY CO.
1885 N. Tustin
Orange, CA 92665
714/998-4460
HOURS: MON-FRI: 9-9   SAT: 9-7   SUN: 10-6
CREDIT CARDS: DISC, MC, V

H & H Floral Craft carries a tremendous line of craft and floral supplies. If you are in need of styrofoam, art supplies, candles, party supplies, macrame, rattan, silk trees, plants and flowers, beads and sequins, floral arrangements, wedding decoration rentals, plasterware, dried flowers, arts and craft books, needlecraft supplies, cake and candy making supplies, wrapping paper or ribbon, this is the place to go. They even have craft and art classes. Last but not least, H & H extends a 10% discount to senior citizens. *Additional Locations: Garden Grove (714/750-9222), Mission Viejo (714/770-5001), Montclair (714/621-3807), Riverside (714/359-1091)*

MIJANOU'S SILK DESIGNS**
718 E. Imperial Hwy.
Brea, CA 92621
714/990-3601
HOURS: MON-SAT: 10-7   SUN: 10-5
CREDIT CARDS: MC, V

Mijanou's is a place that specializes in silk designs. They buy in quantity and pass the savings on to their very satisfied customers. Everything you need in silk greenery, trees, and flowers can be found here for only 15% above cost. They also carry vases, baskets, floral supplies, and brass. If you are a lover of silk arrangements, you'll find them here. Should you want to design your own arrangement, free consultation is available. In addition, Mijanou's makes certain they not only have a great selection of variety and color, but also take pride in stocking the unusual. Make certain you take your BUYING RETAIL IS STUPID coupon with you for an additional 5% discount.

POTTERY AND FLORAL WORLD**
3352 San Fernando Rd.
Los Angeles, CA 90065
213/254-5281
HOURS: 7 DAYS A WEEK: 8-7
CREDIT CARDS: MC, V

Pottery and Floral World has one of the West Coast's largest selections of pots, pottery, dried and silk flowers, and all the accessories that go along with them. They have great macrame supplies, gourmet ware, baskets and wrought iron. They are both a factory outlet and a direct importer, so you can expect discounts of 20 to 50% off retail prices found elsewhere. They have closeouts weekly, so you always find a changing inventory. If you're looking for Christmas decorations, they carry a complete line. You will get an additional 10% off your purchase price when you use your BUYING RETAIL IS STUPID discount coupon.
Additional Locations: Out of the area (San Francisco & Las Vegas)

STAT'S
120 S. Raymond Ave.
Pasadena, CA 91101
818/795-9308
HOURS: MON-SAT: 9-9   SUN: 10-6
CREDIT CARDS: MC, V

At Stat's you will find decorator, arts and crafts, and floral supplies, plus everything for seasonal decorating at prices 20 to 30% below retail. Their selection of artificial flowers are made of silk and of polyester. Demonstrations in floral arrangements are available, and also for many other crafts. Whether you're having a wedding, shower, birthday party, you name it, decorations for any celebration can be found at Stat's. December 26th you can save an additional 50% off already low prices on their seasonal merchandise, and in June they have a huge parking lot sale where everything is marked

as low as 90% off retail! All of their stores are very large, ranging from 20,000 to 40,000 square feet.
Additional Locations: Capistrano Beach (714/493-3752), Downey (213/772-2458), Redondo Beach (213/772-2458), Whittier (213/449-1691)

∞ FABRICS & NOTIONS ∞

AL GREENWOOD BEDSPREAD KING
2750 E. Pacific Coast Hwy.
Long Beach, CA 90804
213/498-9277
HOURS: MON-THUR, SAT: 10-5:30   FRI: 10-7   SUN: 12-5
CREDIT CARDS: ALL MAJOR CREDIT CARDS

When a man calls himself the Bedspread King, you know you are going to find one of the country's largest selections of bedspreads. Well, it's true. In addition to the incredible selection of bedspreads and the terrific savings (20 to 50% off retail), Al Greenwood also carries a huge selection of custom drapes in matching fabrics. You can match your drapes and take them home with you, and get this, with no waiting! If you are handy with a sewing machine, make or create your own accessories to match your new bedspread. Just have them cut the length you need of matching fabric, and you are on your merry way. If you prefer a comforter to a bedspread, check out their Quallofil comforters which have the lightness, warmth and puffiness of down, but without the same price.
Additional Locations: South Gate (213/566-9393)

BIG Y YARDAGE OUTLET
440 S. Main St.
Orange, CA 92668
714/978-3970
HOURS: MON: 9:30-9   TUES-FRI: 9:30-6   SAT: 9:30-5:30
CREDIT CARDS: MC, V

After you have decorated your house with new furniture, stop by Big Y Yardage Outlet for do-it-yourself assistance in making new draperies, bedspreads, valances, tablecloths, cushions, pillows and more. You will find a large assortment of decorator drapery and upholstery fabrics, along with a sales force knowledgeable about the right fabric to use for your needs. For those of us less creative than others, Big Y Yardage Outlet also offers made-to-order services on the items mentioned above. Mini-blinds and Roman shades can be ordered here, too. Ample parking is available and they are close to all major freeways (5, 22, 55, 57, 91). You'll save at least 25 to 50% off the retail price, and remnants are offered at just 25¢ a yard.

CALICO CORNERS
3830 Foothill Blvd.
Pasadena, CA 91107
818/792-4328
HOURS: MON: 9:30-8 TUES-SAT: 9:30-5:30 SUN: 12-4
CREDIT CARDS: MC, V

Wouldn't you love to own a quilted bedspread? Well, you can at 30 to 60% above cost when you shop at Calico Corners. They carry designer fabrics, slip covers, table cloths, feather and down pillows. Upholstery fabrics and books on upholstering are for sale, plus books on slip covers and windows. They have tape for making Roman and Austrian shades, and pleating tape for making curtains. Get on their mailing list so you'll know about their really big sales.

D/M YARDAGE OUTLET
16510 Hawthorne Blvd.
Lawndale, CA 90260
213/772-1800
HOURS: MON-SAT: 9:30-6
CREDIT CARDS: DISC, MC, V

Any day of the week you can save up to 70% off retail prices at D/M Yardage Outlet on thousands of in-stock fabrics, plus discounts on their special order fabrics, too. D/M Yardage Outlet will custom make your draperies and your bedspreads, if you like. They have a beautiful selection of upholstery and drapery fabrics, ready-made draperies, wallpaper, and even discounted mini-blinds.

DESIGNER FABRIC SHOWCASE
10199 Hole Ave.
Riverside, CA 92503
714/354-6684
HOURS: MON-THUR: 10-6 FRI: 10-4 SUN: 12-4
CREDIT CARDS: MC, V

Designer Fabric Showcase is the place to go for spectacular savings on decorative fabrics for the home. They always have at least 1,000 bolts of first quality fabric to choose from. Their fabrics are all kept on rollers enabling you to actually pull out the fabric for a total visual concept rather than only having a little square to look at. If you don't want to do the job yourself, you can order custom draperies, bedspreads and upholstery work. With savings at 50% below manufacturers list and 25% less for labor, you can't go wrong.

FABRIC WAREHOUSE
11612 W. Olympic
W. Los Angeles, CA 90024
213/477-7023
HOURS: MON-FRI: 10-8 SAT: 10-6 SUN: 12-5
CREDIT CARDS: AE, MC, V

For those of us still interested in taking the time to sew our own clothes, decorate our own homes or just feel like being creative, Fabric Warehouse is definitely the place. You'll be in fashion with the newest fabrics purchased from many of the top clothing manufacturers in New York. Fabric Warehouse's inventory is constantly changing year round, so you will always find the latest in fabrics and prints, along with their exclusives such as silk prints from St. Gillian. You will find they carry cotton, linen, wool, silk, drapery and upholstery fabrics, as well as notions and patterns. Some of their fabrics are imported. Whatever you do, don't miss out on any of their special sales by making certain you get on their mailing list. *Additional Locations: Costa Mesa (714/646-4040), La Puente (818/964-2117), Northridge (818/349-3988), Torrance (213/543-5588), Valencia (805/254-8300)*

G. KAGAN & SONS, INC.
750 Towne Ave.
Los Angeles, CA 90021
213/627-9655
HOURS: MON-FRI: 8:30-4:30
CREDIT CARDS: CASH OR CHECKS ONLY

Anyone that does their own sewing or tailoring will find this store to be truly amazing. If you can imagine it, G. Kagan and Sons has it. Apparel construction and fashion products is the proper description of the merchandise they carry. Translated, that means you will find things like beads, laces, pearls, ribbon, sequins, appliques, tassels, webbing, elastics, netting, fringes, ruffling and anything else you need. You have the convenience of finding everything you need under one roof, and because they are wholesalers, you can count on exceptional savings. Please note, they only sell their merchandise in full rolls or boxes, no cut yardage and no samples.

GOLDEN FLEECE DESIGNS INC.**
441 S. Victory Blvd.
Burbank, CA 91502
818/848-7724
HOURS: MON-FRI: 8-5
CREDIT CARDS: MC, V

Canvas, canvas and more canvas. Anything made from canvas can be found here. Canopies, flags, duffle bags, boat covers, sailboat accessories, nautical gift items, marine hardware and hats. They will also custom make any canvas item to suit your needs. You can purchase industrial canvas by the yard and you can also silkscreen and embroider on any item. If you remember to use your BUYING RETAIL IS STUPID coupon and you can sail off with an additional 10% discount.

LINCOLN FABRICS
1600 Lincoln Blvd.
Venice, CA 90291
213/396-5724
HOURS: TUES-FRI: 10-6   SAT: 10-5:30
CREDIT CARDS: MC, V

This family business has been in this location since 1955. Their warehouse, so big it covers an entire block, contains over a million yards of fabric. Lincoln Fabrics has drapery fabrics and hardware, hall runners, and upholstery fabrics. You will be happy to know that you'll be paying at or below wholesale prices! They also carry art and marine canvas, cottons, linens, silks, foam rubber, polyfoam trimmings, notions, vinyl, leather, natural burlap and more. You get good service along with a massive selection of merchandise. It's no wonder they've been in business for so many years!

MICHAEL LEVINE, INC.
920 S. Maple
Los Angeles, CA 90015
213/622-6259
HOURS: MON-FRI: 9-5:30 SAT: 9-4:30
CREDIT CARDS: MC, V

Michael Levine, Inc. has been in business over 20 years; their store occupies one entire block near 9th and Maple in the heart of Los Angeles' garment district. Everything you need in fabrics and notions can be found under one roof. They offer their customers a complete bridal department, upholstery products, and drapery goods. Fun furs, piece goods, and other apparel necessities are also available. Everything is priced at 20 to 50% below retail. Parking is validated with a $5.00 minimum purchase.

OFF THE BOLT
6812 De Soto Blvd.
Canoga Park, CA 91303
818/999-0441
HOURS: MON-FRI: 9-6 SAT: 10-5
CREDIT CARDS: MC, V

All major mills are represented here. Off The Bolt has about 75,000 yards of fabric for your selection. This is a wonderful place to browse through and you can save about 50% off the retail prices. Their selection of decorative fabrics are perfect for drapery and upholstery projects. They have great selections for that new bed-spread or slip cover you've been wanting to make for the last year, along with matching wallcoverings. The salespeople here are most perceptive about your needs, and you really should check out their clearance and remnant tables where you can unearth great fabrics for as low as 50¢ a yard.

ORIENTAL SILK CO.
8377 Beverly Blvd.
Los Angeles, CA 90048
213/651-2323
HOURS: MON-SAT: 9-6
CREDIT CARDS: MC, V

The Oriental Silk Company has exceptional buys on elegant silks and wools. You will discover a large selection of different colors and patterns in this 2,600 square foot store. They import their own products in large quantities and pass the savings on to their customers. You will not only save about 25% off what you'd pay in a fabric store at the mall, but you'll have a lot more to choose from. With prices low and quality good, stock is depleted quickly, so if you see something you like get it now, because it might not be there next time. Call George every now and then to make sure you don't miss out on anything. He'll tell you about his current stock or let you know when his next fabulous shipment will be arriving.

STERN'S DISCOUNT DRAPERY CENTER
308 E. 9th St.
Los Angeles, CA 90015
213/622-3564, 213/622-4894
HOURS: MON-SAT: 9-4
CREDIT CARDS: MC, V

Stern's Discount Drapery Center is a leading wholesaler and retailer (since 1952) of drapery and upholstery fabrics. You will save 40 to 50% off retail and even more on unclaimed items. Custom-made draperies are available, but the savings aren't quite as much as they are on fabrics. Look for their special close out selection of fabrics for more savings.

THE VELVET TOUCH
300 S. La Brea Ave.
Los Angeles, CA 90036
213/933-8363
HOURS: TUES-FRI: 10-5   SAT: 10-3

CREDIT CARDS: MC, V

In business since 1959, Yehuda Handel knows what the public wants when it comes to beautiful drapery and upholstery fabrics. He'll also create window coverings for you. Drapery and upholstery fabrics, drapery hardware, mini-blinds, pleated shades, window shades and roman shades are all available here at savings of at least 20 to 50%.

∞ HOBBIES ∞

– COINS –

ASSOCIATED FOREIGN EXCHANGE, INC.
433 N. Beverly Dr.
Beverly Hills, CA 90210
213/274-7610
HOURS: MON-FRI: 9-4:30 SAT: 10-3
CREDIT CARDS: CASH OR CASHIERS/TRAVELERS CHECKS ONLY

Even if you are buying money, why should you pay retail? Yes, Associated Foreign Exchange sells Krugerrands, Mexican Pesos, Credit Swiss bars, silver coins and bullion, and U.S. gold coins and foreign currency. AFEX offers these foreign currencies and precious metals at the lowest market price available. They buy and sell all gold, silver and platinum investment products, with no commission charges and handle over 120 foreign currencies.

– COMIC BOOKS –

MARKSTU DISCOUNT COMICS
3642 7th St.
Riverside, CA 92501
714/684-8544
HOURS: MON-SAT: 10:30-6 SUN: 11-5
CREDIT CARDS: AE, DISC, MC, V

What do Batman, Spiderman, and Superman have in common? Give up? They can all be found and many more of your comic book favorites at Markstu Discount Comics. The 500,000 comic books they have in their 4,000 square foot store will definitely keep you busy searching for your pastime heros. Since 1954, Markstu has been buying, trading, and collecting comic books of every kind. Their many services offered are special attention to collectors just starting out and locating comic books if they don't have them in stock. Make sure to check out their special tables with values ranging 50 to 60% off retail.

– MODEL TRAINS –

ALLIED MODEL TRAINS
4411 S. Sepulveda Blvd.
Culver City, CA 90230
213/313-9353, 213/475-0463
HOURS: MON-THUR, SAT: 10-6   FRI: 10-9
CREDIT CARDS: AE, MC, V

We have discovered the world's largest model train store! They carry all brands and all sizes of kits, tools, scenery supplies, and die-cast automobile and aircraft models. Most everything you see is priced at 20 to 50% off retail. You will appreciate finding name brands such as Lionel, LGB, Marklin, Fleischman, Bachman, Brio, Playmobil, American Flyer, Aster, Athearn, Atlas, MRC, Delton, REA. Allied Model Trains is located in a brand new building with over 11,600 square feet for hobbyists to explore! For your enjoyment, they have several very interesting, extremely detailed operating displays. They have literally thousands of items in stock at all times. Expert repairs are available, and they also buy old trains and toys. If you are in the neighborhood you should visit Allied Model Trains. You can have a good time here just watching their realistic displays.

DISCOUNT TRAIN WAREHOUSE**
777 W. Imperial Hwy.
Brea, CA 92621
714/255-0185
HOURS: MON-THUR: 11-8   FRI: 11-9   SAT: 10-6   SUN: 11-5
CREDIT CARDS: AE, DISC, MC, V

Located 2 miles west of the 57 Freeway on Imperial Highway in the city of Brea, is Southern California's most complete discount model train store. The Discount Train Warehouse carries thousands of items for the model train hobbyist in their 3,500 square foot store—everything for the beginner to expert. Some brand names you'll find are LGB, Lionel plus many more. They are also an authorized Lionel dealer. If you make tracks to this store, they will give you an additional 5% discount when you use your BUYING RETAIL IS STUPID discount coupon.

THE ROUNDHOUSE TRAIN STORE**
12804 Victory Blvd.
N. Hollywood, CA 91606
818/769-0403
HOURS: MON-THUR, SAT: 8:30-6 FRI: 8:30-9 SUN: 12-5
CREDIT CARDS: AE, DISC, MC, V

No longer are electric train sets a pastime strictly for children. Adults who enjoy collecting trains can be found browsing at one of the largest train stores in Southern California. The Roadhouse Train Store carries such brand names as LGB, Playmobil, Lionel, American Flyer, HO, N & Z Gauge and more. Thousands of HO scale detail parts are in stock. As a matter of fact, the movie industry is constantly buying parts to be used for special effects. Different specials are run every week in addition to their regular discounted prices. Whatever you do, don't forget to bring your BUYING RETAIL IS STUPID coupon for added savings of 10%. Make certain to get on their mailing list for updates on their sales and new merchandise arrivals.

– RUBBER STAMPS –

PARTY KING
6038 Reseda Blvd.
Tarzana, CA 91356
818/343-3343
HOURS: MON-FRI: 6-6:30 SAT: 9-5:30 SUN: 11-5
CREDIT CARDS: MC, V

This 4,000 square foot store has a huge selection of party supplies for every occasion and theme imaginable. Party King consistently has over 150 designer patterns and fashion colors, including an incredible selection of juvenile ensembles, decorations and party favors. You can expect to save 25% off retail prices on wedding invitations, Bar Mitzvah invitations, and 20% off all greeting cards. Rubber stamp collectors will be delighted to know that during their recent renovation, they opened "Stamp Castle," a-store-within-a-store, featuring novelty rubber stamps, ink pads, paper and other accessories. They have been in business since 1979 and can offer you expert advice in party planning.

∞ SPECIALIZED TOOLS & EQUIPMENT ∞

THE JEWELERS SUPPLY WAREHOUSE
18345 Ventura Blvd., Suite 305
Tarzana, CA 91356
818/343-4655
HOURS: MON-FRI: 9-5
CREDIT CARDS: CASH OR CHECKS ONLY

Discerning craftsmen and expert-level hobbyists will thank us for revealing this source to them. Devotees of model trains and model ships will appreciate the time saving instruments available to them at The Jewelers Supply Warehouse, as will those involved with restoring antique toys or furniture. If you make your own jewelry or are a student taking a class in jewelry making, you'll find the necessary supplies here. You can feel comfortable in knowing that you will be purchasing merchandise from trustworthy people. The owners, from a family involved for many generations in the jewelry business, have been supplying professional artisans with premium instruments for no less than 40 years.

AUTOMOBILES & VEHICLES

∞ ALARMS, STEREOS & TELEPHONES ∞

AHEAD STEREO
7426 Beverly Blvd.
Los Angeles, CA 90036
213/931-8873
HOURS: MON-FRI: 11-7 SAT: 10-6
CREDIT CARDS: MC, V

Here are discount prices for home and car stereos and cellular phones, with personalized service, in a store that stocks everything. Their inventory includes names such as Technics, Kenwood, ADCOM, Denon, A.D.S., and lots more. "We dare you to beat our prices," they say. You'll appreciate the full service provided by the nice sales staff. All of this, and they guarantee the best price, too.

AUTO STEREO WAREHOUSE
8376 W. Beverly Blvd.
Los Angeles, CA 90048
213/655-5521
HOURS: MON-SAT: 9-5:30
CREDIT CARDS: AE, DISC, MC, V

They have been doing business since 1977. The wide variety of discounts at Auto Stereo Warehouse (5 to 50%) is attributed to manufacturer close-outs and volume purchasing. Specializing in custom installation, they offer auto stereo systems in such names as Alpine, Blaupunkt, ADS, Fosgate, Denon and Becker. Auto alarm systems are available in passive and manual arming, keypad style, remote control, and pagers. Their auto alarm systems are made by Vehicle Security, Derringer 2, Stealth, Quantum, Alpine, Clifford and more. All brands of cellular phones are heavily discounted due to volume buying. Working models of stereos are on display in their carpeted, soundproof showroom for a more accurate and personal selection. In addition to installing stereos, Auto Stereo Warehouse offers custom woodwork and upholstery. Also available are free estimates for insurance replacement work.

CELLULAR WHOLESALERS**
4200 Lincoln Blvd.
Marina del Rey, CA. 90291
213/827-8885
HOURS: MON-FRI: 7:30-5:30 SAT: 10-4
      (OPEN ON ALTERNATE SATURDAYS)
CREDIT CARDS: AE, MC, V

Cellular Wholesalers specialize in cellular mobile phones for cars, boats and and also handle portable units, fax machines, beepers and car alarms. They offer savings of 20% off retail prices, and they carry all major brands such as Mitsubishi, Oki, Panasonic, NEC, Radiant, Motorola, and others. They have one of the largest customer service departments in Los Angeles, and installers will come to your premises. They can furnish a mobile phone number for you from either Pacific Bell or LA Cellular, and have a national activations department for hook-up anywhere in the U.S. Ask about their "buy 1 get 1 free" plan, and about their special plan designed for large corporations. Your BUYING RETAIL IS STUPID coupon will save you an additional 5%!

INTERSPACE ELECTRONICS, INC.
10854 Washington Blvd.
Culver City, CA 90232
213/836-6018
HOURS: MON-FRI: 10-5 SAT: 10-3
CREDIT CARDS: MC, V

Save from 20 to 50% off retail prices on communications equipment, citizen band radios, cordless telephones, scanners, answering machines, alarm systems for automobiles, flashlights, and even radar detectors. While we haven't begun to name everything Interspace Electronics has in their inventory, we're sure you get the general idea.

ITC ELECTRONICS**
2772 W. Olympic Blvd.
Los Angeles, CA 90006
213/388-0621
HOURS: MON-SAT: 9-6
CREDIT CARDS: MC, V

ITC Electronics is a full line authorized distributor of electronic supplies, computer accessories, auto sound products and electronic test equipment. They also carry close-outs and special purchases at additional savings. You can expect to save anywhere from 10 to 60% off retail on such brand names as Sansui, Pyle auto speakers, Fluke, Sony headphones, and Pioneer. Special pricing is available for quantity purchases and don't forget to use your BUYING RETAIL IS STUPID coupon for an additional 5% discount. Their store in Torrance is the only one open on Sundays (11-5).
Additional Locations: Chatsworth (818/700-0900), Oxnard (805/983-4115), Torrance (213/370-6211)

LEO'S STEREO
10915 Santa Monica Blvd.
Westwood, CA 90025
213/479-8036
HOURS: MON-FRI: 9-9 SAT: 9-6 SUN: 10-6
CREDIT CARDS: MC, V

Psst, want to save big money on a stereo? Leo's is the place to shop! Save up to 60% on stereos for your home or vehicle, television sets, cellular telephones, and CD players. You'll find all the popular brand names such as Sony, TDK, Fuji, and more. They have financing available, and you'll discover they are super people to deal with. For your convenience, they have vehicle installation departments at all 37 of their locations in Southern California. Leo's Stereo also has great sales throughout the year where the bargains are so good you will think they are giving the merchandise away!
Additional Locations: 36 other stores throughout S. CA

OLYMPIC ELECTRONICS
6310 Hollywood Blvd.
Hollywood, CA 90028
213/467-4752
HOURS: 7 DAYS A WEEK: 10-9
CREDIT CARDS: MC, V

Olympic Electronics is right on the corner of Hollywood and Vine. They promise the lowest prices in the area on AM-FM portable radios, cameras, and stereos for the home or car. They have a store full of electronic wonders from all the major manufacturers, and most are priced at just 5 to 10% over cost. They are wholesale to the public, so shop here and save.

RADIOLAND/INGLEWOOD ELECTRONICS
4701 W. Century Blvd.
Inglewood, CA 90304
213/671-7761
HOURS: MON-FRI: 9:30-6 SAT: 9:30-5:30 SUN: 10:30-4
CREDIT CARDS: CASH OR CHECKS ONLY

Radioland/Inglewood Electronics offers discount prices on name brands seven days a week. Their customers save from 25 to 35% off retail on radio and television tubes, transistors, TV antennas, cable TV accessories, as well as stereos and CB radios for vehicles. A few of the other items available here are portable radios, phonograph needles, and most electronic parts.

REGGIE'S STEREO
7820 Santa Monica Blvd.
W. Hollywood, CA 90046
213/656-0111
HOURS: MON-SAT: 10-7 SUN: 11-5
CREDIT CARDS: MC, V

If you want to save 20 to 60% off the suggested manufacturer's list price on home and car stereos, car alarms, car phones, televisions, videos, and answering machines, then all you have to do is visit Reggie's. They carry all the above and much more. Their expert

installation service can work miracles on same-day installation of car stereos, alarms, and phones. They have instant financing on approved credit, and their sales staff is extremely knowledgeable. Watch for their special sales during the year where you can save even more on selected merchandise. If you want to take advantage of their financing service, you can save time by calling Reggie's Instant Credit Hotline at (213/931-4444).
Additional Locations: Van Nuys (818/902-0444)

ROGERSOUND LABS
8381 Canoga Ave.
Canoga Park, CA 91304
818/873-3051
HOURS: MON-FRI: 12-9   SAT-SUN: 12-6
CREDIT CARDS: MC, V

Rogersound Labs carries speaker systems, audio-video components, car stereos, television sets, and much more. Their prices on such brand names as Sony, Kenwood, Yamaha, Mitsubishi, and JVC are 50% below retail prices. You can count on finding a helpful, professional staff at any of the Rogersound Labs.
Additional Locations: 6 other stores throughout S. CA

SOUNDS GOOD STEREO
7218 Topanga Canyon Blvd.
Canoga Park, CA 91303
818/999-4523
HOURS: MON-SAT: 9-6
CREDIT CARDS: AE, MC, V

This discount store offers you a selection of stereo systems for your car or truck, cellular telephones and automobile alarms. You will find their merchandise priced at about 30 to 40% off retail. Since 1978, Sounds Good Stereo has been featuring low prices and high quality with such names as Alpine, Rockford, Fosgate, JBL, Concord, and more. They are equipped for doing repairs and are very proud of their professional, award winning installation department. Sounds good to us.

SPEAKER CITY
10615 Vanowen St.
Burbank, CA 91505
818/508-1908
HOURS: MON-SAT: 10-6:30
CREDIT CARDS: MC, V

We have discovered a virtual candy store for speaker enthusiasts and audiophiles, filled with speakers for the home and complete sound systems for vehicles, at savings of at least 50%! All components needed to build speakers from scratch, and also complete kits for speaker systems can be found here. They do "X-overs" too. One of the great things about Speaker City is you know exactly what you are buying. The price of a speaker already built is no longer a mystery because lining the walls are the individual components that went into the speaker, along with the cost of each item. Though they only carry speakers for the home (no stereos), they do stock complete sound systems for your car (no installations). Customized speaker systems are available for both home and vehicles. Names you'll recognize include, Focal, Dynaudio, Vifa, Peerless and Pyle. If you need any technical advice, talk to Wally Ross. He's not only an expert on sound systems, he's also a professional musician.

∞ BATTERIES ∞

BATTERY DEPOT**
9118 Glenoaks Blvd.
Sun Valley, CA 91352
818/768-7802
HOURS: MON-FRI: 8-6 SAT: 8-3
CREDIT CARDS: CASH OR CHECKS ONLY

New and rebuilt batteries are sold here for autos, trucks, and RV's. On new batteries you'll save 50% off retail. In addition to batteries they sell starters and alternators. The friendly people you'll meet at Battery Depot will do an electrical check for you at no charge. Major brands include Delco, GNB, and many more. If you purchase a new battery, don't forget to use your BUYING RETAIL IS STUPID coupon for a free 40 piece socket set. You'll get a charge out of shopping here!

BATTERY SPECIALIST CO.
21303 Sherman Way
Canoga Park, CA 91303
818/884-2288
HOURS: MON-FRI: 9-6 SAT: 9-4
CREDIT CARDS: ALL MAJOR CREDIT CARDS

The Battery Specialist Co. carries over 1,000 batteries for all applications at extremely competitive prices. Most all major brands are included. Considering themselves problem solvers of any kind of battery needs, they will analyze your problem or concern, recommend a product and check the equipment for you. The Canoga Park store is closed on Sundays, but their Van Nuys store is open every day. Call them for their hours on Sundays.
Additional Locations: Van Nuys (818/988-2288)

LYNWOOD BATTERY MFG. CO., INC.
3171 Fernwood Ave.
Lynwood, CA 90262
213/631-2200
HOURS: MON-FRI: 8-4:30
CREDIT CARDS: CASH OR CHECKS ONLY

Just as the name implies, the Lynwood Co. manufactures their own batteries. They have been selling their merchandise to the trucking industry and marine dealers in California, Arizona and Colorado since the 1930's. Even though they use only the highest quality materials, you can buy your battery at 20 to 50% over cost! That should give you a charge.

∞ FLOOR MATS ∞

ULTIMAT CAR MATS
6734 Reseda Blvd.
Reseda, CA 91335
818/343-2242
HOURS: MON-FRI: 9-5:30 SAT: 10-3
CREDIT CARDS: MC, V

Ultimat Car Mats specializes in mats for any make or any model automobile. If you're sprucing up your car or have just bought a brand new one, you can purchase mats to match from their assortment of 20 colors. They offer same day service for both standard and custom monograms. Look for discounts at 20 to 25% below retail at this factory outlet.

∞ PARTS ∞

ABC MOBIL BRAKE
21360 Deering Court
Canoga Park, CA 91304
818/883-3021
HOURS: MON-SAT: 8-5
CREDIT CARDS: MC, V

ABC Mobile Brake sells all brake parts, shock absorbers, clutches, power steering components, brake drums, disc rotors, machine drums, and machine fly wheels. Name brands include, among others, Bendix, TRW, KYB, and Wagner. Started in 1968, this family operation is reputed to be the most knowledgeable in the business. They have the largest inventory in the San Fernando Valley and offer their customers savings between 20 to 30% off retail prices found elsewhere.

BOB'S AUTO SUPPLY
1539 W. Manchester Ave.
Los Angeles, CA 90047
213/759-1155
HOURS: MON-FRI: 8-6 SAT: 8-5
CREDIT CARDS: MC, V

Instead of running all over town, do-it-yourself mechanics can find everything they need at Bob's Auto Supply. Savings run 30 to 50% on all auto parts and machine shop services. They carry quality AC-Delco parts, brake drums, and can provide engine repair and parts— foreign and domestic. Complete engines are also available for sale.

RAP DISCOUNT AUTO PARTS & MARINE SUPPLY
21407 Vanowen St.
Canoga Park, CA 91303
818/884-3370
HOURS: MON-FRI: 8-10 SAT: 8-5 SUN: 9-5
CREDIT CARDS: CASH OR CHECKS ONLY

Rap is the specialist in reconditioning of cylinder heads for automotive or marine engines. They carry a complete line of spare parts for engines of all types and sell them at 30 to 70% below retail. You'll find products made by Cannon, Adesco, Ditzler paints and supplies, welding goods, and marine accessories. In addition to foreign and domestic parts, they have a complete machine shop for engine work, and they make hydraulic, air conditioning and power steering hoses.

SURPLUS CITY JEEP PARTS
11796 Sheldon St.
Sun Valley, CA 91352
818/767-3666
HOURS: MON-SAT: 9-6
CREDIT CARDS: MC, V

Whether your Jeep is new or used, this is the place to go for all your jeep needs. Expect to find their prices 20–30% below dealer prices. Your vehicle may be all terrain, but you won't need to go over hill and dale to find good prices—just stop here.

– USED PARTS –

MARV'S AUTO
11021 Tuxford St.
Sun Valley, CA 91352
818/767-6615, 213/549-8486
HOURS: MON-FRI: 8-5 SAT: 9-2
CREDIT CARDS: MC, V

Marv's auto carries over 45,000 item numbers in their computerized used parts inventory. All their parts are cleaned and tested and carry a six month guarantee. They have 20 experienced countermen to help you find the part you need. You can save 50 to 65% off the cost of new parts when you buy from Marv's. Why spend more on new parts when Marv's are less and are guaranteed?

∞ RV SUPPLIES & EQUIPMENT ∞

THE SHELL CENTER OF THOUSAND OAKS
3242 E. Thousand Oaks Blvd.
Thousand Oaks, CA 91362
805/373-0259
HOURS: MON-FRI: 8:30-6 SAT: 9-4
CREDIT CARDS: AE, MC, V

When we first heard of this place we pictured it to be a store, with a tropical sort of decor, filled with rare and exotic seashells from all over the world. Boy, were we wrong! The Shell Center of Thousand Oaks carries shells for any kind of pick-up truck. Some of the names carried are Snug Top Brahma, Stockland, Vista Supershells and others. First you start out with a bare bones shell and factory options are passed on at cost—at the very least—you save 50%. All shells start out white and have to be painted. After the paint is dry, things like windows and vents have to be added. Most camper shell stores charge $120–140 for painting their shells. The Shell Center of Thousand Oaks charges only $40. No matter when you go out there, you can expect to find about 110–150 shells in stock. You will not only save money here because of the discounts, you'll also end up contented with a camper reflecting your own tastes, not someone's from the factory.

SIX-PAC FACTORY OUTLET
1450 Pomona Rd.
Corona, CA 91720
714/735-2402
HOURS: MON-FRI: 9-5 SAT: 9-4
CREDIT CARDS: MC, V

Since 1938 Six-Pac Factory Outlet has been serving the RV industry with great buys on RV parts, accessories and shells. Depending on what you are buying, savings run from 5 to 25%. They have unadvertised specials, so call to check out their best deals.

VAN DE CAMPER**
7801 Noble Ave.
Van Nuys, CA 91405
818/780-6361
HOURS: MON-FRI: 9-5   SAT: 10-3
CREDIT CARDS: DISC, MC, V

Okay you van enthusiasts, Van De Camper is the place to get a complete van conversion—everything from running boards, seats, windows, carpeting, paneling, televisions, drink trays, refrigerators, and all the other products needed for the self-contained vehicle. You can do the work yourself, or you can let Van de Camper build and install to your specifications. While you're there, look at their catalogs for automobiles, trucks, vans, and performance and racing cars. Their catalogs feature aftermarket items, accessories and replacement parts. You can save between 30 to 50% off dealer prices at Van de Camper. With your BUYING RETAIL IS STUPID coupon, you can save an extra 5% on van supplies, or an extra 10% off catalog orders!

∞ REPAIR & MAINTENANCE ∞

– BODY WORK –

ASSOCIATED AUTO BODY**
11803 Sherman Way
N. Hollywood, CA 91605
818/764-5884
HOURS: MON-FRI: 8-5
CREDIT CARDS: CASH OR CHECKS ONLY

Associated Auto Body mainly does contract work for insurance companies, combining high quality with thoroughness and consistency. Luckily, they also welcome the individual customer and give them a discount on the labor charges. Serving the public in this area since the late 1960's, they do complete frame, auto body repair, and repainting. Price and time estimates are given in advance. The job usually gets done in the promised time, but if it doesn't, they will let you know. Not only will you find the people at Associated Auto Body accommodating and friendly, their work is guaranteed. You'll save an additional 5% discount on labor charges by using your BUYING RETAIL IS STUPID coupon.

– ENGINE WORK –

FRANCO'S ENGINE REBUILDERS
4989 Huntington Dr.
Los Angeles, CA 90032
213/225-4129
HOURS: MON-SAT: 8-6 SUN: 8-4
CREDIT CARDS: CASH ONLY

A professional engineer supervises the remanufacturing of the engines, and you also get factory-direct, wholesale prices. Franco's services domestic and foreign engines; plus they have a large inventory of engines and a complete line of auto parts. They offer a good warranty and have been in business since 1975.

LA SIERRA AUTO
11019 Hole Ave.
Riverside, CA 92505
714/687-1220
HOURS: MON-FRI: 8-5 SAT: 8-12
CREDIT CARDS: CASH ONLY

Trying to salvage your beautiful 1960 Mercedes, but the engine died? Stop by La Sierra Auto and save on foreign and domestic new, used, and rebuilt engines. They also clean and repair engines. Since 1974, they have been rebuilding engines and have really mastered the technology as well as offering low prices. New radiators are available as well. If for some reason they don't have what you need, these friendly folks will most likely be able to refer you to someone else.

– GLASS REPLACEMENT –

ALL STAR GLASS
14326 Oxnard St.
Van Nuys, CA 90401
818/906-0366
HOURS: MON-FRI: 8-5 SAT: 8-12
CREDIT CARDS: AE, MC, V

All Star Glass specializes in windshield replacement for automobiles. Free mobile service is provided, which means, they'll do
the work at your home at no extra charge. Also available are residential or commercial table tops, shower enclosures, doors, wardrobe sliders, quarters, and vents. If you need an estimate, All Star
Glass will give you one on the phone. They provide written
guarantees and have qualified technicians/installers, maintaining
factory standards.
Additional Locations: 10 other shops throughout S. CA

FEDERATED GLASS CO.
1650 N. Glassell, Unit P
Orange, CA 92665
714/282-8020
HOURS: MON-FRI: 8-5 SAT: 9-1
CREDIT CARDS: CASH OR CHECKS ONLY

Federated Glass Company offers wholesale prices to the public.
They will replace any glass on your automobile or truck and offer
mobile service to your front door. With free estimates and savings
ranging from 10 to 50%, you should definitely give them a call.
They guarantee they have the best price in Riverside or Orange
County.

∞ SALES, LEASING & RENTALS ∞

AUTO NOW!
1916 Riverside Dr.
Los Angeles, CA 90039
213/663-6434
HOURS: MON-FRI: 9-6 SAT: 10-3
CREDIT CARDS: MC, V

Auto Now! uses its group purchasing power to get the best deal on a new car, whether buying or leasing to own. They not only shop for the best price on a car, but also shop banks for the best financing or lease rate. Savings of several thousand dollars is not unusual. All makes and models, foreign and domestic, are included. Auto Now! works for you to get you the best possible deal. Wouldn't it be nice to let someone else do all of the leg work? Call for an appointment or a free consumers car guide at 213/663-6434, or call their 24 hour recorded "Info Line" at 800/322-2886 or 213/663-6363.
Additional Locations: Chatsworth (818/772-4120), Long Beach (213/595-5111), Ontario (714/988-9288)

GAYNOR'S CYCLE SALES
11916 S. Prairie Ave.
Hawthorne, CA 90250
213/644-2900
HOURS: MON-FRI: 8-7 SAT: 8-5
CREDIT CARDS: DISC, MC, V

If you're looking for a low cost means of transportation or just fun on the weekends, visit California's largest selection of used motorcycles at Gaynor's Cycle Sales. You can choose from 500 cycles with such brand names as Suzuki, Yamaha, Kawasaki and Honda.

NATIONAL AUTO BROKERS, INC.
23011 Moulton Pky., Suite I-11
Laguna Hills, CA 92653
714/770-7441
HOURS: MON-FRI: 9-6:30
CREDIT CARDS: MC, V, CASHIERS CHECKS

National Auto Brokers (NAB) has serviced Southern Californians for over a decade . They have sold and leased thousands of cars and trucks to customers at enormous savings. They sell all makes and models, domestic or foreign. Their volume allows them to purchase new vehicles at the lowest prices, and because they operate on a low fixed fee, the savings are really remarkable. You can save between $500 to $5,000 depending on the make or model. They take trade-ins and provide financing and leasing OAC. Leases can be tailored to the buyer's specifications, and National Auto Brokers offers the lowest cost "bumper-to-bumper" extended warranty available anywhere. Cashiers checks are preferred, but bank drafts are accepted.

RENT-A-WRECK
12333 W. Pico Blvd.
Los Angeles, CA 90064
213/478-0676
HOURS: MON-SAT: 7-7 SUN: 8-4
CREDIT CARDS: MC, V

Why not go to Rent-A-Wreck where you can save on car rentals by renting a vintage beauty at 20 to 40% less than standard. You can also rent a van, pick-up truck or classic convertible. Their used cars rent for as little as $19.95 a day, some even have free mileage. If you're curious, they will send additional information.
Additional Locations: 29 other offices in S. CA–Call 800/535-1391

UGLY DUCKLING RENT-A-CAR
10620 Venice Blvd.
Culver City, CA 90230
213/837-7752
HOURS: MON-FRI: 8-6 SAT: 9-5
CREDIT CARDS: AE, MC, V

Save a buck, rent a duck. That's their slogan, not ours. But the fact remains that Ugly Duckling will meet or beat other prices in town. You won't know until you call. All cars are used.
Additional Locations: Santa Monica (213/451-4724), West Hollywood (213/874-0975)

∞ SERVICES ∞

– DRIVING SCHOOL –

FORD DRIVING SCHOOL
4624 Hollywood Blvd.
Los Angeles, CA 90027
213/660-1212
HOURS: MON-FRI: 8-11
CREDIT CARDS: MC, V

This is a full driving school service promising the lowest possible rates in town. Ford says they'll save adults taking their courses 50% and savings run 40% for courses designed for teenagers. Need a traffic school because of a speeding ticket? You'll save 20% at Ford's traffic school. In addition to their 15 years of experience, they have dual control cars, male and female instructors and can handle all languages. They also have fast, economy courses where teens can take driver's education and training in one week at their special, low price.

– INSURANCE –

SURVIVAL INSURANCE
4845 Fountain Ave.
Los Angeles, CA 90029
213/960-8200
HOURS: MON-FRI: 9-9   SAT: 9-6
CREDIT CARDS: MC, V

Richard Acunto says he'll save you 15 to 20% on auto insurance if you give him a call Even if you drive an exotic car or have a few tickets, he says he can still save you money on your insurance needs. Remember, you have to have insurance on your car in California, it's the law! So in order to survive, you may want to call Survival Insurance.
Additional Locations: 6 other offices in S. CA–Call 800/441-5533

– SMOG CERTIFICATION –

HOLLYWOOD SMOG CENTER
5900 Melrose Ave.
Los Angeles, CA 90038
213/462-7606
HOURS: MON-FRI: 8-5 SAT: 8-1
CREDIT CARDS: MC, V (CHECKS NOT ACCEPTED)

Since you have to have your car smog certified when you buy it, and then you're required to do it again every two years, we thought you'd like to know about a place providing this service less expensively than most. Hollywood Smog Center charges $15, which they claim is the cheapest smog certifying rate in LA. We checked a lot of other places, and we were usually quoted $19 or more for the service. No appointment is necessary, but take your credit cards or cash because they don't accept checks. You really 'auto' drive in!

∞ TIRES ∞

BOB'S TIRE TOWN
2478-2484 W. Washington Blvd.
Los Angeles, CA 90018
213/731-6389
HOURS: MON-FRI: 7:30-5:30 SAT: 7:30-3:30
CREDIT CARDS: MC, V

Bob's Tire Town offers B.F. Goodrich, Pirelli, Uniroyal, Michelin, Solar Shocks at 10 to 20% above cost. They also offer brake repair, alignment and front-end work at significant savings. There are great buys on custom wheels for those of you with real hot "rides."

GRAND PRIX AUTOMOTIVE CENTER
2314 S. Atlantic Ave.
Monterey Park, CA 91754
213/723-2082
HOURS: MON-SAT: 9-6
CREDIT CARDS: MC, V

You'll find a veritable treasure house of tires for foreign and domestic cars, trucks, vans and RV's at savings of 25 to 40%. Some of the brands they carry include Goodyear, Uniroyal, Michelin, Pirelli and Dunlop. Grand Prix also does excellent front-end work and alignments, tune-ups, brake work and shocks—and at the same great prices.
Additional Locations: Glendale (213/245-3339)

TELETIRE
17622 Armstrong Ave.
Irvine, CA 92714
714/250-9141
HOURS: MON-FRI: 7-6 SAT: 8-1
CREDIT CARDS: MC, V

Teletire is a mail and phone order operation that will save you 40 to 60% off the manufacturer's suggested retail price on tires from Bridgestone, Dunlop, Continental, Yokohama, Michelin and Pirelli. You can also order wheels from Euki and American Racing. They are a division of 4-Day Tire, based in Irvine, CA. With their phones staffed by tire experts, not just order clerks, you can feel comfortable placing an order with Teletire

BEAUTY SUPPLIES

BALL BEAUTY SUPPLIES
416 N. Fairfax Ave.
Los Angeles, CA 90036
213/655-2330
HOURS: MON-SAT: 8:30-5:30
CREDIT CARDS: MC, V

Ball Beauty Supplies carries everything for your hair and mani-curing needs, and you'll save 30 to 50% by shopping there. They have been serving the public for over 35 years and know what their customers like. You will find everything from hair coloring and cosmetics to brushes and curling irons. Excuse the pun, but you'll have a ball shopping at Ball Beauty Supplies.

BEAUTY SUPPLY WAREHOUSE
743 W. Taft Ave.
Orange, CA 92665
714/921-8482
HOURS: MON-FRI: 9-5
CREDIT CARDS: MC, V

With 5,000 square feet filled with products for nails, hair, make-up, accessories, rollers, and perms, you're bound to find everything you need at the Beauty Supply Warehouse. They carry most major brands including Roux, Clairol, Loreal, and many others. Know what you want and get great prices, usually at 30 to 50% below retail prices charged elsewhere. Don't forget to check out their close-out sales, too.

THE COSMETIC OUTLET
1666 N. Highland Ave.
Hollywood, CA 90028
213/463-6164
HOURS: MON-SAT: 9-5
CREDIT CARDS: MC, V

Here's a wonderful opportunity to buy cosmetics bearing one of the world's most famous names, but we have been sworn to secrecy, so we can't mention any names here. When shopping at The Cosmetic Outlet you can save 10 to 50% off retail on cosmetics worn by so many stars and many of the world's most beautiful women. This wonderful outlet also carries products such as nail polish and perfumes. For everything to make you look your very best, visit The Cosmetic Outlet.

CROWN DISCOUNT BEAUTY SUPPLY**
19228 Ventura Blvd.
Tarzana, CA 91356
818/344-8307
HOURS: MON-FRI: 9:30-6 SAT: 9:30-5:30
CREDIT CARDS: MC, V

Crown Discount Beauty Supply has been serving their customers for the past seven years with hair care, nail care and hair accessories at 10 to 15% off retail. Favorite products such as Sebastian, Paul Mitchell, Joico and Mastey are carried, and if you desire, they'll test your purchases on you at their full service hair salon. Most of Crown's experienced staff have their hair and nail care licenses. You can "trim" an additional 10% off the purchase price when you shop with a BUYING RETAIL IS STUPID coupon here!

JACK SPERLING BEAUTY SUPPLY**
13639 Vanowen St.
Van Nuys, CA 91405
818/985-2225
HOURS: MON-SAT: 10-6

CREDIT CARDS: MC, V

This beauty supply store has been in business at the same location since the late 1960's. They stand behind their products 100% because they carry quality merchandise. You will find every type of beauty supply item you might need at 20% above cost. They cater to the movie and television studios and the general public selling at wholesale prices. Many of their customers are professionals who invest a lot of time and money in their appearances. You can see some of their satisfied customers represented in the over 200 autographed pictures of stars and models covering their walls. Qualified professionals are always available to answer questions on your hair, skin, and nails. Every year Jack Sperling Beauty Supply conducts one of the largest nail shows in the country. All major brand names are available. You'll receive an additional 10% discount on your purchase if you present your BUYING RETAIL IS STUPID coupon.

LORA BEAUTY CENTER
18737 Ventura Blvd.
Tarzana, CA 91356
818/705-4030
HOURS: MON-SAT: 9:30-6:30
CREDIT CARDS: MC, V

Looking for the best prices in town on Lancome products? Sean Miles, the owner of Lora Beauty Center, guarantees to beat anyone's price on Lancome products and fragrances. In addition to Lancome, they carry a complete line of beauty supplies and professional hair care products. You'll also find name brand fragrances such as Halston, Fendi, Paris, Nina Ricci, Chanel, Cartier, Polo, and many others. And last but not least, they provide full salon and nail service. Remember to head for Lora Beauty Center when you run out of one of your Lancome products. You'll save 10 to 50% off retail shopping here.

PFC FRAGRANCE & COSMETICS
906 S. Los Angeles St.
Los Angeles, CA 90015
213/627-9090
HOURS: MON-SAT: 9-5 SUN: 11-4
CREDIT CARDS: MC, V

Revlon, Max Factor, Ultima II, Germaine Monteil, Borghese, Jean Nate, Ciara, Norrell, Maroe, Bill Blass cosmetics and fragrances can be found at 25 to 60% off retail at PFC Fragrance & Cosmetics. They are a factory-direct outlet, so make it a point to check out their prices, service and quality. Additional health and beauty aids and gift items can also be found here.

STERLING BEAUTY SUPPLY CO.
1244 N. Vine St.
Hollywood, CA 90028
213/463-6801
HOURS: MON-SAT: 9:30-7 SUN: 11-5
CREDIT CARDS: MC, V

Save 20 to 40% off retail prices on one of the largest selections of brand-name beauty products, shampoos, hair coloring, permanents, and any other products to make you more beautiful. They also carry products like TCB and Lustra-Silk. You will find that Sterling Beauty Supply Company has a friendly, knowledgeable staff to give you expert advice.
Additional Locations: 7 other stores throughout S. CA

WILSHIRE BEAUTY SUPPLY CO.
5401 Wilshire Blvd.
Los Angeles, CA 90036
213/937-2000
HOURS: MON-SAT: 8-5:30 SUN: 11-5
CREDIT CARDS: MC, V

Your hair really is your crowning glory. You can have on an unbelievable outfit, but if your hair isn't together, forget it. At Wilshire Beauty Supply Company you can purchase all the hair products you need for 20% above cost. If you would like to try a new product someone there will be happy to recommend something suitable for your type of hair. You will also find a selection of cosmetics, nail products, salon equipment and furniture. They have a monthly catalog for professional cosmetologists, as well as seminars and educational classes.
Additional Locations: Arleta (381/891-5745), Beverly Hills (213/276-0627), Simi Valley (805/526-2281), W. Los Angeles (213/475-3531)

∞ SALON EQUIPMENT ∞

GALAXY SALON EQUIPMENT MFG. CO.
5411 Sheila St.
Los Angeles, CA 90040
213/728-3980
HOURS: MON-FRI: 10-5
CREDIT CARDS: MC, V

Have you been seriously considering opening your own beauty salon? Do you need some advice? From a fabulous salon layout to the grand opening, Galaxy Salon Equipment is at your service with factory direct prices. You can expect to save 50% off retail on your salon equipment. If new equipment doesn't quite fit in your budget, you can save even more on their used equipment. Financing is available. In their inventory Galaxy also carries hospital and physician supply equipment.

∞ WIGS ∞

SHAKY WIGS OF HOLLYWOOD
6364 Hollywood Blvd.
Hollywood, CA 90028
213/461-8481
HOURS: MON-SAT: 10-7
CREDIT CARDS: AE, MC, V

If you are looking for that perfect wig, hair accessory or even hairspray, go straight to Shaky Wigs of Hollywood. We flipped our wigs when we saw over 100 wigs to choose from! Don't be shy! Go ahead and try on any number of their wide selection of wigs at a discount of 10 to 20% off retail. By the way, this store isn't just for women. Men will find wigs and toupes made from 100% human hair. Other services offered are braiding and weaving.

BOATING & MARINE PRODUCTS

B & B MARINE EQUIPMENT & SERVICE, INC.
2701 W. Coast Hwy.
Newport Beach, CA 92663
714/646-8901
HOURS: MON-SAT: 9-5   SUN: 10-2
CREDIT CARDS: MC, V

B & B has been doing business at this Newport Beach location since 1977. They carry a full line of communication and navigation equipment, paint and finishes, safety equipment, and all boating accessories. In fact, they say, "Call us for anything marine." Next day delivery is available and also installation service. They carry all major brands including Raytheon, Furuno, Micrologic, Datamarine, Apelco, Marinetech, Sterling, 3M and many others. Call around. All of their products are discounted and the best price is guaranteed. Orders are taken over the phone so, if you already know what you need, give them a call.

GOLDEN FLEECE DESIGNS INC.**
441 S. Victory Blvd.
Burbank, CA 91502
818/848-7724
HOURS: MON-FRI: 8-5
CREDIT CARDS: MC, V

Canvas, canvas and more canvas. Anything made from canvas can be found here. Canopies, flags, duffle bags, boat covers, sailboat accessories, nautical gift items, marine hardware and hats. They will also custom make any canvas item to suit your needs. You can purchase industrial canvas by the yard and you can also silkscreen and embroider on any item. If you remember to use your BUYING RETAIL IS STUPID coupon and you can sail off with an additional 10% discount.

LYNWOOD BATTERY MFG. CO., INC.
3171 Fernwood Ave.
Lynwood, CA 90262
213/631-2200
HOURS: MON-FRI: 8-4:30
CREDIT CARDS: CASH OR CHECKS ONLY

Just as the name implies, the Lynwood Co. manufactures their own batteries. They have been selling their merchandise to the trucking industry and marine dealers in California, Arizona and Colorado since the 1930's. Even though they use only the highest quality materials, you can buy your battery at 20 to 50% over cost! That should give you a charge.

RAP DISCOUNT AUTO PARTS & MARINE SUPPLY
21407 Vanowen St.
Canoga Park, CA 91303
818/884-3370
HOURS: MON-FRI: 8-10 SAT: 8-5 SUN: 9-5
CREDIT CARDS: CASH OR CHECKS ONLY

Rap is the specialist in reconditioning of cylinder heads for automotive or marine engines. They carry a complete line of spare parts for engines of all types and sell them at 30 to 70% below retail prices. You'll find Cannon, Adesco parts, Ditzler paints and supplies, welding supplies, and marine accessories. In addition to foreign and domestic auto parts, they also have a complete machine shop for any kind of engine work, and they make hydraulic, air conditioning and power steering hoses.

BOOKS & MAGAZINES

∞ NEW & USED ∞

BODHI TREE ANNEX
8585 Melrose Ave.
Los Angeles, CA 90069
213/659-3227
HOURS: 7 DAYS A WEEK: 11-7
CREDIT CARDS: MC, V

The people at the Bodhi Tree Annex specialize in homeopathic remedy, herbs, and all metaphysical books. Shoppers will find a good stock of new age and religions of the world books. Discounts of 50% off retail are not unusual. They buy and sell, and they have a substantial inventory of used books. It's a fun place to browse, especially if you are philosophically undernourished.

BOOK MART U.S.A.
12152 Victory Blvd.
N. Hollywood, CA 91606
818/980-2241
HOURS: TUES-SAT: 10-6
CREDIT CARDS: CASH OR CHECKS ONLY

You've been playing the game all your life. Now learn "How to Win at Bingo." This is probably the only store that carries this manual of current Bingo games. Along with this book, you can get complete Bingo game supplies. Book Mart stocks over ten thousand separate titles of paperback books at 20 to 70% off the publisher's printed price, and you'll save 10 to 20% on other merchandise. What other merchandise? Buttons! They have custom made buttons for every occasion. There is also a bargain table with paperbacks priced at 49¢ each.

DISCOUNT READER BOOKSTORE
8651 Lincoln Blvd.
Los Angeles, CA 90045
213/410-1069
HOURS: MON-SAT: 9-9   SUN: 9-6
CREDIT CARDS: MC V

Discount Reader Bookstore offers a 10% discount on paperbacks and a 20% discount on hardcovers. If a book is on the NY Times Best Seller list, you'll get 25% off paperbacks and 35% off hardcovers! They are distributors for North Point Press, one of the best small publishers in California. You'll find a good selection of metaphy-sical, cookbooks and health books. You can save up to 70% in a special section of even further discounted books.

DUTTON'S BOOKS
5146 Laurel Canyon Blvd.
N. Hollywood, CA 91605
818/769-3866
HOURS: MON-FRI: 9:30-9   SAT: 9:30-6   SUN: 11-5
CREDIT CARDS: AE, MC, V

Dutton's Books carries a huge stock of new, used and rare books. This is a book lovers paradise! With a half a million books in stock, you can also trade in your used books and get a 40% discount toward your purchase. They also carry publishers overstock at tremendous discount prices, research and scholarly books on nearly every subject and category, and children's books. To top it all, they have imported greeting cards and free gift wrapping.
Additional Locations: Brentwood (213/476-6263), Burbank (818/840-8003), Los Angeles (213/683-1199)

ENCYCLOPEDIAS BOUGHT & SOLD
14071 Windsor Pl.
Santa Ana, CA 92705
714/838-3643
HOURS: DAILY BY APPOINTMENT ONLY: 10-10
CREDIT CARDS: CASH OR CHECKS ONLY

E N C Y C L O P E D I A—remember when you knew you could spell when you sang Encyclopedia? Well Kathleen Italiane has been singing this song for the last 25 years. She has one of the largest and most varied collection of encyclopedias in the Western United States dating from the late 1800's to 1989. Her collection consists of Britannia, Americana, Colliers, World Book, New Book of Knowledge, Compton, Academic American, and she'll sell them at a savings of 10-60% on used sets and at least 40% on new sets. Harvard Classics and Time-Life books are also available.

VALLEY BOOK CITY
5249 Lankershim Blvd.
N. Hollywood, CA 91601
818/985-6911
HOURS: MON-THUR: 11-7 FRI-SAT: 10-8 SUN: 11-6
CREDIT CARDS: MC, V

There are over 100,000 new and used books here, and you can save 30-90%! That's right—because all new hardback books are sold for 30% off cover price. It pays to become a regular because Valley Book City issues their hard-core patrons a 20% courtesy discount card, and that means savings of 50%! Bargain shelves inside the store and on the sidewalk have hardcover books for as low as 29¢. They buy, sell and trade new, used, rare and collectable books. Here's where you can find scarce and out-of-print titles. They have thousands of new, used, and rare paperbacks, too, at 50% off cover price (some exceptions). Their books are arranged in over 400 categories. They not only accept cash, checks and credit cards, they've been known to haggle on occasion as well. You'll find all of this in a quiet, relaxed atmosphere that encourages browsing.

∞ USED BOOKS ∞

ACRES OF BOOKS
240 Long Beach Blvd.
Long Beach, CA 90802
213/437-6980
HOURS: TUES-SAT: 9:15-5
CREDIT CARDS: CASH OR CHECKS ONLY

Acres of Books, in business since 1934, has an overwhelming selection of books. With 13,000 square feet of floor space and

750,000 books, it's about the largest store of its kind. In fact, it's so big there are maps strategically placed around the store to help their customers find their way around. Acres of Books attracts bookworms from all over Southern California. Head on down to Long Beach if you are searching for a particular book no longer in print. If you love books, you'll find a visit a real treat, and they get new shipments every day.

BOOK CASTLE INC.
200 N. San Fernando
Burbank, CA 91502
818/845-1563
HOURS: MON-FRI: 10-7   SAT-SUN: 10-6
CREDIT CARDS: MC, V

There are over 200,000 used hardbacks, 100,000 paperbacks, and 500,000 magazines stocked in this massive, concrete building that does resemble a castle, and you'll save 20 to 60%. There's a large inventory of comic books and a large, full-service newsstand that has over 1,000 periodicals on sale monthly. Right next to the main store is Book Castle's Movie World store, devoted to selling items of all description related to the history and lore of the cinema. Included in their inventory are photographs, movies posters, lobby cards, movie and TV scripts, books and other memorabilia.

BOOK CITY
6627 Hollywood Blvd.
Hollywood, CA 90028
213/466-2525
HOURS: MON-SAT: 10-10   SUN: 10-6
CREDIT CARDS: MC, V

This truly is a city of books—literally thousands and thousands of them. You can save 20 to 50% on your purchases, and in addition, Book City has one of Southern California's largest selection of used books. If you have a little time to spare, just browse through the book stacks and find reading treasures for as little as 49¢. And, if you are a movie or music buff (and who isn't?), then you must visit their separate collectibles store right next door where you can find photos, magazines, autographs and the like, dating back to 1900!

THE BOOKANEER
6755 Tampa Ave.
Reseda, CA 91335
818/881-6808
HOURS: TUES-SAT: 10-6
CREDIT CARDS: CASH OR CHECKS ONLY

Opened in 1974 by Jim and Shirley, genuine bookworms will have
a hard time leaving this used bookstore. The Bookaneer has over
150,000 titles in their collection of paperbacks, hardbacks, comic
books, biographies, science fiction, romance, western, non-fiction,
and of course children's books. They buy, sell and trade 500 books
a day, so their stock is always changing. Upon purchase of a few
paperbacks no longer in print, we received book credits good
towards future purchases. Though not the largest used bookstore in
the area, it's definitely the friendliest. Jim's sense of humor seems
to rub off on his customers. We can't tell you how refreshing it was
to see people, strangers to each other when they entered the store,
discussing the works of a favorite author like old friends.

BOOKSVILLE
2626 Honolulu Ave.
Montrose, CA 91020
818/248-9149
HOURS: 7 DAYS A WEEK 9:30-7:00
CREDIT CARDS: CASH OR CHECKS ONLY

The proprietress of this charming bookstore is Shirley McCormick.
You'll be able to find special buys in used books for every member
of the family. Start your search here for treasures at bargain prices.

COSMOPOLITAN BOOK SHOP
7007 Melrose Ave.
Los Angeles, CA 90038
213/938-7119
HOURS: MON-SAT: 11:30-6
CREDIT CARDS: CASH OR CHECKS ONLY

After 30 years in business, and 17 years at their present location,
nothing is new at Eli Goodman's Cosmopolitan Book Shop. There
is, however, for those who enjoy rummaging through one of the

West Coast's largest collections of used, out-of-print and anti-quarian books, the possibility of finding the rare, the unusual and the different. Included in the 3,000 square feet of space are paper-backs, select copies of magazines, and LP's of every description. Top prices are offered for whole collections, or they'll make accept-able trades. A customer can expect to save as much as 50% on all purchases, and it's even possible to buy a book for as little as 25¢.

PIK-A-BOOK CO.
8422 W. 3rd St.
Los Angeles, CA 90048
213/651-3566
HOURS: MON-SAT: 9:30-5
CREDIT CARDS: CASH OR CHECKS ONLY

If you're looking for that used or out-of-print book you just can't find elsewhere, then Pik-A-Book Co. is the place for you. Their books range from 50¢ up to $1,000 for a very rare book. If you're interested in good buys or have a collection to sell, then come in and visit with Harry Bierman. He's been in business since 1955 and sells merchandise to many other bookstores, so you know the price is right. You'll find no paperbacks, textbooks, or Book-Of-The-Month Club books here.

MARKSTU DISCOUNT COMICS
3642 7th St.
Riverside, CA 92501
714/684-8544
HOURS: MON-SAT: 10:30-6 SUN: 11-5
CREDIT CARDS: AE, DISC, MC, V

What do Batman, Spiderman, and Superman have in common? They can all be found and many more of your comic book favorites at Markstu Discount Comics. The 500,000 comic books in their 4,000 square foot store will definitely keep you busy searching for your pastime heros. Since 1954, Markstu has been collecting, buying and trading comic books. Their many services offered are special attention to beginning collectors and locating comic books if they don't have it. Make sure to check out their special tables with values of 50–60% savings.

BUILDING & REMODELING

∞ AIR CONDITIONING & HEATING ∞

AIR CONDITIONING EXCHANGE
6900 San Fernando Rd.
Glendale, CA 91201
818/849-2495
HOURS: TUES-FRI: 8:30-5:30 SAT: 8-4
CREDIT CARDS: AE, MC, V

You can find everything you need for central heating and air conditioning equipment at the Air Conditioning Exchange. Whether you are installing a complete system or fixing an old one, you will find prices at 20 to 50% above their cost. Not only do they carry major brand names such as Carrier, Lennox, Payne, Day and Night, and Whirlpool, they also stock supplies, parts, custom sheet metal, and fireplaces.

HOME COMFORT CENTER**
18419 Vanowen St.
Reseda, CA 91335
818/345-9557
HOURS: MON-FRI: 10-6 SAT: 10-4
CREDIT CARDS: MC, V

If you are the handywoman or handyman in your household, you will definitely want to head over to Home Comfort Center, a place geared toward home owners. They carry everything you'll need for do-it-yourself heating and air conditioning at savings of 50 to 60% off retail prices. Whether you're doing repair work or installing an entire system, you'll find everything at Home Comfort Center. Experts on their staff will help you every step of the way, and it's all free. Their showroom has extensive displays designed especially to be unintimidating to do-it-yourselfers, and they will go out of their way to make you feel comfortable doing this kind of work. You'll find extra comfort saving an additional 10% when you use your BUYING RETAIL IS STUPID coupon.

NUTONE PRODUCTS DISTRIBUTOR
14670 Firestone Blvd., #410
La Mirada, CA 90638
213/921-8933
HOURS: MON-FRI: 8-10 SAT: BY APPOINTMENT ONLY
CREDIT CARDS: CASH OR CHECKS ONLY

These people are the factory distributors for all Nutone products.
You'll save 25 to 30% off the retail price on heaters, exhaust fans,
paddle fans, track lighting, intercoms, security systems, door bells,
bath cabinets, mirrors, food centers, central vacuum systems, and
more. They have been in business over 14 years, and they offer
shipping on all items.

∞ BRICKS, BLOCKS & MASONRY ∞

BRICK CORRAL
24100 Orange Ave.
Perris, CA 92370
714/657-1807
HOURS: TUES-FRI: 8-5 SAT: 8-2 (OCT-APR) 8-4 (MAY-SEPT)
CREDIT CARDS: MC, V

Brick Corral is a division of New Davidson Brick Company. This
is their outlet for seconds and overruns so you pay prices that are far
below wholesale! Some of the brick products are 5–15¢ less than
what a contractor would pay. These bricks, blocks and pavers are
perfect for patio and garden projects. They are structurally sound
and are considered cosmetic seconds.

ELLIOTT PRECISION BLOCK CO.
157 N. Rancho Ave.
San Bernardino, CA 92410
714/885-6581
HOURS: MON-FRI: 7-5 SAT: 7-NOON
CREDIT CARDS: MC, V

Elliott Precision Block Co. has been around since 1946 offering first
quality materials for the do-it-yourselfer at factory direct prices.

Their customers are generally professional contractors needing materials for projects such as building walls, fences and courtyards. They carry blocks, brick, cement, pavers, sand, steel and everything needed to build a fireplace from scratch. If you know exactly what you need, they will be happy to quote you prices over the phone.

SHIPS CONCRETE COMPANY
6925 Cherry Ave.
Long Beach, CA 90805
213/630-1775
HOURS: MON-FRI: 7-5:30 SAT: 7-NOON
CREDIT CARDS: CASH OR CHECKS ONLY

Okay, how many times have you been looking for just the right place to buy sand, cement and masonry supplies? Well, search no more because Ships Concrete Company carries all the sand, cement and masonry supplies you need. They have firsts and seconds here at low low prices. Parking is available and free.

∞ CABINETS, CLOSETS & COUNTERTOPS ∞

CLOSET STORE, THE
2801 S. Robertson Blvd.
Los Angeles, CA 90034
213/838-0337
HOURS: MON-SAT: 9-6 SUN: 10-5
CREDIT CARDS: AE, MC, V

At The Closet Store, do-it-yourselfers with an urge to revamp their closets can save up to 30% on closet accessories of all types—hangers, belt holders, shoe racks, custom shelving, basket systems, clothes boxes and zipper bags. As an alternative, custom installation is available if you don't have the time or the inclination to tackle the job yourself. For special savings, there's also a bargain table.
Additional Locations: Lawndale (213/371-1177)

FAIRFAX KITCHEN CABINETS
935 N. Fairfax Ave.
Los Angeles, CA 90046
213/656-1133
HOURS: MON-FRI: 7-4
CREDIT CARDS: CASH OR CHECKS ONLY

Fairfax will plan your cabinets for kitchen and bath. Custom woods include oak and birch, or Fairfax will refinish your existing cabinets with formica or wood. They also do countertops and wardrobes. With their free consultations and expert planning, you will save 30 to 40% on the work—an incredible bargain!

FROCH'S WOODCRAFT SHOP, INC.
6659 Topanga Canyon Blvd.
Canoga Park, CA 91303
818/883-4730
HOURS: AE, MC, V
CREDIT CARDS: MON-THUR: 9-6 FRI: 9-5 SAT: 9-6

Froch's Woodcrafts Shop, a large store with standard and unusual pieces, is by far the best unfinished furniture store we've ever seen. They manufacture their unfinished furniture in the San Fernando Valley with their own craftsmen. This allows for fantastic savings of 50% off retail. You will find a wide assortment of all types of home furnishings, from dining room tables and chairs to huge wardrobes and dressers. You can remodel or build your kitchen with cabinetry available in different styles and sizes. If you're ready to revamp your closets, Froch's has various units you can mix and match to suit your own particular needs. Everything is all wood and of the finest quality, so you won't be able to find any particle board at Froch's Woodcraft Shop.
Additional Locations: Panorama City (818/787-3682)

KITCHEN & BATH CENTER**
8523 Canoga Ave., Units D & E
Canoga Park, CA 91303
818/700-1891
HOURS: MON-FRI: 8-6 SAT: 10-4
CREDIT CARDS: CASH OR CHECKS ONLY

Allow Kitchen & Bath Center, a factory-direct outlet, to bring your old kitchen into the 21st century. They have European kitchen specialists, complete professional design service and a full line of traditional and custom cabinets available. Their prices usually run 20 to 40% below retail. Make sure to use your BUYING RETAIL IS STUPID coupon good for 5% off your purchase.

THE KITCHEN & BATH WAREHOUSE**
2149 W. Washington Blvd.
Los Angeles, CA 90018
213/734-1696
HOURS: MON-SAT: 9-5
CREDIT CARDS: MC, V

Kitchen and bathroom cabinets of all qualities and price ranges, from ultra contemporary to old-world traditional, and from cherry to oak are all available at The Kitchen & Bath Warehouse. They also have marble and formica counter tops. All of this at savings from 10 to 60% off retail! Come in and bring your room measurements with you. An expert kitchen designer will help you create a beautiful kitchen or bathroom, one that maximizes storage space and work flow, while creating a room that you will be proud of. And, believe it or not, the designing is absolutely free! Save another 5% by using your BUYING RETAIL IS STUPID coupon.

MARBLE PRODUCTS OF FULLERTON**
112 W. Commonwealth, Bldg. A
Fullerton, CA 92632
714/738-4384
HOURS: MON-FRI: 10-5
CREDIT CARDS: CASH OR CHECKS ONLY

Vanity tops for bathrooms, shower pans, walls, window sills and table tops can be found here, and John Mezei promises to be 10% lower than anyone in Orange County. They manufacture their own products so they are able to make anything of any size or color. Don't forget your BUYING RETAIL IS STUPID coupon at home or you'll miss out on an additional 5% discount.

NISSAN WOODWORKS INC.
2150 W. Washington Blvd.
Los Angeles, CA 90018
213/731-4883
HOURS: MON-SAT: 10-5
CREDIT CARDS: CASH OR CHECKS ONLY

Alfred Nissan specializes in standard and custom cabinetry for your kitchens, bathrooms, bars, and garages. Whether it's wood or laminate cabinets you are looking for, you will find them here at 20 to 40% below retail prices.

PANEL-IT DISCOUNT STORES
6322 W. Slauson
Culver City, CA 90230
213/839-5213
HOURS: MON-SAT: 8:30-5:30 SUN: 9:30-3
CREDIT CARDS: MC, V

Panel-It Discount Stores specialize in prefinished kitchen cabinets at 50% off retail prices. In addition, you will also find bathroom vanities, glass enclosures, counter tops, doors and windows. Panel-It offers you Diamond and Merillat Cabinets, Formica Counter Tops, and Z Brick. You will be pleased dealing with their well-trained, professional sales staff.
Additional Locations: Hawthorne (213/542-1641)

THRIFTY KITCHENS, INC.
16146 Runnymede St.
Van Nuys, CA 91406
818/286-0984
HOURS: MON-FRI: 8-5
CREDIT CARDS: MC, V

For the complete kitchen remodeling job, Thrifty Kitchens offers up to 25–50% off! Along with great quality, they guarantee the best prices. They offer kitchen remodeling, refacing new counter tops, and they supply design ideas as well as all materials and labor.

Look for familiar names such as Formica, DuPont and Corian, to name a few. So, whether you want your kitchen cabinets refaced with a new look, or want to tear out everything and start over again, Thrifty Kitchens could be the solution.

∞ CERAMIC & STONE TILE ∞

CALIFORNIA WHOLESALE TILE
1656 S. State College Blvd.
Anaheim, CA 92806
714/937-0591
HOURS: MON-SAT: 7:30-5
CREDIT CARDS: MC, V

Whether you're looking for bathroom, kitchen, entryway or patio tiles, California Wholesale Tile is the place to shop. You will find quarry tile, terra cotta tile, pool tile, hand painted tile, small mosaic tile and Italian decorative floor and wall tile at one of the largest ceramic tile showrooms in Orange County. They have over 6,000 square feet of showroom filled with great buys. Although the store names are different, they have two other locations in the same area of Anaheim. So, if one of their stores doesn't have exactly what you have in mind, it's a short distance to another showroom.
Additional Locations: Anaheim (714/533-9800), Anaheim (714/937-1818), San Diego (619/695-0220)

DISCOUNT TILE CENTER
8627 Venice Blvd.
Los Angeles, CA 90034
213/202-1915, 213/202-1939
HOURS: MON-FRI: 8-6 SAT: 9-5
CREDIT CARDS: MC, V

This is a great wholesale, factory-direct center for ceramic tiles of all kinds. Discount Tile Center has tiles imported from all over the world. Hand painted tiles come with such names as Huntington Pacific, Marazzi USA, Royal Tiles of Italy, Monarch and Soto Mexican Pavers. Everything is in stock or can be obtained in just a few days. You'll save at least 30% off retail prices all the time, and they also feature special sales during the year where you could be paying less than wholesale!

NEW METRO TILE COMPANY
5477 S. Alhambra Ave.
Los Angeles, CA 90032
213/221-1144
HOURS: MON-FRI: 7-5 SAT: 8-2:30
CREDIT CARDS: MC, V

This store handles imported and domestic tiles of all major brands like H & R Johnson, Huntington/Pacific, and many more. This is a real do-it-yourselfers headquarters. You can save 20 to 50% on your purchases and they have extra special prices on their discontinued items and seconds. When you buy their tile, you can leave a deposit, and they will loan you tools to complete the job.

TILE OUTLET
1551 S. State College Blvd.
Anaheim, CA 92806
714/937-1818
HOURS: MON-SAT: 7:30-5
CREDIT CARDS: MC, V

This 1,500 square foot showroom is filled with ceramic tiles and marble at savings of 25 to 50% off retail. Tile Outlet is an importer with a 23,000 square foot warehouse. They have marble and ceramic tiles in all colors, shapes and sizes. Whether you're remodeling your kitchen or bathroom, you will find prices that should make you very happy at this outlet.

TILE, MARBLE & GRANITE WAREHOUSE**
7118 Reseda Blvd.
Reseda, CA 91335
818/881-1056
HOURS: MON-FRI: 9-6 SAT: 9-5

CREDIT CARDS: MC, V

You'll find miles of tiles at this business based entirely on great service! And, their prices are still 30% below most tile stores. Owner, Jeff Joss, imports most of the tile himself and passes the savings on to you. You will be pleased with the selection of tile, marble and granite for your floors, walls, trims, counters, kitchen, bathrooms, pool or spa. They have their own in-house designers and all the supplies needed for installation. Not only do they offer free professional advice, they also offer free use of tools. Bring in your BUYING RETAIL IS STUPID coupon and they will give you an additional 10% discount. Now that's a deal carved in stone!
Additional Locations: Glendale (818/240-7555)

TILECLUB**
6945 Reseda Blvd.
Reseda, CA 91335
818/345-2276
HOURS: MON-FRI: 9-6   SAT-SUN: 10-4
CREDIT CARDS: MC, V

Tileclub caters to the homeowner. They have a large inventory, and there is no more than a five to seven day wait on non-stock items. You will find ceramic tile, some marble and granite, and related products for counters, walls and floors. Their staff will teach you how to install ceramic tile, and they have rental equipment and offer tile cutting service too. Savings run 20 to 50% off retail, and you can save more at their January clearance sale. Whatever you do, don't forget to bring along your BUYING RETAIL IS STUPID coupon for an additional 10% discount!
Additional Locations: Encinitas (619/632-1178), Escondido (619/745-9123), La Mesa (619/697-6400), San Diego (619/276-0271)

VALLEY TILE DISTRIBUTORS
1618 S. San Gabriel Blvd.
San Gabriel, CA 91776
213/283-5085
HOURS: MON-SAT: 9-5
CREDIT CARDS: MC, V

One of the largest ceramic tile showrooms in Southern California, Valley Tile is never undersold. Their savings range from 20 to 80% (the 80% is on their closeouts), and they are really "wholesalers to the public". They carry the biggest names, give instructions to the do-it-yourselfers, cut tile, and have tools and setting materials. Valley Tile has been selling tiles from around the world for everything from your kitchen to your swimming pool since 1965.

WESTERN STATES STONE & TILE CO.
1849 E. Slauson Ave.
Los Angeles, CA 90058
213/582-6117
HOURS: MON-FRI: 8-4 SAT: 8-12:30
CREDIT CARDS: CASH ONLY

You won't be able to miss this place because they are a city block long with over 20,000 square feet full of merchandise. They have imported products of glazed and unglazed tile from all over the world—floor tile, sink tile, shower tile, as well as marble, slate and quarry tiles. In the same location since 1949, they have experienced salespeople to help solve your tile questions and problems. Why not take advantage of their large selections and great discounts, usually 35% off retail prices? You'll find bigger bargains on their first quality merchandise that has been discontinued. They also speak Spanish.

∞ DOORS, WINDOWS & MIRRORS ∞

ALL STAR GLASS
14326 Oxnard St.
Van Nuys, CA 90401
818/906-0366
HOURS: MON-FRI: 8-5 SAT: 8-12
CREDIT CARDS: AE, MC, V

All Star Glass specializes in windshield replacement for autos. Free mobile service is provided, which means, they will do the work at your home at no extra charge. Also available are residential or commercial table tops, shower enclosures, wardrobe sliders, doors, quarters, and vents. If you need an estimate, All Star Glass will give you one on the phone. They provide written guarantees and have qualified technicians/installers, maintaining factory standards.
Additional Locations: 10 other shops throughout S. CA

ALL VALLEY SHOWER DOOR CO.
14665 Arminta St.
Van Nuys, CA 91402
818/782-7477
HOURS: MON-FRI: 8-5 SAT: 8:30-12
CREDIT CARDS: CASH OR CHECKS ONLY

Marilyn Singer is the manager of this establishment that offers standard and custom shower enclosures, mirrors, wardrobe doors, and anything in glass. Contractors are welcome. You'll find brochures and samples on display.

OLD WORLD
1915 Elise Circle
Corona, CA 91719
714/272-9600
HOURS: MON-FRI: 7-4
CREDIT CARDS: CASH OR CHECKS ONLY

Doors, doors, doors...1,000 to select from in solid panels to leaded glass. These doors are not seconds, but closeouts on discontinued

- 79 -

lines and are still in factory fresh cartons at savings of 50 to 70%. All doors in their 18,000 square foot warehouse are solid hard-woods, no veneers. Stock is constantly changing.

PREFERRED GLASS
1839 Napa St.
Northridge, CA 91324
818/628-6902
HOURS: MON-FRI: 8-6 SAT: 10-3
CREDIT CARDS: CASH OR CHECKS ONLY

Preferred Glass is your one stop glass shop. Whether you happen to be looking for window panes, mirrors, store fronts, sliding glass doors, or tub and shower enclosures, you'll find them here at about 30% below retail prices. They give free estimates and also one-day mobile service on automobile glass repair.
Additional Locations: 7 other shops throughout S. CA

∞ GATES & FENCING ∞

FENCE FACTORY
29414 Roadside Dr.
Agoura, CA 91301
818/889-2240
HOURS: MON-FRI: 8-5 SAT: 9-3
CREDIT CARDS: MC, V

Save 10–50% below retail on wood fences, ornamental iron fences, chain link fences, fittings, gates, poultry wire and more at the Fence Factory. They have a superb staff to install everything for you, or provide the do-it-yourselfer with all necessary materials. Custom work is available, too.
Additional Locations: Goleta (805/965-2817), Santa Maria (805/928-5848), Ventura (805/485-8831)

J & Y WELDING & IRONWORKS
11151 S. Avalon Blvd.
Los Angeles, CA 90061
213/756-9215
HOURS: MON-SAT: 8-5
CREDIT CARDS: CASH OR CHECKS ONLY

J & Y Welding has been in business since 1980 installing motorized gates for guarded estates or apartments. Specializing in ornamental ironworks such as gates, window bars, pool fences, and handrails, they will also custom design and build to specifications. You can expect savings of at least 15% over what others would charge.

∞ HOME DESIGNS ∞

HIAWATHA HOMES**
16706 Bollinger Dr.
Pacific Palisades, CA 90272-1148
213/454-4809
HOURS: MON-FRI: 9-5
CREDIT CARDS: CASH OR CHECKS ONLY

Looking to save money on building your own home? The first thing you should do is place an order with Hiawatha Homes. Six books filled with 1,000 designs for single family homes will cost you a total of $19.00. After you decide on the home of your dreams, order a set of four working drawings and two outline specifications at a cost ranging from $95 to $600. Some of these plans could easily cost $3,000 to $5,000 prepared by a designer or architect as a custom plan, and yet the quality would be no better than the plans you can buy from Hiawatha Homes. Their plans are designed primarily for the West and meet California building codes. Save time and money on building your next home, and build in an additional 10% discount using your BUYING RETAIL IS STUPID coupon. Remember, the coupon works with the plans, not the house.

∞ ONE-STOP HARDWARE STORES ∞

A–WAHL'S BUILDING MATERIALS
11501 Tuxford St.
Sun Valley, CA 91352
818/767-9400
HOURS: MON-FRI: 7-6 SAT: 8-6 SUN: 8-4:30
CREDIT CARDS: DISC, MC, V

This family owned and operated business is on five and a half acres and has been serving the public for the past 30 years. They carry such brand names as Skil, Makita, Milwaukee, and Armstrong. Everything related to building projects of every kind can be found at A–Wahl's. You'll find great prices on power tools, lumber, roofing material, hardware, sand and gravel, fencing, plumbing materials, electrical, and paint. You name it, and if it has to do with building, they probably have it. Savings run at least 50% off retail.

BUILDER'S DISCOUNT
20914 Nordhoff St.
Chatsworth, CA 91311
818/341-3646
HOURS: MON-FRI: 7-9 SAT: 7-8 SUN: 8-6
CREDIT CARDS: MC, V

This place has everything at low discount prices year round on name brands for the person who knows exactly what he needs. Builder's Discount carries a complete supply of snap-up lumber, paneling, kitchen cabinets, bathroom vanities, toilets, faucets, hand and power tools, doors and windows, water heaters, light fixtures, drill bits, pipes and fittings, all at savings of 20 to 70%. You'll recognize top name brands such as Dasco, Paramount, True Temper, Skil, Weyerhauyser, Makita, Georgia Pacific, GE, Kwikset, and many others.
Additional Locations: Los Angeles (213/938-5656), N. Hollywood (818/982-5900), Simi Valley (805/552-2725)

L.A. WRECKING COMPANY
810 E. 9th St.
Los Angeles, CA 90021
213/622-5135, 213/623-3646
HOURS: MON-SAT: 8-4:30
CREDIT CARDS: MC, V

It's not what you think. You don't hire these people to wreck your house. L.A. Wrecking Company has everything you need in the way of plumbing fixtures and supplies, bathroom vanities, building materials, kitchen cabinets, light fixtures, all new and used—plus used windows, doors, brick and screens. Save 20 to 50% on these items plus an additional 5% discount on purchases of $100 or more paid in cash. Checks are taken with purchases of $25 or more and credit cards are accepted on purchases over $15.

∞ PAINT ∞

A. A. BAKER'S PAINT & HARDWARE
3925 San Fernando Rd.
Glendale, CA 90065
818/242-7467
HOURS: MON-FRI: 7:30-6 SAT: 7:30-5 SUN: 9-4
CREDIT CARDS: MC, V

Baker's is an institution in Glendale, having been there since 1915. They offer the best discount prices on paint and hardware needs.

PAR PAINT COMPANY INC.**
1801 W. Sunset Blvd.
Los Angeles, CA 90026
213/413-4950
HOURS: MON-FRI: 7:30-5 SAT: 7:30-2
CREDIT CARDS: MC, V

Talk about guys that know paint? Par Paint Company has been in business since 1949 selling paints, lacquers, varnishes, compliances coatings, automotive paints, industrial paints and supplies at wholesale prices. They represent 3M, Lilly Industrial, Gemstar, Guardsmen, Purdy, Pittsburgh Paints, Spectrum Paints, Krylon, Zynolite,

Nason, and Ellis Paint Companies. They also have rollers, spray cans, covers, brushes, and all acoustical supplies. Whatever you need in this department, they've got, and their prices are 20% below retail. You will save an additional 5% when you use your BUYING RETAIL IS STUPID coupon.

SCOTCH PAINTS FACTORY STORE
555 W. 189th St.
Gardena, CA 90248
213/329-1259
HOURS: MON-FRI: 7-5 SAT: 8-9
CREDIT CARDS: CASH OR CHECKS ONLY

Scotch Paints Factory Store is the place to go when you know what you want and are eager to get up to 75% off retail. The paints you purchase here are manufactured at their own plant and are the same ones they sell to million dollar construction companies. They have a selection of 32 exterior and 16 interior colors from which to choose. You'll also find everything in equipment and supplies needed for house painting such as ladders, brushes, rollers, drop cloths, and lots of other things. Because Scotch Paints caters mainly to professionals, the best buys come in five gallon containers. If you don't need quite that much, one gallon containers are available for just a few cents more.
Additional Locations: Hesperia (619/244-3477), Lancaster (805/945-8080), Rancho Temecula (714/677-9498)

∞ PLUMBING & ELECTRICAL ∞

FATOR'S APPLIANCES & PLUMBING
533 S. Western Ave.
Los Angeles, CA 90015
213/386-1743
HOURS: TUES-SAT: 9-5
CREDIT CARDS: MC, V

Family owned and operated, Fator's offers all major appliances at 5 to 10% above cost. They carry a large display of refrigerators, washers, dryers and dishwashers. Knowledgeable salespeople are always happy to give useful information and to point customers in the right direction. They also have microwave ovens and outdoor gas barbecues. If you're going to install your new dishwasher yourself, you will be relieved to know that Fator's carries a complete supply of plumbing materials. There is plenty of parking and free delivery to local areas.

LE ELEGANT BATH
470 Princeland Court
Corona, CA 91719
714/734-8084
HOURS: MON-FRI: 8-5 SAT-SUN: BY APPOINTMENT ONLY
CREDIT CARDS: MC, V

Pamper yourself and relax in one of Le Elegant's beautiful bathtubs. Prices start at $395 and go to just under $2,000. The $2,000 tub is a two person whirlpool with 10 jets and 2 separate air controls. This price includes all hardware and the on/off switch (located on the tub itself) for the air pump. Another two person whirlpool that measures 6' x 42", has 8 jets, and sells complete for $1,398. All of their tubs are nonporous and easy to clean. They use the same suppliers and the exact materials (100% acrylic) that American Standard, Jacuzzi and Kohler use for their products. If you have priced whirlpool tubs lately, you know these prices are amazing. Any color is available on their seven models, and if they don't have it in stock, they will make one up for you. If the color isn't a standard color, bring in a sample so they can custom blend the color for you on the premises. At savings of at least 50% off retail, depending on the model you select, you can save hundreds or thousands of dollars at Le Elegant.
Additional Locations: San Diego (800/863-2284)

MC NALLY ELECTRIC
10792 Los Alamitos Blvd.
Los Alamitos, CA 90720
213/598-9438, 714/761-0692
HOURS: MON-FRI: 9-5
CREDIT CARDS: DISC, MC, V

Whatever your lighting needs, McNally Electric can satisfy them. Table and floor lamps, fluorescents, incandescents, HID, track or recessed lighting, low voltage, indoor or outdoor, you'll find them here at 20–50% savings. Whether your needs are commercial, residential, or office, their trained sales personnel will help you with your purchase. They also carry all the "stuff" that goes behind the light fixture such as switches, breakers, fuses, and PVC. If you have a favorite lamp that needs repair, bring it in. We can't begin to list all of the brand names they carry, but some of the brand names they carry are Tivoli, Fredrick Ranond, Hilite, Nutone, Plantation, Melissa, Angelo, Dinico, and Halo Lighting.

SAVE–MOR PLUMBING SUPPLIES
3361 Hamner Ave.
Norco, CA 91760
714/688-2722
HOURS: MON-FRI: 8-5:30
CREDIT CARDS: DISC, MC, V

At Save-Mor Plumbing Supplies, every employee can take the do-it-yourselfers by the hand and help them with their projects. These projects can range from installing a garbage disposal to plumbing an entire house. While their showroom is only 900 square feet, their inventory of supplies and equipment takes up 2-1/2 acres! Prices run about 20 to 40% below prices at hardware chain stores. They have 40 plumbers that make calls at far less than most since they are the material suppliers. Another plus for shopping here is that their personnel appears to be genuinely pleased to serve you.

LARRY & JOE'S PLUMBING SUPPLIES
10955 Sepulveda Blvd.
Mission Hills, CA 91345
818/365-9394
HOURS: MON-FRI: 8-6 SAT: 8:30-5 SUN: 9-4
CREDIT CARDS: DISC, MC, V

In business since 1967, these people know what they are doing. Whatever you happen to need in plumbing, electrical and hardware supplies, they have at 20 to 30% off normal retail prices. They offer free professional advice to all of you do-it-yourselfers and will provide installation, if that's what you need. Service is their priority and service is what you get at Larry & Joe's Plumbing Supplies. *Additional Locations: Northridge (818/349-2540), Reseda (818/345-6103), Simi Valley (805/584-6800)*

∞ **TOOLS** ∞

J & J TRADING POST
354 N. Glendale Blvd.
Los Angeles, CA 91602
213/250-9656
HOURS: MON-SAT: 8-6   SUN: 9-2
CREDIT CARDS: MC, V

Plumbing and electrical needs, paint, tools (new and used), cement, glass and screens plus any hardware supplies can be purchased from 10 to 15% off retail prices here. In addition to used tools, they also carry other used merchandise such as toilets, sinks and water-heaters. You can have all your doors and windows rescreened, too. J & J Trading Post has been trading and buying used tools at very competitive prices since 1949.

SANTA FE TOOL & SUPPLY
3838 Santa Fe Ave.
Vernon, CA 90058
213/588-1255
HOURS: MON-SAT: 8-5   SUN: 10-3
CREDIT CARDS: AE, DISC, MC, V

This is the undisputed leader in discount prices for tools. They say they have no competition because they will beat all prices. What's more, Santa Fe Tool & Supply guaranties everything they sell. What do they sell? TOOLS—power tools, hand tools, air tools, auto tools and shop tools—including such names as Skil, Hitachi, Makita and the rest. They also sell work gloves and work brushes too. Ask to be put on their mailing list so you can hear about special sales. Any day you visit Santa Fe Tool & Supply you'll save 30 to 50% off retail prices. They have been in business since 1975 and have free parking alongside the store.
Additional Locations: 18 other stores throughout S. CA

∞ WOOD STAINING & REFINISHING ∞

RAY'S WOOD FINISHING
10465 San Fernando Rd., Unit 3
Pacoima, CA 91331
818/899-1488
HOURS: MON-FRI: 8-4:30 SAT: 9-3
CREDIT CARDS: CASH OR CHECKS ONLY

Want to add more cabinets to your kitchen? If you do but have had second thoughts because of the cost, or you couldn't match the stain, Ray's Wood Finishing may be just the ticket. Ray Camacho, a man that loves his work, can help you with the finish of any kind of wood, new or antique. He also does minor repair work, but if the job is too big, he will find someone to do it for you. Ray's guarantees the best price around. He's been in business for seven years, and the money you save will surprise you.

CLEANING & STORAGE

BOX CITY**
16159 Sherman Way
Van Nuys, CA 91406
818/901-0336
HOURS: MON-SAT: 9-6 SUN: 10-3
CREDIT CARDS: AE, DISC, MC, V

If you need a box of any kind, this is definitely your kind of place—gift boxes, mailing boxes, shipping boxes and moving boxes. Whatever kind of box you need they have, plus all necessary supplies for shipping and moving. Not only do they have every kind of box imaginable, but you can expect to save big bucks! We can't mention any names, but Box City is 30% lower than a well known do-it-yourself moving business that most of us have used in the past and wait, it gets better! Not only does Box City charge 50% less for their boxes than your major moving companies, the owner will accept a 10% BUYING RETAIL IS STUPID coupon! So, if you need a box, go to Box City.
Additional Locations: Van Nuys (818/982-5675), W. Los Angeles (213/474-5144)

GLOBE DRUM CO., INC.
1149 S. Eastern Ave.
Los Angeles, CA 90022
213/263-2132
HOURS: MON-FRI: 7-3:30
CREDIT CARDS: CASH ONLY

These are not the kind of drums preferred by professional musicians. Globe Drum is a wholesale factory outlet for empty barrels, drums and trash cans. Why would you want one? They make great packing barrels, water barrels, planters, furniture, displays, and whatever else your imagination can come up with.

∞ CLEANING PRODUCTS ∞

INDIVIDUAL PAPER PRODUCTS
5333 Downy Rd.
Vernon, CA 90058
213/583-4121
HOURS: MON-FRI: 7-5
CREDIT CARDS: CASH OR CHECKS ONLY

This store is family owned and has been in business since 1926. This is a no frills warehouse where you can save big bucks on a wide variety of paper, plastic and aluminum products. You will also find some cleaning supplies. If you don't care what is imprinted on the paper plates, napkins and cups, you'll save even more than the usual 25–50% off retail because they buy the overruns from manufacturers. Get on their mailing list for early announcements of their special sales.

RAY LOTTO INDUSTRIAL RAGS
4607 S. Main St.
Los Angeles, CA 90037
213/232-3226
HOURS: MON-FRI: 8-4
CREDIT CARDS: CASH OR CHECKS ONLY

If you have any need for throw-away wiping cloths or shop rags, you should investigate Ray Lotto Industrial Rags. They give quantity discounts and have a delivery service. Samples are available, so you can preview the rags. This is a speciality store, but Steve Lotto says they've gone from "rags to riches."

CLOTHING & ACCESSORIES

∞ ACTIVE WEAR ∞

CHEAP FRILLS**
8036-1/2 W. Third St.
Los Angeles, CA 90048
213/653-9997
HOURS: MON-SAT: 11-6
CREDIT CARDS: AE, MC, V

If you want to be a hit at your local gym, stop by Cheap Frills. Their expert sales staff will help coordinate your entire workout outfit. They carry dance, swim, athletic and sportswear for women and children, a small men's collection, aerobic shoes, ballet and jazz shoes, body hugging cotton/lycra clothing (mini-skirts), leggings, sport bras and bags. All this at 10 to 20% off retail prices and up to 50% off on sales items. Brand names include Dance France, Carushka, Danskin, Flexatard, Nike, Kicks, Marika, Baryshnikov, Olga, EG Smith and Avia. And if you can't stop by the store, they have a catalog for mail orders. You'll be in the pink, tights that is, when you use your BUYING RETAIL IS STUPID coupon here to save an additional 5%!

LOVE MATCH TENNIS SHOP
21781 Ventura Blvd.
Woodland Hills, CA 91364
818/348-8866
HOURS: MON-SAT: 10-6
CREDIT CARDS: AE, MC, V

As the name suggests, this store offers a huge selection of tennis clothing, shoes, and accessories. From arm bands to warm-up suits, you'll find whatever you need for everyone in the family. Everything is at least 15% off retail, and don't overlook their special price racks for even greater savings!

SANDLER OF THE VALLEY**
19009 Ventura Blvd.
Tarzana, CA 91356
818/881-6999
HOURS: MON-SAT: 10-5:30
CREDIT CARDS: DISC, MC, V

Women and children can find shoes discounted between 10 and 20% at Sandler of the Valley. Dancewear is also available and has been since 1969. You'll find L.A. Gear, Keds, Nike, Mia, Mushrooms, Jumping Jacks, and Capezio brands here. Their very large inventory also includes shoes, socks, and tights. Save an additional 10% when you bring in your BUYING RETAIL IS STUPID coupon.

SHELLY'S DISCOUNT AEROBIC & DANCE WEAR
2089 Westwood Blvd.
Westwood, CA 90025
213/475-1400
HOURS: MON: 10-8 TUES-SAT: 10-6 SUN: 11-4
CREDIT CARDS: AE, DISC, MC, V

You'll save from 50 to 70% on leotards, tights and active wear that are perfect for dancing and those strenuous aerobic workouts. Shelly Seeman has them in all sizes and styles and colors—even for mothers-to-be and for children. She has special sales all the time, as well as a parking lot sale once a month. Brand names include Rachelle, Jenni Rose, Softouch, Marika and Cathy George, to name a few. You'll find a complete selection of costumes and accessories, dance shoes, dancewear and activewear in this well stocked 3,000 square foot store. Dressing rooms and parking are available.

SPORTS SPECTACULAR
8859 W. Pico Blvd.
Los Angeles, CA 90035
213/275-5453
HOURS: MON-SAT: 10-6:30 SUN: 11-5
CREDIT CARDS: AE, DISC, MC, V

Are you searching for the right athletic shoe for every member of your family? Sports Spectacular has over 600 models on display. Brand names include Nike, New Balance, Avia, Converse, Reebok,

Fila, Ellesse and more. While you're there, check out their athletic clothing and team outfitters department for men, women and children. Prices here are discounted 20% off retail, and there's always a close out table with exceptional bargains on clothing and shoes. Parking in rear and municipal parking is across the street.

SUPER SWEAT
696 N. Robertson Blvd.
Los Angeles, CA 90069
213/659-7715
HOURS: MON-FRI: 10-9   SAT-SUN: 10-6
CREDIT CARDS: MC, V

Super Sweat has turned the old-fashioned sweatsuit into a fashion statement. They have stores all over Southern California, and their prices are just about unbeatable! You'll find brand names such as Fila, Levi, and Ten K at 40 to 60% off retail prices. When it comes to selection you just can't beat Super Sweat. You will literally find thousands of items to choose from. They seem to carry every color, every size, every selection you could ever want to find in either men's or women's styles. They also carry shorts, socks, sweat bands, and accessories. Finding what you want here is no sweat!
Additional Locations: 19 other stores throughout S. CA

∞ BRIDAL & FORMAL ∞

BRIDAL DESIGNERS DIRECT**
213/375-4592, 800/999-GOWN
CREDIT CARDS: MC, V

Believe it or not, wedding gowns priced up to 70% off! Selling direct to the public, this discounter of fine wedding gowns holds special sales two Sundays per month in various hotels in Los Angeles and Orange Counties. How do they do it? They keep overhead low and buy in volume direct from the designers and manufacturers at a fraction of wholesale costs. Imagine, a thousand exquisite gowns arranged according to size (4–20) with prices from $100 to $1,000. Call for sale dates in your area, and try on and take home the gown of your dreams. Remember to use your BUYING RETAIL IS STUPID coupon for an additional 5% savings!

THE BRIDE'S ALTERNATIVE
19449 Ventura Blvd.
Tarzana, CA 91356
818/345-8702
HOURS: MON-WED, FRI: 12-6 THUR: 12-8 SAT: 10-6
CREDIT CARDS: MC, V

Finally, a bridal store that offers an alternative—bridal attire and bridesmaids gowns that you can afford! The Bride's Alternative features low prices (10 to 30% off retail) on designer gowns and headpieces, with superior attention to detail and alterations to make your wedding attire the best you've ever seen. Mom and Dad, this is one store that won't put you on the path to the poorhouse!

HALF-PRICE HOUSE
12152 Brookhurst
Garden Grove, CA 92640
714/537-1231
HOURS: MON-FRI: 10-9 SAT: 10-6 SUN: 10-5
CREDIT CARDS: MC, V

This missy store is the oldest discount house in Orange County, and it's no wonder it's so popular. New merchandise arrives almost daily from cities like New York, Miami and Chicago. Many are designer originals and samples—plus casual dresses, sportswear coordinates, and swimwear. Their specialty is special occasion dresses, both long and short, for mother of the bride, cruises, clubs. They have the largest inventory of "after five" clothing in Southern California. All items are available in regular, large and half-sizes, and are priced 50 to 70% below retail.

HOLLYWOOD GALLERY
10800 Pico Blvd.
Los Angeles, CA 90064
213/467-3259
HOURS: 7 DAYS A WEEK: 10-9:30
CREDIT CARDS: MC, V

You'll find a vast selection of men's and women's wear at the Hollywood Gallery. Most merchandise is priced about 10 to 30%

above cost. There are markdowns at the end of each season, and you'll always find specials. They specialize in evening, leather and silk clothing and have an excellent shoe selection to match.

LEON MAX FACTORY OUTLET
3535 S. Broadway
Los Angeles, CA 90013
213/234-0510
HOURS: MON-FRI: 10-6   SAT: 10-4
CREDIT CARDS: MC, V

Ladies, here's the store for you. Leon Max used to sell his designs through Bullocks and Nordstrom; he now has two retail stores in Brentwood and Santa Monica. Fortunately for BUYING RETAIL IS STUPID readers, he has a factory outlet where you will find terrific buys. You can buy an entire silk outfit for around $100. Silk blouses that retail for $250 can be purchased for $90. From casual to formal wear, for the missy to the matronly, you can find all styles at less than wholesale. They also have markdowns once a month on already discounted clothing.

POOR SNOB
12524 Ventura Blvd.
Studio City, CA 91604
818/769-9666
HOURS: MON-WED, FRI-SAT: 9:30-6   THUR: 9:30-8
CREDIT CARDS: AE, MC, V

If you want to look like a million dollars but just don't want to spend the money, then the Poor Snob is for you. They carry the "look," not necessarily the label. Designer styles without designer prices is what you'll encounter at the Poor Snob. Get your famous designer look-alike for $800 instead of $7,000 to $10,000. While this boutique isn't inexpensive, it may just be one of the best values in BUYING RETAIL IS STUPID. The collection you'll find at the Poor Snob reflects their philosophy of, "The best dressed women know that style means everything, and labels don't matter." For sophisticated clothing you really must come here!

STYLE BOUTIQUE
2043 Westcliff Dr., #109
Newport Beach, CA 92660
714/642-7878
HOURS: MON-FRI: 10-6 SAT: 10-5
CREDIT CARDS: MC, V

Style Boutique has an expensive upbeat New York look with everyday discount prices on everything, in sizes 3/4 to 14. Prices here are 50% off retail. Complement your new threads from their large selection of fashion accessories, including an extensive collection of Anne Klein costume jewelry. Other brand names include Calvin Klein, A. Vittidini, Perry Ellis, and Lanvin. They also carry formals and wedding gowns at 75% off retail.

∞ FAMILY APPAREL ∞

CALIFORNIA MART MANUFACTURERS' SAT. SALE
CA Mart Exhibit Hall–Los Angeles St. @ Olympic Blvd.
Los Angeles, CA 90015
213/623-5876
HOURS: HOURS VARY–CALL FOR INFORMATION
CREDIT CARDS: CASH ONLY

We think everyone has heard of the California Mart, but the majority of the public is unaware of how to get in. In general, they are not open to the public, but once a month or so, they allow the public in for a small entrance fee. The buys at these special sales are absolutely incredible! You'll have access to 175 brand names, 300 lines of apparel and all kinds of accessories. Most items are either excess stock or samples, and everything is priced at cost, no mark-ups. As home to all major clothing manufacturers and their sales reps, available space must be continually made for the arrival of new lines. The last time we were at this sale, we bought some jeans with leather inserts tagged at $160, but we paid only $30. Just one visit will make you a true believer in our BUYING RETAIL IS STUPID philosophy! Hours vary, so call the phone number listed above to find out about their next sale, or keep an eye out for their ads in major newspapers. Don't forget to take plenty of cash with you because they don't accept checks or credit cards.

CALIFORNIA SOCKS
401 Ocean Front Walk
Venice, CA 90291
213/399-7818
HOURS: MON-SUN: 9-6
CREDIT CARDS: MC, V

California Socks has 1,700 square feet filled with one of the largest selections of socks in Los Angeles. Yes, we said socks. Not only will you find some of the most unusual socks in town, but they also have socks featuring every state in the United States. Instead of being a collector of spoons for every state, you can now collect socks at wholesale prices. Oh, they also carry underwear.

COOPER BUILDING
860 S. Los Angeles St.
Los Angeles, CA 90014
213/622-1139
HOURS: MON-SAT: 9:30-5:30 SUN: 11-5
CREDIT CARDS: CASH OR CHECKS ONLY*

This place is incredible! The Cooper Building is a "Tall Mall" 11 stories high with 8 selling floors all bulging with exciting merchandise in the heart of the wholesale garment district. You will find quite a collection of outlet stores representing various manufacturers, famous retail stores and discount stores. Whether you shop at the Cooper Building once a month or once a year, you always save 25 to 75% off retail prices every single day of the week. Quality and value prevail in over 70 stores featuring current designer and brand-name fashions for men, women and children, leather fashions, shoes, handbags, fashion accessories, lingerie and home fashions all under one roof. Why spend twice the amount on prestigious labels carried in expensive department stores when you can save a bundle buying the identical item at the Cooper Building?
*Some vendors accept credit cards.
Additional Locations: 70 stores at one location

DISCOUNT CLOTHING CENTER
2881 E. Florence Ave.
Huntington Park, CA 90255
213/583-4930
HOURS: 7 DAYS A WEEK: 11-7
CREDIT CARDS: CASH ONLY

Get your cash out! Discount Clothing Center always has the best prices on Levis, Lee and Wrangler jeans, jackets, shirts, coveralls, and overalls. Prices for jeans range from $14.00 to $24.99. You'll also find great buys on additional men's, children's and women's wear. Free parking and dressing rooms are available.

KOALA BLUE OUTLET
18007 Gale Ave. (Puente Hills Plaza)
City of Industry, CA 91748
818/913-4228
HOURS: MON-FRI: 10-7 SAT: 10-6 SUN: 11-6
CREDIT CARDS: AE, MC, V

This outlet is worth a drive to City of Industry where you can get the famous styles found in the Koala Blue Stores. They carry all women's and children's clothing from the past seasons out of their retail stores. Merchandise is constantly changing, so get it while it's hot. Savings are 50 to 70% off retail.

LA FASHION GALLERY
305 E. 9th St.
Los Angeles, CA 90015
213/624-0490
HOURS: MON-SAT: 9-6 SUN: 11-5
CREDIT CARDS: MC, V

Imagine, if you will, 100 stores offering discounts of 30 to 70% off suggested retail prices under one roof. Actually, you don't have to use your imagination because it really exists! You'll enjoy shopping in a comfortable, air conditioned environment complete with escalators, elevators, security guards and validated parking on the premises. Parents can look forward to finding things for the entire

family. Whether you're looking for clothing, lingerie, shoes, complete bridal services, fabrics, beauty supplies, jewelry or bicycles, you will find it here. There are also restaurants and food concessions if shopping makes you hungry.
Additional Locations: 100 stores in one location

NORDSTROM RACK
3900 S. Bristol St.
Santa Ana, CA 92704
714/751-5901
HOURS: MON-FRI: 10-9 SAT: 10-6 SUN: 11-6
CREDIT CARDS: MC, NORDSTROM, V

The Nordstrom Rack stores are filled with last season's sensational garb from their mall stores. You'll find shoes, clothing and accessories for the entire family. This is also the perfect place to pick up designer labels at generic prices. One of the authors had the opportunity to attend the Academy Awards and wore a chic ensemble she purchased at Nordstrom Rack. She paid just $89 for an outfit that originally retailed for over $300. Prices run 30–70% off retail.
Additional Locations: Chino (714/591-0551), Woodland Hills (818/884-6771)

WAREHOUSE OUTLET
100 N. Maclay
San Fernando, CA 91340
818/361-0292
HOURS: 7 DAYS A WEEK: 8:30-5:30
CREDIT CARDS: CASH OR CHECKS ONLY

Barry Seeman and family own and operate this quaint store, keeping expenses to a minimum. This 3,500 square foot store is tightly packed with excellent values. Men's and children's casual wear, jeans, underwear, jackets, coats, shirts, screen printed t-shirts and thermals are all 30 to 50% off retail. They carry Levi's, Wrangler, Fruit of the Loom, Zeppelin, and Pipeline. Levi's basic 501 denims are stocked in sizes 0–50. In addition, they carry a full range of Levi's pants, jackets, cords, 501's in all colors, and Levi's Nuvos, to mention a few.

WEAR ART THOU**
1717 S. Figueroa St.
Los Angeles, CA 90015
213/746-2347
HOURS: MON-FRI: 10-6 SAT: 10-5 SUN: 11-5
CREDIT CARDS: AE, DISC, MC, V

Wear Art Thou is a discount outlet with prices always at least 70% off retail. Labels include: Esprit, Betty and Sheila, AKA, Bugle Boy and Young Edwardian. For children and infants, they carry Serene and Monkey Wear. Here's the place to get wonderful long and short sleeve t-shirts for only $3.00. You'll find plenty of free parking, and there is a cafe downstairs if you get the munchies. Remember to use your BUYING RETAIL IS STUPID coupon to save an additional 10%.

∞ FASHION ACCESSORIES ∞

ANTELOPE
12212 Ventura Blvd.
Studio City, CA 91604
818/980-4299
HOURS: MON-SAT: 9:30-6:30
CREDIT CARDS: AE, MC, V

Antelope carries all kinds of leather goods and purses, especially 24K gold plated evening bags. With about 2,000 bags on display, even the most finicky of shoppers are bound to be satisfied. If they have only one remaining of a certain style bag, it's usually sold at cost. They also carry briefcases, attache cases, organizers, wallets, and overnighters. On most items you'll pay 20 to 50% off retail. In business since the early 1970's, they know how to make their customers happy by standing behind their merchandise for one year. Whether the stitching starts to unravel or the hardware falls off, Antelope will fix it or replace it within one year of purchase. They also repair leather clothing and accessories. Some of the brand names they carry are Viva, Pinky, Il Bisonti, and Marco Ricci.

BAG LADY**
31954 San Luis Rey
Cathedral City, CA 92234
619/323-7272
HOURS: MON-SAT: 9:30-5 SUN: 11-4
CREDIT CARDS: AE, MC, V

Claiming to have the largest selection in the entire Cochella Valley, the Bag Lady has women's handbags, leather jackets, leather accessories and fashion jewelry at great savings 20 to 50% off retail. Carrying at least 4,000 handbags, it would be nearly impossible to walk out without finding that perfect handbag. You will always find a great selection filled with buys on the bargain table. Speaking of great buys, don't forget to bring your BUYING RETAIL IS STUPID discount coupon for an additional 5% off. This is a deal that will keep you from becoming a bag lady!

FASHION WEST
71-846 Highway 111
Rancho Mirage, CA 92270
619/773-3361
HOURS: MON-SAT: 9:30-5 SUN: 11-4
CREDIT CARDS: AE, MC, V

Famous designer labels highlight this great fashion accessory shop. Fashion West is geared toward personal service for your personal style! You can look forward to savings of 20 to 40% off retail prices on ladies accessories, handbags, jewelry, belts, scarves and small leather goods. This is where you need to go to spruce up or complete your wardrobe.

HANDBAG HANGUP
8580 Washington Blvd.
Culver City, CA 90232
213/559-4705
HOURS: MON-SAT: 10-5:30
CREDIT CARDS: MC, V

Someone definitely gave this store the right name. It's hard to visualize, but on the average, Handbag Hangup carries 20,000 to 30,000 handbags! Prices range from $1 to $300. In addition to all of those handbags, they also carry a small selection of luggage, small leather goods, and purse and travel accessories. All merchandise is 25% off retail prices set by manufacturers.

LE CLUB HANDBAG CO.
860 S. Los Angeles St.
Los Angeles, CA 90014
213/623-8709
HOURS: MON-FRI: 10-5:30 SAT: 10-6 SUN: 11-5
CREDIT CARDS: MC, V

You can find every major brand of handbag at Le Club Handbag that you would find in your major department stores. They also carry accessories, gloves, hats, costume jewelry, watches, and small leather goods. Their prices average 30 to 60% off department store prices. You can save even more during their semi-annual sales. If you don't see what you're looking for ask Bill Reich, the owner, and he'll help you out!

MARLENE GAINES HANDBAGS
6000 Reseda Blvd.
Tarzana, CA 91356
818/344-0442
HOURS: MON-SAT: 10-5:30
CREDIT CARDS: MC, V

As the name implies, Marlene Gaines Handbags specializes in handbags and jewelry. You'll find buys at 30 to 50% off the retail prices department stores charge. They carry brand names such as Susan Gails, Aspects, Lissette, and Pantera. The handbags are all leather, and they have sales in June and December with prices discounted even more. They also carry one of a kind jewelry, making this store a worthwhile shopping venture.

MILLIE'S HANDBAGS AND SHOES
101 W. 9th St.
Los Angeles, CA 90015
213/623-6175
HOURS: MON-SAT: 10-6
CREDIT CARDS: AE, DISC, MC, V

Across the street from the California Mart, and one block from the Cooper Building, lies Millie's Handbags and Shoes. Millie carefully follows the world of fashion, and makes certain her 2,000 square foot store has the accessories to complement the latest styles. She's just waiting to put the finishing touches on the new outfits you've found while shopping in the garment district. You'll find discounts of 20 to 50% off the retail price on famous brand names such as Liz Claiborne, Anne Klein, Jazz, 9 West, What's What and many more. This is the place to go to make your new threads shine!

VACA
1301 Ocean Front Walk
Venice, CA 90291
213/392-2552
HOURS: 7 DAYS A WEEK: 10-5
CREDIT CARDS: AE, DISC, MC, V (NO CHECKS)

At Vaca you'll find great buys on leather from Brazil. They come in bright fashionable colors and natural, too. There is a wide variety of merchandise that includes shoes, boots, handbags, fannypacks, and more. A few of their products are made of buffalo leather. Savings range from 30 to 50% off retail. You can use cash or credit cards, but Vaca doesn't accept checks.

∞ INFANT'S & CHILDREN'S APPAREL ∞

CHARADES OF CALIFORNIA
1035 S. Maple Ave.
Los Angeles, CA 90015
213/748-9409
HOURS: MON-SAT: 9-5   SUN: 10-4
CREDIT CARDS: MC, V

This 3,500 square foot warehouse is stacked floor to ceiling with children's wear, sizes newborn to 14 in boys and girls. Charades has a large selection of short sets, dresses, pants, dress suits, shirts, slacks, jeans, jogging suits, coats, diaper bags, blankets, caps, belts and accessories, pajamas, socks, underwear, robes, t-shirts, tops and bathing suits. You'll find savings of 20 to 50% off regular department store prices on such brands as Polly Flinders, Baby Togs and Healthtex. You won't need to wave your arms around to get attention here.

DAVID'S CHILDREN'S WEAR
712 S. Los Angeles St.
Los Angeles, CA 90014
213/683-1622
HOURS: MON-SAT: 9:30-6 SUN: 11-5
CREDIT CARDS: AE, MC, V

David's Children's Warehouse has been offering great savings on children's clothing since 1940. Sizes start with infants and go to 14, preteens, slim, regular and husky. The basement is dedicated to a fantastic selection of boy's wear. With 5,000 square feet of clothing at savings of 20 to 50% off retail, this place is a must for mothers with young children.

FOR KIDS ONLY
19367 Victory Blvd. (Loehmann's Plaza)
Reseda, CA 91335
818/708-9543
HOURS: MON-WED, FRI-SAT: 10-6 THUR: 10-7 SUN: 12-5
CREDIT CARDS: MC, V

How often do you say, "I can't believe how quickly the baby is growing?" Well, For Kids Only is the place to keep taking your baby until they reach size 16. You'll find fine European and American clothing priced 40 to 60% lower than your better clothing stores. Always keeping the most up-to-date fashions in stock, your young ones will be the best dressed children in your neighborhood.
Additional Locations: Los Angeles (213/650-4885)

JUVENILE SHOP
4402 W. Pico Blvd.
W. Los Angeles, CA 90019
213/937-0660
HOURS: MON-SAT: 10-6
CREDIT CARDS: MC, V

This 6,000 square foot store, family owned since 1938, sells everything for the newborn—cribs, car seats, high chairs, baby furniture and accessories. They also carry a wide range of clothing sized 0 to 24. They've been in business for a long time with experienced salespeople, so you'll get the kind of service you deserve such as a shower registry provided for free. You can buy the same brand names found in your better department stores (Simmons, Childcraft, Graco, and Perego Strollers), but at lower prices.
Additional Locations: Sherman Oaks (818/986-6214)

SACKS SFO KIDS
7018 Melrose St.
Hollywood, CA 90036
213/935-2590
HOURS: MON-TUES: 10-6 WED-FRI: 10-7 SUN: 11-6
CREDIT CARDS: MC, V

Sacks SFO Kids is right next door to the main Sacks SFO. Here you will find high fashion and low prices for tots to teens. They cater to children as young as 3 months and as old as 14 years. Dare we hope that one day they will tell us what SFO means?

SID'S DISCOUNT BABY FURNITURE
8338 Lincoln Blvd.
Los Angeles, CA 90045
213/670-5550
HOURS: MON-THUR: 9-6 FRI: 9-7:30 SAT: 9-6
CREDIT CARDS: MC, V

Sid's is an institution where you can find everything in baby furniture and clothing for infants. There are all the necessities, of course, like strollers and car seats. He's probably the largest baby furniture dealer in the state. Sid's carries all the major brands like Simmons, Lullabye, Childcraft, Bassett, Pride and Babyline. They offer free delivery on most major items, free layaway, a most knowledgeable staff and big savings! Sid's has special sales at Christmas and New Years. Families have been shopping for their baby needs at Sid's since 1951.

THE STORK SHOP
1868 S. La Cienega Blvd.
Los Angeles, CA 90035
213/839-2403
HOURS: MON-SAT: 10-5:30
CREDIT CARDS: MC, V

The Stork Shop promises a fun visit. They have everything you could possibly want in furniture and clothes for your baby. In fact, they also carry over 50,000 garments for boys and girls up to age 14. Their layettes are beautiful and you'll love the many designer styles of furniture items and accessories. You'll save 20 to 50% off retail prices on most of your purchases too!

∞ LARGE & HALF SIZES ∞

ESTHER'S FULL FASHIONS
18147 Ventura Blvd.
Tarzana, CA 91356
818/996-8323
HOURS: MON-SAT: 10-6
CREDIT CARDS: AE, MC, V

Esther's Full Fashions caters to the large size woman with a fine selection of blouses, dresses, sweats, skirts, jackets, office wear, undergarments and accessories. Sizes range from 14 to 52, and prices are 20% off the retail prices department stores charge, if you can find the right size.

HALF-PRICE HOUSE
12152 Brookhurst
Garden Grove, CA 92640
714/537-1231
HOURS: MON-FRI: 10-9   SAT: 10-6   SUN: 10-5
CREDIT CARDS: MC, V

This missy store is the oldest discount house in Orange County, and it's no wonder it's so popular. New merchandise arrives almost daily from cities like New York, Miami and Chicago. Many are designer originals and samples—plus sportswear coordinates, swimwear and casual dresses. Their specialty is special occasion dresses, both long and short, for mother of the bride, cruises, clubs. They have the largest inventory of "after five" clothing in Southern California. All items, in regular, large and half-sizes, are priced 50 to 70% below retail.

MORE TO LOVE–LARGE SIZES FOR LESS
1238 S. La Cienega Blvd.
Los Angeles, CA 90035
213/657-5114
HOURS: SUN: 12-5 MON-FRI: 10-6
CREDIT CARDS: MC, V

This store specializes in women's sportswear and dresses. Their prices are 30 to 60% below retail, and they carry sizes 36 to 46 in blouses and dresses. Pants and skirts run in sizes 30 to 40. They handle mostly natural fibers, and have four dressing rooms. You'll find parking in back of the store.

∞ LEATHER GARMENTS & FURS ∞

LEATHER CAPITOL
223 E. 9th St.
Los Angeles, CA 90015
213/629-5079
HOURS: MON-SAT: 9-5
CREDIT CARDS: MC, V

Looking for that special leather jacket for your husband or wife? The Leather Capitol has fine quality leather clothing at discounts of 20 to 30%! Save on purchases of leather skirts, pants, handbags, or briefcases. They've been in business since 1973, so you know you can count on quality and service.

CLOTHING & ACCESSORIES

LEONORE'S FUR OUTLET**
228 S. Beverly Dr., Suite 209
Beverly Hills, CA 90212
213/278-4001
HOURS: TUES-SAT: 10-5
CREDIT CARDS: CASH OR CHECKS ONLY

This is the place for fine furs, new and preowned. The family has been in the fur business since 1927 and have fine fur salons throughout the country. They carry the same merchandise found in most of your high end department stores. Some name brands include Christian Dior, Bill Blass, and Oscar De la Renta. You'll find sable, lynx, mink and other varieties of fur in every design imaginable. The store is small but carries at least 300 fur garments at all times. When you purchase a fur at Leonore's, you will receive a furrier cover as well as your name or initials monogrammed in the lining of the garment. If you can't decide between sable or chinchilla, you can experiment by renting a fur from Leonore's. In addition to selling and renting, Leonore's also buys new and nearly new furs. There is metered parking on the street and free 2 hour parking two doors north of the store in the Beverly Hills multilevel parking structure. Don't forget your BUYING RETAIL IS STUPID coupon good for an additional 10% savings.

SCHENLEY'S WHOLESALE CLOTHING
753 S. Los Angeles St.
Los Angeles, CA 90014
213/623-2696
HOURS: MON-SAT: 9:30-5:30 SUN: 11-4
CREDIT CARDS: AE, DISC, MC, V

Discover Schenley's for handsome suits, sport coats and slacks for men. Look for gorgeous leather and suede coats and jackets for men and women. They also have some super special leather, mink or fox coats for milady. You not only have a terrific selection, you save 30 to 75% below retail prices. Enjoy the great service without pressure here, for everyone from the businessman to the punkers. They carry men's sizes up to 54 with labels such as Yves Saint Laurent, Daniel Hechter and Pierre Cardin. The same owners have been there since 1968 and they'll help you coordinate complete outfits. They have a layaway plan too, so don't hesitate to buy your new favorite outfit.

URBAN ART
11634 Ventura Blvd.
Studio City, CA 91604
818/761-8503
HOURS: MON-FRI: 11-7 SAT: 11-6
CREDIT CARDS: AE

This place is leather heaven! You'll find leather boots, jewelry, jackets, belts, children's jackets, boot straps and even some novelty t-shirts. They design and manufacture their own line which translates to very competitive prices, and they can custom make any item you want. Bring in your leather items and let Renee design your favorite look with rhinestones and studs or by using her airbrush. If you see what you want but it's not in your size, that's no problem; they'll make it for you. All of this is yours at savings of 25 to 50% off retail prices.

∞ LINGERIE ∞

AMORE CREATIONS
645 S. Los Angeles St.
Los Angeles, CA 90014
213/624-8048
HOURS: MON-SAT: 10-5:30
CREDIT CARDS: AE, MC, V

Everyone loves lingerie! Especially when you can buy all those gorgeous creations (Bras, girdles, panties, garter belts, G-strings, teddies and peignoir sets) at 40–75% off retail prices. They have 5,000 square feet of lingerie and are always getting new things. Amore Creations stocks the standard lines from most of the major manufacturers like Playtex, Bali, Lilly of France, Gigi, Trendsetters, and many others. Sometimes they are able to buy an entire discontinued line, which translates into more savings for their customers. As an extra touch, they will always let you know if what you are buying is a regular item or one that has been discontinued. Usually closed on

Sunday, they are open seven days a week during the holiday season. Call during November or December for their holiday hours.

CHIC LINGERIE OUTLET
693 High Lane
Redondo Beach, CA 90236
213/372-9352
HOURS: MON-FRI: 8-3:30
CREDIT CARDS: CASH OR CHECKS ONLY

This is a factory outlet where you will find savings from 40 to 50% on sleepwear, lingerie and loungewear. Their merchandise is the same found in most of your budget department stores. Any flaws are clearly marked on the garments. Don't hesitate to try on anything you like from a selection of 15,000 garments. They have been in business for 50 years, saving people a lot of money on their "unmentionable" products!
Additional Locations: Los Angeles (213/233-7121)

CREATIVE WOMAN
1530 S. Myrtle Ave.
Monrovia, CA 91016
818/358-6216
HOURS: TUES-SAT: 10-6
CREDIT CARDS: DISC, MC, V

Located off the Myrtle Avenue exit from the 210 Freeway, this wholesale and discount store is run by the very personable Ed and Bonnie Kaufman. They carry lingerie, intimate apparel in all sizes, garter belts, stockings, corsets, and feathers. Feathers? They even have a department to live out your fantasies with their sexy costumes. Corsets range in sizes 32A–46DD and backless strapless bras come in sizes 32A–48DD. They also have custom fitted bras in sizes 26BB–52HH. Now that's a selection!! Alterations are done on the premises.

NIGHT DRESSINGS
71-848 Highway 111
Rancho Mirage, CA 92270
619/773-5539
HOURS: MON-SAT: 9-5 SUN: 11-4
CREDIT CARDS: MC, V

Don't go to bed unless you are dressed in one of the many choices of lingerie for men and women at Night Dressings. Prices exist to fit every pocket and sizes to fit every person, petite to xxx-large. They also have a great selection of gifts for weddings, birthdays, and holidays.

THE ROBE FACTORY
6040 N. Figueroa St.
Los Angeles, CA 90042
213/258-8490
HOURS: MON-FRI: 9-3 SAT: 9-2
CREDIT CARDS: CASH OR CHECKS ONLY

Looking for that 100% cotton terry or velour robe as a gift or present? Want to trade in "old faithful" that is so comfortable but is now more than a little worn? The Robe Factory outlet is where you can replace "old faithful" at a savings of 50 to 70% below retail department stores or boutiques. You can find over 200 robes at any given time in the store front of the Robe Factory, with some items being sold at cost. You will get first quality here and they carry both men's and women's robes.

THE ROBE OUTLET
2233-1/2 S. Sepulveda Blvd.
W. Los Angeles, CA 90069
213/478-0197
HOURS: MON-SAT: 10-6 SUN: 12-5
CREDIT CARDS: MC, V

The Robe Outlet has a total of ten stores in the Los Angeles area carrying many of the most gorgeous robes for men and women. You can save 30 to 70% below retail prices on not only robes, but also on loungewear, sundresses, career dresses, aerobic suits,

swimsuits, and sleepwear in sizes petite to extra large. They have special sales four or five times a year, so ask to be put on their mailing list. Their merchandise is current; you can find them in department stores or speciality shops, so come here and save.
Additional Locations: 9 other stores throughout S. CA

∞ MATERNITY ∞

DAN HOWARD'S MATERNITY FACTORY
22817 Hawthorne Blvd.
Torrance, CA 90505
213/375-2640
HOURS: MON, THUR: 10-9 TUES-WED, FRI-SAT: 10-6 SUN: 12-5
CREDIT CARDS: AE, DISC, MC, V

Everything an expectant mother needs in the way of apparel is available through this factory outlet which designs and manufactures their own maternity clothing. There is always a wide selection from sportswear to evening wear, in sizes 4 to 24, at 25% off retail and even lower on special sale items. Professional women will be pleased with the attire they carry suitable for the office. Lingerie and pantyhose are also available. You know you're in experienced hands because Dan Howard's Maternity Factory has been producing stylish and quality maternity clothes for over 50 years.
Additional Locations: 8 other stores throughout S. CA

SHELLY'S DISCOUNT AEROBIC & DANCE WEAR
2089 Westwood Blvd.
Westwood, CA 90025
213/475-1400
HOURS: MON: 10-8 TUES-SAT: 10-6 SUN: 11-4
CREDIT CARDS: AE, DISC, MC, V

You'll save from 50 to 70% on leotards, tights and activewear that are perfect for dancing and those strenuous aerobic workouts. Shelly Seeman has them in all sizes and styles and colors—even for mothers-to-be and for children. She has special sales all the time, as well as a parking lot sale once a month. Brand names include

Rachelle, Jenni Rose, Softouch, Marika and Cathy George, to name a few. You will find a complete selection of costumes and accessories, dance shoes, dance wear and active wear in this well stocked 3,000 square foot store. Dressing rooms and parking are also available.

∞ MEN'S APPAREL & ACCESSORIES ∞

3FM FORWARD FASHION FOR MEN
19522 Ventura Blvd.
Tarzana, CA 91536
818/342-3824
HOURS: MON-FRI: 10-9   SAT: 10-6   SUN: 11-5
CREDIT CARDS: MC, V

Can't keep up with the latest trends in men's fashions? Stop by 3FM Forward Fashion For Men and let them coordinate that specialized "look" especially for you. Their friendly staff will guide you through a selection of nearly 100 brand name fashion sweaters. After you've found a sweater or two you can check out what they have available in shoes, shirts, pants, and even watches. All of their merchandise is priced at 30 to 60% off retail.

ACADEMY AWARD CLOTHES, INC.
811 S. Los Angeles St.
Los Angeles, CA 90014
213/622-9125
HOURS: MON-SAT: 9-5:30
CREDIT CARDS: MC, V

Known as the Gucci of Los Angeles Street, Academy Award Clothes has been in business since 1949. They stock thousands of men's suits, sport coats, slacks, formal wear, and haberdashery, with most designer names available. As you enter the front door you will be assigned a salesman to assist you in your selection. Parking is validated with a purchase of $100.

BRUSSELL'S INC.
114 S. Beverly Dr.
Beverly Hills, CA 90212
213/272-4003
HOURS: MON,WED-FRI: 9:30-8:30 TUES, SAT: 9:30-6 SUN: 12-5
CREDIT CARDS: AE, MC, V

Here is a men's clothing store that specializes in two things—famous brand designer names and saving you money! Snap up the men's suits, sport coats, slacks, dress and sports shirts, sweaters, socks and robes from Givenchy, Bill Blass, Halston, Pierre Cardin, Geoffrey Beene, and more. You'll find typical savings of 35 to 45% every day of the week. Owner William Brussell also has special promotions during the year where you can find super bargains. There are thousands of designer suits starting at $149.88 and oxford cloth shirts start at $13.88. Tailoring is done on the premises.

C & R CLOTHIERS
6301 Wilshire Blvd.
Los Angeles, CA 90048
213/655-6466
HOURS: MON-FRI: 8-9 SAT-SUN: 10-6
CREDIT CARDS: AE, MC, V

If you want a complete selection of handsome menswear from all the major labels at savings of 10 to 50% every day of the year (even during those popular sales), then you can't beat C & R Clothiers. They carry an incredible selection of men's suits, jackets, slacks, and accessories—beautiful fashions you would normally find in designer salons and specialty stores often priced at twice the price. Ask to be put on their mailing list so you will be notified of special sales throughout the year.

Additional Locations: 39 other stores throughout S. CA

COMPAGNIA DELLA MODA INC.
Thousand Oaks, CA
818/706-8177
HOURS: MON-FRI: 9-5 SAT:10-4
CREDIT CARDS: CASH OR CHECKS ONLY

A smart businessman never spends more than he has to! Now you can look as though you've just stepped out of GQ dressed in classically styled, Italian men's clothing of the highest quality without paying Beverly Hills' men's store prices. When describing Compagnia Della Moda, Channel 7's Eye On LA's Chuck Henry said, "This is LA's best kept secret!" He is absolutely right. You will find approximately 4,000 square feet consisting of suits, sport coats, slacks, shirts, ties, and sometimes formal wear priced 50 to 60% below intrinsic value. Most of the garments are made of wool, cashmere, silk or cotton and you can forget about finding any polyester blends. By keeping store traffic to a minimum, Compagnia Della Moda is able to provide their clientele with the special attention they deserve. This is the reason you need to call them for their address and directions. Believe me, if you want to wear the very best, and we do mean the very best, it is well worth a trip out to Thousand Oaks. Please note: Even at savings of 50 to 60%, this merchandise is NOT inexpensive.

GHQ OUTLET
19413 Victory Blvd. (Loehmann's Plaza)
Reseda, CA 91335
818/708-8999
HOURS: MON-FRI: 10-9 SAT: 10-6 SUN: 11-5
CREDIT CARDS: AE, DISC, MC, V

Have you ever shopped at a GHQ Store for Men in your local mall? Would you mind saving 30 to 70% on GHQ clothing? We have discovered a gold mine in modern men's clothing. Everything is first quality, no seconds. The clothing is shipped from the mall stores as room is needed for new merchandise. We know of several

young men in their twenties who won't shop anywhere else. They love the fashions and especially the money they save.
Additional Locations: Simi Valley (805/584-3576)

LEONARDO'S ITALIAN FASHION**
336 N. Beverly Dr.
Beverly Hills, CA 90210
213/275-6677
HOURS: MON-SAT: 10-6
CREDIT CARDS: AE, DISC, MC, V

Leonardo's is a direct importer, so they can pass on some real savings on men's suits, slacks, jackets, dress shirts, sport shirts, and accessories such as shoes, ties, belts, and socks. Even though their store is in Beverly Hills, they have some very good buys. Paying $99 for two pair of Italian loafers is what we call a buy! They carry St. Moritz, Corsini, Cavalini, Bucatchi, and other brand names. Madeleine, the owner, tells us she has quite a following of stars, so you may run into one of your favorites if you shop there! Don't forget your BUYING RETAIL IS STUPID coupon for your additional 10% savings.

MAX LEVINE & SON, INC.
845 S. Los Angeles St.
Los Angeles, CA 90014
213/622-2446
HOURS: MON-FRI: 9-5:30 SAT: 9-5
CREDIT CARDS: MC, V

Max Levine & Sons has been around since 1936 evolving into a discount operation selling men's clothes. You can always find a selection of 6,000 to 8,000 suits and slacks here. They also carry sport coats, formal wear, belts, shoes, ties, and other fashion accessories. Designer names such as Ralph Lauren, Calvin Klein, Yves St. Laurent are available in shorts, regulars, longs, and extra longs, in sizes 35 to 50. The savings are generally 40% below retail department stores.

ROGER STUART CLOTHES, INC.
729 S. Los Angeles St.
Los Angeles, CA 90014
213/627-9661
HOURS: MON-SAT: 9-5:30
CREDIT CARDS: MC, V

Roger Stuart has been one of our husband's favorite men's store for over 20 years. They carry brand names such as Cavelli, Ferrine, San Remo, San Georgio, and many others. Their prices are usually 25 to 62% below retail, so you could pay from $266 to $525 for a $700 Italian wool suit at Roger Stuart. They have over 6,000 square feet of men's clothing and 12 dressing rooms, so you can be sure of the fit. Alterations is not a service they provide, but they will recommend a nearby tailor so you can get your purchases altered the same day. Their customer files are kept on computer, so gifts and accessories can be matched up with previous purchases. They have a huge sale every year; it's worth getting on their mailing list. Gentlemen, unless unusually large or small, will be able to find a good fit here. They carry almost every size (35–54 Regular, 38–54 Long, 42–54 Extra Long, 35–46 Short, 35–42 Extra Short) in suits, sport jackets, shirts, ties, and slacks.

ROSEMAN & ASSOCIATES
2211 E. Olympic Blvd.
Los Angeles, CA 90006
213/622-6266
HOURS: MON-SAT: 10-6
CREDIT CARDS: MC, V

Roseman & Associates is another men's clothing wholesaler that offers quality name brand menswear at prices from 50 to 72% below retail. They carry names such as Nino Cerruti, Pierre Cardin, Jamar, Louis Roth, Adolfo, Givenchy, and many more. Their 15,000 square foot location offers suits, sport coats, dress slacks, sports slacks, shirts, and accessories. There are 10 dressing rooms and plenty of free parking. You'll want to get on their mailing list for advance notice of their warehouse sales.

TRADER RICKS DISCOUNT MEN'S WEAR

2500 N. Palm Canyon (Loehman's Discount Plaza)
Palm Springs, CA 92262
619/327-2336
HOURS: MON-SAT: 10-6   SUN: 11-5
CREDIT CARDS: AE, MC, V

This is what we call an organized men's clothing store. Trader Ricks Discount Men's Wear will save you time and money. His famous brands are offered at 30 to 60% off retail on sport shirts, dress shirts, pants, shorts, dress slacks, jackets, sport coats, sweaters, sophisticated nightclub attire, shoes, suspenders, socks, ties and belts. Names you'll recognize are Gianfranco Ruffini, Gotcha, Henry Grethel, Pierre Cardin, Catalina, Generra, Vivaldi, Monte Roma, Gala and more. Everything is first quality, no seconds or close-outs. Everything is organized into size bays. One half of the store is tops; the other half is all bottoms. Just walk into the bay labeled with your size and everything you need will be surrounding you. This makes buying very convenient. After you've made your purchases, you can head on over to Loehmann's which is right next door.

ZACHARY ALL

5467 Wilshire Blvd.
Los Angeles, CA 90036
213/931-1484
HOURS: MON-FRI: 10-6:30   SAT: 9-6   SUN: 10-5
CREDIT CARDS: MC, V

This fabulous men's store is half a block long and is filled with everything the well-dressed man could want. Save 20 to 40% off the retail price on men's suits, jackets, coats, sweaters, shirts, tuxedos, slacks, and all the accessories. They have every size you can imagine and do their own alterations. Plenty of free parking is available in the rear of the store along with good service and courteous attention, too.

∞ MEN'S & WOMEN'S APPAREL∞

3RD FAZE CLOTHING COMPANY
449 Rose Ave.
Venice, CA 90291
213/392-9599
HOURS: MON-SAT: 10-8   SUN: 11-7
CREDIT CARDS: AE, MC, V

What a place! This clothing store for men and women is always filled with clothing reflecting current fashion trends. You can buy everything from an award winning Italian suit to a casual pair of shorts. To give you a idea of what their merchandise is like, Point Zero is one brand name they carry, and Shang-Hai is another. For those of you allergic to synthetics, most of the clothing in the store is made from natural fabrics. We saved the best part for last. The average price you'll pay at 3rd Faze Clothing Company is a whopping 80% off retail!
Additional Locations: W. Hollywood (213/851-5447)

FUNKY & DAMNEAR NEW
123 S. 1st St.
La Puente, CA 91744
818/330-0303
HOURS: MON-SAT: 10-6   SUN: 12-5
CREDIT CARDS: MC, V

Their specialty is "remanufactured", repaired and new Levis. What's great about this place is that you don't have to worry about how the pants you buy will fit after you wash them. Why won't they shrink? All new Levi's at Funky & Damnear New are all laundered and high heat dried to remove all shrinkage. And, if you have a backlog of old Levi's, trade them in for Funky Bucks which can be spent on any merchandise in the store. You'll also find Levi jackets, western shirts, sweats and t-shirts there. Custom length alterations are available on the spot for $3.00.

HARRIS & FRANK CLEARANCE CENTER
13451 Sherman Way
N. Hollywood, CA 91605
818/764-4872
HOURS: MON-SAT: 10-6 SUN: 12-5
CREDIT CARDS: ALL MAJOR CREDIT CARDS

This 6,000 square foot outlet store gives you the best buys on Harris & Frank clothing. Merchandise is brought in from their 19 stores, so you'll find top quality men's and women's clothing, casual to formal wear, shirts, ties, hosiery and hats with names such as Halston, Lanvin, Cricketeer, Jaymar, Dior and Members Only. Though the merchandise is always changing, discounts of 35% off retail are guaranteed at this outlet. Dressing rooms are available.
Additional Locations: Los Angeles (213/933-5701)

HOLLYWOOD GALLERY
10800 Pico Blvd.
Los Angeles, CA 90064
213/467-3259
HOURS: 7 DAYS A WEEK: 10-9:30
CREDIT CARDS: MC, V

You'll find a vast selection of men's and women's wear at the Hollywood Gallery. Most merchandise is priced about 10 to 30% above cost. There are markdowns at the end of each season, and you'll always find specials. They specialize in evening, leather and silk clothing and have an excellent shoe selection to match.

PIC-A-SHIRT
10918 W. Pico Blvd.
Los Angeles, CA 90064
213/475-0088
HOURS: MON-SAT: 10-5:30
CREDIT CARDS: AE, MC, V

Without even trying, you can save at least 20 to 30% on shirts, athletic sweats, t-shirts, and short sleeved dress shirts. But, if you look a little harder you'll find savings up to 75% on men's and women's shirts. Nate Lasner has been in business for over 20 years. His people are helpful, and they'll even do custom lettering and transfers on your jerseys and T-shirts. Shop at Pic-A-Shirt for your shirt needs.

PILLER'S OF EAGLE ROCK
1800 Colorado Blvd.
Los Angeles, CA 90041
213/257-8166
HOURS: FRI-SAT: 10-5:30 SUN: 12-5
CREDIT CARDS: MC, V

Would you like to find a good deal on men's or women's clothing? How about 50% off the retail price of nationally advertised brands just for a start? During the year they have sales on merchandise with prices up to 90% off retail. No hole-in-the-wall, Pillar's of Eagle Rock has nearly 25,000 square feet of merchandise on display. In the shoe department, you'll find about 2,500 pairs of brand names like Bruno Magli, Bally, Johnson and Murphy, Izod, and many more. You'll find first rate quality in a variety of styles and sizes. Dressing rooms are provided, so you can be sure of the fit. Piller's has been in business since 1949, so you know they're reliable.

RAY'S TAILORING & EUROPEAN FASHION CNTR**
4434 Cerritos Ave.
Los Alamitos, CA 90720
714/236-0525
HOURS: MON-FRI: 8-8 SAT: 8-7
CREDIT CARDS: MC, V

Ray's Tailoring is a unique combination store. You'll find clothing, shoes and fashion accessories for both men and women, along with expert tailoring and alterations. They make women's suits and dresses, and are specialists in men's suit lapels. Their clothing line includes dresses, pants, sports clothes, blouses and sweaters for the ladies. The men's clothing line includes suits, jackets, sportswear, jumpsuits, jogging suits, shirts and sweaters. You will see brand names such as Bostonian, Freeman, L. A. Gear, Armani, Gitano, Pro Test, and many more. Their showroom covers over 3,800 square feet, and there is plenty of available parking. You can save

20 to 50% off retail prices, and if you use your BUYING RETAIL IS STUPID coupon, you'll save an additional 10%.
Additional Locations: Long Beach (213/425-9795)

ROCKSTAR
7280 Melrose Ave.
Los Angeles, CA 90046
213/939-STAR
HOURS: MON-SAT: 11-7   SUN: 12-5
CREDIT CARDS: MC, V

If you are a rock star or want to dress like one, this is the place for you. They sell clothing and accessories for present or future stars. If Prince, Berlin, Kiss, or Iron Maiden is your clothing idol, you'll find specialized clothing items such as animal prints, spandex outfits, and leather in custom design work at savings up to 50% off retail. Rockstar has special sales during the year, so you can dress like you're about to go on stage, at half the price.

SACKS SFO INC.
652 N. La Brea
Hollywood, CA 90036
213/939-3993
HOURS: MON-TUES: 10-6 WED-FRI: 10-8 SAT: 10-7 SUN: 11-6
CREDIT CARDS: MC, V

Six great locations, open seven days a week, so you can save a bundle of money all the time on men's and women's fashionable and trendy clothing. Save 40 to 70% on great ready-to-wear items with a special emphasis on natural fibers. Much of their merchandise is designer clothing. Sacks SFO also has leather jackets, pants, and fashion accessories such as jewelry, belts and ties. For your convenience they have private dressing rooms. Get on their mailing list for bimonthly fashion newsletters and sales notices. If you'd like, they'll even coordinate your wardrobe for you. David Sacks goes out of his way to make certain he has the nicest salespeople in all Sacks SFO stores.

Additional Locations: Culver City (213/559-5448), Tarzana (818/609-9282), Studio City (818/506-4787), W. Hollywood (213/659-1771), W. LA (213/312-0388)

SCHENLEY'S WHOLESALE CLOTHING
753 S. Los Angeles St.
Los Angeles, CA 90014
213/623-2696
HOURS: MON-SAT: 9:30-5:30 SUN: 11-4
CREDIT CARDS: AE, DISC, MC, V

Discover Schenley's for handsome suits, sport coats, slacks for men. Look for gorgeous leather and suede coats and jackets for men and women. They also have some super special leather, mink or fox coats for milady. You not only have a terrific selection, you save 30 to 75% below retail prices. Enjoy the great service without pressure here, for everyone from the businessman to the punkers. They carry men's sizes to 54 with labels such as Yves Saint Laurent, Daniel Hechter and Pierre Cardin. The same owners have been there since 1968 and they'll help you coordinate complete outfits. They have a layaway plan too, so don't hesitate to buy your new favorite outfit.

THEL'S CLOTHES**
4334 Sepulveda Blvd.
Culver City, CA 90230
213/390-2144
HOURS: MON-FRI: 10-6 SAT: 10-5
CREDIT CARDS: AE, DISC, MC, V

You can get all kinds of jeans here—Lee, Calvin Klein, Levis, Wrangler and Sedge Field. They specialize in jeans and you save 10 to 30%. Free alterations are provided while you wait. All the work is performed by expert tailors who will also work on clothing not purchased at Thel's. They've been keeping their customers happy in jeans since 1976. Bring along your BUYING RETAIL IS STUPID coupon for an additional 5% discount!

∞ RENTALS ∞

DRESSED TO KILL
8762 Holloway Dr.
West Hollywood, CA 90069
213/652-4334
HOURS: BY APPOINTMENT ONLY
CREDIT CARDS: AE, MC, V

How many times have you wished you could wear a knock-out designer gown for just one evening? Well, your wish can come true because Dressed To Kill offers you just that, an opportunity to rent a gorgeous haute couture gown for just pennies on the dollar. Rental fees run between $75–350 per day for gowns that retail in the four and sometimes five figure range. In addition to the gowns, you can also rent matching accessories. So, when the next invitation to an important gala arrives in the mail, make an appointment at Dressed To Kill. You'll knock 'em dead when you make your appearance in your Bob Mackie or Chanel evening gown.

LEONORE'S FUR OUTLET**
228 S. Beverly Dr., Suite 209
Beverly Hills, CA 90212
213/278-4001
HOURS: TUES-SAT: 10-5
CREDIT CARDS: CASH OR CHECKS ONLY

This is the place for fine furs, new and preowned. The family has been in the fur business since 1927 and have fine fur salons throughout the country. They carry the same merchandise found in most of your high end department stores. Some name brands include Christian Dior, Bill Blass, and Oscar De la Renta. You'll find sable, lynx, mink and other varieties of fur in every design imaginable. The store is small but carries at least 300 fur garments at all times. When you purchase a fur at Leonore's, you will receive a furrier cover as well as your name or initials monogrammed in the lining of the garment. If you can't decide between sable or chinchilla, you can experiment by renting a fur from Leonore's. In addition to selling and renting, Leonore's also buys new and nearly new furs. There is metered parking on the street and free 2 hour parking two doors north of the store in the Beverly Hills multilevel parking structure. Don't forget your BUYING RETAIL IS STUPID coupon good for an additional 10% savings.

∞ RESALE STORES ∞

– INFANTS & CHILDREN –

EVERYTHING FOR KIDS
24407 Hawthorne Blvd.
Torrance, CA 90505
213/373-4863
HOURS: TUES-SAT: 10-5
CREDIT CARDS: CASH OR CHECKS ONLY

Located near the Palos Verdes area, this store gets a lot of look-like-new clothing and furniture for babies to teenagers. All of the items in the store are sold on consignment. This results in customers paying a fraction of the original price. There are dressing rooms and a play area for the kids. Not only will you find top brand-names, friendly service is always available. Mark the 1st and the 15th of every month on your calendars for their special markdown sales. If you have some items you'd like to put on consignment, call Pat Benson to set up an appointment.

KID'S CLOSET
5316 Lankershim Blvd.
N. Hollywood, CA 91601
818/505-8555
HOURS: MON-SAT: 10-5
CREDIT CARDS: CASH ONLY

You'll find some new items, but most are used quality names in children's clothing from sizes 0 to 14. You'll pay at least half of what you would pay if purchasing the items new. There is also a selection of baby furniture such as high chairs, playpens, cribs, car seats, and walkers. Call Kid's Closet, too, if you are selling your goods. They pay cash.

MAKE ROOM FOR BABY
12324 Venice Blvd.
Mar Vista, CA 90066
213/389-7177
HOURS: TUES-SAT: 10-5
CREDIT CARDS: CASH OR CHECKS ONLY

You can save at least 50% on most of your baby purchases when you shop here. They have a large selection of children's clothing, sizes 0-10. You can also find maternity clothes, furniture, lamps, toys, and more! They have some merchandise on consignment and very special buys. Parking in the front and rear of the store.

MOTHER GOOSE GARMENT EXCHANGE
22474 Barton Rd.
Grand Terrace, CA 92324
714/783-4666
HOURS: TUES-SAT: 10-5
CREDIT CARDS: CASH OR CHECKS ONLY

Mother Goose Garment Exchange, located outside of Riverside, is very selective about the clothing it carries. The selection of resale merchandise will clothe a mother to be and her newborn. Sizes for children run from infant to size 14. In addition to clothing, you will find an assortment of baby necessities such as car seats, receiving blankets, walkers, carriers. The selection varies from visit to visit. Sometimes they even have baby furniture. If you have items you no longer need, you may be able to exchange them for store credits to be used in the store at your convenience (by appointment only).

ROSES KIDDIE CLOSET
3408 W. Victory Blvd.
Burbank, CA 91505
818/848-5437
HOURS: TUES-FRI: 10-4   SAT: 10:30-4

CREDIT CARDS: CASH OR CHECKS ONLY

Roses Kiddie Closet carries quality clothing that children have outgrown. Sizes range from infants to teens for both girls and boys. Brands include Guess, Esprit, Bugle Boys, Gennerra and more. They have some clothing for adults as well as a selection of baby furniture and toys. Don't worry about the kids when you shop here; there's a playroom. Consignments taken in on Tuesday only.

– MEN'S & WOMEN'S RESALE –

GENTLEMEN'S EXCHANGE
24066 Neece Ave.
Torrance, CA 90505
213/375-4148
HOURS: TUES-SAT: 11-5
CREDIT CARDS: CASH OR CHECKS ONLY

Let Patricia Benson, owner of Gentlemen's Exchange, dress you in her gently worn suits, sportswear, shoes and accessories. The labels you'll find will include Nino Cerruti, Nordstrom, Daniel Hechter, Christian Dior, and Hart. Half-off sales are held four times a year. She also takes men's clothing on consignment by appointment.

RECYCLED RAGS
2731 E. Coast Hwy.
Corona Del Mar, CA 92625
714/675-5553
HOURS: MON-FRI: 10-8:30 SAT: 10-6 SUN: 12-5
CREDIT CARDS: MC, V

When Audrey Patterson set up her shop in Corona del Mar before 1969, she was one of the first to specialize in recycled designer clothing. With such a major price difference between new, and worn only once or twice, why not wear designer clothes previously owned by the rich and famous? She carries both men's and women's clothes, all at a fraction of the original cost. This shop has clothing, furs, and jewelry from many of the world's top designers. On the last Sunday of every month, she has a parking lot sale where you save even more. She serves hot dogs and lemonade, and shoppers can participate in a drawing for $100 of free merchandise.

– WOMEN'S RESALE –

THE ADDRESS
1116 Wilshire Blvd.
Santa Monica, CA 90403
213/394-1406
HOURS: MON-SAT: 10-6 SUN: 12-5
CREDIT CARDS: AE, MC, V

The AdDress, considered to be one of the most elegant women's resale shops in Southern California, features after-five clothing for those special occasions. Some of the accoutrements found here may have been previously owned by one of your favorite Hollywood stars. In addition to resale, they also have new designer samples at big discounts. You won't be disappointed by the selection, savings, service or hospitality.

CLOTHES HEAVEN
110 E. Union St.–Pasadena Old Town
Pasadena, CA 91103
818/440-0929
HOURS: TUES-SAT: 11-5
CREDIT CARDS: AE, DISC, MC, V

Owner Larayne Brannon says, "Clothes Haven is where good clothes go when they're passed on." They have been serving their long term clientele for the past seven years with a store filled primarily with gently worn designer clothing. Some of the garments, with store tags still intact, have never been worn. Their women's designer clothing and accessories have been passed on from some great closets in New York, Scottsdale, San Francisco, La Jolla, Santa Barbara and Los Angeles. Their labels include Anne Klein, Yves St. Laurent, Valentino, Ungaro, G. Armani, Albert Nipon, Maud Frizen, Krizia, Fendi, Calvin Klein, Chanel, Diane Freis,

Nancy Heller, Liz Claiborne, Carole Little, Ellen Tracy, Gucci, and many other well known designer names. You can save about 67% of the original purchase price shopping here. They are experts in making customers feel special, as well as helping to coordinate their wardrobe. It's been said that Clothes Heaven is a dangerous place, because shopping there can become an addiction (price wise, designer wise and service wise).

DRESS UP
2043 Westcliff Dr., #102
Newport Beach, CA 92660
714/631-8290
HOURS: MON-FRI: 10-6   SAT: 10-5
CREDIT CARDS: MC, V

Dress Up is well established (since 1981) and well known in Newport Beach. They take in only better merchandise and do many buy-outs from other shops (brand new goods at greatly discounted prices). They carry sportswear, career and formals, and also have a large costume and vintage department. The last Saturday of every month they have an 80% off sale on already low priced goods (this is on selected merchandise). They also carry fine jewelry, both antique and contemporary. Their designer corner includes names such as Valentino, Chanel, Zandra Rhodes and Gucci.

THE GREAT NAME
311 Wilshire Blvd.
Santa Monica, CA 90401
213/395-2217
HOURS: MON-SAT: 11-6
CREDIT CARDS: MC, V

About 15 years ago, the five Frost sisters had a great idea; they opened The Great Name and have been stocking it ever since with new and barely-used designer clothing and accessories for women. You can save 50 to 80% off retail prices on such labels as Yves St. Laurent, Missoni, Calvin Klein, Perry Ellis, Chloe, Kamali, Dior, Chanel, Halston, Givenchy, and many more. You'll love the natural fabrics (silks, woolens and cottons) that are featured, and you'll find clothes ranging from casual to formal in sizes 4 to 14. This is a bright, cheerful shop with private dressing rooms and a helpful staff.

JEAN'S STAR APPAREL
15136 Ventura Blvd.
Sherman Oaks, CA 91403
818/789-3710
HOURS: TUES-SAT: 10-6
CREDIT CARDS: AE, MC, V

According to owner Janet, the store was started in 1958 and stocks only the finest designer fashions previously owned by wealthy women. Prices are way below cost. You'll find women's wear from dressy to casual (with a selection of shoes and handbags), from Chanel, Ungaro, Yves Saint Laurent, Anne Klein, Chloe, Adolfo, Ralph Loren, Valentino, Bill Blass, and more. Some of these items are less than a couple of months old. Women have actually flown across the country just to buy clothes from Jean's. Why? The savings are astronomical. A Chanel evening gown that retailed for $9,000 and worn only one hour for a photo session sold for $400!!! You might find a $5,000 Halston gown tagged at $350, a $1,600 Adolfo suit priced at $140 and a pair of $300 shoes priced as low as $2.50! Is the picture a little clearer now? Although the shop has an established celebrity clientele, Jean's Star Apparel caters to a woman's every whim and fantasy by offering exclusive attire for every occasion, sizes range from 3 to 14, and all at affordable prices. A 45 day layaway plan is available and while shopping you can munch on cheese, crackers and beverages. Jean's Star Apparel invites you to come in and indulge yourself.

LABEL'S HI-FASHION RESALE
6268 W. 3rd St.
Los Angeles, CA 90036
213/938-8868
HOURS: MON-FRI: 11-6:30   SAT: 10-5:30   SUN: 12-5
CREDIT CARDS: MC, V

This store is so popular that it just keeps expanding, so hurry to see the fabulous selection of current fashions. Most of the fashions here are for ladies. Save 50 to 80% off the original prices. The secret to Label's success is very simple. They get the best clothing and sell it at great prices. Would you like an example? How about Mary McFadden dresses that retail for $3,000? At Label's you'd pay $600. There are unique resale items from movie sets, fashion houses and actresses. You will find a large variety of famous designers including Anne Klein, Joanie Char, YSL and Kritzia.

PATSY'S CLOTHES CLOSET
1525 N. Main St.
Santa Ana, CA 92701
714/542-0189
HOURS: TUES-FRI: 10-5:30   SAT: 10-4
CREDIT CARDS: MC, V

Like designer clothing but can't stand the prices? Patsy's Clothes Closet is the place for you. How about an Albert Nipon dress for as little as $40, or a two-piece Carole Little silk for $45. Half of Patsy's stock consists of designer samples; the remainder is slightly used, gently worn resales. Sitting prominently in the center of the store is a large case of sample and vintage jewelry, from costume to the real thing, and all at good discounts. They also carry a huge selection of hats and belts. In the same location since 1972, you'll find Patsy's Clothes Closet in what used to be a large, rambling home, built after the turn of the century. There are seven rooms to explore, filled with merchandise, and six dressing rooms. Should you need a bit of a rest, hot coffee is always available.

THE PLACE & COMPANY
8820 S. Sepulveda Blvd.
Los Angeles, CA 90045
213/645-1539
HOURS: MON-SAT: 10-5:30
CREDIT CARDS: MC, V

Newsweek says, "This is the finest resale store in the country." The Place is regularly featured on AM Los Angeles with names such as Ungaro, Adolpho, Chanel, and Valentino. Joyce Brock, the owner, has over 3,000 square feet of everything from formals to sports-wear. She carries furs, jewelry, shoes, handbags, and all the accessories. You need to get on her mailing list to be informed of the super sales that take place in February and July. There's free parking in the rear, so come on down.

SECOND TIME AROUND #2
432 32nd St.
Newport Beach, CA 92663
714/675-2864
HOURS: CASH OR CHECKS ONLY
CREDIT CARDS: MON-FRI: 11-5   SAT: 10-5

Second Time Around is a resale store that deals in consignments. They accept like-new garments, shoes, purses and jewelry. Sizes in clothing range from 5-20. There are savings of 25 to 50% on names like Picone, Anne Klein, Jordache, Dior, Blackwell and more. All items are carefully inspected before being accepted for sale. There are four special sales each year and you'll find ample parking in the rear of the store.

THAT SPECIAL SHOP
8749 La Tijera Blvd.
Westchester, CA 90045
213/670-3441
HOURS: TUES-SAT: 10-5:30
CREDIT CARDS: AE, DISC

Want to meet some great guys? You will here. Ralph Lauren, John Henry, Calvin Klein, Willy Smith, Perry Ellis, Oscar De la Renta are all hanging around this store, and it won't cost you a fortune to get them to come home with you either. You will also find a few creative women hanging around these guys, too. Liz Claiborne has been known to drop in, as well as Carol Little, Anne Klein and Diane Fries. This store's sportswear, shoes, hats, handbags, formals, jewelry, and lingerie are up to 50% off retail prices. The staff at That Special Shop emphasizes courtesy, friendliness, and very special care of their customers. That's probably how they got their name. Their clothes sizes range from 0 to 22-1/2.

∞ SERVICES ∞

– DRY CLEANING –

RITZ DRY CLEANERS
6022 Woodman Ave.
Van Nuys, CA 91401
818/902-1108
HOURS: MON-FRI: 7:30-6:30 SAT: 8:30-5
CREDIT CARDS: CASH OR CHECKS ONLY

Tired of paying more than $5.00 for your suits or dresses to be cleaned? If your answer is yes, then Ritz Cleaners is where you'll want to take your dry cleaning from now on. With the exception of suede, leather, or formal wear, all your articles are dry cleaned for $1.50. Hard to believe? Ritz has another topper—no extra charge for their one day service. So, it's time to start saving on your dry cleaning now!

– TAILORING –

RAY'S TAILORING & EUROPEAN FASHION CNTR**
4434 Cerritos Ave.
Los Alamitos, CA 90720
714/236-0525
HOURS: MON-FRI: 8-8 SAT: 8-7
CREDIT CARDS: MC, V

Ray's Tailoring is a unique combination store. What you will find is clothing, shoes and fashion accessories for both men and women, along with expert tailoring and alterations. They make women's suits and dresses, and are specialists in men's suit lapels. Their clothing line includes dresses, pants, sports clothes, blouses and sweaters for the ladies. The men's clothing line includes suits, jackets, sports clothes, jump suits, jogging suits, shirts and sweaters. You will see brand names such as Bostonian, Freeman, L. A. Gear, Armani, Gitano, Pro Test, and many more. Their showroom covers over 3,800 square feet. You can save 20 to 50%

off retail prices, and if you use your BUYING RETAIL IS STUPID coupon, you'll save an additional 10%.
Additional Locations: Long Beach (213/425-9795)

REYES ADOBE TAILORING
30313 Canwood St. , #27–Plaza Reyes Adobe
Agoura Hills, CA 91301
818/707-1967
HOURS: MON-FRI: 9-6 SAT: 9-5
CREDIT CARDS: MC, V

Every once in a while you find really nice people with whom you want to do business even though their prices aren't the least expensive. Reyes Adobe Tailoring and Eli Midler is one of those places. Eli has been a custom tailor for over 40 years; he does extremely high quality work at very reasonable prices. If you've got a very special article of clothing that needs special tailoring, bring it to Eli. He specializes in men's and women's alterations, reweaving, and restyling. He's in Agoura Hills, but it's definitely worth the drive. Between his charming personality and the twinkle in his eyes, you'll have a hard time leaving once you get there.

∞ SHOES ∞

– FAMILY –

CONVERSE FACTORY OUTLET
423 S. Lincoln Blvd.
Venice, CA 90291
213/396-0719
HOURS: MON-FRI: 10-8 SAT: 10-6 SUN: 11-6
CREDIT CARDS: MC, V

This is the only Converse Factory Outlet in Southern California. You'll find 25 to 70% savings off retail on most types of sport shoes from infant size to 17. And if you have a group, school or business that wants to buy in quantity, you'll receive an even greater discount. They have a friendly knowledgeable staff to help you

SAV-MOR SHOES
16919 Devonshire St.
Granada Hills, CA 91344
818/360-4488
HOURS: MON-THUR: 9:30-7 FRI: 9:30-8 SAT: 9:30-6 SUN:11-5
CREDIT CARDS: MC, V

You'll find brand shoes for the entire family at Sav-More Shoes. Don't be surprised when you see name brands such as Rockport, SAS, Bass, Sperry Topsider, Naturalizer, French Shriner, Candies, Cherokee, Penalgo, Fila, Nike, L.A. Gear, Reebok, Avia, Keds and New Balance. They also carry wide and extra wide shoes. Sav-Mor offers sale racks of odds and ends, too. If you join their Lucky 13 Club, you'll get the 13th pair of shoes you buy for FREE! At the same location since 1964, Sav-Mor Shoes is family owned and operated by the father and two sons.

SHOES HERE "WEST, INC."
19015 Parthenia St.
Northridge, CA 91324
818/772-4697
HOURS: SUN-THUR: 9:30-7 FRI-SAT: 9:30-8
CREDIT CARDS: CASH OR CHECKS ONLY

You'll find prices at 20 to 50% below retail at Shoes Here "West" on men's, women's and children's shoes, boots and athletics. All the great name brands can be purchased such as Reebok, Nike, L.A. Gear, Adidas, Capezio, 9 West, Evan Picone and much more. You can also look forward to $1.00 sales, Red Dot sales and 1/2 price sales. Be sure to get your name on their mailing list, so you will be notified in advance about all of their special sales.

SPORTS SPECTACULAR
8859 W. Pico Blvd.
Los Angeles, CA 90035
213/275-5453
HOURS: MON-SAT: 10-6:30 SUN: 11-5
CREDIT CARDS: AE, DISC, MC, V

Are you searching for the right athletic shoe for every member of your family? Sports Spectacular has over 600 models on display. Brand names include Nike, New Balance, Avia, Converse, Reebok, Fila, Ellesse and more. While you are there, check out their athletic clothing and team outfitters department for men, women and children. Prices here are discounted 20% off retail, and there's always a close out table with exceptional bargains on clothing and shoes. Parking in rear and municipal parking is across the street.

TOP TO TOP
1434 Westwood Blvd.
Westwood, CA 90024
213/470-4700
HOURS: MON-FRI: 11-9 SAT: 11-10 SUN: 11-6
CREDIT CARDS: MC, V

Here's a place you may want to try for athletic shoes of any kind. You can expect a wide variety of styles for your entire family with a discount of 15 to 25% off retail. Nike, Asics, New Balance, Reebok, L.A. Gear and even Keds are just a few of the many different brand names represented at Top To Top. Be sure to get your name on their mailing list, so you will be notified of their special sales. These salespeople know about shoes and the proper fit, so you're in good hands.
Additional Locations: Los Angeles (213/829-7030)

CLOTHING & ACCESSORIES

– MEN'S SHOES –

MR. BURKE'S SHOES
6424 Hollywood Blvd.
Los Angeles, CA 90028
213/462-3419
HOURS: MON-SAT: 10-7 SUN: 12-5
CREDIT CARDS: AE, MC, V

You will find only the finest in men's fashionable shoes and boots from all over the world at Mr. Burke's Shoes. Some brand names you'll find are Franco, Pirelli, Freeman, Giorgio, Brutine, Le Jazz, and Nunn Bush. They have 2,000 styles in total and a special sale rack which guaranties a pair of shoes for $25.00 and two for $45.00.

– MEN'S & WOMEN'S SHOES –

ADLER SHOES
1411 Wilshire Blvd.
Santa Monica, CA 90401
213/394-6102
HOURS: MON-FRI: 10-9 SAT: 10-7 SUN: 10-5
CREDIT CARDS: AE, MC, V

There are more than 20,000 pairs of women's and men's shoes in each Adler Shoes store, and you'll always save 10 to 40% below department store prices. They have handbags and hoisery, too. Each week there are specials where you can save 40 to 70%, and there are two big sales every year. All styles are current in just about every major brand you can name. You'll find Candies, Westies, Jacques Cohen, Romance, Zodiac, Ciao, Nike, Adidas, Bass, Nunn Bush, Bill Blass, Puma, and dozens more. Adler Shoes provides great service, too. They will place special orders for you and still give you discount prices. Everything is bought direct from the manufacturer, so you save big bucks. Women's sizes are 5 thru 10, men's sizes are 6 thru 14, all widths. If you find another store selling a non-sale shoe for less, Adler will beat it.
Additional Locations: 15 other stores throughout S. CA

HENRY'S SHOE FETISH
18055 Chatsworth St.
Granada Hills, CA 91344
818/360-2010
HOURS: TUES-WED: 10-6 THUR: 10-8 FRI-SAT: 10-6 SUN: 12-4
CREDIT CARDS: DISC, MC, V

If you're on a strict budget and looking for a good pair of shoes, go to Henry's Shoe Fetish where the most expensive pair is $38. You'll find a selection of 5,000 pairs of shoes from which to choose. Men's shoes range from $28 to $38 and women's from $18 to $28. Women can find brand names such as Evan Picone, Liz Claiborne, 9 West, Bandolino, Nina, and Caressa. Men will find shoes made by London Fog, Bally, Nunn Bush, and Florsheim. Their inventory is always changing.

NESS SHOES
6440 Hollywood Blvd.
Hollywood, CA 90028
213/460-6435
HOURS: MON-SAT: 10-8 SUN: 12-6
CREDIT CARDS: AE, MC, V

You can save as much as 70% on shoes for men and women. They import most of their merchandise from European countries such as Italy, Spain, France and Morocco. Their buyers are in Europe five or six times a year purchasing the newest styles in dressy and casual shoes and boots.

PILLER'S OF EAGLE ROCK
1800 Colorado Blvd.
Los Angeles, CA 90041
213/257-8166
HOURS: FRI-SAT: 10-5:30 SUN: 12-5
CREDIT CARDS: MC, V

Would you like to find a good deal on men's or women's clothing? How about 50% off the retail price of nationally advertised brands just for a start? During the year they have sales on merchandise with prices up to 90% off retail. No hole-in-the-wall, Pillar's of Eagle Rock has nearly 25,000 square feet of merchandise on display. In the shoe department, you'll find about 2,500 pairs of brand names like Bruno Magli, Bally, Johnson and Murphy, Izod, and many more. You'll find first rate quality in a variety of styles and sizes. Dressing rooms are provided, so you can be sure of the fit. Piller's has been in business since 1949, so you know they're reliable.

SHIRLEY'S DISCOUNT SHOES**
31930 San Luis Rey
Palm Springs, CA 92262
619/323-3737
HOURS: 7 DAYS A WEEK: 9:30-5:00
CREDIT CARDS: MC, V

Men's and women's top name brand discounted shoes are waiting for you at Shirley's. You won't believe this, but there are over 10,000 pairs of shoes here with names like Bruno Magli, Bally and Mr. Seymor. And, you'll get an additional 10% off with your BUYING RETAIL IS STUPID coupon. Now that's what we call a great deal and great selection!

WAREHOUSE SHOE SALES
19507 Business Center Dr.
Northridge, CA 91324
818/701-6847
HOURS: MON-SAT: 10-6 SUN: 11-5
CREDIT CARDS: MC, V

They say they're the largest discount shoe store for men and women in the San Fernando Valley and we believe it. There are 5,000 square feet of selling space and 50,000 pairs of shoes at all times. Save 20 to 80% off retail prices on their shoes in all sizes, narrow and wide widths, too. They also have a large selection of purses.

– WOMEN'S SHOES –

CALIFORNIA SHOE CENTER
19407 Victory Blvd.
Reseda, CA 91335
818/345-9576
HOURS: 7 DAYS A WEEK: 10-6
CREDIT CARDS: MC, V

There are savings of 20 to 50% on ladies name brand shoes at California Shoe Center, where each store has 15,000 pairs of shoes on display. There are many in-store promotions, and the shoes tagged in red have been marked down after 12 weeks in the store. There is a once-a-year carnival sale, and $2.00 discount coupons throughout the year. Brand names include Air Step, Life Stride, Nike, Cherokee, and many more. They have many satisfied customers as indicated by their mailing list of 35,000 persons.
Additional Locations: Westlake Village (818/991-3834)

FOOTSTEPS
12508 Riverside Dr.
N. Hollywood, CA 91607
818/509-9092
HOURS: MON, FRI: 10-7 TUES, THUR: 10-8 SAT: 10-6
CREDIT CARDS: AE, MC, V

Better ladies' shoes and bags, from names like Bruno Valenti, Castori, Cities, Jazz, Sacha of London and others are Footsteps specialties. You can also find clothing and jewelry for completing an outfit. By the way, they carry sizes 5 to 10 in shoes in this one stop shop for women. With the 20 to 25% off retail prices, you may want to buy two pairs at a time.

MAXIM WAREHOUSE SHOES
7303 Lankershim Blvd.
N. Hollywood, CA 91605
818/765-2800
HOURS: MON-THUR: 10-6 FRI: 10-4 SUN: 12-5
CREDIT CARDS: MC, V

Maxim's is heaven for all you shoe-aholics who just can't resist Charles Jourdan, Bruno Magli, Oleg Cassini, 9 West or Sacha of London shoes. You will be in shock when you see their low low prices. Wouldn't you adore paying only $39.99 instead of $150 for a pair of Charles Jourdan pumps? Maxim's also has a $9.99 room full of fabulous shoes and they even have a 2-for-$10 table. Don't hesitate to walk right in and enjoy!

SHOES BY SHIRLEY
17037 Ventura Blvd.
Encino, CA 91316
818/788-1195
HOURS: TUES, THUR: 11-7 WEDS, FRI-SAT: 10-5
CREDIT CARDS: MC, V

Shoes By Shirley has 1,400 square feet of women's handbags and shoes. They have all famous brands in leather and canvas at 40 to 50% off retail. Most sizes are stocked and they specialize in narrows up to size 12. What can $10 buy these days? At Shoes by Shirley there's always a $10 table offering regularly stocked items. The Boutique Corner features t-shirts, shorts, slacks and sweaters at discount prices. Shoes by Shirley gives cash refunds and free parking in the rear.

TIFFANY DESIGNER SHOES
8220 Santa Monica Blvd.
Hollywood, CA 90046
213/654-3462
HOURS: MON-SAT: 10-7
CREDIT CARDS: AE, MC, V

They have so many women's shoes here (5,000 styles) that they divided themselves into two adjoining stores, one for casual and one for dressy. You save about 50 to 70% on everything here. They carry brand names, too, like Charles Jourdan, Dior, Cassidy, Yves St. Laurent, and many more. You'll find styles, sizes, designs and colors to please everyone's taste. Tiffany also carries handbags to coordinate with their shoes, and great service is another plus for shopping at Tiffany Designer Shoes.

CLOTHING & ACCESSORIES

∞ SWIMWEAR ∞

KIRKPATRICK SALES CORP.
8592 Washington Blvd.
Culver City, CA 90232
213/839-6455
HOURS: MON-SAT: 10-6
CREDIT CARDS: MC, V

You can find great buys on women's swimwear, beachwear and sportswear. Catalina and Jantzen are a couple of brand names among many carried here. Instead of paying retail, the 25 to 70% you save can be spent on your cruise! Call them for their extended hours during March thru September.

THE OUTLET
6015 Bandini Blvd.
City of Commerce, CA 90040
213/724-4693
HOURS: MON-FRI: 10-5 SAT: 10-4
CREDIT CARDS: MC, V

The Outlet carries ladies sportswear, swimwear, men's sportswear, swimwear, and junior and children's swimwear. They carry all the famous manufacturers found in your better department stores and have over 20,000 items for sale at 50 to 75% off the retail price. They have plenty of dressing rooms for you to try on those great buys. Carlyn Silva says they have over 400 customers a day, so their merchandise turnover means a good selection for you.
Additional Locations: Northridge (818/894-3422)

TIME-OFF APPAREL
6022 Reseda Blvd.
Tarzana, CA 91356
818/344-2825
HOURS: MON-SAT: 10-6
CREDIT CARDS: MC, V

- 142 -

Ladies, you will find resort and casual sportswear at Time-Off Apparel, but the real draw is their enormous stock of over 4,000 swimsuits all year round! Whether you're looking for a size 3 or size 20, Time-Off Apparel has that perfect swimsuit and cover-up for you. Catalina, Cole, La Blanca, Too Hot Brazil, and Roxanne are a few of the brand names you can look forward to buying at savings from 50 to 80% off retail.

∞ UNIFORMS ∞

GLAMOUR UNIFORM SHOP**
4951 W. Sunset Blvd.
Hollywood, CA 90027
213/666-2122
HOURS: MON-FRI: 10-6 SAT: 10-5
CREDIT CARDS: AE, DISC, MC, V

Whether you're buying a uniform just for yourself or for all your employees, you can save 20 to 50% here. You can find uniforms for nurses, doctors, waitresses, beauticians, barbers and chefs. The uniforms come in white and colors, and in sizes 3 to 56. Glamour Uniform will even give you a greater discount on group orders. Save an additional 10% when you use your BUYING RETAIL IS STUPID coupon. They have two other stores in Los Angeles.
Additional Locations: Owl Uniform-LA (213/233-1830), Parisian Store-LA (213/753-7539)

LOS ANGELES UNIFORM EXCHANGE
5239 Melrose Ave.
Los Angeles, CA 90038
213/469-3965
HOURS: MON-FRI: 9-5 SAT: 9-6
CREDIT CARDS: MC, V

A lot of foreign items here: Army uniforms, British drill pants, British, American, French army shorts. They carry a wide variety of military items, including Army field jackets and Navy pea coats. You can also buy flight suits, coveralls, jackets, military insignia patches and accessories. With a tailor shop on the premises, you can have your uniform tailored right there. Parking is available, and they insist their prices are the cheapest in town!

NADINE OF CALIFORNIA
18552 Sherman Way
Reseda, CA 91335
818/343-7554
HOURS: MON-FRI: 9:30-5 SAT: 11-4
CREDIT CARDS: MC, V

If you're in need of uniforms and you haven't shopped here, you've missed a good bet! Nadine of California carries one of the largest selection of uniforms in the area. Whether you want coveralls, shop smocks, lab coats, nurses uniforms, tuxedo shirts, or aprons, Nadine of California carries it. In the past they custom designed uniforms for Charlie Browns, Bobbie McGees, and some for Disneyland, so they definitely know what they are doing! Their regular prices are 10 to 30% below other stores, plus additional discounts on their specials will save you even more money. They've been around since 1948, and at their current location since January of 1981.

SAM COOK UNIFORMS
2727 S. Flower St.
Los Angeles, CA 90067
213/748-4800
HOURS: MON-FRI: 9-5 SAT: 9-1
CREDIT CARDS: MC, V

Uniforms of all kind—police, waiters, chefs, security guards, mailmen, bus drivers, foods servers, and many different varieties of industrial garb are available at Sam Cook Uniforms. Over 3,000 individual items are in their inventory including such brand names as Dickies, Wrangler, and shoes from Rocky and Thoro-Good. You'll find a good selection of jackets, that even someone who doesn't need a uniform would look good in. They also have a nice selection of blazers, shirts and sportswear. Here's a place to go to get dressed for work or leisure. You will save about 15% off retail making your uniform purchases at Sam Cook Uniforms.

∞ VINTAGE CLOTHING ∞

AARDVARK'S ODD ARK
7579 Melrose Ave.
Los Angeles, CA 90046
213/655-6759
HOURS: MON-SAT: 11-9   SUN: 11-7
CREDIT CARDS: MC, V

Find your way to Aardvark's Odd Ark when you want to find the "unique in antique" or used clothing. This place is an adventure! You can find discarded treasures for a couple of dollars or spend a lot more on a rare antique item. When in need of certain styles of clothing for their plays, some theater groups head straight for Aardvark's. It's a great place to browse away the hours, and their sales folks will be happy to help you find a special item if you'd like.
Additional Locations: Canoga Park (818/999-3211), Venice (213/392-2996)

GRUBB & GRUBB'S GENERAL STORE
18523 Sherman Way
Reseda, CA 91335
818/996-7030
HOURS: MON-SAT: 9:30-5:30
CREDIT CARDS: AE, MC, V

This is a one stop shop for vintage clothing and antiques. They have an extensive line of clothing for men and women, costume jewelry, vintage shoes, purses and hats.

∞ WESTERN APPAREL ∞

BOOT HILL SQUARE DANCE APPAREL**
7610 Balboa Blvd.
Van Nuys, CA 91406
818/901-9544
HOURS: MON, WED-FRI: 11-6   TUES: 11-8   SAT: 10-5
CREDIT CARDS: MC, V

Grab you're partner and do-si-do on over to Boot Hill Square Dance Apparel where they dress men and women from head to toe for a good old fashion square dance. Their large store has a tremendous selection of such brands as H.B.C Western Wear, Karman, Mesquite, Coast Shoes, Promenaders, Jeri Bee, Rockmount Ranchwear, Square Up Fashions and others. Dress sizes run from 4 to 20. Be the one to stand out in the crowd with a custom designed, one of a kind dress or two piece outfit! Check out their accessories and petticoats, too! Their prices are 20 to 50% off retail, and you can use your BUYING RETAIL IS STUPID coupon to save an additional 5%. A layaway plan is also available.

CAROL'S COUNTRY CORNER
21932 Schoenborn
Canoga Park, CA 91304
818/347-1207
HOURS: MON-TUES, THUR-FRI: 11-6   WED: 11-8   SAT: 10-5
CREDIT CARDS: MC, V

Swing your partner and two step down to Carol's Country Corner for the best in western and square dance apparel. They offer quality at discount prices on items from the least expensive to the most exclusive. Save 10 to 30% on shoes, moccasins, square dance shoes, jewelry, accessories and a large belt selection. Carol can design a custom piece made especially for you. For year round unadvertised specials and additional discounts for all callers and groups, give Carol's Country Corner a twirl.

PARIS GO
8432 Sunset Blvd.
Los Angeles, CA 90069
213/650-8295
HOURS: MON-FRI: 10:30-8:30   SAT: 11:30-8:30   SUN: 12:30-4
CREDIT CARDS: MC, V

Looking for western wear, boots, shirts, and the accessories that go with them? Paris Go has it all. Justin, Tony Lama, and Larry Mahan are just a few of the brands they carry. Don't be surprised by the French accent. Simon and Pierre have been at this location for more than 14 years with prices from 30 to 60% below retail. Parking is in the rear and around the corner, so stop, buy and save.

∞ WOMEN'S APPAREL ∞

7TH AVENUE WEST
71-842 Highway 111
Rancho Mirage, CA 92270
619/340-6555
HOURS: SUN-SAT: 9:30-5
CREDIT CARDS: MC, V

Their concept is simple. They sell current New York designer fashions at 20 to 50% below department and specialty store prices. All merchandise is first quality, with new shipments arriving daily. Brand names include: Suzelle, R.G. Arnold, Oscar de la Renta, Adolfo, Needleworks, Semplice, Ann W., Vivanti, Tony Lampert, Ultrasport, Spree, Saint Germain, Pierre Cardin and Stephanie, to name a few. Their motto is, "We've redesigned designer prices."

THE BACK ROOM
840 Santee St.
Los Angeles, CA 90014
213/624-3513
HOURS: 7 DAYS A WEEK 10-5
CREDIT CARDS: MC, V

You'll find California designers of women's clothing such as Michelle Lamy and Leon Max at exceptional savings, some up to 70% off retail. Most merchandise isn't higher than $25.00 and with their huge inventory in their 5,000 square foot store you'll be able to acquire your entire wardrobe for very little money. The stock is always changing so you should make this a regular stop for the up-to-date fashions at wholesale prices or below.
Additional Locations: Los Angeles (213/652-7141ß), Tarzana (818/996-0684)

BACKDOOR BOUTIQUE
14331 Chambers Rd.
Tustin, CA 92680
714/544-9360
HOURS: THUR-FRI: 12-4 SAT: 10-4
CREDIT CARDS: CASH OR CHECKS ONLY

If you are into natural fabrics, this factory outlet is a good source for sportswear and separates made of 100% cotton. They carry a variety of dresses, jackets, tops, and bottoms in sizes 6 to 18. We know their hours are limited, but at savings of 40 to 80%, we can't complain. Sometimes leftover fabric and notions are for sale, too.

BELL FASHIONS STUDIO
3908 Wilshire Blvd.
Los Angeles, CA 90010
213/389-1672
HOURS: MON-FRI: 10-5 SAT: 10-4:30
CREDIT CARDS: MC, V

Bell Fashions Studio is quite a place to shop. Not only do they carry brand name merchandise, with sizes ranging from size 4 to 20, they always offer a wide selection that will please just about everyone. With dresses, suits, blouses, skirts, sweaters, slacks, and sportswear at 30 to 50% below retail, how can you go wrong? Free parking is available in back of the store.

BLACK & WHITE WHOLESALERS
1250 S. Broadway
Los Angeles, CA 90015
213/746-5841
HOURS: MON-SAT: 10-5:30
CREDIT CARDS: MC, V

At Black & White Wholesalers you'll see the same designer made garments found in major departments stores hung on warehouse pipe racks, and there is one large group dressing room. Because nothing is tagged, you must ask about pricing. Although this can be a bit frustrating at times, saving 40 to 60% off retail is definitely

worth the small inconvenience. This is a favorite haunt for style and quality at truly bargain basement prices. Make sure you get on their mailing list so you can get in on their annual sales.
Additional Locations: Woodland Hills (818/992-1814)

BUKY'S**
5550 Wilshire Blvd., Suite 302
Los Angeles, CA 90036
213/934-7878
HOURS: WED-SAT: 11-5
CREDIT CARDS: MC, V

You can find uptown fashions at downtown prices at Buky's. Savings run 30 to 50% off retail on current merchandise. They have fine quality clothing for the discriminating woman and pride themselves on providing special service. Although Buky's is normally closed on Sunday, they'll open the store on their day of rest if you set up an appointment in advance. Now that's what you call service! In addition to their standard discounts, Buky's will accept your BUYING RETAIL IS STUPID coupon that will save you an additional 5%!

CONTEMPO CASUALS OUTLET
1507 S. Riverside Ave
Rialto, CA 92376
714-877-0560
HOURS: MON-FRI: 10-9
CREDIT CARDS: MC, V

Here's a place where you could probably walk out with an entire wardrobe and spend only $50.00. Contempo Casuals Outlet has weekly specials with $1.00, $3.00 and $5.00 racks of their trendy clothing consisting of sportswear, swimsuits, active wear and formal wear. Some items on the $1.00 rack are valued at $50.00. All jewelry is $1.00. Check out their regular merchandise at 50 to 75% off retail on brand names such as Betsy Johnson and Guess.
Additional Locations: Huntington Beach (714/841-0869)

CS X 2**
5610 Lake Lindero Dr.
Agoura, CA 91301
818/991-3281
HOURS: MON-FRI: 9-9
CREDIT CARDS: CASH OR CHECKS ONLY

CS x 2 offers their customers a variety of interesting services. In addition to specializing in updated misses sportswear, one-of-a-kind samples, a full range of sizes, and personalized service, they are available for house parties with incentive prices for the party givers. "Party of four, we come to your door." Some of the lines they carry are A.C. Sport (career clothing), Carducci (sweaters and t-shirts), and Marsha Sportswear (casual). All of their merchandise is sold at 50% below retail. It gets better. The owners, Carole Stewart and Cheryl Shaffer (CS x 2), provide group discounts and will give you an additional 5% discount on your purchase when you use your BUYING RETAIL IS STUPID coupon.

DESIGNER'S FASHIONS, INC.
4201 W. Alameda
Burbank, CA 91505
818/848-2076
HOURS: MON-FRI: 10-7 SAT: 10-6 SUN: 12-5
CREDIT CARDS: MC, V

Attention all mothers. Here's a place to shop and you can bring your children. While you browse through their great selection of Gerron, Paris Blues and Tahasa labeled clothing, your children can be in their large play area. The assortment they have includes clothes for play and work. You'll save at least 25% off retail shopping at Designer's Fashions. They also have special sales when their merchandise is 50 to 80% off retail.

DONNA'S PLACE**
6000 Reseda Blvd., Unit G
Tarzana, CA 91356
818/343-3958
HOURS: WED-SAT: 10:30-5:00
CREDIT CARDS: CASH OR CHECKS ONLY

Donna's Place is the place to shop for the woman who's always on the go. All merchandise is machine washable and goes from casual to evening wear. Their high fashion modular (interchangeable units) and figure slimming concept clothing range in sizes from 6–16. Donna's prices are manufacturer direct, usually 30 to 50% below the retail prices department stores and boutiques charge. She has a professional sales staff that really care about their customers. They have been in business over five years and will take an additional 10% off the purchase price when you use your BUYING RETAIL IS STUPID coupon. (Coupon not redeemable on special sale items and accessories.)

FANTASTIC DESIGNER ROOM
860 S. Los Angeles St.
Los Angeles, CA 90014
213/627-4536
HOURS: MON-SAT: 9-5
CREDIT CARDS: CASH OR CHECKS ONLY

Only top designer clothing is found here! You can get Norma Kamali, plus Beverly Hills Polo, Lanvin, Pierre Balmain, and Leon Max for 40 to 80% less than retail department store prices! They are located in the garment district in downtown Los Angeles.

THE GREAT GATSBY**
14437 Ventura Blvd., Sherman Oaks Town Center
Sherman Oaks, CA 91403
818/789-7701
HOURS: MON-SAT: 10-6
CREDIT CARDS: AE, MC, V

Want that cosmopolitan European look? Then you should stop by The Great Gatsby where you can find better women's fashions from such places as France, Belgium and Italy. Most of their chic looks are done in 100% fine cotton. They also have unique accessories, belts, earrings, and bracelets. Even with fluctuations in the dollar, you'll save 20 to 40% off retail. Use your BUYING RETAIL IS STUPID coupon and save an additional 10% on your purchase. Their store in Encino is called Gaby's.

Additional Locations: Encino (818/986-5584)

HARPER'S LADIES WHOLESALE CLOTHING
15616 Ventura Blvd.
Encino, CA 91316
818/789-5837
HOURS: MON-SAT: 10-6
CREDIT CARDS: MC, V

Because the prices are so low here (you can save 50 to 70%), we can't mention any brand names. In sizes 2 to 20, women will find dresses, suits, pants, blouses, sweaters, t-shirts, jogging suits, tennis clothes, silks, knits, and more. For super bargains, watch for Harper's special sales held during the year. A woman with good fashion sense can completely outfit herself at Harper's for almost every occasion. Each store has free parking.
Additional Locations: Culver City (213/839-8507), Thousand Oaks (805/495-8344), Woodland Hills (818/347-3633)

JUDY'S OUTLET
19411 Victory Blvd.
Reseda, CA 91335
818/344-2044
HOURS: MON-FRI: 10-9 SAT: 10-6 SUN: 11-6
CREDIT CARDS: MC, V

Judy's is the organization responsible for starting warehouse sales featuring unbelievable prices. They still have those great warehouse sales, but having so many stores has made it necessary for them to open up Judy's Outlet Stores. All items found in Judy's chain stores can be found here at savings of 30% on some things, and usually 50 to 70% on everything else. All items are first quality, no seconds. Whatever you do, when you go in don't forget to get on their mailing list. This is the only way to be notified of Judy's semi-annual warehouse sales that occur during spring and early fall. These sales take place only at South Coast Plaza and Judy's main office in Van Nuys. Their Los Angeles outlet, located in the Cooper Building, is open Monday thru Friday 9 to 5, and Sunday hours are from 11 to 5.
Additional Locations: Los Angeles (213/627-9173), Simi Valley (805/581-1518)

LEON MAX FACTORY OUTLET

3535 S. Broadway
Los Angeles, CA 90013
213/234-0510
HOURS: MON-FRI: 10-6 SAT: 10-4
CREDIT CARDS: MC, V

Ladies, here's the store for you. Leon Max used to sell his designs through Bullocks and Nordstrom; he now has two retail stores in Brentwood and Santa Monica. Fortunately for BUYING RETAIL IS STUPID readers, he has a factory outlet where you will find terrific buys. You can buy an entire silk outfit for around $100. Silk blouses that retail for $250 can be purchased for $90. From casual to formal wear, for the missy to the matronly, you can find all styles at less than wholesale. They also have markdowns once a month on already discounted clothing.

LEONARD'S FASHION FAIR

18946 Ventura Blvd.
Tarzana, CA 91356
818/342-3151
HOURS: MON-SAT: 10-6 SUN: 12-5
CREDIT CARDS: AE, DISC, MC, V

In about 1924, Leonard Shapiro's family started retailing in Southern California, and his Leonard's Fashion Fair is the result of all that expertise. It's filled with one of the town's largest selections of women's clothing and sportswear. You can find such names as Liz Claiborne, St. Germain, Adrienne Vittadini, Metropole, Gene Ewing, Nancy Heller, Chaus, Richard & Co., and we could go on and on. Brand names are always changing depending on what's hot for the season. Sizes range from 4 to 16 plus petites and they also carry accessories. The savings vary because Leonard's marks down an outfit after it has been in the store a certain number of days. Visit often and make certain to be added to their mailing list for special sales. For your convenience they have private dressing rooms.

LILA'S GOURMET BASKET
31938 San Luis Rey
Cathedral City, CA 92234
619/325-7383
HOURS: MON-SAT: 9:30-5:00 SUN: 11-3
CREDIT CARDS: MC, V

Yes, even in Palm Springs you can find some good bargains. The name of this store might make your mouth water, but you won't find any gourmet foods here. Lila's Gourmet Basket is a charming store that discounts their merchandise 20 to 25% off retail. You can always find something glamorous to wear in their women's clothing department. If you're feeling generous, you can buy a surprise for someone special from their many unusual gift items located around the store. Lila's also offers sensational gift wrapping.

LOEHMANN'S
6220 W. 3rd St.
Los Angeles, CA 90017
213/933-5675
HOURS: MON-SAT: 10-5
CREDIT CARDS: MC, V

Professional shoppers have been shopping at Loehmann's since the 1930's for dresses, blouses, skirts, slacks, suits, evening wear, coats, jackets, and fashion accessories. They guarantee savings of at least 33% over department store prices, 20% less than discount stores, and savings on fashion accessories run even higher. After an item has been in the store for a little less than eight weeks, the price is marked down, and then continues to be marked down every two weeks until the item is sold. When all is said and done, your savings actually average about 45 to 50% off retail. Whenever you need something extra special to wear, Loehmann's Back Room is the first place you should visit. This is where they keep their finer designer clothing for day and evening wear. You will be pleased to know that Loehmann's is not only a great place to shop, they also appreciate their customers. To make certain their prices stay low for their loyal clientele, Loehmann's goes to the trouble of generating

about 35 comparison shopping reports every month. Look for their special sale on furs held every January in selected stores.
Additional Locations: 6 other stores throughout S.CA

M. FREDERIC & CO. OUTLET STORE
2251 S. Sepulveda Blvd.
W. Los Angeles, CA 90069
213/478-4240
HOURS: MON-SAT: 10-6   SUN: 11:30-6
CREDIT CARDS: MC, V

You can buy all your favorite junior labels at 40% off retail. They carry a large assortment of career and casual separates. Enhance your wardrobe from M. Frederic's.huge selection of sweaters and accessories at 20 to 50% off retail. They have free parking at all locations.
Additional Locations: Beverly Hills (213/657-2021), Marina del Rey (213/305-7059)

MS. FASHIONS
3877 Pacific Coast Hwy.
Torrance, CA 90505
213/373-4622
HOURS: MON-SAT: 10:30-6
CREDIT CARDS: MC, V

If your looking for variety, Ms. Fashions is the place to shop! This store offers a surprising 50 to 70% discount below retail on pants, dresses, blouses, sweaters, and bathing suits. Their inventory is constantly changing, so you always have a huge selection. They also carry earrings, belts, hosiery, scarves, hats, and unique costume jewelry. A dressmaker is on the premises so alterations are no problem. Ms. Fashions is truly a one-stop fashion outlet for ladies; best of all you can use a BUYING RETAIL IS STUPID coupon to save an additional 5% when you shop here!

MS. FITS
310 Vista Del Mar
Redondo Beach, CA 90277
213/378-6998
HOURS: MON-SAT: 10-5:30
CREDIT CARDS: MC, V

Ms. Fits is a cute, personal boutique. This store carries casual wear, dresses, sweaters, and other really fun clothing. Their clothes are "IN", very trendy, new-to-the-scene. You can save 30–50% off retail prices when you shop here, so Ms. Fits is a really fun place!

MY FAIR LADY**
6000 Reseda Blvd., Unit O
Tarzana, CA 91356
818/881-1651
HOURS: MON-SAT: 10-5
CREDIT CARDS: MC, V

My Fair Lady carries name brand women's sweaters, tees, knits, cottons, dresses, and designer pantsuits at 40 to 70% below retail prices. Owner, Jonathan Rick, says, "We're not fancy, just top lines at the greatest bargains going." Their Blow-out Room has super mark-downs up to 90% off retail!. A mailer is sent out four times a year, so you'll want to get on their mailing list. Last but not least, you can save an additional 10% when you use your BUYING RETAIL IS STUPID coupon. (Coupon not valid on items from Blow-out Room or parking lot sales.)

N.E.A.
1801 Bundy Dr.
W. Los Angeles, CA 90041
213/826-2601
HOURS: MON-FRI: 10-9   SAT: 10-7   SUN: 10-7
CREDIT CARDS: DISC, MC, V

This is the largest store in the chain of N.E.A., which stands for North East Apparel. Savings of up to 60% can be found on all their misses clothing, casual to formal wear in sizes 3 to 16, hoisery,

belts and accessories. Stop by and check out their unadvertised sales too.
Additional Locations: 30 other stores throughout S. CA

POOR SNOB
12524 Ventura Blvd.
Studio City, CA 91604
818/769-9666
HOURS: MON-WED, FRI-SAT: 9:30-6 THUR: 9:30-8
CREDIT CARDS: AE, MC, V

If you want to look like a million dollars but just don't want to spend the money, then the Poor Snob is for you. They carry the "look," not necessarily the label. Designer styles without designer prices is what you'll encounter at the Poor Snob. Get your famous designer look-alike for $800 instead of $7,000 to $10,000. While this boutique isn't inexpensive, it may just be one of the best values in BUYING RETAIL IS STUPID. The collection you'll find at the Poor Snob reflects their philosophy of, "The best dressed women know that style means everything, and labels don't matter." For sophisticated clothing you really must come here!

THE PRISM
5001 E. 2nd St.
Long Beach, CA 90803
213/434-6494
HOURS: MON-THUR: 10-6 FRI: 10-8 SAT: 10-6 SUN: 11-5
CREDIT CARDS: MC, V

The Prism is a fun store with a wide of selection for the miss or junior. They carry updated looks in "fun" clothing at savings of 30 to 50% off retail. You'll find three dressing rooms to assure the fit, and they carry fancy and basic lingerie, plus jewelry and fashion accessories. The service is great, and new stock arrives weekly. The Prism is a big package in a small store.

THE SILK FACTORY
3100 Wilshire Blvd.
Los Angeles, CA 90010
213/487-0087
HOURS: MON-SAT: 10:30-6:30
CREDIT CARDS: MC, V

Women love this shop where they can find gorgeous silk, polyester, cotton and linen dresses and suits at 50–70% below retail. You'll also occasionally find separates. The Silk Factory carries famous name brands in sizes 4 to 16. Silk is their specialty, of course, but they have other beautiful bargains as well. They have private dressing rooms for your convenience. Get your name on their mailing list, so you'll know about special sales, new merchandise and extra discounts.

STYLE BOUTIQUE
2043 Westcliff Dr., #109
Newport Beach, CA 92660
714/642-7878
HOURS: MON-FRI: 10-6 SAT: 10-5
CREDIT CARDS: MC, V

Style Boutique has an expensive upbeat New York look with everyday discount prices on everything, in sizes 3/4 to 14. Prices here are 50% off retail. Complement your new threads from their large selection of fashion accessories, including an extensive collection of Anne Klein costume jewelry. Other brand names include Calvin Klein, A. Vittidini, Perry Ellis, and Lanvin. They also carry formals and wedding gowns at 75% off retail.

UNCLE JER'S
4447 Sunset Blvd.
Los Angeles, CA 90027
213/662-6710
HOURS: MON-FRI: 11-7 SAT-SUN: 11-5
CREDIT CARDS: V, MC

Located at the Sunset and Hollywood Boulevard junction, Jerry Morley and Helen Sloan's Uncle Jer's offers savings of 20 to 50%

on clothing items by OK Sam, Surya Imports, Bila, What's Happening?, Solange and many others. A one-stop shopping place, you can buy a frock for auntie, an unusual boutique item for mom, a plaything for junior or junior miss, and greeting cards for all. You will find their folk and ethnic items a great source for unusual gifts. They are proud to state that most of their clothing is made of natural fibers. Uncle Jer's donates 10% of their profits to the Alliance for Survival and also supports many anti-nuclear and environmental organizations.

THE WILD PRICE BOUTIQUE
3680 Wilshire Blvd.
Los Angeles, CA 90010
213/388-4823
HOURS: MON-SAT: 10-6
CREDIT CARDS: AE, DISC, MC, V

Rayons, silks, lace, cotton and cotton knits are the fabrics used for the fine quality clothing you'll find at the Wild Price Boutique. Their casual and exciting styles are sold at wholesale prices and below. During special sales, savings can run as much as 80% off retail. These are the outlet stores for high fashion retail chains and manufacturers. Though most of their merchandise is for women (size 3–14), some unisex clothing is also carried. You can truly find some wild prices at the Wild Price Boutique. Their Los Angeles store is located in the USC University Village Shopping Center.
Additional Locations: Los Angeles (213/747-3148), Venice (213/396-8911)

THE YELLOW BALLOON
2140-E W. Artesia Blvd.
Torrance, CA 90504
213/638-4257
HOURS: MON-FRI: 10-6 SAT: 9:30-5
CREDIT CARDS: MC, V

The Yellow Balloon is a delightful store where you can find junior miss and ladies' fashions at savings of 20 to 50% off retail. Owner Fay Goldfarb has dresses and sportswear with brand names of

Loubella, Jonathan Martin, Teddi, Graff, and more. You'll enjoy the personalized attention, and if you can't get to the store, Fay has been known to load up her car with clothing and bring them to your house.

COMPUTERS

∞ HARDWARE & SOFTWARE ∞

ADRAY'S
6609 Van Nuys Blvd.
Van Nuys, CA 91405
818/908-1500
HOURS: MON-FRI: 10-7   SAT-SUN: 10-6
CREDIT CARDS: MC, V

You will save about 40% on almost everything at Adray's. They are the discount headquarters for major brands of televisions, VCR's, camera equipment, answering machines, stereo systems, computers and computer equipment, small and major appliances, jewelry, cosmetics, perfumes and colognes, china and crystal, pots and pans, sporting goods, exercise equipment, furniture, linens and just about anything else that comes to mind. You will find the salespeople courteous and knowledgeable, but they are usually very busy. If you are looking to make a major purchase, we suggest that you do your homework about the product you are interested in before going to Adray's. Shopping here is much different than shopping in a retail department store, but once you see their prices, adapting won't be a problem.
Additional Locations: Canoga Park (818/348-2600), Los Angeles (213/935-8191), W. Los Angeles (213/479-0797), Torrance (213/378-6777), Ventura (805/644-1111)

THE COMPUTER DEALER
10454-1/2 National Blvd.
W. Los Angeles, CA 90034
213/558-1778
HOURS: MON-SAT: 10-6 OR BY APPOINTMENT
CREDIT CARDS: MC, V

Save 10 to 40% on computers, printers, modems, disk drives, supplies, computer furniture, and other accessories. This is the place for discount hardware. They also have a full service department.

COMPUTER PALACE
22401 Ventura Blvd.
Woodland Hills, CA 91364
818/347-3430
HOURS: MON-SAT: 9-7
CREDIT CARDS: AE, MC, V

Computer Palace carries a wide range of IBM compatible products and will guarantee the best prices. Friendly and patient salespeople will give you excellent service and can help arrange financing.
Additional Locations: 6 other stores throughout S. CA

COMSOFT
8125 San Fernando Rd.
Sun Valley, CA 91352
818/768-5017
HOURS: MON-FRI: 10-6   SAT: 10-5
CREDIT CARDS: ALL MAJOR CREDIT CARDS

If you are hard pressed to come up with a birthday present for your 14 year old, Comsoft carries one of the largest selections of Atari and Commodore software. They also carry IBM compatibles at 20 to 50% below retail.
Additional Locations: Reseda (818/996-8206)

DATA TECHNOLOGY
632 S. Victory Blvd.
Burbank, CA 91502
818/569-4929
HOURS: MON-FRI: 10-6   SAT: 11-4
CREDIT CARDS: CASH OR CHECKS ONLY

Data Technology will not be undersold on their computer equipment, and they will also give you a free loaner when you bring in your computer for repairs. Their brand names include IBM, Compaq, Toshiba, NEC, Zenith, Advance, Every, Acer, Advance Logic Research, Seiko, Sharp and software too numerous to list. Make sure to check them out on their prices and service.

EGGHEAD DISCOUNT SOFTWARE
4264 Lincoln Blvd.
Marina del Rey, CA 90292
213/823-2727
HOURS: MON-SAT: 10-7 SUN: 12-5
CREDIT CARDS: AE, DISC, MC, V

Looking for good service and the best deal in computers? Egghead Discount Software says they will match and beat by one dollar any retail price on products from another store and do it with a smile. Their regular prices on software will give you savings of up to 50% off retail on brand names such as Microsoft, Lotus, Claris, Hayes, AST and Ashton Tate. There are 200 stores nationwide, so you're always near enough to get advice from an Egghead store's experienced staff. Among their 46 stores in California, 2 of them are clearance centers. One is located in Los Angeles (213/473-8115), and the other is located in Pasadena (818/568-0324).
Additional Locations: 45 other stores in S.CA–Call 800-EGGHEAD

ESPANORE LTD.**
7270 Bellaire Ave.
N. Hollywood, CA 91605
818/765-0526
HOURS: MON-FRI: 8:30-5:30
CREDIT CARDS: MC, V

Can't find a ribbon for your new or old printer? Espanore has ribbons for over 10,000 types of printers, many in colors. All of their ribbons are manufactured to meet or exceed OEM specifications. Defective ribbons purchased at Espanore are replaced for free. They carry a wide range of diskettes for all types of computers, such as IBM-PC or Apple, and volume discounts are available. Their no-name and brand-name diskettes in bulk are guaranteed to be 100% error free. Not only do they have diskettes, but they also carry printer labels, paper, disk storage cases and many other accessories for all your computer needs. They ship UPS within the USA and orders from Southern California are shipped the same day. Savings on their merchandise runs 30 to 50% off retail. You can save an additional 5% on your purchase when you use your BUYING RETAIL IS STUPID coupon.

HW COMPUTERS
6840 Havenhurst Ave.
Van Nuys, CA 91406
818/781-0300
HOURS: MON-FRI: 8:30-5:30
CREDIT CARDS: MC, V

Manager Rich Wilson says they have the lowest prices in Los Angeles when it comes to computers, computer furniture and peripherals. In business since 1977, they carry AST, HP, Epson, NEC, IBM, and Compaq. Their knowledgeable sales staff will assist you in selecting the computer that is right for you.

PERSONAL COMPUTER CENTRE
16811 Hawthorne Blvd.
Lawndale, CA 90260
213/214-1501
HOURS: MON-TUES, THUR-SAT: 9-6 WED: 9-8
CREDIT CARDS: AE, MC, V

Looking for a computer for your home or office? Personal Computer Centre is the answer. They have knowledgeable salespeople to demonstrate their Apple and IBM personal computers, printers, accessories and software. Apple software is discounted 10 to 40% everyday, and up to 60% during special sales. Repairs are done in-house and financing is available on approved credit. Get on their monthly newsletter to be notified about special sales and new products. You'll usually find prices to be 10% below most authorized dealers. Personal Computer Centre will meet or beat any advertised special, and urge you to see them before making your new computer purchase.
Additional Locations: 8 other stores throughout S. CA

PERSONAL SUPPORT COMPUTERS
10431 Santa Monica Blvd.
W. Los Angeles, CA 90015
213/474-1633
HOURS: MON-SAT: 10-6   SUN: 11-5
CREDIT CARDS: MC, V

Personal Support Computers has the highest rating in Los Angeles
for service and support . They guarantee lowest package prices and
will train you on the use of your computer purchases. As their name
states, "support" is their middle name. They are recognized as the
largest Macintosh retailer in the United States and carry a large
selection of computer accessories and software. You will also find
many IBM compatibles, Hewlett Packard printers and other brands
such as Epson, NEC and Hyundai. Their large service department
is open seven days a week, with five certified technicians and an
inventory of 150,000 spare parts. Get on their mailing list, so they
can inform you of their super blowouts. You can't go wrong here.
They have been in business for ten years and sell, lease, and service
their products. The owners, Dr. Peter Huber and Debbie Reid, have
received considerable publicity on their successful operation.

SOFT WAREHOUSE
9380 Warner Ave.
Fountain Valley, CA 92708
714/965-1169
HOURS: MON-FRI: 10-9   SAT: 9-6   SUN: 12-5
CREDIT CARDS: MC, V

Soft Warehouse is a computer superstore and they are user friendly!
At 30 to 80% below retail, they make friends easily. These people
really want to save their customers money. That's why there is no
membership fee. This is a complete warehouse stocked with computers, software, printers, drives, monitors, modems, accessories
and everything else needed to allow you and your computer to live
happily ever after. Would you like a few brand names? Okay, we'll
name just a few. You'll find ALR, Toshiba, Panasonic, Packard
Bell, Macintosh, Epson, NEC, Mitsubishi, Everex, Sony and Fuji.
Additional Locations: Hawthorne (213/540-1460)

∞ REPAIR & MAINTENANCE ∞

COMPLETE COMPUTER CURE
16618 Ventura Blvd.
Encino, CA 91436
818/783-1120
HOURS: MON-FRI: 8-5
CREDIT CARDS: CASH OR CHECKS ONLY

If your computer should come down with a dreaded cold or flu, or even a virus, give these folks a call because they have the cure. They will pick up and deliver your computer for free; they even have loaners and offer maintenance contracts as well. So, for fast turn-around at a low cost (about 20% less than others), they will repair and do maintenance on all personal computers, terminals, printers and drives.

Additional Locations: Compton (213/637-6549/South Bay Coverage), Placentia (714/996-0174/Orange County Coverage)

DEPARTMENT & WAREHOUSE STORES

ADRAY'S
6609 Van Nuys Blvd.
Van Nuys, CA 91405
818/908-1500
HOURS: MON-FRI: 10-7   SAT-SUN: 10-6
CREDIT CARDS: MC, V

You will save about 40% on almost everything at Adray's. They are the discount headquarters for major brands of televisions, VCR's, camera equipment, answering machines, stereo systems, computers and computer equipment, small and major appliances, jewelry, cosmetics, perfumes and colognes, china and crystal, pots and pans, sporting goods, exercise equipment, furniture, linens and just about anything else that comes to mind. You will find the salespeople courteous and knowledgeable, but they are usually very busy. If you are looking to make a major purchase, we suggest that you do your homework about the product you are interested in before going to Adray's. Shopping here is much different than shopping in a retail department store, but once you see their prices, adapting won't be a problem.
Additional Locations: Canoga Park (818/348-2600), Los Angeles (213/935-8191), W. Los Angeles (213/479-0797), Torrance (213/378-6777), Ventura (805/644-1111)

COSTCO
6110 Sepulveda Blvd.
Van Nuys, CA 91411
818/989-5256
HOURS: MON-FRI: 12-8:30   SAT: 9:30-6   SUN: 11-5
CREDIT CARDS: CASH, CHECKS OR COSTCO CREDIT CARD

Costco is truly for people who love to save money, lots of money. Each of their membership wholesale distribution centers operates in a 100,000 square foot warehouse. They carry only quality name

brands at substantially lower prices than other wholesale sources. Whether you need clothing, major appliances, books, furniture, groceries, toys, hardware, tires, liquor, jewelry, you name it, they've got it. Costco guarantees great brands, products and value. So, for those of you who really want to save big bucks, call for information on how to become a Costco member.
Additional Locations: 14 other stores throughout S. CA

HARTMAN JEWELRY & GIFTS**
2535 S. Fairfax Ave.
Culver City, CA 90232
213/938-3211
HOURS: MON-SAT: 10-6 SUN: 12-5
CREDIT CARDS: AE, MC, V

Come in, phone or send in your order. Hartman has quality name brand merchandise, personalized service, and low low prices. There are over 4,500 products on hand for immediate delivery— jewelry, watches, appliances, portable electronics, cameras, crystal, microwave ovens and so much more. They will be happy to send you their frequent newsletters with new specials, sale items, and even bigger savings. Make sure you ask about their preferred customers $10.00 lifetime membership card which saves you an additional 10% on all merchandise. The Hartman family has been providing their customers with great service since 1922. Not only can you expect savings of 50% off retail, they will accept your BUYING RETAIL IS STUPID coupon for an additional 10% discount off your purchase.

J. C. PENNEY CATALOGUE OUTLET STORE
6651 Fallbrook Ave.
Canoga Park, CA 91607
818/883-3660
HOURS: MON-FRI: 10-9 SAT: 10-7 SUN: 11-6
CREDIT CARDS: AE, J.C. PENNY, MC, V

This is where J.C. Penney's sells overstocked or discontinued items featured in their catalogues. You will find this enormous store literally packed with first quality merchandise. Choose from clothing for the entire family, toys, furniture, stereos, linens and more. We even spotted some exercise equipment. In addition to the selection, you'll love the 50% savings off retail on most items. Because they want to move this merchandise in a hurry (new merchandise arrives weekly), original prices are slashed dramatically before being put on the floor. You will find higher savings at the spe-cial sales they hold during the the year. So, if you are a faithful J.C. Penney shopper, now you know where to go for terrific bargains on their merchandise.

THE LIQUIDATION CLUB**
19032 S. Vermont Ave.
Gardena, CA 90248
213/715-6500
HOURS: SAT-WED: 11-6 THUR-FRI: 11-8
CREDIT CARDS: MC, V

BUYING RETAIL IS STUPID shoppers unite! The Liquidation Club, which operates through membership only, is extending a FREE MEMBERSHIP to all owners of this book, and this is definitely a place you want to check out. Not only do they have the lowest prices on most major department store brand names, but you'll save an additional 10% using your BUYING RETAIL IS STUPID coupon. Brand names include Liz Claiborne, Ann Klein, Bill Blass, Ralph Lauren, Bally, Georgio Armani, Perry Ellis, London Fog, Osh-kosh, and more. You'll find over 50,000 items of clothing for the entire family, housewares, bedding, accessories, gift items and much more at savings of 60 to 85% off retail. New merchandise accounts for 75% of their inventory, and the remaining 25% of their merchandise is slightly damaged (such as a garment label being removed). Stock changes daily, so make sure to put The Liqui-dation Club on your check list for shopping. Remember to cut out the coupon in back of the book for your free membership and 10% additional discount!

MR. PRICE
5500 Wilshire Blvd.
Los Angeles, CA 90036
213/934-2266
HOURS: MON-FRI: 10-7 SAT: 10-6 SUN: 12-5
CREDIT CARDS: MC, V

Mr. Price is a shopper's paradise, jammed to the rafters with small appliances of every description. You will find every brand name you can think of when you take yourself shopping in this 20,000 square foot showroom for television sets, VCR's, stereos, china, crystal, camera equipment, and an assortment of wonderful gift items too numerous to name. Their prices are 30 to 60% below retail, and they are easy to find since they have been in the same location since 1984.

PRICE CLUB
900 S. Harbor Blvd.
Fullerton, CA 92632
714/441-0584
HOURS: MON-FRI: 11-8:30 SAT: 9:30-6 SUN: 11-5
CREDIT CARDS: CASH OR CHECKS ONLY

Though it can be dangerous, one of our favorite things to do is wander around Price Club. How can shopping be dangerous? With over 100,000 square feet of everything imaginable—groceries, computers, televisions, VCR's, stereo equipment, clothing, office supplies, furniture, appliances, housewares, hardware, books (you name it and it's there)—the danger of spending much more than you had planned lurks along every aisle. At Price Club, the prices are so fantastic you many end up buying things you don't actually need. So before you go shopping, make out out a list of things you need in order to avoid impulse buying, unless of course impulse buying is your thing. Also, if you have never been to Price Club, make sure you schedule enough time so that you can leisurely walk this enormous warehouse and not have to rush through the place (you might miss something). With savings up to 80% off retail, you will recoup the $25 annual membership fee very quickly. All of the

salespeople are friendly and helpful, and their return policy is quite good.
Additional Locations: 17 other locations throughout S. CA

SEARS OUTLET STORE
1030 Celis St.
San Fernando, CA 91340
818/361-7121
HOURS: MON-FRI: 9-9 SAT: 9-6 SUN: 10-6
CREDIT CARDS: DISC, SEARS

Just about everything found at your neighbood Sears store can be found here at huge savings of 20 to 70% off the original retail prices. Merchandise from their stores and catalogues is sent to the surplus stores to make room for new stock. Because so much of their merchandise is seasonal, you'll find something new on every visit. It's pretty much self-service in the various departments that include clothing, appliances, housewares, linens, sporting goods, carpeting, and other various goods. Inventory changes constantly, so when you see something you want, buy it! It might not be there tomorrow.
Additional Locations: 10 other stores throughout S. CA

TOWN FAIR BAZAAR
317 S. Crocker St.
Los Angeles, CA 90013
213/626-4611
HOURS: 2ND SATURDAY OF EACH MONTH
CREDIT CARDS: CASH OR CHECKS ONLY

If you love great bargains and want to feel great about spending money at the same, shop at the Town Fair Bazaar. Every dollar you spend here goes to the City of Hope. You will find brand new merchandise that has been donated by grocery, drug, department, hardware and furniture stores throughout the area. The bazaar is divided into 21 departments featuring unbelievable prices. Don't be surprised to see a $300 lamp for $50 or a pair of L.A. Gear high-tops on sale for $10. The Town Fair Bazaar, which has been operating for more than 60 years, is a make-shift discount department store set up in a huge warehouse owned by the City of Hope. You can expect to save lots and lots of money, but be prepared for a crowd. Call 213/626-4611 for hours and and any other needed information.

DISCOUNT "SHOPPING CENTERS"

CALIFORNIA MART MANUFACTURERS' SAT. SALE
CA Mart Exhibit Hall–Los Angeles St. @ Olympic Blvd.
Los Angeles, CA 90015
213/623-5876
HOURS: HOURS VARY–CALL FOR INFORMATION
CREDIT CARDS: CASH ONLY

We think everyone has heard of the California Mart, but the majority of the public is unaware of how to get in. Generally speaking, they are not open to the public, but once a month or so, they allow the public in for a small entrance fee. The buys at these special sales are absolutely incredible! You will have access to 175 brand names, 300 lines of apparel and all kinds of accessories. Most items are either excess stock or samples, and it's all priced at cost, no mark-ups. As home to all major clothing manufacturers and their sales reps, available space must be continually made for the arrival of new lines. The last time we were at this sale, we bought some jeans with leather inserts tagged at $160, but we paid only $30. Just one visit will make you a true believer in our BUYING RETAIL IS STUPID philosophy! Hours vary, so call the phone number listed above to find out about their next sale, or keep an eye out for their ads in major newspapers. Don't forget to take plenty of cash with you because they don't accept checks or credit cards.

COOPER BUILDING
860 S. Los Angeles St.
Los Angeles, CA 90014
213/622-1139
HOURS: MON-SAT: 9:30-5:30 SUN: 11-5
CREDIT CARDS: CASH OR CHECKS ONLY*

This place is incredible! The Cooper Building is a "Tall Mall" 11 stories high with 8 selling floors (400,000 square feet) all bulging with exciting merchandise in the heart of the wholesale garment district. You'll find quite a collection of outlet stores representing various manufacturers, famous retail stores and discount stores. Whether you shop at the Cooper Building once a month or once a year, you always save 25 to 75% off retail prices every single day of the week. Quality and value prevail in over 70 stores featuring current designer and brand-name fashions for men, women and children, leather fashions, shoes, handbags, fashion accessories, lingerie and home fashions all under one roof. Why spend twice the amount on prestigious labels carried in expensive department stores when you can save a bundle buying the identical item at the Cooper Building? *Some vendors accept credit cards.

FACTORY MERCHANTS OUTLET STORES
2837 Lenwood Rd.
Barstow, CA 92311
619/253-7342
HOURS: MON-SAT: 10-9 SUN: 10-6
CREDIT CARDS: VARIES WITH VENDOR

If brand name factory outlets are your favorite sources for discount shopping, you will find an oasis at Factory Merchants Outlet Stores. The many leading manufacturers found here not only sell their merchandise direct but also own and operate these stores. Because you are buying direct, savings run 20–70% off retail. Some of the stores featuring various styles of wearing apparel are Anne Klein, Bennetton, Polo/Ralph Lauren, London Fog, Oshkosh, Hanes Activewear, Barbizon, L'Eggs/Hanes/Bali, Van Huesen, Gant, Evan Picone, Gitano, Leggoons, Monet/Izod/Ship 'n Shore, Polly Flinders, G.H. Bass and Banister Shoes. For your home, you'll find Wearever and Proctor Silex products at Kitchen Collection, Magnalite items at General Housewares, and linens at Fieldcrest/Cannon. Both Oneida and Royal Doulton have stores here, and Lenox will be opening an outlet in the near future. You'll find other individual outlets selling small leather goods, luggage, toys, light fixtures, greeting cards and paper products, perfume, and even a store that carries ribbons in every color of the rainbow. Your friends might think you're crazy driving to Barstow to go shopping, but after they've seen your purchases and have heard what you paid, they'll want to hitch a ride on your next trip . If you're like us, you might be wondering why Barstow was the city of choice for this shopping plaza. Well, over 70 million people pass through this area every year. So, the next time you're on your way to or from Las Vegas, stop by the Factory Merchants Outlet Stores.

GRAND CENTRAL PUBLIC MARKET
317 S. Broadway
Los Angeles, CA 90013
213/624-2378
HOURS: 7 DAYS A WEEK: 10-7
CREDIT CARDS: CASH ONLY, SOME VENDORS ACCEPT CHECKS

A visit to the historic Grand Central Public Market is a shopping and cultural experience at an international level. You'll find 58 vendors (in about 80,000 square feet) providing a multitude of foods and services. Along with 9 snack bars, you'll see people selling fresh produce (99¢ will buy 8 lbs. of tomatoes, 5 lbs. of bananas or 3 lbs. of grapes), eggs, dried fruits, health foods, natural juices, nuts, bakeries, delicatessens (American, Italian, Latin American and European), poultry, seafood and hard-to-find spices and herbs. You can buy choice cuts of beef, veal and lamb as well as ethnic delicacies such as beef cheeks, brains, pig snouts and lamb heads. We said this was an experience, didn't we? The basement has a complete grocery store and the kids can watch tortillas being made at a tortilla factory located on the main floor. Other stalls provide fresh flowers, toys, sundries, fresh flowers, haircuts, and jewelry repair. Don't worry if English isn't your native tongue. More than 20 languages are spoken here including Arabic, Chinese, Japanese, Jordanian, Korean, Portugese, Spanish, Tagalog, Yiddish and of course, English. Savings run about 10–40% off what you'd pay at your local grocery store. You'll need to take your own shopping bags because right now they don't have shopping carts. Porters are available for assistance if you buy in large quantities. In early 1991 they'll have an 11 story parking structure, but until then, parking is available across the street and adjacent to the market. You'll receive validation for one hour of free parking with a minimum purchase of $15. The Grand Central Public Market, opened in 1917, has never closed, not even during the Great Depression. Many of the vendors have been here for more than 40 years continuing a sense of family, tradition, quality and low prices. Wear comfortable shoes and don't forget your shopping bags.

INDOOR SWAPMEET OF STANTON
10401 Beach Blvd.
Stanton, CA 90680
714/527-1234
HOURS: FRI: 12-8 SAT-SUN: 10-6
CREDIT CARDS: VARIES WITH VENDOR

Find over 170 vendors selling everything from haircuts to fresh roasted coffee beans. Some of the brand names carried include Reebok, Panasonic, Phone Mate, Levi, Jordache, Christian Dior, Kenwood, Oscar de la Renta, Toshiba, Guess, Magnavox, and Bugle Boy. As you can see by the small sampling of brand names, you are in for a shopping treat. This two story, air conditioned 42,000 square foot building was designed especially for swapmeets and they have thought of everything. Even the aisles were made extra wide to accommodate wheelchairs. Parking is ample and free.

LA FASHION GALLERY
305 E. 9th St.
Los Angeles, CA 90015
213/624-0490
HOURS: MON-SAT: 9-6 SUN: 11-5
CREDIT CARDS: MC, V

Imagine, if you will, 100 stores offering discounts of 30 to 70% off suggested retail prices under one roof. Actually, you don't have to use your imagination because it really exists! You'll enjoy shopping in a comfortable, air conditioned environment complete with escalators, elevators, security guards and validated parking located on the premises. Parents can look forward to finding things for the entire family. Whether you're looking for clothing, lingerie, shoes, complete bridal services, fabrics, beauty supplies, jewelry or bicycles, you will find it all here. There are also restaurants and food concessions if shopping makes you hungry.

MELROSE ANTIQUE MALL
7201 Melrose Ave.
Los Angeles, CA 90046
213/965-9424
HOURS: MON-SAT: 11-6 SUN: 12:30-5:30
CREDIT CARDS: MC, V

The Melrose Antique Mall has 66 antique dealers who stock their own merchandise in large showcases. There is a huge assortment of antiques, and their inventory is constantly changing. Each dealer gives their own discount and you can usually save 20 to 25% over most stores and antique shows. If you have a resale card, you can save an additional 10%. You'll find antique jewelry, pottery, china, silver, dolls, books, clothing, toys, luggage, and other collectibles. Some of the brand names you'll find are Miriam Haskell, Eisenbach, Tiffany, Roseville-Hall, Bauer Limoges, Lalique, Baccarat, and Waterford. All the people are knowledgeable and friendly.

ST. VINCENT JEWELRY CENTER
650 S. Hill St.
Los Angeles, CA 90014
213/629-2124
HOURS: MON-SAT: 9:30-5:30
CREDIT CARDS: VARIES WITH VENDOR

St. Vincent Jewelry Center, the single largest jewelry exchange in the world, is home to over 400 wholesalers and manufacturers. This is the place to go for jewelry of any kind, we don't care what you want—it's here! Opened in 1982, the individual jewelry stores offer you factory-direct prices at savings of 40 to 70% below retail. Would you like a gold chain, a bracelet or maybe a diamond watch? Perhaps you have a coronation to attend and need a matched set (perhaps in diamonds and rubies) that includes a tiara, choker, pair of earrings, bracelet and ring to compliment your new Ungaro gown. Whatever you need or desire is here to fit any budget. You can spend $25 or $1,500,000. True jewelry lovers will think they have hit buried treasure. Aside from ready-made jewelry, you'll find businesses specializing in custom design, loose stones, repair, restoration, and you'll also find gold, precious metal and jewelry buyers. It's hard to believe that this fabulous selection is all under one roof, and when you see the prices, you won't believe the savings either. St. Vincent Jewelry Center is located on 7th and S. Hill, with validated parking at 725 S. Hill. Call to obtain a free directory listing all stores.

TOWN FAIR BAZAAR
317 S. Crocker St.
Los Angeles, CA 90013
213/626-4611
HOURS: 2ND SATURDAY OF EACH MONTH
CREDIT CARDS: CASH OR CHECKS ONLY

If you love great bargains and want to feel great about spending money at the same, shop at the Town Fair Bazaar. Everything you spend goes to the City of Hope. You'll find brand new merchandise that has been donated by grocery, drug, department, hardware and furniture stores throughout the area. The bazaar is divided into 21 departments featuring unbelievable prices. Don't be surprised to see a $300 lamp for $50 or a pair of L.A. Gear high-tops on sale for $10. The bazaar, which has been operating for more than 60 years, is a make-shift discount department store set up in a huge warehouse owned by the City of Hope. Expect to save lots and lots of money, but be prepared for a crowd. Call 213/626-4611 for details.

VALLEY INDOOR SWAPMEET**
14650 Parthenia St.
Van Nuys, CA 91402
818/892-0183
HOURS: FRI-SUN: 10-6
CREDIT CARDS: VARIES WITH VENDOR

As the name implies, the Valley Indoor Swap Meet is located inside; it's air conditioned during the summer and protected from the elements during the winter. This makes shopping a definite pleasure. Each location features hundreds of shops that display a huge array of top quality goods such as clothes, fine jewelry, home furnishings, plants, art, antiques and much more. Vendors sell top quality merchandise for 20 to 50% off retail prices. If you bring along your BUYING RETAIL IS STUPID discount coupon, you'll get FREE admission on any Friday, at any of their locations!
Additional Locations: Canoga Park (818/340-9120), Pomona (714/620-4792)

ELECTRONICS

∞ ENTERTAINMENT & COMMUNICATION ∞

ABC PREMIUMS
7266 Beverly Blvd.
Los Angeles, CA 90036
213/938-2724
HOURS: MON-FRI: 10-7 SAT: 9-6
CREDIT CARDS: MC, V

This discount house has been delighting knowledgeable shoppers in the Los Angeles area for more than 10 years with very low prices on all the top name brands in televisions, stereos, video sets, household items, appliances and so much more. It's worth a visit because you will find plenty of bargains, and they guarantee the lowest prices.

AFFORDABLE PORTABLES
1110 Gayley Ave.
Westwood, CA 90024
213/208-6996
HOURS: MON, WED, FRI: 11-9 TUES,THUR: 11-7 SAT: 11-6
        SUN: 1-7
CREDIT CARDS: AE, DC, DISC, MC, V

You'll save between 20 to 50% off retail prices on cordless phones, portable CD players, answering machines, small stereos, and short wave radios at Affordable Portables. They're reported to have the largest Walkman and portable selections in Southern California. You'll find in stock complete lines of Sony, and AIWA personal elec-tronics. They also stock plenty of accessories for walkman and CD players. Affordable Portables, considered to be among the most knowledgeable in the field of small electronics, will quote prices over the phone.
Additional Locations: Costa Mesa (714/650-1100), Torrance (213/370-7877), Sherman Oaks (818/784-1191)

BEL AIR CAMERA, AUDIO & VIDEO
1025 Westwood Blvd.
Los Angeles, CA 90024
213/208-5150
HOURS: MON-FRI: 9-6 SAT: 9:30-6
CREDIT CARDS: MC, V

Bel Air is one of the largest camera, audio, and video stores on the West Coast. They offer cameras and camera accessories, video cameras and recorders, audio components, tape recorders, televisions, enlargers and more. Two or three times a year, they have a large Expo & Sale where they invite representatives from over 40 companies to show their products. Shows are usually in May or December, but you can get the above items daily at 10% above their cost and sometimes at cost. They have Nikon, Minolta, Pentax, Vivitar, Olympus, Panasonic, Sony, Speedotron, Hasselblad and others. Feel free to write a check or charge your purchases at Bel Air, but these people give special discounts if you pay in cash.

DISCOUNT SALES
12004 W. Pico Blvd.
Los Angeles, CA 90064
213/473-5015
HOURS: MON-THUR: 10-7 FRI-SAT: 10-6 SUN: 11-5
CREDIT CARDS: MC, V

Discount Sales has to be visited to be believed. You pay prices that are generally just 10 to 15% above cost and you get top brands in microwave ovens, ceiling fans, stereos, television sets, VCR's and camcorders. They buy in huge quantities for all eight of their stores and sell in volume. Announcements are sent out to their customers when they have clearance sales on floor stock, so be sure to get on their mailing list.

Additional Locations: 7 other stores throughout S. CA

HOLLYTRON
4641 W. Santa Monica Blvd.
Los Angeles, CA 90029
213/668-1800
HOURS: MON-SAT: 11-9 SUN: 12-7
CREDIT CARDS: MC, V

You will find a visit to Hollytron to be worthwhile because of their low prices on brand-name televisions, radios, cameras, the popular Sony Walkman, and a selection of jewelry. There are two technicians on staff to service and repair things, often while you wait.

INTERSPACE ELECTRONICS, INC.
10854 Washington Blvd.
Culver City, CA 90232
213/836-6018
HOURS: MON-FRI: 10-5 SAT: 10-3
CREDIT CARDS: MC, V

At Interspace Electronics you can save from 20 to 50% off retail prices on communications equipment, citizen band radios, cordless telephones, scanners, answering machines, auto alarms, flashlights, and even radar detectors. While we haven't begun to name everything they carry, we're sure you get the idea.

L.A. TRONICS
17921 Ventura Blvd.
Encino, CA 91316
818/344-4104
HOURS: MON-FRI: 10-7 SAT-SUN: 10-6
CREDIT CARDS: AE, MC, V

L. A. Tronics has a wide variety of major brand consumer electronics. The overall concept is "guaranteed lowest price." They will meet or beat any price in Los Angeles County, subject to verification. Paying basically 10% over cost, you can get television sets, videos, stereos, cameras, household appliances, and even beauty products and jewelry.
Additional Locations: Huntington Beach (714/964-4400), Torrance (213/373-2020)

LEO'S STEREO
10915 Santa Monica Blvd.
Westwood, CA 90025
213/479-8036
HOURS: MON-FRI: 9-9 SAT: 9-6 SUN: 10-6
CREDIT CARDS: MC, V

Psst, want to save big money on a stereo? Leo's is the place to shop! Save up to 60% on stereos or your home or car, television sets, cellular telephones, and CD players. You'll find all the popular brand names like Sony, TDK, Fuji, and more. They have financing available, and you'll find they are super people to deal with. For your convenience, they have car installation departments in all of their stores. The sales they have throughout the year feature buys so good you'll think they're giving the merchandise away!
Additional Locations: 36 other stores throughout S. CA

MIKO PHOTO-AUDIO-VIDEO CENTER
1259 3rd Street Promenade
Santa Monica, CA 90401
213/393-9371
HOURS: MON-THUR: 9-6 FRI: 9-7 SAT: 9-6 SUN: 12-4
CREDIT CARDS: AE, DISC, MC, V

Miko Photo-Audio-Video Center prides itself in its high repeat customer business, so you know they are doing something right. They have everything for your home entertainment center, video cameras, portable audio systems, stereos, electric games and more. In addition to their camera equipment and supplies, you can have your film processed there, too. They also have cordless telephones, answering machines, and video editing equipment.
Additional Locations: Manhattan Beach (213/546-5491), Santa Monica Place (213/395-8185)

NATIONAL STEREO
6672 Hollywood Blvd.
Los Angeles, CA 90028
213/463-0772
HOURS: 7 DAYS A WEEK: 10:30-8
CREDIT CARDS: AE, DC, MC, V

National Stereo will meet or beat any price in town. This store is filled to the brim with a vast selection of television sets, radios, watches, the Sony Walkman, and so much more. They carry all brand names at tremendous savings. You'll like the friendly, courteous service they give their customers, too.

OLYMPIC ELECTRONICS
6310 Hollywood Blvd.
Hollywood, CA 90028
213/467-4752
HOURS: 7 DAYS A WEEK: 10-9
CREDIT CARDS: MC, V

Olympic Electronics is right on the corner of Hollywood and Vine. They promise the lowest prices in the area on AM-FM portable radios, cameras, and stereos for the home or car. They've got a store full of electronic wonders from all the major manufacturers, and most are priced at just 5 to 10% over cost. They are wholesale to the public, so shop here and save.

REGGIE'S STEREO
7820 Santa Monica Blvd.
W. Hollywood, CA 90046
213/656-0111
HOURS: MON-SAT: 10-7 SUN: 11-5
CREDIT CARDS: MC, V

If you want to save 20 to 60% off the suggested manufacturer's list price on home and car stereos, car alarms, car phones, televisions, videos, and answering machines, then all you have to do is visit Reggie's. They carry all the above and more. Their expert installation service can work miracles on same-day installation of car stereos, alarms, and phones. Instant financing on approved credit is available, and their sales staff is extremely helpful. Watch for their special sales during the year where you can save even more on selected items. If you want to take advantage of their financing service, you can save time by calling Reggie's Instant Credit Hotline (213/931-4444).

Additional Locations: Van Nuys (818/902-0444)

ROGERSOUND LABS
8381 Canoga Ave.
Canoga Park, CA 91304
818/873-3051
HOURS: MON-FRI: 12-9 SAT-SUN: 12-6
CREDIT CARDS: MC, V

Rogersound Labs has speaker systems, audio-video components, car stereos, television sets, and much more. Their prices on such brand names as Sony, Kenwood, Yamaha, Mitsubishi, and JVC are 50% below retail prices. You can be sure of a helpful, professional staff at any of the Rogersound Labs.
Additional Locations: 6 other stores throughout S. CA

SHELLY'S STEREO HI-FI CENTER
2212 Wilshire Blvd.
Santa Monica, CA 90403
213/453-4451
HOURS: MON-WED, SAT: 10-6 THUR-FRI: 10-8
CREDIT CARDS: AE, DISC, MC, V

Owner Robert Coyle has been in business since 1964 and can save you money on quality, brand-name stereo components, plus you get old-fashioned home service for custom wiring. Shelly's has some used equipment, accepts trade-ins, and also has an excellent service department. They guarantee the best prices on their merchandise.
Additional Locations: Canoga Park (818/716-8500)

SPEAKER CITY
10615 Vanowen St.
Burbank, CA 91505
818/508-1908
HOURS: MON-SAT: 10-6:30
CREDIT CARDS: MC, V

We have discovered a virtual candy store for speaker enthusiasts and audiophiles, filled with speakers for the home and complete sound systems for vehicles, at savings of at least 50%! All components needed to build speakers from scratch, and also complete kits for speaker systems can be found here. They do "X-overs" too. One of the great things about Speaker City is you know exactly what you are buying. The price of a speaker already built is no longer a mystery because lining the walls are the individual components that went into the speaker, along with the cost of each item. Though they only carry speakers for the home (no stereos), they do stock complete sound systems for your car (no installations). Customized speaker systems are available for both home and vehicles. Name brands include, Focal, Dynaudio, Vifa, Peerless and Pyle. If you need any technical advice, talk to Wally Ross. He's not only an expert on sound systems, he's also a professional musician.

∞ PARTS, SUPPLIES & EQUIPMENT ∞

ALL ELECTRONICS CORP.
905 S. Vermont Ave.
Los Angeles, CA 90006
213/380-8000
HOURS: MON-FRI: 9-5 SAT: 9-4
CREDIT CARDS: AE, DISC, MC, V

This is a big surplus outlet for electronic parts and supplies. If you are handy with that sort of thing and know your way around semiconductors, relays, speakers, and transformers, you can save from 25 to 75% off retail prices on all of your purchases! As they have been in business since 1968, the folks at All Electronics Corp. know everything and have everything in their stores.
Additional Locations: Van Nuys (818/997-1806)

AMERICAN ELECTRONICS SUPPLY
1200 N. Vine St.
Hollywood, CA 90033
213/464-1144
HOURS: MON-FRI: 8:30-5:30 SAT: 8:30-5 SUN: 11-3
CREDIT CARDS: MC, V

A one-of-a-kind operation! American Electronics Supply covers nearly a city block with 60 parking places available for your convenience. Known throughout the nation as the "Supermarket of

Electronics", they are relied upon by both business and industry for those hard-to-get items. We won't even try listing the contents of this huge place, but rest assured, they have everything electrical that you could possibly need. Some brand names are Sony, Mcintosh, RCA, Zenith, Panasonic, NAD, Revox, Teac, Electro-Voice, Bogen, Sunheiser, AKG, Neumann, University Sound plus many others. Go in; get what you want at only 20 to 40% above cost. Should you end up not buying anything, you can make your trip worthwhile by registering for a free drawing. We almost forgot to tell you about another service they offer. Are you in search of a few props for the concert scene in the latest movie you're producing? Must you have several closed circuit televisions added temporarily to your security system when Charles and Di visit next month? You can rest easy. They rent just about anything to do with electronics. For rental rates and availability, the phone number is 213/466-4321.

ITC ELECTRONICS**
2772 W. Olympic Blvd.
Los Angeles, CA 90006
213/388-0621
HOURS: MON-SAT: 9-6
CREDIT CARDS: MC, V

ITC Electronics is a full line authorized distributor of electronic supplies, computer accessories, auto sound products and electronic test equipment. They also carry close-outs and special purchases at additional savings. You can expect to save anywhere from 10 to 60% off retail on such brand names as Sansui, Pyle auto speakers, Fluke, Sony headphones, and Pioneer. Special pricing is available for quantity purchases and don't forget to use your BUYING RETAIL IS STUPID coupon for an additional 5% discount. Their store in Torrance is the only one open on Sundays (11-5).
Additional Locations: Chatsworth (818/700-0900), Oxnard (805/983-4115), Torrance (213/370-6211)

RADIOLAND/INGLEWOOD ELECTRONICS
4701 W. Century Blvd.
Inglewood, CA 90304
213/671-7761
HOURS: MON-FRI: 9:30-6 SAT: 9:30-5:30 SUN: 10:30-4
CREDIT CARDS: CASH OR CHECKS ONLY

Radioland/Inglewood Electronics offers discount prices on name brands every day, and you save 25 to 35% on radio and television tubes, transistors, antennas, cable TV accessories, car stereos and CB radios. They also carry portable radios, phonograph needles, and most other electronic parts.

SANDY'S ELECTRONIC SUPPLY
21305 Saticoy St.
Canoga Park, CA 91303
818/346-8353
HOURS: MON-FRI: 8-6 SAT: 9-6
CREDIT CARDS: MC, V

Want to fix your own television or radio? Go to Sandy's, one of the largest outlets in the San Fernando Valley, for all your electronic needs. They have a full line of over 1,000 different items and you'll save 20 to 50% on things like connectors, surge protectors, cables and battery back-ups. Electronic test equipment is also available.
Additional Locations: North Hollywood (818/765-8585)

∞ REPAIR & MAINTENANCE ∞

HOOK UPS R US
18540 Plummer St., #210
Northridge, CA 91324
818/349-0901
HOURS: MON-SAT: 9-9
CREDIT CARDS: CASH OR CHECKS ONLY

For those of us with two left hands needing to hook up a new VCR, television or stereo equipment, call Hook Ups R Us. They'll come to your home and set things right, add cable from one room to another and make sure it's all working properly. They'll also clean your video and audio sets for a flat fee of $15.95. You'll save about 10% when you use their services.

T.V. WORLD DISCOUNT SALES & SERVICE**
20963 Devonshire St.
Chatsworth, CA 91311
818/700-0546
HOURS: MON-FRI: 9-6 SAT: 9-4
CREDIT CARDS: CASH OR CHECKS ONLY

If your television or VCR or audio equipment needs a tune up, these people will service or repair it, and they guarantee their work. T.V. World will give you a free estimate on anything you carry in, and you can expect to save about 20%. Senior citizens receive an additional 5% discount. As an added incentive, T.V. World Discount Service will honor your BUYING RETAIL IS STUPID coupon for an additional 10% savings!

FOOD & BEVERAGE

∞ BAKERY GOODS ∞

ABC DONUTS
1528 W. Olympic Blvd.
Los Angeles, CA 90015
213/381-2328
HOURS: 7 DAYS A WEEK–24 HOURS A DAY
CREDIT CARDS: CASH ONLY

Just imagine, these are the people who produced and delivered 1,200 dozen donuts to the Rose Parade! So if you're having a huge party, or the local Brownie troop is coming over for donuts, don't worry; these are the people who can handle the job. Call in your order of one dozen or dozens of dozens the day before and receive wholesale pricing! They'll even deliver with a minimum order. They are also open for over-the-counter sales but at a little higher price. Christmas and New Years are the only days they are closed.

MEYER COOKIE CO.
8735 Remmet Ave.
Canoga Park, CA 91303
818/341-0409
HOURS: MON-FRI: 8-4
CREDIT CARDS: CASH OR CHECKS ONLY

The Cookie Monster loves this store and you will too. Save 50% or more on the cookies you purchase. They carry about 30 varieties of cookies and you can buy them buy the dozen or 1,000 dozen. One of their specialities is old fashion sugar cookies and they've been making them since 1963. They also make a line of dietetic cookies, so you can satisfy your sweet tooth without the calories.

OLD COUNTRY BAKERY
4324 W. Magnolia
Burbank, CA 91505
818/841-2832
HOURS: MON-SAT: 9-5:30
CREDIT CARDS: CASH OR CHECKS ONLY

A tradition of its own, Old Country has been around for over half a century baking breads, pastries, cakes and cookies in their Kosher bakery. Everything is freshly baked, and the ones that didn't come out looking picture perfect are sold at 50% off retail, however, they taste just fine. Seniors, make sure you ask about your additional 10% savings.
Additional Locations: 9 other stores throughout S. CA

VAN DE KAMPS THRIFT STORE
11180 Lucerne
Los Angeles, CA 90230
213/391-9116
HOURS: MON-SAT: 9-6
CREDIT CARDS: CASH OR CHECKS ONLY

When the urge hits you, there's nothing you can do but succumb to the feeling. Right here is where you can find satisfaction with baked products like cheese Danish, flaky buttery rolls, cream or fruit filled pastries, iced cinnamon rolls, and lots of other goodies. By taking advantage of their overproduction, or when the baked goods don't come out looking quite as perfect as they'd like, you can buy these delicious baked goods at up to 70% off.
Additional Locations: 15 other stores in S. CA–Call 213/255-0171, extension 311 for one near you.

∞ DIETETIC & BULK FOODS ∞

AMERICAN BULK FOODS
19836 Ventura Blvd.
Woodland Hills, CA 91364
818/346-1653
HOURS: MON-SAT: 8:30-9   SUN: 10-7
CREDIT CARDS: CASH OR CHECKS ONLY

American Bulk Foods is one of our favorite places to shop. If you want healthy but tasty food, this is the place. They specialize in low fat, low calorie, gourmet "healthful" foods of high quality. Aside from the bakery goods and frozen desserts, just about everything is sold in bulk. There are bins filled with everything from numerous varieties of dry soup mixes, flour, legumes, spices, granola, pasta, and rice, to old fashioned candies, gummies, jelly bellys, dried fruit without sulfate, and nuts (raw, roasted, unsalted). When you see what the bulk goods cost, you'll never want to pay prepackaged prices ever again! To give you an idea of what we mean, we bought some sugar-free taffy at 75% less per pound than what we had paid at a local candy store. Their slogan is, "Home of the Guilt Free Sundae." We're talking about an 8 ounce hot fudge sundae with only 74 calories. With 3,000 square feet of merchandise, they have the largest selection of sugar free, lo-cal items in the Los Angeles area. Another plus is the special attention paid to diabetics. Baked or prepared daily on the premises, their diabetic line is sugar and salt free, and very low in oil. Aside from being low in calories, their diabetic line is also kosher. Also in stock are unsalted snacks, no oil Mandel Bread, Meusalis, and freshly baked muffins with NO cholesterol, NO eggs, NO animal fats and kosher, too! Health conscious, "how to" recipes are available throughout the store. For those of you with special dietary needs, American Bulk Foods will make special orders of delicious cakes and desserts.

∞ HEALTH FOODS & VITAMINS ∞

DISCOUNT HEALTH FOODS
14427-1/2 Ventura Blvd.
Sherman Oaks, CA 91423
818/995-7684
HOURS: MON-SAT: 9-9   SUN: 10-7
CREDIT CARDS: MC, V

For all of you health conscious people, which includes almost everyone living in California, you must stop by Discount Health Foods and see their display of supplements, 230 feet wide and 6 feet high. They also carry organic produce, vitamins, herbs, homeopathics and a full line of cosmetics. Savings go up to 50% off retail.

NATURE MART
2080 Hillhurst Ave.
Los Angeles, CA 90027
213/660-0052
HOURS: MON-SAT: 9-10   SUN: 9-9
CREDIT CARDS: MC, V

Fresh carrot juice and a good vegie burger always makes one feel wholesome. That's why we're happy to tell you about Nature Mart. Shop for all your vitamins, produce, grains, nuts and cosmetics at discounted prices, and then take a break at their health food restaurant. Seniors receive an additional 10% off their regular low prices.

∞ MARKETS ∞

GRAND CENTRAL PUBLIC MARKET
317 S. Broadway
Los Angeles, CA 90013
213/624-2378
HOURS: 7 DAYS A WEEK: 10-7
CREDIT CARDS: CASH ONLY, SOME VENDORS ACCEPT CHECKS

A visit to the historic Grand Central Public Market is a shopping and cultural experience at an international level. You'll find 58 vendors (in about 80,000 square feet) providing a multitude of foods and services. Along with 9 snack bars, you'll see people selling fresh produce (99¢ will buy 8 lbs. of tomatoes, 5 lbs. of bananas or 3 lbs. of grapes), eggs, dried fruits, health foods, natural juices, nuts, bakeries, delicatessens (American, Italian, Latin American and European), poultry, seafood and hard-to-find spices and herbs. You can buy choice cuts of beef, veal and lamb as well as ethnic delicacies such as beef cheeks, brains, pig snouts and lamb heads. We said this was an experience, didn't we? The basement has a complete grocery store and the kids can watch tortillas being made at a tortilla factory located on the main floor. Other stalls provide fresh flowers, toys, sundries, fresh flowers, haircuts, and jewelry repair. Don't worry if English isn't your native tongue. More than 20 languages are spoken here including Arabic, Chinese, Japanese, Jordanian, Korean, Portuguese, Spanish, Tagalog, Yiddish and of course, English. Savings run about 10–40% off what you'd pay at your local grocery store. You'll need to take your own shopping bags because right now they don't have shopping carts. Porters are available for assistance if you buy in large quantities. In early 1991 they'll have an 11 story parking structure, but until then, parking is available across the street and adjacent to the market. You'll receive validation for one hour of free parking with a minimum purchase of $15. The Grand Central Public Market, opened in 1917, has never closed, not even during the Great Depression. Many of the vendors have been here for more than 40 years continuing a sense of family, tradition, quality and low prices. Wear comfortable shoes and don't forget your shopping bags.

SOUTHLAND FARMERS' MARKET ASSOCIATION
1010 S. Flower St., Room 402
Los Angeles, CA 90015
213/749-9551
HOURS: OPEN 1 DAY PER WEEK
CREDIT CARDS: CASH OR CHECKS ONLY

Markets range in size from 15 to 70 farmers and all products are sold directly by the producer, catcher or collector. Shoppers save from 20 to 30% over local markets on items including fresh fruits, fresh vegetables, nuts, eggs, honey, fish, live plants, beefalo products, dried fruits, juices, olives, dates, sprouts. The markets are open one day a week. Contact the Southland Farmers' Market Association at 213/749-9551 for hours and information regarding the market nearest you.
Additional Locations: 10 markets in S. CA–Call 213/749-9551

∞ MEAT & SEAFOOD ∞

PACIFIC AMERICAN FISH CO., INC.
838 E. 6th St.
Los Angeles, CA 90021
213/623-3433
HOURS: MON-FRI: 6AM-2 SAT: 6AM-1
CREDIT CARDS: CASH ONLY

Now you can buy direct from one of the largest fish distributors in Southern California. Pacific American Fish Company will sell you any type of frozen or fresh fish at 10 to 25% less than supermarkets. Varieties in stock include shark, mahi mahi, orange roughy, salmon, catfish, tuna, swordfish, all sizes of shrimp, whitefish, lobsters, clams, oysters, and more. If you have a special recipe calling for some type of unusual seafood they don't usually carry, they'll do their best to locate it for you. When buying fish, you generally must buy it whole, but don't worry, a filleting service is available. The filleted price is normally 15 to 20% higher, depending on the weight loss, but you pay only for the weight of the fillets. Shopping at Pacific American Fish Co. is the easy way to catch fish!

WESTERN EXCHANGE MEAT MARKET
544 W. Arbor Vita
Inglewood, CA 90301
213/678-1872
HOURS: MON-SAT: 9-6
CREDIT CARDS: MC, V

The more you buy, the more you save, so go in with a friend or friends because there are discounts on pounds purchased. Western Exchange is your freezer order specialists selling sides of beef, hind quarters, large deli selections and fresh seafood. In business since 1956, they will fill your freezer with whatever you choose or cater a party from 10 to 500 people with personalized service.

∞ MEXICAN FOODS & PRODUCTS ∞

DOS BANDERAS
3721 E. Slauson Ave.
Maywood, CA 90270
213/589-3311
HOURS: MON-FRI: 6-2:30
CREDIT CARDS: CASH OR CHECKS ONLY

In business since the early 1980's, this family owned and operated manufacturer offers wholesale prices to the public. They specialize in handmade tamales. Yes, we said handmade. They have five different kinds—beef, pork, chicken, green chili and cheese, and sweet tamales. Other quality Mexican food is also available. All of their products are USDA inspected. You can call your order in 24 hours a day, and if no one is available you can leave your order on their machine. Buy by the case for even greater discounts.

MONTERREY FOOD PRODUCTS
3939 Brooklyn Ave.
Los Angeles, CA 90033
213/263-2143
HOURS: MON-FRI: 8-5
CREDIT CARDS: CASH ONLY

This large warehouse of wholesale groceries and restaurant supplies specializes in Mexican foods. Even though it's a giant warehouse, 8,000 square feet, they pride themselves in personal attention to each customer. There are over 40 varieties of spices available by the pound, dry chiles, tamale steamers, Mexican grinding stones, and they can make up custom blends of spices for that special dish. They will even mail the merchandise to you. This place is a must for the Mexican gourmet!

∞ NUTS & CANDY ∞

THE CANDY FACTORY
12510 Magnolia Blvd.
N. Hollywood, CA 91607
818/766-8220
HOURS: TUES-SAT: 10-5
CREDIT CARDS: MC, V

The Candy Factory has one of the most complete inventories of candy making supplies and molds anywhere. Candy is sold by one pound packages or in bulk by the 40 and 47 pound case. They also have candy making classes and will do custom candy. You'll even find "x-rated" molds in a discreet location of the store. Name brands carried here include Merckens, Nestles, and Guittard. Mark your calendar for the special sales they hold in July.

CANDY STORE**
707 W. 17th St.
Long Beach, CA 90813
213/436-5106
HOURS: MON-SAT: 9-5
CREDIT CARDS: MC, V

The Candy Store carries all kinds of candy and gift items at savings of 20 to 50%. They take pride in saying that their candies are the "best in the U.S.A." They have sugar-free and salt-free candies, also. Name brands include Miss Saylors, Jelly Bellys and Chocolate Roses. Chocolate prices start at $2.50 a pound. Pricing for candy starts at $1.95 a pound and is sold by the piece or in unlimited pounds. Satisfy your sweet tooth and get a "sweet" deal at the same time by using your BUYING RETAIL IS STUPID coupon for an additional 10% discount!

CHRISTOPHER'S NUT CO.
14333 Bessemer
Van Nuys, CA 91401
818/787-6303
HOURS: MON-FRI: 7-5   SAT: 9-3
CREDIT CARDS: CASH AND CHECKS ONLY

Having a party? Even if you just need something to munch on, stop by Christopher's Nut Company where you purchase all kinds of nuts, dried fruit, sugarless and regular candy, all at 35 to 55% below retail. Savings are even higher if you buy in bulk. One pound of macadamia nuts costs $7.95 here, while you might pay $12 to $14 elsewhere. They are the largest distributor for major brand nuts in Los Angeles. Some brands you might recognize are Blue Diamond, Mauna Loa and Dole. They only deal with top of the line products. You can save even more when buying in bulk. They also carry spices.

GUST PECOULAS & CO.
746 Towne Ave.
Los Angeles, CA 90021
213/627-2008
HOURS: MON-FRI: 7-4:30
CREDIT CARDS: CASH OR CHECKS ONLY

Who can resist nuts that are fresh roasted daily? A person could actually go nuts trying to make a selection from all the nuts, seeds, candy, trail mix, dried fruit, glazed fruit, chocolate coated nuts and more. If you make your own candy, you can buy several varieties of chocolate. Buy it in 10 pound blocks and you'll save even more money. Gust Picoulas & Co. has been around since 1907. Not only will you be saving 10 to 25% below retail, you will be dealing with a company that really knows their nuts.

NUTS TO YOU
644 E. 9th St.
Los Angeles, CA 90015
213/627-8855
HOURS: MON-SAT: 8-5
CREDIT CARDS: MC, V

If you go nuts over nuts like we do, then you can really save money when you buy your nuts from Nuts To You. When we sit down to watch a football game or some other sporting event, the cashews and pecans just seem to disappear. You'll save 20 to 50% off retail prices, but you have to buy 5 pounds at a time. The good news is you can buy an assortment to get to the 5 pound minimum. Even better news is that all their nuts are roasted right on the premises. You can grind your own peanut butter, and they also have a large selection of dried fruit.

SILVER ROSES NUTS
4621 Pacific Blvd.
Vernon, CA 90058
213/581-8283
HOURS: MON-FRI: 8-4

CREDIT CARDS: CASH OR CHECKS ONLY

Imagine, 48,000 square feet of NUTS! We're referring to the kind you eat! They wholesale 20 different varieties of nuts, cashews, almonds, peanuts and sunflowers to name a few. Custom roasting can be requested, and they will also ship anywhere in the world. These folks are "nutty" enough to sell their merchandise at 30% below retail.

∞ SPIRITS ∞

LIQUOR BANK & DELI
3600 Stocker
Los Angeles, CA 90008
213/296-7467
HOURS: SUN-WED: 7-12 THUR-SAT: 7-2
CREDIT CARDS: MC, V

Looking for that special bottle of wine after 10 p.m. and hungry too? The Liquor Bank and Deli is the place for you! They have great prices on liquor and party catering. Their special kosher-style deli platters are perfect for a Saturday night poker game. Stop in weekly as there is always something on special besides the prices.

LOS ANGELES WINE CO.
4935 McConnell Ave., #8
Los Angeles, CA 90066
213/306-WINE (9463)
HOURS: MON-SAT: 10-6 SUN: 12-5
CREDIT CARDS: MC, V

Do you need to find a vintage wine bottled the same year your parents were married? Not only can you find it at the Los Angeles Wine Co., you'll find it at 35 to 50% off retail prices! Oenologists will appreciate the fact that these folks are the largest, single-store volume purveyor of fine wines in the state of California. They also produce a monthly newsletter announcing new items in their inventory. Whether you are looking for a private reserve Cabernet, a vintage Port, or a wine opener, you'll find it at the right price at the Los Angeles Wine Co.

THE WINE HOUSE
2311 Cotner
W. Los Angeles, CA 90064
213/479-3731
HOURS: MON-SAT: 10-7   SUN: 12-6
CREDIT CARDS: MC, V

You can always save 10 to 50% at the Wine House. They probably have one of the most complete selections assembled here. If it has been brewed or bottled as a wine, liquor or beer, you're almost sure to find it here. Sometimes the savings go up as high as 75 to 90%. If you are interested they will show you wine books and tell you about wine tours. True connoisseurs should inquire about the wine locker rentals available for their own precious collection of private stock. Be sure to sign up for the informative newsletter they send to their customers. They also have free tastings.

∞ WAREHOUSES ∞

BINGO CASH & CARRY
10864 Cantara
Sun Valley, CA 91352
818/768-7846
HOURS: MON-FRI: 7-5   SAT-SUN: 8-4
CREDIT CARDS: CASH ONLY, NO CHECKS

Are you a baseball card collector? Buy them by the case at Bingo Cash & Carry. You will find everything you'd need if you wanted to open a grocery store. They stock a full line selection of groceries, candy, health and beauty aids, tobacco, soft drinks and food service and frozen foods. They sell mainly to stores, and items are sold strictly by the case. The public is welcome, but they don't really

cater to the individual consumer. As this business generally fills case orders placed by stores stocking their shelves, customer service is practically nonexistent. Know what you want to buy a case at a time before going down there. No membership fees are required. This store falls somewhere between the Price Club and Smart and Final, but remember, it's cash and carry, no checks.
Additional Locations: Northridge (818/349-6522)

COSTCO
6110 Sepulveda Blvd.
Van Nuys, CA 91411
818/989-5256
HOURS: MON-FRI: 12-8:30 SAT: 9:30-6 SUN: 11-5
CREDIT CARDS: CASH, CHECKS OR COSTCO CREDIT CARD

Costco is truly for people who love to save money, lots of money. Each of their membership wholesale distribution centers operates in a 100,000 square foot warehouse. They carry only quality name brands at substantially lower prices than other wholesale sources. Most of the food and grocery items are available only by the case, in very large sizes or are packaged in multiples. So, for those of you who really want to save big bucks, call for information on how to become a Costco member at one of their 15 locations in Southern California.
Additional Locations: 14 other stores throughout S. CA

LA BREA BARGAIN CIRCUS
852 N. La Brea
Los Angeles, CA 90038
213/466-7231
HOURS: MON-SAT: 9:30-8:30 SUN: 10-8
CREDIT CARDS: MC, V

A grocery store and so much more! In addition to food products, La Brea Bargain Circus features knives, silver, beer and an assortment of ceramic planters and dishes. The stock changes weekly, so it's like going to a new store every week. They buy inventory close-outs and job lots, so the prices are terrific; the people are nice and friendly, too. With this store having over 80,000 square feet, not only do you have a large assorted selection, you have lots of area to cover. Watch for their newspaper ads for their latest specials.

PRICE CLUB
900 S. Harbor Blvd.
Fullerton, CA 92632
714/441-0584
HOURS: MON-FRI: 11-8:30 SAT: 9:30-6 SUN: 11-5
CREDIT CARDS: CASH OR CHECKS ONLY

Whatever you do, make sure you walk into the Price Club with a full stomach if you're headed for the grocery section. You'll find most of the same brands and items stocked by your local super-market, but just about everything comes in larger sizes or quantities than you're probably accustomed to buying. Also, if you've never been to Price Club, make sure you schedule enough time so that you can leisurely walk through this enormous warehouse and not have to rush through the place (you might miss something). Prices can run up to 80% off retail at the Price Club, so you'll recoup the $25 annual membership fee very quickly.
Additional Locations: 17 other stores throughout S. CA

WAREHOUSE FOOD MART
8035 Webb Ave.
N. Hollywood, CA 91605
818/767-2234
HOURS: 7 DAYS A WEEK: 8-10
CREDIT CARDS: MC, V

This is a full, giant-size grocery supermarket, where you can get all your groceries and meats and save 30 to 40% on your order. Check them out for everyday savings because you'll save more than a few pennies. Since their opening in March of 1984, people have been driving miles just to grocery shop at the Warehouse Food Mart.

HOME FURNISHINGS

∞ CHINA, SILVER & TABLEWARE ∞

AAA EXTERNAL STAINLESS STEEL CORP.**
430 S. San Bernardino Rd.
Covina, CA 91723
818/331-7204
HOURS: MON-FRI: 9-5
CREDIT CARDS: AE, MC, V

They carry a wide variety of household and kitchenware stainless steel products, including such items as waterless cookware and china. There are between 100 to 200 different items from which to choose. Depending on the item, you can expect to save 20 to 50% below retail. Regal Products are among the many name brands represented in their inventory. Special close out items are offered at prices below the standard discounts. For any large scale buying, you can arrange to have sales people come to you. Under their lifetime guarantee policy, they will replace any defective item for the rest of your life. Make sure to use your BUYING RETAIL IS STUPID coupon and save an additional 10% on your next purchase.

ALMOST PERFECT ENGLISH CHINA
14519 Ventura Blvd.
Sherman Oaks, CA 91423
818/905-6650
HOURS: MON-SAT: 10-5
CREDIT CARDS: MC, V

Don't let the name fool you. The Lalique, Waterford and Baccarat crystal is first quality and you save 15 to 20% off retail prices. You can save up to 80% on the English bone china because the firsts and seconds are mixed together. Frankly, the seconds are of excellent quality, and most have unnoticeable flaws. During their January and July sales, crystal is discounted an additional 5% and some china an additional 15%! Stock is on open shelves so you can pick what you want. You don't have to pay for entire place settings thus saving even more money by purchasing only the items you need. You will find Royal Doulton, Wedgewood, Toby Mugs, Coalport, and lots more. They will special order any out-of-stock item.

DANSK FACTORY OUTLET
2550 N. Palm Canyon Dr. (Loehmann's Plaza)
Palm Springs, CA 92662
619/320-3304
HOURS: MON-SAT: 9:30-5:30 SUN: 12-5:30
CREDIT CARDS: MC, V

Are you a lover of the Dansk products? The elegant simplicity of Dansk always makes a perfect wedding or anniversary gift. Now you can pay factory direct prices at their factory outlet located in Palm Springs. You will find quite a selection of merchandise in various colors and patterns.

MIKASA FACTORY STORE
20642 S. Fordyce Ave.
Carson, CA 90749
213/537-9344
HOURS: MON-THUR: 9-5 FRI: 9-8 SAT: 9-5 SUN: 12-5
CREDIT CARDS: MC, V

The Mikasa Factory Store isn't just for discontinued patterns. They have over 25,000 square feet of floor space, with more than 200 patterns in stock. You can buy new and discontinued patterns at 30 to 70% below retail prices. They carry china, crystal, gifts, flatware, stemware, silk flowers, candles, and table linens in a variety of brand names. Mikasa, Studio Nova, Home Beautiful, and Christopher Stuart are just a few of the manufacturers found at this store. They are close to the 710, 91, and the 405 freeways. You can place special orders, and they will ship your purchase anywhere for a nominal fee.
Additional Locations: Palm Springs (619/778-1080), San Diego (619/428-2022)

MUNN'S SILVER & JEWELRY SHOP
209 W. Wilson
Glendale, CA 91203
818/241-2776, 818/241-1909
HOURS: TUES-SAT: 10-5:30
CREDIT CARDS: MC, V

What we have here is gold and silver jewelry, silver flatware, plated flatware, and silver hollowware at an unbelievable 15% over cost. Ruth and Ted Munn also carry diamond rings, and rings with precious or semiprecious stones. You'll also find a variety of souvenir spoons and they do watch and clock repair as well. They are a franchise dealer of Gorham, International Kirk-Stieff, Lunt, Reed & Barton, Towle, and Wallace.

POTTERY RANCH, INC.
248 W. Huntington Dr.
Monrovia, CA 91016
818/358-1215
HOURS: MON-SUN: 9-6
CREDIT CARDS: MC, V

You'll find everything you need for your table at the Pottery Ranch in Monrovia. Dinnerware, gardenware, glassware, baskets, silk and dried flowers, and ceramic giftware are all sold here at discounts averaging 20% or more. They have a bridal registry, and specials are run all year. Brand names carried include Mikasa, Noritake, Houtake, and Sango. They're nice people with good buys.

∞ DECORATOR ITEMS ∞

THE 2NDS SHOP**
1975 S. Sepulveda Blvd.
Los Angeles, CA 90025
213/477-7229
HOURS: MON-FRI: 10-5 SAT: 9-5
CREDIT CARDS: MC, V

You'll find outstanding buys at The 2nds Shop which carries all seconds from the manufacturer of Los Angeles Pottery. There is always a vast array of glazed ceramics for your home and kitchen. Most merchandise is priced at or below wholesale, with even bigger savings in the Bargain Room. They have a potpourri of decorator merchandise. Perfect for gift giving, these various items are made of brass, silver, glass, wood, crystal, and more. Some of the items are duplicates that were on display at the LA Mart. For even greater savings make use of your 10% BUYING RETAIL IS STUPID coupon.

BRASS AND SILK FLOWER DISCOUNT
23625 El Toro Rd., Suite D
El Toro, CA 92630
714/951-8200
HOURS: MON-SAT: 10-6 SUN: 10-4
CREDIT CARDS: MC, V

Here you can find an array of beautiful silk flower arrangements to permanently decorate your home. They also make silk plants and trees that look so real it's eerie. You may not know this, but silk plants and trees are real time savers. Not only do they offer beauty without the worries of watering, fertilizing or light exposure, they are also very difficult to kill. You may want to purchase a few delicate ceramic pieces to give as gifts. All this plus a wide selection of classic brass items are 50 to 80% below retail prices.

THE GIFT CORNER
2547 Pacific Coast Hwy.
Torrance, CA 90505
213/539-5011
HOURS: MON-SAT: 10-6 SUN: 12-5
CREDIT CARDS: AE, MC, V

For a unique selection of better quality collectibles and giftware, try The Gift Corner. You will see such brand names as Waterford, Goebel and Baccarat, all at 10 to 20% savings. They also have a great selection of dolls such as Effanbee at 40% off retail. Later in the year, The Gift Corner turns itself into a Christmas store full of wonderful gift ideas to go under the tree. Make sure to call them in February and August to find out about their sidewalk sales for even greater savings.

THE GLASS GARAGE
414 N. Robertson Blvd.
Los Angeles, CA 90048
213/855-9064
HOURS: MON-SAT: 10:30-6:30 SUN: 12-6
CREDIT CARDS: MC, V

The Glass Garage is a low-price interior decorator outlet which is open to the public. They offer a variety of crystal vases, in every size and color, to suit any color scheme. There is a wide selection of silk flowers and a resident silk floral designer who can arrange your flowers just the way you'd like. They stock an impressive collection of barware, stemware, candles, candle holders, oil lamps, and other decorator items. Shoppers can expect to save 30–70% on favorite brands such as Mikasa, Colony, Toscany, Sven Jensen and Krosno. Baccarat is also offered at lower than usual prices.

ISLAND PRODUCTS DISTRIBUTING
4050 Chandler
Santa Ana, CA 92704
714/540-6597
HOURS: MON-FRI: 8:30-4:30
CREDIT CARDS: AE, DISC, MC, V

Get ready for a real treat. Eli Coloma, owner of Island Products, has handmade rattan from the Philippines and China, plus lots of baskets too. You can shop in his 13,000 square foot warehouse in Santa Ana, which is open to the public, but the best buys to be had are found at the Orange County Swapmeet on Saturdays and Sundays. Eli says when you get there to ask anyone who works there, "Where's the crazy Filipino?" Eli offers an early bird special at the swapmeet. From 7–9:30 a.m. you get an additional 15% off his regular 35–50% below retail prices. From 10–11 a.m. you get an additional 10% discount. However, there's one hitch! If you don't remember to ask for the discount before you pay for the merchandise, it's sorry Charlie! As an added bonus, no matter what time it is at the swapmeet, if you are pregnant and showing or wearing green pants (this includes men), Eli will give you an additional 15% discount but you have to bring it up before money changes hands. No one said this would be easy. You can also find Island Products at the swapmeet held at Golden West College in Huntington Beach.

MAINLY SECONDS–POTTERY, PLANTS & THINGS
12144 Magnolia Blvd.
N. Hollywood, CA 91607
818/985-4499
HOURS: MON-FRI: 9-9 SAT: 9-6 SUN: 10-6
CREDIT CARDS: MC, V

If you're looking for those room accessories that make your house a home, that displays your personality, then this is where you need to shop. Mainly Seconds carries pottery (clay, stoneware, ceramic), baskets, indoor plants, plant foods, potting soils, cacti, silk flowers, vases, dried flowers, macrame, and wrought iron at 40–60% below retail. Each of their locations has over 6,000 square feet always stuffed with goodies.
Additional Locations: Buena Park (714/994-0540), Costa Mesa (714/548-7710)

MIJANOU'S SILK DESIGNS**
718 E. Imperial Hwy.
Brea, CA 92621
714/990-3601
HOURS: MON-SAT: 10-7 SUN: 10-5
CREDIT CARDS: MC, V

Mijanou's is a place that specializes in silk designs. They buy in quantity and pass the savings on to their very satisfied customers. Everything you need in silk greenery, trees, and flowers can be found here for only 15% above cost. They also carry floral supplies, vases, baskets, and brass. If you are a lover of silk arrangements, you'll find them here. Should you want to design your own arrangement, free consultation is available. In addition, Mijanou's makes certain they not only have a great selection of variety and color, but also take pride in stocking the unusual. Make certain you take your BUYING RETAIL IS STUPID coupon with you for an additional 5% discount.

POTTERY AND FLORAL WORLD**
3352 San Fernando Rd.
Los Angeles, CA 90065
213/254-5281
HOURS: 7 DAYS A WEEK: 8-7

CREDIT CARDS: MC, V

Pottery and Floral World has one of the West Coast's largest selections of pots, pottery, dried and silk flowers, and all the accessories that go along with them. Macrame supplies, gourmet ware, baskets and wrought iron products can also be found here. They are both a factory outlet and a direct importer, so you can expect discounts of 20 to 50% off retail prices found elsewhere. Close-outs occur weekly, so you always find a changing inventory. If you're looking for Christmas decorations, they carry a complete line. You'll get an additional 10% off your purchase price when you use your BUYING RETAIL IS STUPID Coupon.

SHE'S FLOWERS
712 S. Olive St.
Los Angeles, CA 90014
213/689-1372
HOURS: MON-SAT: 7:30-6
CREDIT CARDS: AE, MC, V

Save up to 50% on flowers and plants for all occasions. She's Flowers grows many of their own flowers and imports others directly; then She's Flowers wholesales them to the public. You can also buy silk flowers, dried flowers, trees, baskets, and even balloons for weddings, birthdays and holidays. They deliver, and you can charge your purchase by phone. They've been in business since 1980, and they are always very helpful.

WORLD OF PLANTS AND GIFTS**
3716 Motor Ave.
Los Angeles, CA 90034
213/838-4100
HOURS: MON-FRI: 9-7 SAT-SUN: 9-6
CREDIT CARDS: MC, V

Beautiful fresh cut flowers, indoor plants, trees, baskets, pottery, macrame, flowering plants, plant stands and framed prints, are all available at discount prices. Their plants are purchased directly from growers in San Diego, so they can offer the best prices and a wide selection. If you use your BUYING RETAIL IS STUPID coupon with your purchase, your discount blossoms an additional 10%.

∞ FLOOR COVERINGS ∞

– CARPETING, LINOLEUM & TILE –

AAA CARPET EXCHANGE
2045 S. La Cienega Blvd.
Los Angeles, CA 90034
213/204-6061
HOURS: MON-SAT: 9-6 SUN: 12-5
CREDIT CARDS: MC, V

Levelor blinds are oh-so-chic. Apartment owners even advertise them as rental features. You can get Levelor and mini-blinds at AAA Carpet Exchange as well as vinyl, wood and tile flooring, draperies and a full line of carpeting. Save 20-70% on most every-thing! This huge showroom/warehouse stocks miles and miles of carpets, plus thousands of remnants in all sizes and colors. Special sales occur all the time, so check often for extra savings on their vast and varied merchandise. All employees are professionally trained and are most helpful. They have a second store in Los Angeles on Crenshaw Boulevard.
Additional Locations: Los Angeles: 213/290-3414

ABLE CARPETS
5843 W. Pico Blvd.
Los Angeles, CA 90019
213/933-9251
HOURS: MON-SAT: 9-5
CREDIT CARDS: DISC, MC, V

All major brands of carpets are discounted for you and they have been in business here since 1959; quotes are cheerfully given. You can carry out your carpet purchases, or they will deliver. They have expert installation service, plus a good selection of vinyl flooring and mini-blinds to complement your decor. In addition to the huge stock of full rolls, there are always good remnants to check out.

CARPET BAZAAR
7833 Canoga Ave.
Canoga Park, CA 91304
818/713-9220
HOURS: MON-FRI: 9-6 SAT: 9-5
CREDIT CARDS: MC, V

With over 15,000 square yards of carpet in stock and hundreds of styles and colors to choose from, in a showroom/warehouse of 6,600 square feet, the Carpet Bazaar is a place you should shop before making a decision. Special prices on mill close-outs and slightly irregulars are below their everyday low prices. Their truck-load buying power saves you money. They offer volume discounts, and prompt installations are available. Name brands include Cabin Crafts, Royale Weave, Tuftex, Royalty, Galaxy and Classique. Both residential and commercial customers are welcome.
Additional Locations: Agoura (818/706-2353)

CARPET COLLECTION**
12124 Sherman Way
N. Hollywood, CA 91605
818/982-4554
HOURS: MON-FRI: 8-6 SAT: 9-5 SUN: 11-5
CREDIT CARDS: MC, V

Carpet Collection carries a large inventory of floor coverings—carpeting, vinyl, tile and linoleum—and also window coverings. According to the owners, any carpet a customer might want is avail-able and for any budget. They say they will beat any legitimate price. Service is emphasized and immediate installation is available. They carry a large selection of name brands such as Philadelphia, Salem, Royalty, El Dorado, Catalina, Armstrong, Horizon and more. Their 3,500 square foot showroom is housed in a 10,000 square foot warehouse. The public is welcome and special low discounts are offered to contractors and interior decorators. You can save an additional 5% off your purchase price when you use your BUYING RETAIL IS STUPID coupon.

CARPET LAND MILLS
6951 Reseda Blvd.
Reseda, CA 91335
818/609-0339
HOURS: MON-FRI: 10-8 SAT: 10-6
CREDIT CARDS: CASH OR CHECKS ONLY

In their 1,500 square feet of showroom, there are more than 100 mills represented and over 2,000 samples from which to choose. They also carry hardwood, vinyl and tile flooring, and vertical or mini-blinds. Their prices are at about 5% above cost and phone quotes are welcomed. Among the name brands carried are Stainmaster and Weardated carpets. They offer immediate delivery. Don't forget to ask about their 18 month replacement guarantee.

CARPET MANOR**
18314 Sherman Way
Reseda, CA 91335
818/344-2277
HOURS: MON-FRI: 9-6 SAT: 10-5 SUN: 12-5
CREDIT CARDS: MC, V

In business since 1953, Carpet Manor offers a wide selection of carpets, remnants, wood and vinyl flooring and window coverings. All fashion colors are available. Selling prices are up to 70% off retail, and they guarantee best price. They carry all major brands and offer prompt delivery and service as well as free advice to those ambitious customers who want to do it themselves. They will roll out the carpet for an additional 5% discount if you use your BUYING RETAIL IS STUPID coupon!

CARPET MARKET OUTLET
5916 Kester Ave.
Van Nuys, CA 91411
818/989-0940
HOURS: MON-SAT: 9-5:30
CREDIT CARDS: AE, MC, V

The Carpet Market Outlet is just what their name describes—they are an outlet for most major brands of carpeting, linoleum, and ceramic tile. They carry only major brands such as Anso V, Stainmaster, and DuPont Certified. Joe Zeldin says he has the guaranteed best price anywhere.

CARPET WAREHOUSE
3390 Tyler St.
Riverside, CA 92503
714/359-6967
HOURS: MON-FRI: 9-8 SAT: 9-6 SUN: 10-6
CREDIT CARDS: MC, V

In business since 1969, Carpet Warehouse offers unbeatable prices and expert installations. The higher the price of carpet, the more you save because the profit margin stays the same whether it's low or high end carpeting. Installation is included in the price of the carpet. In addition to the five year warranty from the carpet manufacturer, Carpet Warehouse gives their customers a five year installation warranty. They also sell flooring in wood, ceramic and linoleum. Look for savings of 30–50% from Carpet Warehouse.

CULVER CARPET CENTER
4026 S. Sepulveda Blvd.
Culver City, CA 90230
213/398-2458
HOURS: MON-SAT: 8:30-6
CREDIT CARDS: MC, V

Culver Carpet Center is a large discount carpet and vinyl warehouse, one of LA's largest volume dealers. You can save 25 to 40% off retail on first-quality, name-brand rolls and remnants of carpets. You'll also find a complete line of custom wood flooring, linoleum and a fine vinyl selection. They have a department for window coverings, too, and these experts can install everything they sell. In business since 1952, they offer selection, service, and big savings.

FLOOR COVERING UNLIMITED
8480 W. 3rd St.
Los Angeles, CA 90048
213/651-5290
HOURS: MON-FRI: 8-5:30
CREDIT CARDS: MC, V

Whatever you want to put on the floor, including the floor, Floor Covering Unlimited has it and at wholesale prices. Custom hardwood floors, vinyl and tile, Levelor blinds, wallpaper and draperies are available in an almost limitless array of choices. They have been in business since 1971 and give free estimates. There's always a pile of carpet doormats and remnants for $1 to $2.

FLOORMART
401 W. Los Feliz Rd.
Glendale, CA 91204
818/243-6241
HOURS: MON-FRI: 7:30-4:30 SAT: 8:30-3:30
CREDIT CARDS: MC, V

Because Floormart is a specialist in buyer close-outs, most of their inventory is priced below cost. They handle carpeting and vinyl coverings and you'll pay less than department store sale prices on items they have in inventory. If you want to special order floor coverings, you can expect to pay 12% above cost. Installation can be provided, depending on the job to be done.

LESTER CARPET CO., INC.
7811-7815 Beverly Blvd.
Los Angeles, CA 90036
213/934-7282
HOURS: MON-SAT: 8-5
CREDIT CARDS: MC, V

Whether you want to cover your floors, windows, or doors, Lester Carpet Co. guarantees the lowest price! They've been in business since 1954; with that kind of experience and over 13,000 square feet of warehouse, they definitely know how to buy in volume and pass the savings on to you. You can carpet your home with name brands such as Tuftex, Armstrong, Hollytex, Tarkett, and Queen. Other items carried are draperies, blinds, shutters, mini-blinds, vertical blinds, quilts, upholstery, linoleum sheets, tiles and wood flooring. Custom work is available as well.

LINOLEUM CITY
5657 Santa Monica Blvd.
Hollywood, CA 90038
213/469-0063, 463-1729
HOURS: MON-THUR: 8:30-5:30 FRI: 8:30-7 SAT: 9-5
CREDIT CARDS: MC, V

Since 1948, Linoleum City has been serving the needs of L.A.'s shoppers for floor coverings. They have a combination warehouse and showroom in Hollywood of over 10,000 square feet. Claiming to have the largest selection of vinyls and carpeting in the city, you can find brand names such as Armstrong, Congoleum, Mannington, Tarkett, Kentile, Hartco, Caronet, Royalweave, Wellington, as well as many others. In addition to the thousands of rolls of vinyl floor covering in stock, they have a huge inventory of commercial and residential tiles, rolls of carpets, and hundreds of carpet samples. Their sales staff is very knowledgeable and installation is available through independent contractors.

M & H
7111 Arlington Ave., Suite E
Riverside, CA 92503
714/688-0193
HOURS: MON-FRI: 9-5 SAT: 10-2
CREDIT CARDS: MC, V

Don't worry if the kids spill chocolate sauce on your white carpets, M & H carries Anso V Worry Free Carpets and Genesis, as well as several other brand names, at 40% below retail. Bring in any written estimate and they will beat the price.

MELROSE DISCOUNT CARPET
7951 Melrose Ave.
Los Angeles, CA 90046
213/653-4653
HOURS: MON: 9-7 TUES-FRI: 9-5
CREDIT CARDS: MC, V

If you're going to replace your old vinyl floor in the kitchen, here's the place for you. Melrose Discount Carpet carries carpet, hardwood flooring, linens, tile, and area rugs. You can save 50% over most places, and they have remnants for sale. They are located one block west of Fairfax and parking is on the street only.

OBALEK TILE & WALLPAPER
2301 S. Hill St.
Los Angeles, CA 90007
213/748-4664
HOURS: MON-FRI: 8-6 SAT: 9-5
CREDIT CARDS: MC, V

If you want to find great discount prices on a huge stock of tiles from around the world, visit Obalek Tile & Wallpaper. They have approximately 500,000 square feet of ceramic and vinyl tiles in stock. The savings found here are fantastic. For example, tiles that retail for $1.79 to $1.89 at other stores cost as little as 59¢ to $1.29 per tile. If the price is $3.89 at other stores, you pay only $1.99 at Obalek. In addition to tile, they have 250,000 rolls of wallpaper in stock. They carry all the tools necessary for do-it-yourselfers, and their professional staff will be glad to instruct you on the how-to. General manager Bill Cochran and his staff are extremely helpful.

PICO CARPET CO.
1647 La Cienega Blvd.
Los Angeles, CA 90035
213/274-7846
HOURS: MON-FRI: 8-5 SAT: 8-4
CREDIT CARDS: MC, V

Pico Carpet Company is a discount warehouse selling carpets primarily from major mills at 20 to 50% off retail. In addition to the many rolls of carpet in stock, they also have remnants, linoleum, wood flooring, custom blinds, and expert installation. Make the time to look here before you make your next carpet purchase.

ROYAL DISCOUNT CARPETS
529 N. Fairfax St.
Los Angeles, CA 90036
213/653-6043
HOURS: MON-SAT: 9-4
CREDIT CARDS: CASH OR CHECKS ONLY

This shop is stuffed with wonderful buys on carpeting, loose rugs and oriental carpets. Most of the merchandise is priced at 10% over cost. If you're looking for carpeting, then this shop is a must because the prices are really hard to beat. Go on over and check out what Royal Discount Carpets has to offer.

– ORIENTAL RUGS –

EMBASSY AUCTIONEER, INC.
18517 Ventura Blvd.
Tarzana, CA 91356
818/996-9244
HOURS: MON-FRI: 9:30-5
CREDIT CARDS: AE, MC, V

Take a ride on a flying carpet. This store has quite a selection of handmade Persian and Oriental rugs. Take one home and wait for the magic to happen. If there's no magic, then you'll just have to settle for the envy of your friends. Their handmade rugs come from countries such as China, India, Iran, Afghanistan, Romania, Pakistan, and Turkey.

HAROUTUNIAN ORIENTAL RUGS
7910 Santa Monica Blvd.
W. Hollywood, CA 90046
213/656-7575
HOURS: MON-FRI: 9-5:30 SAT: 10-4
CREDIT CARDS: MC, V

Jack Haroutunian says he'll sell you his beautifully crafted rugs from countries such as Iran, India, Pakistan, China and Turkey at the best prices in Los Angeles. He has new, used and antique rugs in such brand names as Chinese Pagoda, Sarouk, Tabriz, Isfahan and many more. They also do an excellent job on repairs, weaving and hand washing.

ORIENTAL RUG EXCHANGE**
339 N. La Cienega Blvd.
Los Angeles, CA 90048
213/657-1100
HOURS: MON-SAT: 10-6 SUN: 12-6
CREDIT CARDS: MC, V

The Oriental Rug Exchange carries over 7,000 handmade rugs from all around the world. They carry modern, and antique rugs from China, Persia, India, Pakistan, Russia, and many other countries. You'll also find intricate tapestries and needlepoint. Walk through their large 5,000 square foot showroom and a huge warehouse near by. This store is truly an exchange because they buy or trade in used rugs. Need your rug repaired or cleaned? The Oriental Rug Exchange offers expert service on any handmade rug. They will also appraise your rugs. Jacob Shabtai guarantees the best price in town, 50–75% below retail prices, and he'll accept your BUYING RETAIL IS STUPID coupon for additional savings of 5%.

∞ FURNITURE ∞

– BEDROOM –

A-1 FURNITURE OUTLET
6002 S. Broadway
Los Angeles, CA 90003
213/758-3963
HOURS: BY APPOINTMENT ONLY, MON-FRI: 10:30-5
CREDIT CARDS: CASH OR CHECKS ONLY

On their showroom floor are at least 100 bedroom sets, and 100 mattress and box spring sets. On top of that, they also carry living room furniture, dining room sets, dinette sets, occasional tables and much more. Many different brands are represented and they encourage customers to first check prices elsewhere. After you've decided what you want, take the brand name and model number to A-1 Furniture Outlet where you can get values as low as 10% over cost. They're open to the public by appointment only, so remember to check out the other stores before giving them a call.

ALPERT'S BEDROOM CITY WAREHOUSE**
7631 Canoga Ave.
Canoga Park, CA 91304
818/888-5060
HOURS: MON-FRI: 10-8 SAT: 10-6 SUN: 12-5
CREDIT CARDS: AE, DISC, MC, V

Alpert's has been selling at discount prices since 1962. They stock a large selection of bedroom furniture, specializing in solid oak products, wall units, waterbeds, flotation units, four poster beds, canopy beds, innerspring mattresses; also, contemporary lacquer upholstered beds, futons, air beds, foam beds, and youth furniture such as chest beds, and bunk beds. Everyday discounts range from 18–55% off original prices with a 30 day price guarantee. Major brands include Simmons, Beautyrest, Sealy, Somma, Sunbeam (waterbed heaters) and many others. The Canoga Park store covers 13,000 square feet of every type of sleeping surface imaginable.

(Their two other locations aren't quite as large, but you'll still find a terrific selection.) With such large inventories, most items are available for delivery within 24 hours. You'll save an additional 5% when you use your BUYING RETAIL IS STUPID coupon.
Additional Locations: Thousand Oaks (805/497-4529), Van Nuys (818/787-6010)

BED BROKER**
300 E. Orangethorpe
Placentia, CA 92670
714/993-9953
HOURS: MON-FRI: 10-8 SAT: 10-6 SUN: 12-5
CREDIT CARDS: DISC, MC, V

Having almost 8,000 square feet of showroom, with a warehouse on the premises, makes them the largest bedroom furniture store in Orange County. Over 50 mattresses are on display with 22 different manufacturers from which to choose. They have 60 white iron and brass beds displayed and a selection of over 600. There are over 45 day beds and bunk beds with more than 400 from which to choose. Most major brands are available, including Sealy, Aireloom, Stearns & Foster, Concorde, Lady Americana, Tempo and many more. The Bed Broker offers savings of 50 to 70% off list price and guarantees lowest prices. They advertise "never undersold" and emphasize quality and courtesy as much as price. Don't forget to use your BUYING RETAIL IS STUPID coupon for an additional 5% savings.

BRASS BED FACTORY**
5953 Sepulveda Blvd.
Van Nuys, CA 91411
818/989-5006
HOURS: MON-SAT: 10-5
CREDIT CARDS: AE, DISC, MC, V

The Brass Bed Factory carries a vast selection of brass beds, day-beds, mattresses, and white iron beds. Because they are the manu-facturer, they are able to do custom orders, refinish all brass items and do repairs in just two weeks or less! In addition to their own brand you'll find such names here as Elliotts Designs, Diamond, Restonic and Flamingo. You can use your new mattress to hide the money you save because the Brass Bed Factory will take an addi-

tional 10% off the purchase price when you present your BUYING RETAIL IS STUPID coupon.
Additional Locations: Agoura (818/706-1202), Culver City (213/313-0145)

BRASS BEDS DIRECT
4866 W. Jefferson Blvd.
Los Angeles, CA 90016
213/737-6865
HOURS: MON-SAT: 10-5
CREDIT CARDS: AE, DISC, MC, V

Brass Bed Direct offers the highest quality of brass beds and accessories available at 65% off retail prices. Call and inquire about specific items. Layaway and financing plans are available.

ELECTROPEDIC ADJUSTABLE BEDS
15600 Roscoe Blvd.
Van Nuys, CA 91406
818/909-0077
HOURS: MON-FRI: 9-5   SAT: 9-4   SUN: 11-4
CREDIT CARDS: AE, MC, V

When one of our husbands unfortunately threw his back out while playing paddle tennis, we decided an electric bed was one of the answers for a quick recovery. And it was. Electropedic Adjustable Beds is a factory outlet and sells these comfortable beds at savings of 40 to 50% off retail. The beds are available in twin, full, queen, king, dual queen, and dual king.

F B WATERBEDS
6311 Laurel Canyon Blvd.
N. Hollywood, CA 91606
818/763-5586
HOURS: MON-SAT: 11:30-7:30
CREDIT CARDS: AE, MC, V

Looking for a change from your standard sleeping mattress? F B Waterbeds says, "Shop us last.you'll be glad you did." They claim to have the best prices on waterbeds, airbeds and floatation beds, along with a complete selection of frames, heaters, linens, bedroom furniture and all accessories at 40 to 70% off. They also run terrific specials on their demos. Financing is available.

MATTRESS WAREHOUSE
4825 W. Rosecrans
Hawthorne, CA 90250
213/675-5400
HOURS: MON-FRI: 10-8 SAT: 10-5
CREDIT CARDS: MC, V

The Mattress Warehouse carries name brand mattresses and box springs in every size available. They also carry bed frames, brass beds, headboards, sofa sleepers, and an excellent variety of sheets and mattress covers. All of this at 40–50% off retail! They have quality merchandise and pass on the manufacturer's warranty. Look for additional savings on factory overruns and cancellations on merchandise with major department store labels. Immediate delivery is available, but you'll save more if you can handle delivery yourself.
Additional Locations: Torrance (213/375-5400)

RICHARD PRATT'S MATTRESS WAREHOUSE
18717 Parthenia St.
Northridge, CA 91324
818/349-8118
HOURS: 7 DAYS A WEEK: 9-6
CREDIT CARDS: MC, V

Why pay department store prices when you can buy bedding at Richard Pratt's Mattress Warehouse? They carry King Koil, Restonic, Simmons, Aireloom, Serta, Sealy, Englander, and more. You can get all sizes and models, from bunk beds to rollaways, from twin sized to California king. Buying up what others can't sell results in savings for their customers of 30 to 70% off retail. You're likely recognize department store labels on many of their products. Also to be found are barely used mattresses purchased from stores that offer a trial period to their customers. These beds were either too hard, too soft or too something and were returned. We'll bet those store owners hate seeing Goldilocks pulling up to their store fronts.

RTC MATTRESS WAREHOUSE
5142 Clareton Dr., Unit 140
Agoura, CA 91301
818/991-5868
HOURS: MON-FRI: 10-6 SUN: 11-5
CREDIT CARDS: DISC, MC, V

You'll save 15 to 40% off retail prices when you shop here for Simmons, Beautyrest, Maxipedic, Bassett, or Stearns & Foster. Savings are even higher on mismatched mattress sets at RTC Mattress Warehouse. They offer same-day, local delivery and will even haul your old mattress away. All sizes of mattress sets are available, plus trundle beds, roll-aways and bed frames.

SIT'N SLEEP
3880 Culver Center
Culver City, CA 90230
213/870-1374
HOURS: MON-FRI: 10-8 SAT: 10-6 SUN: 11-5
CREDIT CARDS: AE, MC, V

You'll find 20 to 40% savings off manufacturer list prices here. Sit'n Sleep carries name-brand mattress sets in all sizes and firmnesses. They stock the largest selection of futons and futon frames in Los Angeles, at guaranteed best prices. Sofa beds, platform beds, oak wall units, bookcases, bedroom sets and more, are available. Sit'n Sleep offers a 30 day price guarantee and a 30 night sleep trial. The 500 mattresses they have in stock means, "Buy it today and try it tonight."

VALLEY MATTRESS & BUNK BED CENTER**
6875 Beck Ave.
N. Hollywood, CA 91605
818/765-6451 213-875-2107
HOURS: MON-FRI: 9-5:30 SAT: 9-5 SUN: 12-5
CREDIT CARDS: DISC, MC, V

With a motto like "Comfort is our most important product," you know you'll be taken care of at Valley Mattress & Bunk Bed Center. Selling at "warehouse to you" prices, they have California's largest selection of space saving children's bedroom furniture and over 50 bunk beds and lofts on display in their 5,000 square foot store. Many items are in stock, so you can take them with you or take advantage of their delivery service. Some of their more unusual styles are hard to find space-savers, trundle bunks that sleep three, chest bunks that include 9 drawers of storage, and study centers which include a loft bed, desk and chest below. And if you want to be creative, try out their space shuttle and fire engine bunks. Make sure you bring in your BUYING RETAIL IS STUPID coupon for an additional 5% discount.

WOODEN SHIPS WATERBED DISCOUNT WAREHOUSE
2933 University Ave.
Riverside, CA 92507
714/781-8112
HOURS: MON-SAT: 9-6
CREDIT CARDS: AE, DISC, MC, V

Bargain hunters paradise is the nickname they give to Wooden Ships Waterbed Discount Warehouse. Riverside's oldest waterbed store features factory close-outs and damaged goods at huge savings from their retail store. A waterbed priced at $499 (already a 10–30% discount) at their retail store sold for $250 here. With about 10,000 square feet of waterbeds, furniture and accessories, shoppers have a large variety from which to choose.

WOODEN SHIPS WATERBEDS
10181 Indiana Ave.
Riverside, CA 92503
714/359-3131
HOURS: MON-FRI: 10-8 SAT: 10-6 SUN: 12-5
CREDIT CARDS: AE, DISC, MC, V

This is the retail outlet for Wooden Ships Waterbed Discount Factory Warehouse. Here you'll find downright honest salespeople who tell you like it is and won't try to sell you something you don't need. Wooden Ships wants their clients to be satisfied for life and makes sure they are. A customer, trying to decide whether to replace their waterbed at a cost of several hundred dollars or to repair it, was advised by a Wooden Ships salesperson to patch it at a cost of $10.00. They work on a lower profit margin than most waterbed stores, so you'll save 10 to 30% on your purchases. You'll find excellent buys on their waterbed accessories, too. All military people get an added 10% discount on nonsale items.

– HOME –

AL'S DISCOUNT FURNITURE**
4900 Lankershim Blvd.
N. Hollywood, CA 91601
818/766-4289 213/877-4783
HOURS: MON-SUN: 10-9
CREDIT CARDS: AE, DISC, MC, V

Al's has been in business since 1962 selling every kind of furniture and bedding for the home; top name brands included are Sealy Posturepedic, Berkline, Basset, Schweiger, Lea, Somma, Ashley, and many more. Al's claims the reason for their success and longevity is that they sell quality furniture at the lowest price in Southern California and give "full service." As a direct result of their selling philosophy, they report that over 70% of their customers are repeat or referral. Be sure to use your BUYING RETAIL IS STUPID coupon, and you'll save an additional 5%. They're awfully nice people, and knowledgeable too!

ANGELUS FURNITURE WAREHOUSE
3650 E. Olympic Blvd.
Los Angeles, CA 90023
213/268-5171
HOURS: WED-SUN: 10-6
CREDIT CARDS: AE, MC, V

Angelus Furniture Warehouse, in the same location since 1928, is probably one of the largest discount warehouses in Los Angeles. They have 385,000 square feet of inventory, showrooms equal to 135,000 square feet, and 4 stories of merchandise. The clearance center on their top floor, a bargain hunter's dream, offers you even greater savings. That's where you'll find discontinued or damaged items, dining room sets missing a piece or two, a bedroom set with only one of its original pair of night stands, and all kinds of other odds and ends. On our last visit we saw a beautiful bedroom set made by a famous, high-end furniture maker marked at less than half price. What was wrong with the set? No damage, just some of the hardware was missing. Some smart person, simply by replacing or matching up the hardware, could have a quality bedroom set for about the same price a set of much lesser quality would cost retail. If you don't need the entire set, or if a large scratch nobody will ever see after the bookcase is filled won't cause you any sleepless nights, then the top floor is for you. At Angelus Furniture Warehouse you can save up to 60% off the manufacturer's suggested retail price in every department, and if you can't find what you want here, it doesn't exist. You'll find a selection of 250 brand names. Make sure to check out their parking lot sales held in January and July.

BYRNE HOME FURNISHINGS
3516 W. Magnolia Blvd.
Burbank, CA 91505
818/845-0808
HOURS: MON-SAT: 9-5
CREDIT CARDS: MC, V

Located in Burbank, Byrne Home Furnishings' showroom is 7,000 square feet of displays in room like settings. Feast your eyes on many beautiful and unique decorator items including antiques, mirrors, clocks, lamps and many samples from the various manufacturers that are available at a 25–40% savings below retail prices. Thomasville, Century, Henredon, Sealy, Aireloom, Simmons, Stiffel, Lane, and Stanley are a few of the many quality brand names they carry. Find out about their floor sample sale held in the month of January.

COLORMART FURNITURE
1207 N. Western
Los Angeles, CA 90027
213/646-3397
HOURS: MON-SAT: 8-6 SUN: 10-6
CREDIT CARDS: MC, V

Dealing in upholstered furniture they manufacture themselves, Colormart has prices that are easily affordable. You can save up to 80% off retail. Customers get a variety of styles and fabrics to choose from in sofas, sofa beds, playpens and/or conversation pits, and side or occasional chairs.

CONSUMERS GUILD, INC.
17034 Devonshire St.
Northridge, CA 91325
818/363-3900
HOURS: MON-SAT: 9-5
CREDIT CARDS: MC, V

Consumers Guild in Northridge has been specializing in catalogue discount sales for more than 20 years. With low overhead, no fancy showroom, no warehousing, fewer salespersons and less advertising, they are able to pass on discounts of 20 to 50% off retail to their customers on such quality brand names of furniture as Bassett, Lane, Henredon, Simmons, Sealy, Stanley, Universal and almost 200 additional manufacturers. In addition to furniture, they carry lamps and window treatments. Delivery and installation are also available.

ELEGANCE FURNITURE
19404 Business Center Dr.
Northridge, CA 91324
818/993-4416
HOURS: MON-FRI: 10:30-7 SAT: 10:30-6 SUN: 12-5
CREDIT CARDS: MC, V

Are you in a redecorating, throw-out-the-old-bring-in-the-new kind of mood? Yes? Then Elegance Furniture is the place to go. Grab your checkbook (it's okay, they take checks) and rush over while the force is still with you. They have Thomasville, Hare, Lane, and Burlington to name a few at 20–25% off retail.

FMSA (FURNITURE MFG SALES AGENCY INC.)
2027 S. Figueroa Ave.
Los Angeles, CA 90007
213/746-3663
HOURS: TUES-FRI: 10-6 SAT: 9-5 SUN: 12-5
CREDIT CARDS: AE, DISC, MC, V

This is where you can turn visions of your home into reality. Since 1949, FMSA had only been open to the trade. Fortunately for us, in 1989 owner Bernie Hoffman opened the doors to the public. You will know you are getting a good buy when you walk into 65,000 square feet of furniture, carpets and drapes. Some brand names you can find here are Bernhart, Stanley, Dixie, Line Taylor and Henry Link. They have professional designers on staff for free designing assistance. You'll not only save 10 to 40% off retail department stores prices, because FMSA provides or carries everything needed for complete home decorating, you'll save time not having to run around to different stores. FMSA also has two other services for their clientele. You can gain admittance to any of the professional decorator showrooms in the area, but only by setting up an appointment with FMSA. You can also save on major appliances and televisions ordering through their catalogue service.

GOOCHEY'S FURNISHINGS & LIGHTING
14241 Ventura Blvd.
Sherman Oaks, CA 91423
818/986-4772
HOURS: MON-FRI: 10-6 SAT. AND EVENINGS BY APPOINTMENT
CREDIT CARDS: CASH OR CHECKS ONLY

Goochey's Furnishings & Lighting can help you decorate your entire home or office. They carry wallpaper, carpeting, furniture, light fixtures, draperies, blinds and even art for your empty walls. You'll save at least 30% off retail on all your decorating needs at this one-stop shop.

KRAUSE'S SOFA FACTORY
17512 Studebaker Rd.
Cerritos, CA 90701
213/924-7871
HOURS: MON-FRI: 10-9   SAT-SUN: 10-6
CREDIT CARDS: MC, V

Here is top quality at factory prices for all you sofa lovers! Krause's Sofa Factory has a vast selection of sofas, loveseats, sectionals and sofa-beds, all at 20 to 25% savings! One visit and you are sure to find what you're looking for. Several times during the year, they have special sales where you can save even more money. Check your local phone directory for a Krause's Sofa Factory in your neck of the woods.
Additional Locations: 18 other stores throughout S. CA

LEON'S FURNITURE
5700 Lankershim Blvd.
N. Hollywood, CA 91601
818/506-6881
HOURS: MON-SAT: 10-8   SUN: 12-5
CREDIT CARDS: MC, V

From coffee tables and corner groups, to bunkbeds, playpens, sofas and rollaways, they have it here. You can save as much as 50% on all types and styles of furniture. You'll find Broyhill, Bassett and many other major brands.

MANUFACTURER'S CLEARANCE WAREHOUSE
4601 So. Soto St.
Los Angeles, CA 90058
800/321-0502, 213/583-1836
HOURS: MON-FRI: 9-5
CREDIT CARDS: MC, V

If you are looking for furniture for your dining needs, then look no further! This store has thousands of square feet of low priced merchandise from which to choose. They claim the largest assortment of dining chairs, tables, barstools, and outdoor furniture anywhere in Los Angeles.

MARK FRIEDMAN FURNITURE
1437 4th St.
Santa Monica, CA 90404
213/393-2338
HOURS: MON-FRI: 11-7 SAT: 11-5
CREDIT CARDS: CASH ONLY

This store has home furnishings for every room in the house. They carry every style including contemporary, traditional, country and classic. You can get bedrooms, living rooms, dining rooms, mattresses and box springs, dinettes, carpeting, lamps, wall hangings, curios, leather, and occasional items. They have all famous national brand names at 10% above cost. And for even greater savings check out their floor sample sales.

METZLER'S HOME FURNISHINGS
22637 Ventura Blvd.
Woodland Hills, CA 91364
818/346-4610
HOURS: TUES-SAT: 10-5:30
CREDIT CARDS: MC, V

This store offers the creme de la creme in home furnishings for the San Fernando Valley at 20 to 50% off retail prices. They offer decorating service, and top quality merchandise at their 4,000 square foot showroom in Woodland Hills. They also carry carpeting, draperies, wallpaper, shutters, and blinds. Metzler's Home Furnishings has excellent service, and you must get on their mailing list for their Spring and Fall sales.

NAT DIAMOND EMPIRE FURNITURE**
4431 W. Adams
Los Angeles, CA 90011
213/732-8128
HOURS: MON, FRI: 10-7 TUES-THUR, SAT: 9:30-6
CREDIT CARDS: MC, V

This store has been in business over 50 years selling furniture and appliances at 20–50% below retail. They carry a huge inventory of General Electric appliances which include refrigerators, freezers, stoves, washers, dryers, and more. The latest in furniture trends and styles can be also found here. Use your BUYING RETAIL IS STUPID coupon for another 10% off their already terrific prices.

ROSCOE FURNITURE LIQUIDATORS**
21300 Sherman Way
Canoga Park, CA 91303
818/719-0220
HOURS: SUN-MON, FRI: 10-6   TUES-THUR: 10-8
CREDIT CARDS: MC, V

"Quality at Discount" is the theme at Roscoe Furniture Liquidators, and that's just what you'll find. Their prices range from 50 to 70% below major department stores and 20 to 30% below other discount furniture stores. In their 20,000 square foot store, you'll find savings on all types of furniture, bedding, lamps, decorator items, and tables featuring brand names such as Universal, BP John, Sterns & Foster, Klausner, Kincaid, Lane Recliners and Douglas. Financing is also available. Make sure to use your BUYING RETAIL IS STUPID coupon for an additional 5% discount.

SITTING PRETTY INC.
7115 Darby
Reseda, CA 91335
818/881-3114
HOURS: MON-SAT: 10-6   SUN: 12-5
CREDIT CARDS: MC, V

Sitting Pretty offers factory discounts on bars, bar stools, dinettes, game sets and chairs. They have over 18,000 square feet of beautiful merchandise in decorator designs. Expect to save 25% off retail prices on brand names like Cal Style, Chrome Craft, Cardinal, S K Products, Dino, Studio K, and many more.

WHOLESALE FURNITURE DISTRIBUTORS
68-845 Perez Rd., #19
Cathedral City, CA 92234
619/324-5451
HOURS: MON-SAT: 9-5   SUN: 11-4
CREDIT CARDS: MC, V

Save up to 50% off on all your furniture and accessories for the kitchen, dining room, living room, den, bedroom, restaurants, snack bars or hotels at Wholesale Furniture Distributors. They have an enormous selection in their nine unit showroom (Units #15–23), featuring such brand names as Cal-Style, Parkview, Pacific Rattan, I.M. David, Singer, and Diamond Mattress.

WHOLESALE FURNITURE OUTLET
407 W. Chevy Chase Dr.
Glendale, CA 91204
818/242-5734   213/622-8991
HOURS: MON-FRI: 11-8   SAT-SUN: 10-6
CREDIT CARDS: MC, V

If you're newly married, just starting out and looking for the best prices in town so you can fill every room with furniture, look no further! The Wholesale Furniture Outlet is just what their name implies, decent furniture at terrific prices. You won't get a high pressure sales pitch here; this is a warehouse filled to the gills with furniture at great prices, 20 to 40% below retail. Financing is available with 10% down and approved credit.

– INFANTS & CHILDREN –

BABY TOYTOWN, INC.
16800 E. Gale Ave.
Industry, CA 91745
818/333-6440
HOURS: MON-SAT: 10-6   FRI: 10-9   SUN: 12-5
CREDIT CARDS: DISC, MC, V

These stores carry everything you may need for a baby up until they are six or seven years old. They have such items as cribs, strollers, chests, lamps, mobiles, toys, bottles, teen furniture, wall decor, and more. Major brands, including Simmons, Bassett, Lullabye, Red Calliope, Nojo, and Childcraft, are available at 20% above COST. Each store offers ample parking. There is free delivery (within a specified area). Major sales take place each year, where customers are willing to wait two hours just to come in the door.

Additional Locations: 6 other stores throughout S. CA

CAROUSEL BABY FURNITURE
1726 E. Colorado Blvd.
Pasadena, CA 91106
213/684-0457
HOURS: MON-THUR, SAT: 9:30-6 FRI: 9:30-9
CREDIT CARDS: MC, V

Roll those dice. Baby needs a new pair of shoes. If not, then a new car seat might be in order. You won't have to take any gambles at Carousel Baby Furniture. They have everything you need—strollers, playpens, mattresses, clothing, layettes and many other furniture items. For brand new mommies, there are breast pumps, diapers, and bassinettes. You'll find bunkbeds, mirrors, head-boards, books, lamps, replacement pads and parts. They have wicker items too! When buying your Simmons, Childcraft, or Aprica you can expect to pay up to 50% off retail prices.

CHARLIE'S WAREHOUSE
7742 Edinger Ave.
Huntington Beach, CA 92647
714/848-0682
HOURS: WED-THUR: 10-6 FRI: 10-8 SAT: 10-5:30 SUN: 11-5
CREDIT CARDS: MC, V

Everything parents need in furniture and accessories for babies and children alike can be found at Charlie's Warehouse at savings of 20–30% off retail. For infants they have 60–65 different models of cribs with matching chests and dressing tables. Bedding, strollers, high chairs, car seats, lamps, portable cribs, and play pens are a few more of the items you'll find. They even have rocking chairs and gliders for new mothers. Their complete line of name brands include Childcraft, Evenflo, Aprica, Cosco, Graco, and many others. For your older children you'll find all kinds of beds and furniture made specifically with juveniles in mind. Two of the many brands they stock are Stanley and Bassett.. If you don't see an item you want, you can place special orders by selecting goods from their many catalogs. Owners Leonard and Judy Small (a.k.a. Mr. & Mrs. Charlie) started this wonderful enterprise after they "retired." They encourage comparison shopping and have writing pads spread all over the store for their customers. This 20,000 square foot store also carries a complete line of patio furniture and accessories. You'll always find 50–60 patio sets on display and in stock. Delivery service is extra.

ENCINO DISCOUNT PATIO & BABY FURNITURE**
17563 Ventura Blvd.
Encino, CA 91316
818/986-1074
HOURS: MON-FRI: 9-6 SAT: 9-5 SUN: 11-4
CREDIT CARDS: MC, V

Looking for that perfect outdoor swing for your baby while you're entertaining guests at your backyard garden party? Encino Discount Patio and Baby Furniture has it all. Patio and baby furniture and accessories. They carry Innova, California Umbrella, Homecrest, Pacific Sun, O.W. Lee, Kettler in patio furniture and Childcraft, Century, No-Jo, Lambs and Ivy, and Creative Playthings for baby furniture. Owner Mackie Singer says her customers tell them that they have the best selection and prices (30 to 50% off retail) and have been coming back to the store since 1939. They will also give you for an additional 5% discount when you use your BUYING RETAIL IS STUPID coupon, except on already marked sale items.

SID'S DISCOUNT BABY FURNITURE
8338 Lincoln Blvd.
Los Angeles, CA 90045
213/670-5550
HOURS: MON-THUR: 9-6 FRI: 9-7:30 SAT: 9-6
CREDIT CARDS: MC, V

Sid's is an institution where you can find everything in baby furniture and clothing for infants. There are all the necessities, of course, like strollers and car seats. He's probably the largest baby furniture dealer in the state. Sid's carries all the major brands like Simmons, Lullabye, Childcraft, Bassett, Pride and Babyline. They offer free delivery on most major items, free layaway, a most knowledgeable staff and big savings! Sid's has special sales at Christmas and New Years. Families have been shopping for their baby needs at Sid's since 1951.

STORK SHOP, THE
1868 S. La Cienega Blvd.
Los Angeles, CA 90035
213/839-2403
HOURS: MON-SAT: 10-5:30
CREDIT CARDS: MC, V

The Stork Shop promises a fun visit. They have everything you could possibly want in furniture and clothes for your baby. In fact, they also carry over 50,000 garments for boys and girls up to age 14. Their layettes are beautiful and you'll love the many designer styles of furniture items and accessories. You'll save 20 to 50% off retail prices on most of your purchases too!

– LEATHER –

LEATHER FACTORY
11970 Wilshire Blvd.
W. Los Angeles, CA 90025
213/820-8477
HOURS: MON-SAT: 10-6 SUN: 12-6
CREDIT CARDS: AE, DISC, MC, V

Save 40 to 60% when you buy factory direct! The Leather Factory manufactures their own products and sells them out of their showrooms throughout California. They have more than 50 different styles of leather sofas and loveseats, sleepers, chairs, ottomans, recliners and office furniture. Everything is made to order, and you have a choice of over 100 colors. They also carry lamps, tables and accessories. Best of all, you get a lifetime warranty on the frame, springs and construction. Financing is available with 24 months to pay, or you can go with their 90 day financing which is interest free. *Additional Locations: 18 other stores in S. CA*

– PATIO –

ABC POOL & PATIO**
24449 Hawthorne Blvd.
Torrance, CA 90505
213/373-0935
HOURS: MON-SUN: 10-6
CREDIT CARDS: MC, V

Established in 1958, ABC now has 10,000 square feet of patio furniture, barbecues, fireplace accessories, pool and spa supplies and gifts. Trapitone furniture and Ducane barbecues are among the various brand names represented. You can expect to save 35% off retail prices on patio furniture. You'll save 10 to 15% off their barbecues and other items. Don't miss their bargain room located upstairs, and special sales held on the Fourth of July and Labor Day. Be sure to use your BUYING RETAIL IS STUPID coupon and you'll save an additional 5%!

BERKS
2520 Santa Monica Blvd.
Santa Monica, CA 90404
213/828-7447
HOURS: MON-SAT: 9-6   FRI: 9-9   SUN: 10-5
CREDIT CARDS: MC, V

If you're looking for a complete selection of outdoor and casual indoor furniture, and you'd like to pocket savings of 20–60%, then shop at Berks. Since the 1950's, they've been selling everything you need to furnish your patio or porch. They stock things like tables, chaise lounges, and umbrellas by makers such as Brown Jordan, Samsonite, Kenneth James and others. Their customers always find variety of styles and colors, and Berks offers immediate, free delivery. If you find it advertised cheaper anywhere else, show it to them; if they have it in stock they'll meet it or beat it. Check out their special sales during the year for extra big savings.

COTTAGE SHOPS
7922 W. 3rd St.
Los Angeles, CA 90046
213/658-6066
HOURS: MON-SAT: 9:30-6 SUN: 11-5
CREDIT CARDS: AE, MC, V

This discount store, in business since the late 1940's, has a complete selection of chairs, tables, lamps, pool and patio furniture, lounges, umbrellas, and so much more. A division of Scotty's Casual Furniture, the Cottage Shops will save you about 20% and more off retail on most items and they really stand behind what they sell. Brand names include Tropitone, Allibert, Ducane, and Barlow Tyrie Teak. Delivery and layaway services are available, and they can refurbish your old pool and patio furniture. You'll find free parking in back of the store and a free catalog is available.

WOODLAND CASUAL
19855 Ventura Blvd.
Woodland Hills, CA 91364
818/348-6000
HOURS: MON-SAT: 10-6 SUN: 11-5
CREDIT CARDS: MC, V

Well here it is, the largest selection of patio furniture in the San Fernando Valley. There are four entire floors of wicker, rattan, dinette sets, sofa sets, bedroom furniture and entertainment centers to choose from. You can expect to find such brands as Tropitone, Grosfillex, Pacific Rattan and Thypon Wicker to name a few. With a purchase of $500 or more they'll even deliver. You can look forward to saving 30% off retail on most items.

– *RATTAN & WICKER* –

MASTERCRAFT
350 N. Pacific Coast Hwy.
Redondo Beach, CA 90277
213/379-1794
HOURS: MON-FRI: 9-7 SAT: 9-6 SUN: 10-5
CREDIT CARDS: DISC, MC, V

You can save 20 to 40% when you stop here for your wicker and rattan furniture. They carry all styles of end tables, baskets, lamps, and oriental rugs. Mastercraft is wonderful for gifts because they will ship anywhere. They carry wicker and rattan designs for every room of the house, inside or out.
Additional Locations: Torrance (213/316-6616)

RATTAN DEPOT
10588-1/2 W. Pico Blvd.
Los Angeles, CA 90064
213/839-9003
HOURS: MON-FRI: 10-6 SAT: 10-5 SUN: 12-5
CREDIT CARDS: MC, V

Rattan Depot carries rattan and wicker for the living room, dining room, and bedroom. Their prices are 20 to 50% below retail department store prices. You'll find a good selection, and they are very helpful in assisting you with your decorating decisions.

RATTAN DISTRIBUTION WAREHOUSE
8010 Wheatland Ave., Unit I
Sun Valley, CA 91352
818/504-0119
HOURS: FRI-SUN: 10-4
CREDIT CARDS: CASH OR CHECKS ONLY

Have you ever wondered why the rattan furniture purchased by interior decorators look so much better than what you are able to find? Rattan Distribution Warehouse, selling only to decorators, not stores, is the reason. Open to the public only on Friday, Saturday, and Sunday, this 4,000 square foot outlet is a direct importer of the finest rattan from the Phillipines. Everything they carry is 100% rattan, and even in the places you can't see, no wood is used. They carry very high quality rattan furniture for the living room and dining room and also have bar stools, and wall units. The custom sets they sell will allow you more decorating control than you thought possible. You have the option of not only selecting the stain for the rattan, you also have the option of using one of their fabrics or supplying your own for the upholstery work. Prices are 40 to 50% below retail and you can save even more on floor samples. Delivery on custom orders takes 2 to 3 weeks.

RATTAN RARITY SHOP
14257 Ventura Blvd.
Sherman Oaks, CA 91423
818/789-8751
HOURS: MON-SAT: 10-5:30   SUN: 12-5
CREDIT CARDS: MC, V

There are 4,000 square feet of rattan and wicker furniture to be found here. The wide variety will make it easy for you to find items for any room in your home. Hard to find items, such as a wicker lamp or a room screen, are Rattan Rarity's specialty. They have great prices all year round (25% off retail) and 90 day financing is available with no interest. Rattan and wicker lovers have been going to this store in Sherman Oaks since 1951.

WICKER MART
36 W. Main St.
Alhambra, CA 91801
818/576-1313, 818/281-4711
HOURS: MON-FRI: 9:30-6   SAT: 10-6
CREDIT CARDS: MC, V

If you want wicker furniture, custom rattan furniture, cane planters, cane seat repairs and accessories, come to Wicker Mart and save 20 to 50% off retail and enjoy their extensive selection. Custom upholstery and a layaway plan is also available. For even higher discounts, keep your eyes open for their summer sales.

– *UNFINISHED* –

FROCH'S WOODCRAFT SHOP, INC.
6659 Topanga Canyon Blvd.
Canoga Park, CA   91303
818/883-4730
HOURS: AE, MC, V
CREDIT CARDS: MON-THUR: 9-6 FRI: 9-5 SAT: 9-6

Froch's Woodcrafts Shop is by far the best unfinished furniture store we have ever seen. They manufacture their unfinished furniture in the San Fernando Valley with their own craftsmen. This allows for the fantastic savings of 50% off retail. You'll find a wide assortment of all types of home furnishings, from dining room tables and chairs to huge wardrobes and dressers. You can remodel your kitchen with cabinetry available in different styles and sizes. If you are ready to revamp your closets, Froch's has various units you can mix and match to suit your own particular needs. Everything is all wood and of the finest quality, so you won't be able to find any particle board at Froch's.
Additional Locations: Panorama City (818/787-3682)

∞ INTERIOR DECORATING SERVICE ∞

ACCESS DESIGN
6313-1/2 Orange St.
Los Angeles, CA 90048
213/937-3736
HOURS: BY APPOINTMENT ONLY
CREDIT CARDS: CASH OR CHECKS ONLY

At last, the integrated spectrum of interior architecture, design and decorating! Access Design provides full-scope design, programming and planning services for new construction and major remodeling with a significant twist. They have the ability to purchase from all "to-the-trade-only" design showrooms at near designer's cost. Their fees for design services are extremely competitive and provide flexible options and arrangements with regard to most design projects, both residential and commercial. Access

Designs' fees are nearly half what architects, designers and decorators attach to the wholesale purchase price they are charged for furnishings, fabrics, wallcoverings, materials, and decorative accessories. They provide the incentive to buy the very finest in furnishings and goods without sacrificing professional service and expertise. Access Design is affiliated with both AIA and ASID.

∞ LAMPS & LIGHT FIXTURES ∞

CASTLE CHANDELIERS & LIGHTING CO.
7045 Topanga Canyon Blvd.
Canoga Park, CA 91303
818/340-0681
HOURS: MON-SAT: 9-6 SUN: 11-5
CREDIT CARDS: AE, DISC, MC, V

If it has to do with lighting fixtures, Castle has it all. They stock lamps, fans, chandeliers, track lights, exterior lighting, shades, and more. Products they haven't manufactured themselves are imported from Europe. All merchandise is offered at factory-direct prices. With the biggest showroom in Southern California, you are bound to find what you are looking for with over 1,000 of the finest lamps from which to choose.
Additional Locations: 7 other stores throughout S. CA

HANSEN WHOLESALE FAN CO.**
5169 N. Douglas Fir Rd., #1
Calabasas, CA 91302
818/883-7511
HOURS: MON-FRI: 9-4
CREDIT CARDS: CASH OR CHECKS ONLY

This is a wholesale house where you can get rock bottom prices on ceiling fans and light fixtures. All you have to do is step up to their order desk and place your order. Working only with catalogs, they will process your order for Casablanca and Hunter fans and light fixtures. Sometimes they will have the item you want in stock, but normally an order takes two to four weeks. The money you save will be well worth the wait, and on top of that, they'll give you an additional 5% discount when you use your BUYING RETAIL IS STUPID coupon.

LAMPMART
5821 S. Main St.
Los Angeles, CA 90003
213/234-5320
HOURS: MON-FRI: 9-5:30   SAT: 9-3
CREDIT CARDS: MC, V

One of the largest lamp and lighting fixture inventories in the greater Los Angeles area can be found here. Their prices are 33% below retail on lamps, lampshades, chandeliers, fans, and mirrors. If you've got a lamp that needs to be fixed, they can do it right on the premises, or if you need your fixtures installed, they can handle that too. Not only does Lampmart offer terrific pricing, they also carry top name brands.

MC NALLY ELECTRIC
10792 Los Alamitos Blvd.
Los Alamitos, CA 90720
213/598-9438, 714/761-0692
HOURS: MON-FRI: 9-5
CREDIT CARDS: DISC, MC, V

Whatever your lighting needs, McNally Electric can satisfy them. Table and floor lamps, fluorescents, incandescents, HID, low voltage, track or recess lighting, indoor or outdoor you'll find them here at 20 to 50% savings. Whether your needs are commercial, residential , or office, their trained sales personnel will help you with your purchase. They also carry all the "stuff" that goes behind the light fixture such as switches, breakers, pipe, fuses, and PVC. If you have a favorite lamp that needs repair, bring it in. We can't begin to list all of the brand names they carry, but some of the names are Tivoli, Fredrick Ranond, Hilite, Nutone, Plantation, Melissa, Angelo, Dinico, and Halo Lighting.

RAY FERRA'S IRON & ANTIQUE ACCENTS
342 N. La Brea Ave.
Los Angeles, CA 90036
213/934-3953
HOURS: TUES-FRI: 10-5   SAT: 10-3
CREDIT CARDS: V, MC

If you've been looking for replacement glass for an old antique lamp, then Ray Ferra can come to your rescue. If the problem isn't replacement glass, he also does rewiring for most lamps, ceiling fixtures, and crystal chandeliers. Commercial and residential lighting are also specialties. If you are looking to find more of an antique look for your home or office, you'll find Ray Ferra carries reproduction and original Tiffany lamps, handles, and many hard to find lighting items. He has been providing excellent service since 1967, and you can save 20% or more off retail prices, even if you could find it elsewhere.

∞ LINENS ∞

AL GREENWOOD BEDSPREAD KING
2750 E. Pacific Coast Hwy.
Long Beach, CA 90804
213/498-9277
HOURS: MON-THUR, SAT: 10-5:30   FRI: 10-7   SUN: 12-5
CREDIT CARDS: ALL MAJOR CREDIT CARDS

When a man calls himself the Bedspread King, you know you are going to find one of the country's largest selections of bedspreads. Well, it's true. In addition to the incredible selection of bedspreads and the terrific savings (20 to 50% off retail), Al Greenwood also carries a huge selection of custom drapes in matching fabrics. You can match your drapes and take them home with you, and get this, with no waiting! If you are handy with a sewing machine, make or create your own accessories to match your new bedspread. Just have them cut the length you need of matching fabric, and you are on your merry way. If you prefer a comforter to a bedspread, check out their Quallofil comforters which have the lightness, warmth and puffiness of down, but without the same price.
Additional Locations: South Gate (213/566-9393)

BED 'N BATH
19804 Ventura Blvd.
Woodland Hills, CA 91364
818/702-9301
HOURS: MON-FRI: 9:30-9 SAT: 9:30-6 SUN: 10-6
CREDIT CARDS: MC, V

With their prices, Bed'n Bath says, "We make you laugh at white sale prices." Their large stores are filled with giant selections of sheets, towels, bedspreads, comforters, pillows, kitchenware, dinnerware, cookware, gift items, toss pillows, shower curtains, everything! You'll find Martex, Fieldcrest, Wamsutta, Nettlecreek and Mikasa, just to name a few, and the prices are way below department store sale prices.
Additional Locations: Huntington Beach (714/842-0068), Redondo Beach (213/370-1225), San Diego (619/295-9888), Studio City (818/980-0260), W. Los Angeles (213/478-5767)

BEDSIDE MANNER
2247 S. Sepulveda Blvd.
W. Los Angeles, CA 90064
213/478-3519
HOURS: MON-SAT: 10-6 SUN: 12-5
CREDIT CARDS: MC, V

Bedside Manners is just the spot you've been searching for if you are ready to redecorate your bedroom. Save anywhere from 10 to 50% off what department stores charge on sheets, Southhampton comforter sets, down comforters, Swishee pillows in over 50 colors, and other various products. For bigger savings, make certain you don't overlook the bargain tables filled with close-outs and discontinued items.

BEDSPREAD CREATIONS**
14054 E. Firestone Blvd.
Santa Fe Springs, CA 90670
213/802-7938
HOURS: MON-SAT: 10:30-5
CREDIT CARDS: AE, DISC, MC, V

As the manufacturer for their own stores, Bedspread Creations is able to offer wholesale prices to people lucky enough to know about them. They have about 3,500 square feet with more than 1,000 bedspreads in stock. With over 2,000 different fabrics to choose from, they'll make anything you want, even if you wish to furnish your own fabric. They carry comforters, pillows, mini and vertical blinds, and all the other items necessary to make them a one-stop bedroom decorating center. Name brands include Bedspread Creations, Pacific Designs, India Ink, Laurel Wood, and many others. You'll save an additional 5% with your BUYING RETAIL IS STUPID coupon. Deals don't get much better than this.

BEDSPREAD WAREHOUSE
6949 Topanga Canyon Blvd.
Canoga Park, CA 91303
818/887-4347
HOURS: MON-SAT: 10-6 SUN: 12-5
CREDIT CARDS: MC, V

Bedspread Warehouse offers a wide variety of bedspreads, comforters, pillows, day bed sets, and bath accessories at 20 to 60% off retail. They specialize in custom-made window treatments and bedspreads. You'll find a full line of quality merchandise with brand names such as Dakota, India Ink, Laurel Wood, and Croscille. Stressing customer service, their experts will provide assistance in helping you to color coordinate your rooms in style.

CALICO CORNERS
3830 Foothill Blvd.
Pasadena, CA 91107
818/792-4328
HOURS: MON: 9:30-8 TUES-SAT: 9:30-5:30 SUN: 12-4
CREDIT CARDS: MC, V

Wouldn't you love to own a quilted bedspread? Well, you can at 30 to 60% above cost when you shop at Calico Corners. They carry designer fabrics, slip covers, table cloths, feather and down pillows. Upholstery fabrics and books on upholstering are for sale, plus books on slip covers and windows. They have tape for making Roman and Austrian shades, and pleating tape for making curtains. Get on their mailing list so you'll know about their really big sales.

COUNTRY LINENS**
18 Fashion Square
Sherman Oaks, CA 91423
818/995-7417
HOURS: MON-FRI: 10-9 SAT: 10-6 SUN: 12-5
CREDIT CARDS: AE, MC, V

Not only will you find a large selection of top of the line bed and
bath accessories at 20% below department store prices, but they also
specialize in monogramming and creating custom bedding. Country
Linens knows how to take care of their customers with complimen-
tary gift wrapping and friendly service. You'll find a large selection
of imported soaps and toiletries and hard to find items such as vanity
benches and vanity mirrors. Their selection is so good that the
movie studios frequently come in to shop. Save an extra 10% when
you use your BUYING RETAIL IS STUPID coupon.

EVER-RICH BEDDING**
22135 Sherman Way
Canoga Park, CA 91303
818/999-2184
HOURS: MON-SAT: 10:30-6
CREDIT CARDS: MC, V

Trying to keep cool in the summer and warm in the winter? Stop by
Ever-Rich Bedding, and check out their goose down comforters and
pillows. They have designer toss pillows, bedspreads, daybed sets,
waterbed and regular sheets, and complete comforter sets. Some of
the brand names you'll find are Crown Craft, Purofied Down, Max
Rawicz Designs and Hollander Home Fashions. If your purchase is
over $100, they will take off an additional 10% when you use your
BUYING RETAIL IS STUPID discount coupon.

THE LINEN ROOM
860 S. Los Angeles St., Rm. 430
Los Angeles, CA 90014
213/627-3333
HOURS: MON-SAT: 9:30-6 SUN: 11-5
CREDIT CARDS: AE, MC, V

Victor, the owner of The Linen Room, guarantees not to be undersold. If you're looking for bedspreads, comforters, sheets, or towels, look no further. This 8,000 square foot showroom is filled with linens, including most designer names, at savings of 35 to 70% off retail. You will also find accessories for your powder room. If you need a warm comforter for your Aunt Tilley in Montana, you can phone your order in and have it shipped just in time for her birthday. They have been satisfying their customers since the late 1970's, so they must be doing something right.

MR. SATIN, INC.
2236 S. Barrington Ave.
Los Angeles, CA 90064
213/879-3353
HOURS: MON-FRI: 8:30-4 SAT: 12-5
CREDIT CARDS: CASH OR CHECKS ONLY

This factory outlet specializes in satin sheets, comforters, shams, dust ruffles, boudoir pillows, and dust covers. You can save 30 to 70% off retail shopping here. They also carry seconds in excellent condition. Feel like a King or Queen when you sleep between satin sheets without paying regal prices!

∞ WALL & WINDOW TREATMENTS ∞

– WALLPAPER –

OBALEK TILE & WALLPAPER
2301 S. Hill St.
Los Angeles, CA 90007
213/748-4664
HOURS: MON-FRI: 8-6 SAT: 9-5
CREDIT CARDS: MC, V

If you want to find great discount prices on a huge stock of tiles from around the world, visit Obalek Tile & Wallpaper. They have approximately 1/2 million square feet of ceramic and vinyl tiles in stock. In addition to tile, they have 250,000 rolls of wallpaper in stock. They carry all the tools necessary for do-it-yourselfers, and their professional staff will be glad to instruct you on the how-to. General manager Bill Cochran and his staff are extremely helpful.

WALLPAPER BIN
8969 Tampa Ave.
Northridge, CA 91324
818/886-1291
HOURS: MON-SAT: 10-6
CREDIT CARDS: MC, V

If you're looking for "high-quality" decorator and famous maker wallcovering, how would you like to save up to 80% off original book prices! That's exactly what you can save on items in stock at Wallpaper Bin. They carry brands like Mitchell Designs, James Seamans, Astor, Jonap, Sinclair, Bolta, Wallex and Sanitas. You'll be able to make your selection from a variety of vinyls, mylars, textures, handprints, strings, grasscloths and more. Most all of these absolutely marvelous buys are from factory, mill and distributor inventories (out of production goods). The Wallpaper Bin, located in the Tampa Plaza Shopping Center in Northridge, can save you big bucks on your next wallpapering project!

WALLPAPER CITY
1320 Lincoln Blvd.
Santa Monica, CA 90401
213/393-9422
HOURS: MON-FRI: 8:30-5:30 SAT: 10-5 SUN: 12-5
CREDIT CARDS: MC, V

There are more than 1,000 rolls of different wallpaper in stock at any one time, 800 wallpaper books to order from, and you can save 20–60% on your selection. Manager Lotte Hanock has this large stock of wallpaper which she can match to shades and drapery treatments. Fabric can also be ordered to match your designer paper from companies such as Shumacker, Waverly and Charles Barone. At Wallpaper City you can purchase vinyls, grasscloths, custom bedding, pillows and window coverings, all at big savings.

– WINDOW TREATMENTS –

AERO SHADE
8404 W. 3rd St.
Los Angeles, CA 90048
213/655-2411
HOURS: MON-FRI: 8:30-5
CREDIT CARDS: MC, V

Aero Shade has everything for windows, except drapes. If you're looking for pleated or laminated shades, shutters, Levolor or vertical blinds, they have a complete stock and quick service. You're buying factory direct at Aero Shade, and can save 10 to 25%. Some of the styles available are custom, decorative and simple. They'll provide new rollers or put the new cloth on your old rollers. You can also have your fabrics laminated. In business for over 50 years, and free estimates are offered upon request.

BARON WINDOW COVERINGS
7449 Woodley Ave.
Van Nuys, CA 91046
818/994-9995, 213/873-7273
HOURS: MON-FRI: 8-5 SAT: 10-2
CREDIT CARDS: MC, V

Whether you live in a mansion or have your office in a highrise on the 30th floor, Baron Window Coverings has everything you need to cover or accent all of your windows. Claiming to have the lowest prices on all major brands of window coverings for home and business, they have name brands that include Levolor, Bali, M&B, Louver Drape, Hunter Douglas, Graber, and Kirsch. They feature Baron Vertical Blinds manufactured in their own plant. These blinds come with a 10 year warranty, along with extremely low prices. Constructed with 2" heavy duty headrails and self-aligning carriers, these blinds are truly far superior to all other brands. Baron carries all qualities of mini-blinds, but most sales are directed to durable 8 gauge for better wear. Also check with them for pleated shades and "Duette" shades. In addition, you'll find various types of draperies are available, suitable for all needs.

BEVERLY WESTERN INTERIORS
336 N. Western Ave.
Los Angeles, CA 90004
213/463-3192
HOURS: MON-FRI: 8-6
CREDIT CARDS: CASH OR CHECKS ONLY

Save 20 to 40% and get the best of interior design selection, too. Beverly Western has draperies, carpeting, bedspreads and furniture for your consideration. Your draperies will be custom-made and of the finest quality at factory-to-you prices. Established in 1965, you receive expert advice and years of experience.

BLIND FAITH**
13165 Sherman Way
N. Hollywood, CA 91605
800/222-2300, 818/765-2345, 213/277-9566
HOURS: MON, THUR: 10-8   TUES-SAT: 10-5   SUN: 12-5
CREDIT CARDS: MC, V

L.A. Magazine (Oct. 87) called them the "biggest bargain in town." They have a 4,000 square foot showroom filled with factory direct products. Their custom vertical blinds with custom inserts (fabric inserted in the groovers) are 65% off retail. Made at their own mill are custom sofas made with hardwood frames, in any size, any style, and any fabric (can work from a photograph). Also made at their mill are hide-a-beds, sectional chaises, chairs, benches, headboards, and cornice boxes. Delivery from the mill usually takes 2 to 4 weeks. Their Levolor products are always 58% off. Blind Faith will beat any verified quote on any product they sell—Louverdrape, M & B Kirsch, Hunter Douglas, Duette, Levelor, and many more. You'll save an additional 5% when you shop here with your BUYING RETAIL IS STUPID coupon.

BLUE CHIP DRAPERY, INC.
2139 Stoner Ave.
Los Angeles, CA 90025
800/BLUE-CHP, 213/477-2421
HOURS: MON-SAT: 8:30-5
CREDIT CARDS: DISC, MC, V

You will usually save 50% or more on draperies and blinds at Blue Chip Drapery. This company is California's largest discount drapery manufacturer, with eight wholesale window covering showrooms throughout greater Los Angeles and Orange County. Blue Chip carries the state's largest, in-stock, inventory of ready-to-hang draperies. There are 120 sizes in a great variety of textures and colors, always available at factory-direct prices in each showroom. All Blue Chip ready-mades (standard, elegant, luxury and close-out lines) are sold on a satisfaction guaranteed basis, allowing a 10 day exchange or refund. When you order custom draperies from Blue Chip's huge stock of discounted decorator fabrics, there is no labor charge added to most selections. Major brands of mini blinds, verticals, drapery rods and other kinds of window treatments are also featured at discounted prices in the Blue Chip super-showrooms.
Additional Locations: 7 other stores in S. CA–Call 800/BLUE-CHP

DIAMOND V INTERIORS
4145 Indus Way
Riverside, CA 92503
714/736-6055
HOURS: MON-FRI: 8-5
CREDIT CARDS: CASH OR CHECKS ONLY

Diamond V Interiors carries custom draperies and bedspreads direct from the manufacturer. They have thousands of samples to choose from, and you can save 20% off retail on your purchases. They have been in business for over 10 years, so you can expect to find knowledgeable help.

INTERIOR MOTIVES
8362 W. 3rd St.
Los Angeles, CA 90048
213/658-6017
HOURS: MON-FRI: 9-5
CREDIT CARDS: MC, V

Interior Motives is really a window covering specialist, but they also offer 20 to 50% discounts on office furniture, carpets and window tinting. You will find an extensive selection of mini-blinds, vertical blinds, woven blinds, shutters, Levolors, Roman shades, pleated shades and custom draperies. They give free estimates, have a helpful home shopping service and have been in business since 1979 doing custom work at discount prices. Also included at Interior Motives is Baby Motives which is a full service baby and children furniture store.

MELROSE DRAPERIES
7748 Santa Monica Blvd.
Los Angeles, CA 90046
213/653-1601
HOURS: MON-FRI: 8:30-5
CREDIT CARDS: CASH OR CHECKS ONLY

These folks have been in business over 30 years selling, manufacturing, and installing window coverings. Want your bedspread to match your bedroom drapes? Look no further! Want to see how the fabrics will look in your home? They'll bring out samples for you to choose in your home. Draperies, bedspreads, window shades, and true discount prices. What a combination!

MORAN WAREHOUSE STORE
4631 S. Huntington Dr.
Los Angeles, CA 90032
213/221-4141
HOURS: TUES-SAT: 10-6
CREDIT CARDS: MC, V

You can get ready-made draperies, quality custom-made draperies, bedspreads, sheets, curtains, panels, mini-blinds, vertical blinds, drapery yardage, and remnants at 40 to 50% below retail prices. These discounted products are the discontinued items from their 17 retail stores. They buy direct from their vendors and pass these savings on to you. They also have a parking lot sale in July.

STAR DRAPERIES MFG.
111 S. Western Ave.
Los Angeles, CA 90004
213/383-1318, 800/541-7827
HOURS: MON-SAT: 9-5:30
CREDIT CARDS: AE, DISC, MC, V

Star will come to your home, measure your windows and give you a free estimate. When your order has been completed, their pro will handle the installation. Vertical blinds are their specialty and they make mini-blinds, pleated shades and wood blinds. Draperies are also custom-made. Look forward to factory direct prices with savings as much as 60 to 70% off retail prices. They have been in business since 1974.
Additional Locations: Anaheim (714/827-3260), La Puente (818/965-0688, 714/595-8666), Van Nuys (818/787-7841)

SUPERIOR WINDOW COVERINGS, INC.**
10731 Chandler Blvd.
N. Hollywood, CA 91601
818/762-9033
HOURS: MON-SAT: 9-5
CREDIT CARDS: MC, V

Wholesale prices on draperies, vertical blinds, mini-blinds, pleated shades, wood blinds, draperies, roman shades, balloon shades, cloud shades and cornice boxes are found in Superior Window Coverings' factory showroom. They carry such brand names as Bali, Duette, and Superior. You will find extra special sales during the months of February and March. Bring in your BUYING RETAIL IS STUPID coupon and you can get an additional 10% discount!

VASONA INTERIORS
8732 Tampa Ave.
Northridge, CA 91324
818/993-9248
HOURS: MON-FRI: 9-5 SAT: 9-4
CREDIT CARDS: AE, DISC, MC, V

Vasona Interiors has window coverings to fit any room in your house. They can fix you up with mini-blinds, shades, vertical blinds, and verosol blinds with brand names such as Levolor, LouverDrape and Kirsch. You can also get draperies, bedspreads, wallpaper and personalized service. All orders are custom-made. Service is most important to them. Customer satisfaction is guaranteed. You can appreciate a 50% discount off retail items.

JEWELRY

ALEX LAZAR JEWELERS, INC.**
3648 Central Ave.
Riverside, CA 92506
714/683-1149
HOURS: MON-FRI: 10-6 SAT: 10-2
CREDIT CARDS: CASH OR CHECKS ONLY

So you've set the wedding date, and you're in search of that perfect diamond for your his and her rings. Consider stopping by Alex Lazar Jewelers and selecting those perfect rings or loose stones. You'll find everything in the store at about 20% below retail, and loose stones are an even better buy at 40% below retail. Appraisals are given with purchase. These folks have been in Riverside since 1964 and they know their stuff! Use you BUYING RETAIL IS STUPID coupon and you'll receive another "jewel" of an additional 5% discount!

BES INTERNATIONAL JEWELRY
607 S. Hill St., #334
Los Angeles, CA 90014
213/626-1075
HOURS: MON-FRI: 9:30-5 SAT: 10-3
CREDIT CARDS: MC, V

Here's a complete line of jewelry at wholesale prices. You will save at least 50% in their glittering showroom filled with 14 and 18 karat gold! Owner Evelyn LeVine has bracelets, necklaces, chains, rings, wedding rings, engagement sets, earrings, and more. Custom designing is available, and repairs are done while you wait. In fact, if you are bored with some of your old jewelry lying around, let Bes redesign or remount it for you in a new modern style. They've been in business since 1977, so you can rely on them.

CALIFORNIA JEWELSMITHS
250 S. Beverly Dr.
Beverly Hills, CA 90025
213/272-5364
HOURS: MON-SAT: 9:30-5:00
CREDIT CARDS: MC, V

California Jewelsmiths has been in business since the 1940's and has maintained two and three generations of clients strictly by word of mouth. They don't advertise about the great savings, usually 30% off retail, on their fine diamond jewelry, bracelets, necklaces, rings, precious and semi precious stones, charms, pendants, chains and watches. Check them out when shopping for a dependable jewelry store. Repair work for jewelry and watches is done on the premises.

CLAYDON'S JEWELERS
2772 Artesia Blvd.
Redondo Beach, CA 90278
213/542-0501
HOURS: WED: 10-7 MON-FRI: 10-6 SAT: 10-4:30
CREDIT CARDS: AE, MC, V

We found Claydon's Jewelers from a woman's letter saying she was their new customer for life. Why? She saved $500 there on a diamond and didn't write to us about it until she had done some apples-to-apples comparison shopping. Claydon's can do everything for you from custom designing a piece of jewelry using rare gemstones in unusual shapes, to repairing silver and pewter items such as candle holders, tea sets, or frames. All this is done on their premises. They also do watch repairs, string pearls and engrave your merchandise. Always wanting to do just a little more for their customers, Claydon's will schedule special appointments during and after their normal business hours. Now we'd say that this is a one stop jewelry shop.

COLLECTOR'S EYE
18564 Sherman Way
Reseda, CA 91335
818/996-3100
HOURS: MON-SAT: 10:30-6:30
CREDIT CARDS: AE, MC, V

This is definitely one of our favorites. Walking into the Collector's
Eye is like walking through a rainbow and finding the pot of gold.
All of their elegantly displayed vintage jewelry is arranged by colors
and/or style. You might find an antique vanity draped in pearl
brooches, earrings, bracelets, chokers, necklaces, rings and ropes.
Another display might consist of 75 various styles in shades of blue
or perhaps, sterling silver. The antique jewelry, real and costume,
is from the early 1800's up through the early 1960's and all at 50%
to 70% below retail. You can literally spend hours browsing
through this oasis of jewelry acquired from estate sales, swap meets
and retirement homes. If you can bring yourself to look away from
the jewelry (it took us three visits), you'll find a selection of
paintings, needlework and prints. The Collector's Eye does jewelry
repair and will also buy your vintage jewelry. A definite stop when
in the San Fernando Valley!

DARVA JEWELERS
18410 Ventura Blvd.
Tarzana, CA 91356
818/881-GOLD
HOURS: MON-FRI: 9:30-5:30 SAT: 10-5
CREDIT CARDS: MC, V

Darva Jewelers offers quality jewelry at 25 to 60% below retail and
watches at 30 to 40% off retail. Their motto is service, and they
offer a money back guarantee if not satisfied within 14 days. They
even will add a 5% discount for each can of food you bring in (up to
a 25% discount) during their Annual Sale to help the Homeless.
Make sure to call and find out when the sale is, not only to save
money, but to help the homeless. Appraisals and repairs done on
the premises.

DESIGNER JEWELRY MART
18456 Clark St.
Tarzana, CA 91356
818/345-0535
HOURS: TUES-SAT: 10-6
CREDIT CARDS: AE, DISC

The owner of Designer Jewelry Mart, Nick Dembowich, is the reason people enjoy shopping here for jewelry and watches. Nick runs his business with a philosophy that is rare in today's world. He believes in making a lifetime happy customer, not a quick sale. Nick carries most anything you need and if he doesn't have it, he will get it for you. Diamonds are bought direct resulting in higher savings for his customers. Prices on jewelry run approximately 10% above cost, and you can save up to 50% on Seiko watches. Custom designing and repairs are also available.

THE DIAMOND MINE
1060 Hamner Ave.
Norco, CA 91760
714/735-7447
HOURS: MON-FRI: 10-5 SAT: 9-6
CREDIT CARDS: AE, DISC, MC, V

Why not save yourself at least 50% below mall jewelry store prices by checking out The Diamond Mine? You can buy on sight or design what you want in 14K and 18K gold. In addition, they carry loose diamonds and gemstones, and they do their own castings. If you are longing for a solid gold watch in 14K or 18K gold, with or without diamonds, head for the Diamond Mine. Though owner Dan Shevitski doesn't keep expensive watches like this in stock, he'll get one for you for only 10% over what he is charged for the watch. Knowing that the same item costing $100 at retail jewelry stores, will cost only $40 at The Diamond Mine, why would anyone want to pay $100?

ENCINO JEWELRY EXCHANGE
17143 Ventura Blvd.
Encino, CA 91316
818/990-8944
HOURS: MON-SAT: 10-5:30
CREDIT CARDS: AE, MC, V

First the freebies: free jewelry cleaning, free verbal appraisals and free parking. The Encino Jewelry Exchange has a large selection of watches like Seiko, Citizen, Pulsar, Omega, and others at 50% off retail prices. Their collection of 14K and 18K gold jewelry is priced 50 to 70% less than you'd pay at department stores or chain jewelry stores. Jewelry and watch repair is done on the premises. Many jobs can be done while you wait.

LORD OF THE RINGS**
607 S. Hills St.
Los Angeles, CA 90014
213/488-9157
HOURS: BY APPOINTMENT ONLY
CREDIT CARDS: AE, DISC, MC, V

Lord of the Rings offers all types of fine jewelry, precious stones, diamonds, engagement rings and wedding bands to the public at wholesale prices. Generally, your savings will run about 33 to 50% below retail. They are open six days a week and some evenings if requested. Please call them to set up an appointment. They will also accept your BUYING RETAIL IS STUPID coupon for an additional 5% discount on your purchase.

M. WEINSTEIN INC.
9720 Wilshire Blvd.
Beverly Hills, CA 90212
213/276-0696
HOURS: MON-FRI: 10-4:30
CREDIT CARDS: MC, V

Previously in Los Angeles, Mr. Weinstein has been in the jewelry business for over 60 years. He offers his clientele new and used jewelry at all different price levels, so don't let the Beverly Hills address intimidate you. You'll discover exceptional values on everything from a simple gold chain to fabulous estate pieces. If you want to start from scratch, M. Weinstein's also carries loose diamonds and gemstones. Satisfaction is guaranteed.

MARVIN HIME & CO., INC.
228 S. Beverly Dr.
Beverly Hills, CA 90212
213/275-5211
HOURS: MON-SAT: 9:30-5
CREDIT CARDS: AE, MC, V

Don't let the Beverly Hills address fool you! You will save 50% off retail when you shop here. They carry a line of imported watches, gold novelties, pearls, and a wide variety of men's and women's jewelry. Have an old piece of jewelry you want updated? They're equipped to do it right on the premises. They have three gemologists on staff, do appraisals, and repairs. They buy their pearls direct from Japan, so they can pass on the savings to you. Need a 14K gold whistle, a gold cigar cutter? You'll find the usual and unusual here. If you don't see what you're looking for, chances are they can make it for you. Marvin Hine & Co. has been in business since 1946. There is no substitute for experience.

MAYA
7614 Melrose Ave.
Los Angeles, CA 90046
213/655-2708
HOURS: MON-THUR: 11-7 FRI: 11-9 SAT: 12-6
CREDIT CARDS: AE, MC, V

Maya says she has the greatest earring show on earth. With over 4,000 pairs to choose from, she may be correct. Earrings in gold, silver, enamel, copper, and brass, whatever you're looking for, you can find it here. This unique store also carries some clothing items, necklaces, and other gift items. You'll always save about 20%, and Maya will usually have some specials to entice you.

MUNN'S SILVER & JEWELRY SHOP
209 W. Wilson
Glendale, CA 91203
818/241-2776, 818/241-1909
HOURS: TUES-SAT: 10-5:30
CREDIT CARDS: MC, V

What we have here is gold and silver jewelry, silver flatware, plated flatware, and silver hollowware at an unbelievable 15% over cost. Ruth and Ted Munn also carry diamond rings, and rings with precious or semiprecious stones. You'll also find a variety of souvenir spoons and they do watch and clock repair as well. They are a franchise dealer of Gorham, International Kirk-Stieff, Lunt, Reed & Barton, Towle, and Wallace.

SHANES JEWELRY STORE
1065 Broxton Ave.
Los Angeles, CA 90024
213/208-8404
HOURS: MON-SAT: 10:30-6   SUN: 12-6
CREDIT CARDS: AE, DISC, MC, V

This business offers their customers a complete jewelry service. Not only do they carry an incredibly large stock of 14K gold and diamond jewelry at all times, they also supply the following services: special orders, jewelry designing, jewelry repair, and a very convenient layaway plan. Any alterations a customer may want, on any piece of merchandise, can be done quickly and professionally. Shanes also has sapphires, rubies, emeralds, opals, and sterling silver at wholesale prices. They offer 50% off on gold and diamond jewelry.

ST. VINCENT JEWELRY CENTER
650 S. Hill St.
Los Angeles, CA 90014
213/629-2124
HOURS: MON-SAT: 9:30-5:30
CREDIT CARDS: VARIES WITH EACH VENDOR

St. Vincent Jewelry Center, the single largest jewelry exchange in the world, is home to over 400 wholesalers and manufacturers.

This is the place to go for jewelry of any kind, we don't care what you want—it's here! Opened in 1982, the individual jewelry stores offer you factory-direct prices at savings of 40 to 70% below retail. Would you like a gold chain, a bracelet or maybe a diamond watch? Perhaps you have a coronation to attend and need a matched set (in diamonds and rubies) that includes a tiara, choker, pair of earrings, bracelet and ring to complement your new Ungaro gown. Whatever you need or desire is here to fit any budget. You can spend $25 or $1,500,000. True jewelry lovers will think they've hit buried treasure. Aside from ready made jewelry, you'll find businesses specializing in custom design, loose stones, repair, restoration, and you'll also find gold, precious metal and jewelry buyers. It's hard to believe that this fabulous selection is all under one roof, and when you see the prices, you won't believe the savings either. St. Vincent Jewelry Center is located on 7th and S. Hill, with validated parking at 725 S. Hill. Call to get a free directory listing all stores.

STEVEN & CO. JEWELERS
437 N. Bedford Dr.
Beverly Hills, CA 90210
213/274-8336
HOURS: MON-FRI: 10-5:30
CREDIT CARDS: AE, MC, V

Dreams turn into reality here. Steven & Co. has jewelry with diamonds, emeralds, rubies, sapphires and pearls at 10 to 20% above cost, as well as watches, clocks, and gold jewelry. They carry such brand names as Rolex, Cartier, Ebel, Movado and others. Expert repairing of watches and jewelry, custom designing, redesigning and ear piercing is available. They also purchase and appraise estates. Free parking at 461 Bedford. Get on their private mailing list for special sales.

MEDICAL NEEDS

∞ DRUG STORES & PHARMACIES ∞

CONSUMER DISCOUNT DRUGS
6542 Hollywood Blvd.
Hollywood, CA 90028
213/461-3606
HOURS: MON-SAT: 9-9 SUN: 10-6
CREDIT CARDS: DISC, MC, V

You can save an average of 30% off the retail price on most items in this fully stocked drug store. Consumer Discount Drugs carries everything from vitamins and brand name cosmetics, to health and beauty aids. Every week, they feature at least 10-20 special sale items, so check those out for extra savings!

P X DRUGS NO. 2**
6318 Van Nuys Blvd.
Van Nuys, CA 91406
818/785-0441
HOURS: MON-FRI: 8:30-6:30 SAT: 9-1
CREDIT CARDS: MC, V

Everything you buy in this drug store is discounted. Prescriptions, hair and skin care products, greeting cards, cosmetics, health aids and food items such as soft drinks, ice cream and lots of munchies. P X Drugs honors most insurance plans in their pharmacy. Presentation of your BUYING RETAIL IS STUPID coupon will get you an additional 10% discount on anything in the store but prescriptions.

∞ SUPPLIES & EQUIPMENT ∞

ANDERS ORTHOPEDICS & PROSTHETICS
1825 N. Western Ave.
Los Angeles, CA 90027
213/461-4279
HOURS: MON-FRI: 9-5
CREDIT CARDS: CASH OR CHECKS ONLY

From braces to wheelchairs, Anders carries everything in orthopedic and prosthetics lines. They have more than 25 years of experience so you will receive knowledgeable, professional service plus savings of 30 to 50% off retail. They also have corsets, trusses, orthopedic shoes, surgical stockings, crutches, and many other necessary items. Just ask for Johnny Anders.

ELECTROPEDIC ADJUSTABLE BEDS
15600 Roscoe Blvd.
Van Nuys, CA 91406
818/909-0077
HOURS: MON-FRI: 9-5   SAT: 9-4   SUN: 11-4
CREDIT CARDS: AE, MC, V

When one of our husbands unfortunately threw his back out while playing paddle tennis, we decided an electric bed was one of the answers for a quick recovery. And it was. Electropedic Adjustable Beds is a factory outlet and sells these comfortable beds at savings of 40 to 50% off retail. The beds are available in twin, full, queen, king, dual queen, and dual king.

GALAXY SALON EQUIPMENT MFG. CO.
5411 Sheila St.
Los Angeles, CA 90040
213/728-3980
HOURS: MON-FRI: 10-5
CREDIT CARDS: MC, V

Have you been considering opening your own beauty salon? Do you need some advice? From salon layout to the grand opening,

Galaxy Salon Equipment is at your service with factory direct prices. You can expect to save 50% off retail on your salon equipment. If new equipment isn't in your budget, you can save even more on their used equipment. Financing is available. They also carry hospital and physician supply equipment.

MEDCHOICE WAREHOUSE CLUB**
10910 Talbert Ave.
Fountain Valley, CA 92708
714/963-4838
HOURS: MON-FRI: 9-7 SAT: 10-6
CREDIT CARDS: MC, V

Now you can shop where the doctors shop, and get the same wholesale prices. MedChoice Warehouse Club is one of the answers to rising costs of health care. You can save 10 to 50% on everything from aspirin to wheelchairs. MedChoice carries only the best brand-name products. Are you a parent caring for a growing family? Are you a fitness enthusiast? Under special medical supervision or do you need a reliable source for low-cost medical supplies such as vitamins, bandages or baby diapers? If you answered yes to any of these questions, then you can save at MedChoice. If addition, you can get advice from their medical, dental and home care specialists who are dedicated to giving you personal service. It isn't mandatory for you to become a member to shop there, but members receive an additional 10% off their purchases. Your BUYING RETAIL IS STUPID coupon is good for a one day pass, along with receiving membership prices (10% off) on your purchases. Why not give MedChoice a shot?
Additional Locations: Woodland Hills (818/347-9779)

QUICKMED SUPPLIES INC.
3421 San Fernando Rd.
Los Angeles, CA 90065
800/336-3660, 213/259-1000
HOURS: MON-FRI: 8:30-5
CREDIT CARDS: CASH OR CHECKS ONLY

Quickmed Supplies is your one-stop shop for all medical supplies such as wheelchairs, orthopedic goods, portable commodes, gauze, bandaids, and cotton. They carry back supports, canes, knee braces, and other related products. This is a discount warehouse where you can save 20 to 30% off retail prices. If it's portable, you'll find everything related to medical recuperation at Quickmed Supplies.

∞ USED EQUIPMENT ∞

KAGAN SURPLUS SALES**
8050 Webb Ave.
N. Hollywood, CA 91605
818/768-1422
HOURS: MON-THUR: 8:45-5:45 FRI: 8:30-5:15 SAT: 10-4:30
CREDIT CARDS: CASH OR CHECKS ONLY

Kagan Surplus Sales specializes in used office furniture, hospital furniture, home care items, and material handling equipment. This 4,000 square foot warehouse offers items that have been completely refurbished (repaired, painted and recovered if necessary). Savings range from 50 to 90% off what you would pay normally if these items were brand new. The price is the only way to tell that the wheelchairs (always a large selection) and Geri-chairs are used. In addition, Kagan Surplus Sales carries desks, credenzas, chairs, file cabinets, shelving, casters, carts, lockers, storage cabinets, medical, lab and x-ray equipment. Don't forget to use your BUYING RETAIL IS STUPID coupon for additional savings. You'll save 5% if your purchase is under $100, and 10% if your purchase is over $100.

MEMBERSHIP STORES

COSTCO
6110 Sepulveda Blvd.
Van Nuys, CA 91411
818/989-5256
HOURS: MON-FRI: 12-8:30 SAT: 9:30-6 SUN: 11-5
CREDIT CARDS: CASH, CHECKS OR COSTCO CREDIT CARD ONLY

Costco is truly for people who love to save money, lots of money. Each of their membership wholesale distribution centers operates in a 100,000 square foot warehouse. They carry only quality name brands at substantially lower prices than other wholesale sources. Whether you need clothing, major appliances, books, furniture, groceries, toys, hardware, tires, liquor, jewelry, you name it, they've got it. Costco guarantees great brands, products and value. So, for those of you who really want to save big bucks, call for information on how to become a Costco member.
Additional Locations: 14 other stores throughout S. CA

THE LIQUIDATION CLUB**
19032 So. Vermont Ave.
Gardena, CA 90248
213/715-6500
HOURS: SAT-WED: 11-6 THUR-FRI: 11-8
CREDIT CARDS: MC, V

Buying Retail Is Stupid shoppers unite! The Liquidation Club, which operates by membership only, is extending a FREE MEMBERSHIP to all owners of this book, and this is definitely a place you want to check out. Not only do they have the lowest prices on most major department store brand names, but you'll save an additional 10% using your BUYING RETAIL IS STUPID coupon. Brand names include Liz Claiborne, Ann Klein, Bill Blass, Ralph Lauren,

Bally, Georgio Armani, Perry Ellis, London Fog, Oshkosh, and more. You'll find over 50,000 items of clothing for the entire family, housewares, bedding, accessories, gift items and much more at savings of 60 to 85% off retail. New merchandise accounts for 75% of their inventory, and the remaining 25% of their merchandise are slightly damaged (such as label removed). Stock changes daily, so make sure to put The Liquidation Club on your check list for shopping. Don't forget to take the coupon from the back of the book for your additional 10% discount and free membership!

MEDCHOICE WAREHOUSE CLUB**

10910 Talbert Ave.
Fountain Valley, CA 92708
714/963-4838
HOURS: MON-FRI: 9-7 SAT: 10-6
CREDIT CARDS: MC, V

Now you can shop where the doctors shop, and get the same wholesale prices. MedChoice Warehouse Club is one of the answers to rising costs of health care. You can save 10 to 50% on everything from aspirin to wheelchairs. MedChoice carries only the best brand-name products. Are you a parent caring for a growing family? Are you a fitness enthusiast? Under special medical supervision or do you need a reliable source for low-cost medical supplies such as vitamins, bandages or baby diapers? If you answered yes to any of these questions, then you can save at MedChoice. If addition, you can get advice from their medical, dental and home care specialists who are dedicated to giving you personal service. It isn't mandatory for you to become a member to shop there, but members receive an additional 10% off their purchases. Your BUYING RETAIL IS STUPID coupon is good for a one day pass, along with receiving membership prices (10% off) on your purchases. Why not give MedChoice a shot?

Additional Locations: Woodland Hills (818/347-9779)

THE OFFICE CLUB
15385 Oxnard St.
Van Nuys, CA 91411
818/988-2582
HOURS: MON-FRI: 8-7 SAT: 9-5
CREDIT CARDS: CASH OR CHECKS ONLY

The Office Club is a membership warehouse that costs $10 a year, and you don't have to sacrifice service for savings. Their knowledgeable and helpful sales staff will assist you or answer any questions you may have about office supplies, equipment or furniture at this one-stop shop. They offer wholesale prices every day on thousands of best selling, top quality, name brand office products in their huge, no frills warehouse stores. Delivery is available, and you can place your order by telephone with your Office Club Credit Card. You will find Office Clubs in Los Angeles, Orange and San Diego Counties.
Additional Locations: 9 other stores throughout S. CA

PRICE CLUB
900 S. Harbor Blvd.
Fullerton, CA 92632
714/441-0584
HOURS: MON-FRI: 11-8:30 SAT: 9:30-6 SUN: 11-5
CREDIT CARDS: CASH OR CHECKS ONLY

Though it can be dangerous, one of our favorite things to do is wander around Price Club. How can shopping be dangerous? With over 100,000 square feet of everything imaginable—groceries, computers, televisions, VCR's, stereo equipment, clothing, office supplies, furniture, appliances, housewares, hardware, books (you name it and it's there)—the danger of spending much more than you had planned lurks along every aisle. At Price Club, the prices are so fantastic you many end up buying things you don't need. So before you go shopping, make out out a list of things you need in order to avoid impulse buying, unless of course impulse buying is your thing. Also, if you've never been to Price Club, make sure you schedule enough time so that you can leisurely walk this enormous warehouse and not have to rush through the place (you might miss something). With savings up to 80% off retail, you will recoup the $25 annual membership fee very quickly. The salespeople are friendly and helpful, and their return policy is quite good.

Additional Locations: 17 other stores throughout S. CA

MUSIC & MOVIES

∞ CD's, Records, Tapes & Videos ∞

ARON'S RECORD SHOP
1150 N. Highland
Hollywood, CA 90038
213/469-4700
HOURS: MON-SAT: 10-10 SUN: 11-7
CREDIT CARDS: AE, DISC, MC, V

You'll always save 30 to 50% off new items such as cassettes and LP's. Aron's Record Shop has everything in current releases, plus a wide selection of Japanese and European imports, audiophile pressings, and small local labels. They put out at least 1,000 used records each day, at special discount prices. Blank audio and video tapes are offered at big savings. Check out the buys on video games, soundtracks and Broadway shows. Bring in your old albums for trade value towards the purchase of new merchandise.

CD BANZAI!
8250 W. 3rd St.
Los Angeles, CA 90048
213/653-0800
HOURS: MON-SAT: 10-10 SUN: 12-6
CREDIT CARDS: AE, DISC, MC, V

For everything in CD's, visit CD Banzai! New CD selections at savings of 10 to 20% include rock, jazz, classical, movie sound tracts, show tunes, reggae, collector items and world beat music. What they don't have in stock will be researched and special-ordered for you. They also carry hundreds of used CD's with good up-to-date titles. Joining their yearly membership program offers you further discounts and many other benefits. Trade-ins are accepted. They are very customer service oriented and additional discounts are given on all new CD's if you pay in cash.

DISC-CONNECTION RECORDS & COMPACT DISCS
10970 W. Pico Blvd.
W. Los Angeles, CA 90054
213/208-7211
HOURS: MON-THUR, SAT: 11-7 FRI: 11-9 SUN: 12-6
CREDIT CARDS: AE, MC, V

Eighty thousand albums in one room. Find me a sales clerk, quickly. Of course, with that many records, you'll always find what you want, especially since they specialize in hard-to-find movie soundtracks and Broadway show tunes or original cast albums. At only 6% above cost, you'll want to replace all the records where you've worn out the grooves over the years. They also carry cassettes (blank and prerecorded), CD's and records, plus tape cleaning paraphernalia, books and record collecting magazines. But that's not all, ladies and gents, they have a large stock of comedy and personality albums. Here's a switch. This store gives you money!   Bring in your unwanted LP's or cassettes, and they'll pay you cash or give you credit towards purchases.

OFF THE RECORD CD & CASSETTE
2621 Wilshire Blvd.
Santa Monica, CA 90403
213/829-7379
HOURS: 7 DAYS A WEEK: 10-10
CREDIT CARDS: AE, MC, V

Off The Record, this is the place to find great bargains on CD's and cassettes. You can find those compact disks and tapes you couldn't find elsewhere. You'll save 20 to 30% over other store's prices. They carry too many compact disks to count and over 7,000 cassettes. You can also find used compact disks at low prices. We spent a lot of time just browsing, they have an amazing inventory!

PENNY LANE
62 Windward Ave.
Venice, CA 90291
213/399-4631
HOURS: 7 DAYS A WEEK: 10-7
CREDIT CARDS: AE, MC, V

With new music groups popping up more and more every day, one truly needs to be educated in all the current sounds. Penny Lane is a place that keeps you updated in rock, heavy metal and rap. New and used records, tapes and CD's are bought and sold. Bored with some of your old sounds? Take them to Penny Lane's and trade them in for store credit. Make sure you check out their 99¢ section of tapes and records.

SECOND TIME AROUND RECORDS**

7704 Melrose Ave.
Los Angeles, CA 90046
213/852-1982
HOURS: MON-SAT: 11-9 SUN: 12-7
CREDIT CARDS: AE, MC, V

Love isn't the only thing better the second time around. Go to Second Time Around Records and you'll see what we're talking about. Shoppers will find new and used records, CD's, tapes, videos as well as used stereo equipment. Because they love a good challenge, they will hunt down and find any record you want. Elvis and Beatles lovers will find objects to add to their collections among the memorabilia and collectibles found here. Used records sell for as little as 99¢. Don't forget to bring your BUYING RETAIL IS STUPID coupon to receive an additional 5% discount. In addition to this store, they have six other stores in the Los Angeles, Orange County and San Diego areas.
Additional Locations: 6 other stores throughout S. CA

TOWER RECORDS

8801 Sunset Blvd.
Los Angeles, CA 90069
213/657-7300
HOURS: SUN-THUR: 9-MIDNIGHT FRI-SAT: 9-1AM
CREDIT CARDS: AE, MC, V

Tower has the largest selection of records in the western United States, and they have every conceivable tape and cassette you can mention. Usually, tapes and records are $1 to $3 off list price, but there are big savings on everything at Tower Records. They have a separate building on Sunset just for their classical selections and a separate building for videos. They sell cases and accessories too.

Oh, there is something else you should know. Unless an urge hits you in the wee hours of the morning, Tower Records is open 365 days a year for immediate music gratification.
Additional Locations: 10 other stores throughout S. CA

∞ MOVIES ∞

ODYSSEY VIDEO
11910 Wilshire Blvd.
Los Angeles, CA 90025
213/477-2523
HOURS: 7 DAYS A WEEK: 9-12
CREDIT CARDS: AE, DISC, MC, V

If you've felt like it's been an odyssey lately finding that special movie you've wanted to see, then look no more! The Odyssey carries over 10,000 movies from which to choose. You won't believe the prices. They have the lowest prices in town! Tuesday through Thursday their movies are only 99¢ per day. They charge only $2.50 on the other days. Musicals, westerns, children's films, and selected new releases are 99¢ everyday. It takes no Herculean effort to get there, so you can cocoon the whole weekend.

– MOVIE THEATER –

SUPER SAVER CINEMAS
12343 Seal Beach Blvd.
Seal Beach, CA 90740
213/594-9411
HOURS: CALL THEATER FOR SCHEDULE
CREDIT CARDS: CASH ONLY

Imagine, going to the movies for only $1.50. No, we aren't in a time warp. No matter what time of day it is or what first run movie is playing, that's what you pay at Super Save Cinema. So, if you are a movie buff who still enjoys the sights, sounds and smells of a real movie theater, this is the place for you. Their are seven theaters at the Seal Beach location and eight theaters at the Pomona location.
Additional Locations: Pomona (714/620-1036)

MUSICAL INSTRUMENTS

∞ MUSIC STORES ∞

ABC MUSIC CENTER
4114 W. Burbank Blvd.
Burbank, CA 91505
818/849-2793
HOURS: TUES-FRI: 10-7 SAT: 10-5
CREDIT CARDS: MC, V

In business for over 32 years, ABC Music Center takes pride in selling "Tomorrow's Instruments for Today's Musicals." All major brands are carried, and they specialize in high tech equipment such as PA systems and new electronics. Noted for their excellent service on everything they sell, many musicians won't shop any place else. If you need an item fixed or adjusted, they have in-house repair. Discounts start at about 20% and financing is available.

ACE MUSIC
1714 Wilshire Blvd.
Santa Monica, CA 90403
213/828-5688
HOURS: MON-SAT: 10-6
CREDIT CARDS: MC, V

Finally, a store that quotes discount prices over the telephone without hemming and hawing. Just tell those customers what they want to hear. That may be because this store has had continuous ownership since 1964, guaranteeing interest in the customer after the sale. They have brand name musical instruments like Fender, Gibson, Martin and Guild, and all makes and models of electric and acoustic guitars, amps, pianos, synthesizers, plus PA equipment. Service is provided on all products they sell. They offer a special in-store warranty beyond what the manufacturers offer. You can expect to save 20 to 50% off retail prices.

AMENDOLA MUSIC, INC.
1692 Centinela Ave.
Inglewood, CA 90302
213/645-2420
HOURS: MON-FRI: 11-7   SAT: 10-5:30
CREDIT CARDS: AE, MC, V

At Amendola Music, you can save up to 50% off the manufacturer's retail price on musical instruments, amplification systems, professional sound systems, recording equipment and other accessories. They carry such names as Fender, Gibson, Guild, Ovation, JBL, Yamaha, Peavey, Ibanez, Tama, Ludwig, Rogers, Zildjian, Paiste, Shure, Armstrong, Bach, Elmer, and more. They also have a complete repair center. Says Mr. Amendola, "We discount anything, anytime!" Financing is also available.

AMERICAN MUSIC
5100 Lankershim Blvd.
N. Hollywood, CA 91601
818/762-7949, 213/465-6455
HOURS: MON-WED: 11-7   THUR-FRI: 12-9   SAT: 11-4
CREDIT CARDS: AE, MC, OPT, V

They carry everything musical for the musician, from amateur to professional. You'll find a good selection of musical instruments, recording equipment, computers, software, guitars, amplifiers, electronic keyboards (synthesizers, digital home pianos, multi effect signal processors). Believe it or not, you can count on savings of 20 to 50% off retail and sometimes more. Call occasionally to ask about their next blowout pricing sale. Most major brands are available. American Music provides after sale product support and will teach you how to work any piece of equipment purchased at the store without charge. They have a full service center and can fix anything in musical electronics.

BETNUM MUSIC
403 N. Larchmont Blvd.
Los Angeles, CA 90004
213/464-7468
HOURS: MON-SAT: 10:30-6 SUN: 12-4
CREDIT CARDS: AE, MC, V

Betnum carries over 1,000 instruments, with one of the largest selections around of winds and horns. They consider themselves the number one saxophone dealer on the West Coast. In addition to band and orchestra instruments, they also have guitars, synthesizers, amps and electronic pianos, in most name brands. Savings range from 20% to 30% off retail on new instruments. Rentals are available and you can also have repair work done at Betnum Music. Since they've been in business since the early 1960's, I guess they are entitled to "toot" their own horn.

THE GUITAR STORE
496 E. Holt Ave.
Pomona, CA 91767
714/623-6448
HOURS: MON-FRI: 11-7 SAT: 11-6
CREDIT CARDS: MC, V

This discount music store, offering up to 50% off retail prices, is a dream come true for professional bands. They have 10,000 square feet stocked with a full line of guitars, amplifiers, drums, sound systems, keyboards, recording equipment, stage lighting and accessories. With their seven departments staffed by experts, you'll get straight answers to your questions. Some of the brands carried are Yamaha, Roland, JBL, Tama, Fender, Gallen Krueger and Ibanez. They handle both new and used items. Trade-ins are accepted, and they buy used equipment. Financing is available.

MUSICAL INSTRUMENTS

HOUSE OF DRUMS AND GUITARS
17046 Devonshire St.
Northridge, CA 91325
818/360-7100
HOURS: AE, DISC, MC, V
CREDIT CARDS: MON-SAT: 11-7   SUN: 12-3

The House of Drums and Guitars carries drums, guitars, PA systems, keyboards, synthesizers and recording equipment at savings of 20 to 50% off retail price. During the year they hold special clinics for musicians. One of their clinics for drummers featured "the 8 year old wunderkid," Jacob Armen, who performed and shared techniques. Major brands such as Fender and Ovation guitars, Yamaha keyboards, and Ludwig drums are always in stock. They are the Valley's largest Peavy distributor, and lessons are also available at a nominal charge.
Additional Locations: Canyon Country (805/252-5324)

SAWYERS & SAWYERS
5263 Lankershim Blvd.
N. Hollywood, CA 91604
818/761-5781
HOURS: MON-SAT: 10-6
CREDIT CARDS: CASH ONLY

At Sawyers & Sawyers you'll find a rather strange combination of sporting goods and musical instruments. Joe used to sell wholesale only to the studios, but he now sells to the public out of a 2,500 square foot store located in North Hollywood. The brand name merchandise is sold at 50% below name store sale prices. If you know the merchandise you want and have the model number, call Joe and he can order it for you. He can't accept coupons or credit cards because his discounts are so high!

SIGHTSINGER MUSIC
3203 S. Harbor Blvd.
Santa Ana, CA 92704
714/540-1441
HOURS: MON-FRI: 10-8   SAT: 10-6   SUN: 12-5

CREDIT CARDS: AE, DISC, MC, V

Looking for 20 to 50% off on the best in electronic keyboards, synthesizers, music computers, music software, guitars (acoustic and electric), amplifiers, PA systems, drums or accessories? At Sightsinger Music you'll find name brands like Roland, Yamaha, Korg, Kurzwell, Fender, Guild, Martin, Takamine, Ovation, JBL, Ricken Backer, Sunn, Marshall, Ampeg and Atari. They have one of the largest selections in musical gear along with a very service oriented and knowledgeable staff. Satisfied musicians have been getting their equipment at Sightsinger Music since 1964.
Additional Locations: Orange (714/639-3940)

UNITED BAND INSTRUMENT CO.
3370 Verdugo Rd.
Los Angeles, CA 90065
213/257-7514
HOURS: TUES-SAT: 10-5
CREDIT CARDS: CASH OR CHECKS ONLY

Musicians and future musicians will find used brass and woodwind instruments here. They sell and repair, so you can be sure to get a good buy. They have been in business since 1954 and know their stuff! You'll find 20 to 30% savings here on their used equipment. They do carry some new instruments, but the best buys are on the used ones. We can definitely say that good deals are blowing in the wind, or brass, or woodwind.

WEST L.A. MUSIC
11345 Santa Monica Blvd.
Los Angeles, CA 90025
213/477-1945, 818/905-7020
HOURS: MON-FRI: 11-7 SAT: 10-6
CREDIT CARDS: AE, MC, V

This is THE music store where you can find everything in professional audio equipment, everything in musical instruments, and everyone who is anyone in the music or recording industry. The recording stars aren't on Hollywood Boulevard or Sunset. They're at West L.A. Music, buying the equipment they need for their studios, their band members, their tours. West L.A. Music will beat any deal you can get anywhere else, and they have guitars, drums, speakers, microphones and stands, keyboards, synthesizers, computers and music software, recording equipment and all accessories. They are usually the first in town to get the newest items, and they have frequent special sales, so check them out often if music is your beat. You'll find helpful,and knowledgeable sales people to assist you in every department.

WOODLOWE MUSIC CENTER
21410 Ventura Blvd.
Woodland Hills, CA 91364
818/883-0050
HOURS: MON-FRI: 10-5:30 SAT: 10-3:30
CREDIT CARDS: MC, V

Woodlowe Music Center offers a terrific range of merchandise and service, at 20 to 40% off retail prices. In addition to selling quality instruments such as guitars, drums, clarinets, flutes, violins, trumpets and any other type of musical instrument, they have one of the finest teaching staffs in the San Fernando Valley. Amplifiers, sheet music and books are also available. They have provided fantastic service since 1965 along with instruments, lessons and repairs.

∞ PIANOS, ORGANS & KEYBOARDS ∞

ABEL'S DISCOUNT PIANO OUTLET
5456 Centinela Ave.
Mar Vista, CA 90066
213/827-7837
HOURS: BY APPOINTMENT ONLY, MON-SUN: 11-5
CREDIT CARDS: CASH OR CHECKS ONLY

James Abel, owner of Abel's Discount Piano Outlet, offers you Steinway at cost to 25% above cost. They carry everything from spinets to grands. So if you're ready to accompany Itzhak Perlman, or if your goal is just to get through your exercises without missing a note, they've got you covered. There are always 15 grand pianos, and up to 20 vertical pianos on hand at any given time. The assortment available ranges from beginner practice pianos to concert grands. Other brand names carried are Baldwin, Yamaha, Kawai and Hanil. They also have electronic keyboards and synthesizers. Financing and credit are available. As part of his excellent customer service, Mr. Abel offers free delivery and tuning. Buy one of their used pianos or wait for one of their special sales offered three to four times a year. Remember to call for an appointment.

HOLLYWOOD PIANO RENTAL CO.
1647 N. Highland Ave.
Hollywood, CA 90028
213/462-2329
HOURS: MON-FRI: 9-5:30 SAT: 9-4
CREDIT CARDS: MC, V

Family owned since 1928, Hollywood Piano Rental offers savings of 10 to 20% on all types of pianos and organs for home or professional needs. They have about 2,000 pianos for rent which makes them one of the largest private collectors of pianos in the world. They also sell both new and used pianos in all styles. In-house financing is available for your purchases.
Additional Locations: Burbank (818/848-0222)

KEYBOARD EXCHANGE
30613 Canwood St.
Agoura, CA 91301
818/889-9780
HOURS: MON-SAT: 10-6 SUN: 12-5
CREDIT CARDS: AE, DISC, MC, V

For the past 10 years Keyboard Exchange has been serving the community with exclusive, factory-direct pianos and electronic keyboards made by Baldwin, Kawai, Young Chang. Whether you are in search of a grand piano or a spinet, you'll find that their prices average 25 to 50% off the retail prices charged in most stores. Lessons, repair work and financing are also available.

KEYBOARD LIQUIDATORS
6600 Telegraph Rd.
Commerce, CA 90018
213/724-2828
HOURS: MON-SAT: 10-6
CREDIT CARDS: MC, V

Pianos and organs are the only game in town here, and you'll save 30 to 50% on high quality instruments at wholesale prices. There are spinets and there are grands. If they don't have it, they'll order it for you. Pianos start at $200 and organs at about $400. You know you've got plenty to choose from with styles that include pianos that would retail for as much as $20,000. They carry brands such as Baldwin, Yamaha, Kawai, Hammond, Samick, Kimball, Story & Clark and have been in business since 1915. They also handle churches and recording studios. Their work is primarily by appointment, and 75% of all their business comes from word-of-mouth because they specialize in satisfied customers. You can save even more on their used pianos and organs, and also at their special sales held twice a year.

THE LITTLE PIANO SHOP
16145 Roscoe Blvd.
Sepulveda, CA 91343
818/891-4389
HOURS: MON: 10-8 TUES-FRI: 10-6 SAT-SUN: 2-5
CREDIT CARDS: AE, DISC, MC, V

You will definitely feel Boris Bernards' love for the piano as you walk into his store, The Little Piano Shop. He has been selling new and used pianos since 1961. One of the latest inventions featured in his shop is the new Yamaha Disklavier. A what? It's an acoustic piano that not only plays prerecorded discs, it can also record and playback. They are a factory authorized dealer for Yamaha and other fine brands. And yes, Mr. Bernards will even give BUYING RETAIL IS STUPID readers a gift, valued at $30 to $60, when a new piano is purchased.
Additional Locations: Lancaster (805/945-0969)

OFFICE & BUSINESS NEEDS

∞ ONE-STOP SUPPLIERS ∞

A 'N B STATIONERY
12408 Ventura Blvd.
Studio City, CA 91604
818/760-0244
HOURS: MON-FRI: 9-5:30 SAT: 10-5
CREDIT CARDS: AE, MC, V

This is a small, personal store but their stock and service are large. They carry a complete line of office supplies, office furniture, rubber stamps, accounting and computer supplies, and even greeting cards. You will discover all major brands and all at a 20 to 50% savings. Call to find out about A 'N B Stationery's quarterly sales for even bigger discounts.

BUDGET OFFICE PRODUCTS
19553 Parthenia St.
Northridge, CA 91324
818/993-3211 or 213/873-4545
HOURS: MON-FRI: 9-5:30 SAT: 10-4
CREDIT CARDS: MC, V

This company has a friendly, knowledgeable staff headed by Barbara Bakley, and they offer immediate free delivery of office supplies, furniture, equipment and printing. Everything at Budget Office Products is discounted from 10 to 80% and they guarantee meeting or beating the competition with ad proof within 30 days of purchase. You may place your order by phone and Ms. Bakley invites commercial charge accounts.

COMMERCIAL OFFICE PRODUCTS & PRINTING CO.
610 S. Berendo
Los Angeles, CA 90005
213/386-5144
HOURS: 7 DAYS A WEEK: 8-6
CREDIT CARDS: MC, V

Save 20% or more off retail prices on all your office supplies at
Commercial Office Products & Printing Company. One stop here
and you'll find everything you need including business machines,
business forms, computer supplies, xeroxing and instant offset
printing.

DISCOUNT DESK CENTER
21035 Sherman Way
Canoga Park, CA 91303
818/883-2112, 800/227-8571
HOURS: MC, V
CREDIT CARDS: MON-FRI: 9-6 SAT: 10-5

At Discount Desk Center you can save 40% off list price on most
items, and they have a full catalogue of desks, chairs, credenzas,
sofas for the lobby, bookshelves, storage and filing cabinets, stationery, and a lot more. Each year, they purchase millions of dollars
worth of desks, so they get great savings which they can afford to
pass on to you. You can get in-stock items immediately; others will
take just three days or so. Their warehouse is on the premises and
there is 10,000 square feet of showroom space. Ask to be put on
their mailing list.

HQ OFFICE SUPPLIES WAREHOUSE
10822 Jefferson Blvd.
Culver City, CA 90230
213/202-6493
HOURS: MON-FRI: 7-9 SAT: 8-6 SUN: 10-6
CREDIT CARDS: AE, MC, V

HQ Office Supplies Warehouse is your one-stop office supply center with over 8,000 items at guaranteed lowest prices! You won't believe your eyes when you see the incredible variety and selection of merchandise. This isn't merely an office supply store, HQ can outfit an entire office building or your child's school supplies. You can look forward to saving up to 70% off list prices on everything from furniture to fax machines. This huge warehouse of merchandise is well stocked and organized. To save time, just about everything is efficiently displayed for self service. Their sales staff is very helpful and will happily offer any assistance you may need. So, if you're looking for computer paper, supplies, blackboards, file cabinets, briefcases, office machines, telephones, furniture, or even pens and pencils, head on over to HQ Office Supplies Warehouse.

Additional Locations: 10 other stores throughout S. CA

MEYER'S OFFICE PRODUCTS
1534 S. Figueroa St.
Los Angeles, CA 90015
213/749-7138
HOURS: MON-FRI: 8:30-5 SAT: 11-3
CREDIT CARDS: AE, MC, V

Meyer's Office Products has been serving the Southern California business community for over 38 years with discount prices and quality personalized service. Their store is located just south of the Los Angeles Convention Center. On display are many styles of desks, chairs, files, computer furniture, data supplies, and general office supplies. Over 15,000 items are available in one day from their catalogs. Everything you need is discounted 10–50% below retail. Ken Meyer and his staff specialize in personal service and offer expert product knowledge.

MODERN SERVICE OFFICE SUPPLY CO., INC.
1345 East 16th St.
Los Angeles, CA 90021
213/748-4171, 800/672-6767
HOURS: MON-FRI: 8-5
CREDIT CARDS: MC, V

This store offers you business necessities such as fax machines, copier supplies, typewriter ribbons, micro computer supplies, calculators, office furniture, writing instruments, word and data processing supplies, and computer furniture. You can save 20 to 50% off retail prices when you shop here. Modern Service Office Supply Company offers free delivery in California, Arizona, and Nevada with a minimum order.

THE OFFICE CLUB
15385 Oxnard St.
Van Nuys, CA 91411
818/988-2582
HOURS: MON-FRI: 8-7 SAT: 9-5
CREDIT CARDS: CASH OR CHECKS ONLY

The Office Club is a membership warehouse that costs $10 a year, and you don't have to sacrifice service for savings. Their knowledgeable and helpful sales staff will assist you or answer any questions you may have about office supplies, equipment or furniture at this one-stop shop. They offer wholesale prices everyday on thousands of best selling, top-quality, brand name office products in their huge, no frills warehouse stores. Delivery is available, and you can place your order by telephone with your Office Club Credit Card. You will find Office Clubs in Los Angeles, Orange and San Diego Counties.
Additional Locations: 9 other stores throughout S. CA

OFFICE SUPPLY CO.
6141 Kester Ave.
Van Nuys, CA 91411
818/786-1660
HOURS: MON-FRI: 8:30-5:30
CREDIT CARDS: MC, V

The Office Supply Company has been doing business for over 35 years. Their inventory is so vast you have to see it to believe it. You can save a lot of money if you are furnishing a new office or restocking your present one. Save up to 50% on office furniture and at least 10% or more on office supplies. With all those years of experience, you know you'll get professional help here.

ROYAL OFFICE SUPPLIES
600 N. La Brea Ave.
Los Angeles, CA 90036
213/930-1770
HOURS: MON-FRI: 8-5
CREDIT CARDS: MC, V

Royal Office Supplies carries a full line of business necessities including furniture, calculators, clocks, and more. You'll find their prices range from 10 to 40% off retail. Check out their bargain table with monthly specials where you can save 50% or more off retail. There's limited free parking, but don't let that deter you from checking out the savings you can get here.

SAVE MORE ON OFFICE SUPPLIES
18021 Ventura Blvd.
Encino, CA 91316
818/996-7870
HOURS: MON-FRI: 8:30-6:00 SAT: 9-5
CREDIT CARDS: AE, MC, V

This store has everything in office supplies, and more, and you can save 20 to 50%. Look through their office supplies, then check out their business machines, art and engineering supplies, furniture, gift items, and card and party shop. This 18,000 square foot facility has all the leading brands. They have a telephone order desk and delivery service. Also, ask about charge accounts and extra discounts on quantity orders.

∞ BUSINESS MACHINES ∞

ABM ART TYPE BUSINESS MACHINES
12216 Victory Blvd.
N. Hollywood, CA 91606
818/980-3010
HOURS: MON-FRI: 9-6 SAT: 9-3
CREDIT CARDS: MC, V

It takes longer to say their name than it does to get a good deal on all types of office equipment. ABM has copiers, fax machines, typewriters, word processing calculators and supplies. Andrew Katz guarantees the lowest prices around, and they handle most name brands such as IBM, T/A Adler-Royal, Sharp, Brother, and Panasonic. ABM has friendly knowledgeable service.
Additional Locations: Granada Hills: 818/893-8066

CITY TYPEWRITER OF WESTWOOD
10867 W. Pico Blvd.
W. Los Angeles, CA 90064
213/478-7282
HOURS: MON-FRI: 8:30-5:30 SAT: 9-5
CREDIT CARDS: MC, V

Do you have a problem trying to work your new answering machine, word processor, typewriter, Fax machine or calculator? Then make your next investment at City Typewriter of Westwood where you'll find such brand names as Smith Corona, Sanyo, Sony, Norelco and Brother. Their prices are very low, and they will give you lessons on how to operate every machine you purchase. They will make sure you know exactly how your new machine works. These days, even typewriters and calculators have so many different options you need some instructions other than those printed in the manual. City Typewriter does repairs on the premises and is an authorized center for Smith Corona.

COMMERCIAL TYPEWRITER CO.
641A S. Spring St.
Los Angeles, CA 90014
213/622-1323
HOURS: MON-FRI: 8:30-5
CREDIT CARDS: DISC, MC, V

If you are a person that prefers dealing with experience, Commercial Typewriter has been serving Los Angeles since 1911. Today they offer typewriters at savings of 40% below retail prices. Choose from IBM, Olympia, Olivetti, SCM, and others. You know you'll get a good deal, as Commercial Typewriter also offers big savings on calculators, computers, and copiers. They also have maintenance agreements, and they have an excellent service department.

COPIERLAND**
821 E. Broadway
Glendale, CA 91206
818/956-5988
HOURS: MON-FRI: 7-6
CREDIT CARDS: ALL MAJOR CREDIT CARDS

For the last 11 years Copierland has been selling their office equipment and furniture all over the country. They have over 1,000 pieces of equipment in their open warehouse, and they say they can beat any price in Southern California with their "lowest price guarantee." Some brand names in stock are Sharp, Ricoh, Panasonic, Murata, Mita, Cannon, Iwatsu, and Sony. They sell at 10% above cost, but you can save that 10% when you use your BUYING RETAIL IS STUPID coupon.

Additional Locations: 11 other stores in S. CA

DISCOUNT OFFICE MACHINES
11351 Santa Monica Blvd.
Los Angeles, CA 90025
213/477-6091
HOURS: MON-FRI: 9:30-6 SAT: 10-5
CREDIT CARDS: MC, V

You can save up to 50% on typewriters, answering machines, cash registers, dictating machines, calculators, copy machines, and more. Discount Office Machines carries Canon, IBM, Sanyo, Olympia, Sharp, Texas Instruments, and provide in-house service.

∞ USED FURNITURE & EQUIPMENT ∞

AMERICAN SURPLUS TRADERS**
18643 Parthenia St.
Northridge, CA 91324
818/993-5355
HOURS: MON-FRI: 8:30-5:30 SAT: 10:30-3:30
CREDIT CARDS: MC, V

They specialize in Holga office furniture and have 6,000 square feet of desks, secretarial chairs, executive chairs, file cabinets, lateral files, storage cabinets, shelf files, bookcases, and computer furniture. You'll find new furniture, which are factory seconds, used furniture, and industrial shelving. You can anticipate saving 15 to 60% off retail, but if you use your BUYING RETAIL IS STUPID coupon, you'll save an additional 10%!

FRANCO SURPLUS
8652 Amigo Ave.
Northridge, CA 91324
818/349-7631
HOURS: MON-FRI: 9-5:30
CREDIT CARDS: MC, V

Save about 20% on a kaleidoscope of things in Rich Franco's place and even more on used office furniture. They have file cabinets, desks, computer furniture, floor mats for shops, chairs, safes, clocks, tables, folding tables, fans and more. You should definitely check them out for file cabinets since they say they have the largest selection in the San Fernando Valley. Delivery is extra .

KAGAN SURPLUS SALES**
8050 Webb Ave.
N. Hollywood, CA 91605
818/768-1422
HOURS: MON-THUR: 8:45-5:45 FRI: 8:30-5:15 SAT: 10-4:30
CREDIT CARDS: CASH OR CHECKS ONLY

Kagan Surplus Sales specializes in used office furniture, hospital furniture, home care items, and material handling equipment. This 4,000 square foot warehouse offers items that have been completely refurbished (repaired, painted and recovered if necessary). Savings range from 50 to 90% off what you would pay normally if these items were brand new. The price is the only way you can tell their wheelchairs (always a large selection) and Geri-chairs are used. In addition, Kagan Surplus Sales carries desks, credenzas, chairs, file cabinets, shelving, casters, carts, lockers, storage cabinets, medical, lab and x-ray equipment. Don't forget to use your BUYING RETAIL IS STUPID coupon for additional savings. You'll save 5% if your purchase is under $100, and 10% if your purchase is over $100.

∞ SERVICES ∞

– PRINTING –

BUDGET PRINTING
6019 Sunset Blvd.
Hollywood, CA 90028
213/467-6048
HOURS: MON-FRI: 9-5
CREDIT CARDS: CASH OR CHECKS ONLY

In a bind because you needed something yesterday? Here's the place to get money saving prices and rush services on all types of printing and typesetting. Budget Printing also has one day service on business cards and will handle all your photocopying needs. So stay within your budget, Budget Printing that is!

WHOLESALE PRINTING FACTORY 1**
17523 Ventura Blvd.
Encino, CA 91436
818/789-1055
HOURS: MON-FRI: 8:30-6   SAT: 10-5
CREDIT CARDS: CASH OR CHECKS ONLY

The Wholesale Printing Factory will handle all of your printing and copying needs. They offer one day service on most items, and you will save 20% off the prices most other printers charge. They also have a 20% off membership club that is worth looking into if you have a lot of printing done. A fax service is available for that document that just has to get there fast! Not only do you save on printing, you will save an additional 5% when you present your BUYING RETAIL IS STUPID coupon.

– SECRETARIAL –

AUTOMATED OFFICE SERVICES
10616 Bothwell Rd.
Chatsworth, CA 91311
818/368-4261
HOURS: MON-SAT: 8-5
CREDIT CARDS: CASH OR CHECKS ONLY

Automated Office Services offers complete secretarial services mandatory in today's business world. They can provide you with business letters, mailings, financial reports, resumes, and form letters at very competitive prices. One day service is available and they have the capability of "desk top publishing". In business since 1981, they are customer oriented and easy to deal with. If you need a secretary, but really don't want to hire one, then Automated Office Services may be the answer for you!

OPTICAL SERVICES

DR. M. FRIEDMAN AND ASSOCIATES**
10724 Washington Blvd.
Culver City, CA 90230
213/870-2848
HOURS: TUES, THUR-SAT: 9:30-6 WED: 9:30-7
CREDIT CARDS: AE, DISC, MC, V

Computerized eye exams. Hmmm, that sounds interesting. Well, there are also three doctors and ten assistants to give you traditional eye exams. Contact lenses are available plus glasses with consumer discount frames or designer, high-fashion frames. Services are 30% less than other offices, and they have a laboratory on the premises. Presenting your BUYING RETAIL IS STUPID coupon to Dr. Friedman will get you a general eye exam for just $19.00.

DR. THOMAS KUTROSKY**
5308 Lankershim Blvd.
N. Hollywood, CA 91601
818/769-2020
HOURS: MON-SAT: 9-6
CREDIT CARDS: AE, MC, V

You can get lenses, frames, and contacts from Dr. Tom at discount prices. While his storefront is not as large as some, his discounts are bigger than most. You'll save 25% and receive personalized service at the same time at Dr. Tom's office. Your BUYING RETAIL IS STUPID coupon will give you additional 5% discount, so don't leave it at home.

OPTICAL SERVICES

FOR EYES OPTICAL OF CALIFORNIA, INC.
18724 Ventura Blvd.
Tarzana, CA 91356
818/705-4020
HOURS: MON-WED, FRI: 10-6 THUR: 10-8 SAT: 10-5
CREDIT CARDS: CASH OR CHECKS ONLY

This full-service optical company sells prescription, sun, sport and other eyewear in its own stores coast-to-coast. It was started in the early 1970's by two opticians who decided to save the public money. As a result, you can now visit any For Eyes and save 25 to 50% on all prescription and nonprescription glasses. Each pair is custom made but the stores maintain a "one price" policy of $39 for regular line frames and lenses. High-fashion frames and lenses start at $49. There are no added charges for plastic lenses, tinted lenses or oversized lenses. You can select such designer names as Anne Klein, Pierre Cardin, Oscar de la Renta and Gloria Vanderbilt. We have good news for moms and dads. A guarantee is provided for one year against breakage on children's glasses!
Additional Locations: 6 other stores throughout S. CA

FRAME-N-LENS
7914 Sunset Blvd.
Los Angeles, CA 90046
213/851-2068
HOURS: MON-SAT: 10-7
CREDIT CARDS: MC, V

You should know about these convenient, price worthy stores if you're in the market for eyeglasses. Frame-N-Lens will make you two pair of single vision glasses for $63 and two pair of bifocals for $81. With over 400 frames to choose from, there are styles sure to please everyone. Designer frames are also available at additional cost. And, they do eyeglass repairs, too.
Additional Locations: Over 100 stores–Call 800-GLASSES

PARTIES & CELEBRATIONS

∞ COSTUMES ∞

AARDVARK'S ODD ARK
7579 Melrose Ave.
Los Angeles, CA 90046
213/655-6759
HOURS: MON-SAT: 11-9 SUN: 11-7
CREDIT CARDS: MC, V

When you want to find the "unique in antique" or used clothing, go to Aardvark's Odd Ark. This place is an adventure! You can find discarded treasures for a couple of dollars or spend a lot more on a rare antique item. When in need of certain styles of clothing for their plays, some theater groups head straight for Aardvark's. It's a great place to browse away the hours, the sales folks will be glad to help you find a special item if you'd like.
Additional Locations: Canoga Park (818/999-3211), Venice (213/392-2996)

CREATIVE WOMAN
1530 S. Myrtle Ave.
Monrovia, CA 91016
818/358-6216
HOURS: TUES-SAT: 10-6
CREDIT CARDS: DISC, MC, V

Located off the Myrtle Avenue exit from the 210 Freeway, this wholesale and discount store is run by the very personable Ed and Bonnie Kaufman. They carry lingerie, intimate apparel in all sizes, garter belts, stockings, corsets, and feathers. Feathers? They even have a department to live out your fantasies with their sexy costumes. Corsets range in sizes 32A–46DD and backless strapless bras come in sizes 32A–48DD. They also have custom fitted bras in sizes 26BB–52HH. Now that's a selection!! Alterations are done on the premises.

DRESS UP
2043 Westcliff Dr., #102
Newport Beach, CA 92660
714/631-8290
HOURS: MON-FRI: 10-6 SAT: 10-5
CREDIT CARDS: MC, V

Dress Up is well established (since 1981) and well known in Newport Beach. They take in only better merchandise and do many buy-outs from other shops (brand new goods at greatly discounted prices). They have a large costume and vintage department. The last Saturday of every month they have an 80% off sale on selected merchandise. They also carry fine jewelry.

GRUBB & GRUBB'S GENERAL STORE
18523 Sherman Way
Reseda, CA 91335
818/996-7030
HOURS: MON-SAT: 9:30-5:30
CREDIT CARDS: AE, MC, V

This is a one-stop shop for vintage clothing and antiques. Grubb & Grubb's General Store has an extensive line of clothing for men and women, costume jewelry, shoes, purses and hats. After you've put together the perfect outfit, take a look at what they have to offer in antique furniture, kitchenware, and art.

LOS ANGELES UNIFORM EXCHANGE
5239 Melrose Ave.
Los Angeles, CA 90038
213/469-3965
HOURS: MON-FRI: 9-5 SAT: 9-6
CREDIT CARDS: MC, V

Need an emergency costume for a party? Los Angeles Uniform Exchange might be the answer. A lot of foreign items can be found here: Army uniforms, British drill pants, British, American, and French army shorts. They carry a wide variety of military items, including Army field jackets and Navy pea coats. You can also buy flight suits, coveralls, jackets, military insignia patches and accessories. A tailor shop is on the premises. Parking is available, and they insist their prices are the cheapest in town!

PARTY CORNER DISCOUNT CENTER**
11422 Laurel Canyon Blvd.
Mission Hills, CA 91345
818/365-6909
HOURS: MON-SAT: 10-6 SUN: 11-4
CREDIT CARDS: MC, V

Can't think of anything to wear as a costume for that come-as-you-are party? You'll find it at Party Corner Discount Center and much much more. They rent and sell costumes, along accessories, wigs, masks, and pinatas. Party planning is a cinch with their large selection of party supplies which includes decorations, wedding invitations, crepe paper, garlands, decorations for autos, balloons and wrapping paper. They will blow your balloons up for you or you can rent a helium tank and blow them up yourself. Expect to find discounts in the neighborhood of 10 to 20% off retail prices, and wedding invitations are 25% off retail. When you use your BUYING RETAIL IS STUPID coupon you'll save 10% more on your purchase. They have an inventory of over 1,000 costumes at Party Corner, so you can definitely appear at your party in style!

VAN NUYS ARMY & NAVY STORE
6179 Van Nuys Blvd.
Van Nuys, CA 91401
818/781-3500
HOURS: MON-SAT: 8:30-9 SUN: 9-6
CREDIT CARDS: MC, V

You will find this to be one of the best stocked surplus stores in the area. Filled with items for both men and women, it shouldn't be too difficult to come up with a costume. You can find Schott leather jackets, MA-1 and M65 field jackets in both nylon and leather. Their complete military department stocks camouflage from at least six different companies. In business since 1950, Carol and Joe head the Van Nuys store and Dave oversees the one in Reseda. Both stores will meet or beat their competitors' prices. Check out their Air Force sunglasses and Halloween costumes too.
Additional Locations: Reseda (818/344-0237)

∞ FLOWERS & BALLOONS ∞

BALLOON FACTORY
8600 W. Third St.
Los Angeles, CA   90048
213/225-5666, 800/BALLOON
HOURS: MON-SAT: 8-6 SUN: 10-2
CREDIT CARDS: AE, MC, V

What a great way to liven up that special occasion with balloons! These folks aren't filled with hot air either. They describe themselves as "LA's most innovative and affordable balloonists." With brilliant balloon bouquets, in over 50 selections for all occasions, arches, centerpieces, sculptures and more, this place can really add a "lift" to your next party. They also have unique gifts, stuffed toys, popcorn, champagne, fun candies and cards. If you are a do-it-yourselfer you can rent a tank and fill your own balloons. In the surrounding Los Angeles area, the Balloon Factory will come to your party and decorate. For savings of 20 to 30% off retail, call 213-BALLOON or 1-800-BALLOON.
Additional Locations: Studio City (818/509-9910)

KIM-E'S FLOWERS**
818/885-6957
HOURS: BY APPOINTMENT ONLY
CREDIT CARDS: CASH OR CHECKS ONLY

With 15 years experience in the floral industry, Michael and Kim Holtzer will definitely put the cherry on the top of your next affair with exceptional floral arrangements at discounted prices. They will personally come to your home or office and work with you in the selection of perfect floral designs for weddings, banquets or parties. You'll have one less headache when the big day arrives because the Holtzers will make certain the arrangements are displayed to your satisfaction. Their specialties include preparing floral arrangements for weddings from bridal bouquet, table centerpieces, and ceremony arrangements, to stands along the aisle. Their prices average about 50% off retail. And don't forget, you can use your BUYING RETAIL IS STUPID coupon and receive even greater savings of 10%.

SHE'S FLOWERS
712 S. Olive St.
Los Angeles, CA 90014
213/689-1372
HOURS: MON-SAT: 7:30-6
CREDIT CARDS: AE, MC, V

Save up to 50% on flowers and plants for all occasions. She's Flowers grows many of their own flowers and imports others directly; then She's Flowers wholesales them to the public. You can also buy silk flowers, dried flowers, trees, baskets, even balloons for weddings, birthdays, holidays. They will deliver, and you can charge your purchase by phone. They have been in business since 1980, and they are very helpful.

∞ PARTY COORDINATING SERVICE ∞

THE WRITE PLACE
213/839-1340, 213/839-6794
HOURS: BY APPOINTMENT ONLY
CREDIT CARDS: CASH OR CHECKS ONLY

Too busy to plan your party? The Write Place will do it all—from addressing your invitations to finding the right caterers, bands, photographers, even writing your "thank you" notes at savings of 10 to 20%. Calligraphy is their specialty.

∞ PARTY & PAPER SUPPLIES ∞

ALIN PAPER COMPANY
4929 Woodruff Ave.
Lakewood, CA 90713
213/925-5501
HOURS: MON-FRI: 9-9 SAT: 9-6 SUN: 11-5
CREDIT CARDS: MC, V

This store is the greatest! Whatever you need for your next celebration can be found at Alin Paper Company at only 10–40% above their cost. They carry a complete line of supplies for banquets, parties, weddings, and receptions, including invitations (regular,

religious, photograph holders, Spanish, Mormon, Jewish). You'll find Christmas cards and supplies for all specialty parties including 25th, 40th, and 50th wedding anniversaries, showers, luaus, Bar Mitzvahs, Quince Anos, and more. Have a wedding coming up in the future? Select your invitations from more than 20 sample books, all of which are available at full priced competitors, and save up to 30% on your order. They have an unbelievable selection of wrapping paper at wholesale prices in jumbo rolls along an entire wall. Buy as much or as little as you need. Business owners may want to stop by and choose from many full rolls available.
Additional Locations: Downey (213/862-1661), Riverside (714/354-9680)

INDIVIDUAL PAPER PRODUCTS
5333 Downy Rd.
Vernon, CA 90058
213/583-4121
HOURS: MON-FRI: 7-5
CREDIT CARDS: CASH OR CHECKS ONLY

This store is family owned and has been in business since 1926. This is a no frills warehouse where you can save big bucks on paper, plastic and aluminum products. They also carry cleaning supplies. If you don't care what is imprinted on the paper plates, napkins and cups, you will save even more than the usual 25 to 50% off retail because they buy the overruns from manufacturers. Get on their mailing list so you'll be in on their special sales.

PARTY KING
6038 Reseda Blvd.
Tarzana, CA 91356
818/343-3343
HOURS: MON-FRI: 6-6:30 SAT: 9-5:30 SUN: 11-5
CREDIT CARDS: MC, V

This 4,000 square foot store has a huge selection of party supplies for every occasion and theme. They have over 150 designer patterns and fashion colors including an incredible selection of juvenile ensembles, decorations and favors. Party King offers 25% off retail prices on wedding invitations, Bar Mitzvah invitations, and 20% off all greeting cards. During their recent renovation, Party King opened "Stamp Castle," a-store-within-a-store, featuring novelty rubber stamps, pads, paper and other accessories. They've been in business since 1979 and can offer you expert advice.

PARTY WORLD
19450 Business Center Dr.
Northridge, CA 91324
818/993-3033
HOURS: MON-SAT: 9:30-5:30
CREDIT CARDS: MC, V

There are 10 Party World stores in Southern California. Each store is a one-stop center for all your party needs. Save 10 to 70% on everything from invitations, to helium tanks and balloons. If you're going to have a party for your child, they have over 27 patterns available. To give your next bash a personal touch, make sure to inquire about their custom imprinting service. Whether you are having a party for 2 or 2,000, Party World has it all.
Additional Locations: 9 other stores throughout S. CA

SAVE MORE ON OFFICE SUPPLIES
18021 Ventura Blvd.
Encino, CA 91316
818/996-7870
HOURS: MON-FRI: 8:30-6:00   SAT: 9-5
CREDIT CARDS: AE, MC, V

This store has everything in office supplies, and more, and you can save 20 to 50%. Look through their office supplies, then check out their gift items, and card and party shop. Ask about charge accounts and extra discounts on quantity orders.

STAT'S
120 S. Raymond Ave.
Pasadena, CA 91101
818/795-9308
HOURS: MON-SAT: 9-9   SUN: 10-6
CREDIT CARDS: MC, V

At Stat's you will find decorator, arts and crafts, and floral supplies, plus everything for seasonal decorating at prices 20 to 30% below

retail. It doesn't matter if you are having a wedding, shower, birthday party, you name it, decorations for any celebration can be found at Stat's. December 26th you can save an additional 50% off already low prices on their seasonal merchandise, and in June they have a huge parking lot sale where everything is marked as low as 90% off retail! All of their stores are very large, ranging from 20,000 to 40,000 square feet.
Additional Locations: Capistrano Beach (714/493-3752), Downey (213/772-2458), Redondo Beach (213/772-2458), Whittier (213/449-1691)

WILBURN'S DISCOUNT PARTY CENTER
8730 Santa Fe
South Gate, CA 90280
213/569-7169
HOURS: TUES-FRI: 9-5:30 SAT: 9-5
CREDIT CARDS: MC, V

Discounts of 10 to 25% on paper and plastic items, and 30% below retail on printed invitations are the tail end of the story at Wilburn's, where they can service any kind of party from 8 to 800 from start (printed invitation) to finish (plastic garbage bags). They can usually fill your order from available stock. Brand names include: Paper Art, Beach, American, Reed, Dixie, Amscan and Van Brode. A complete and varied assortment of favors and decorations includes such hard-to-get items as pinatas, and glass wedding cake decorations. Among their unique birthday ensembles for children you will find a complete line of Mickey Mouse and Batman goodies. You can also get punch concentrate and snow-cone base available in 13 flavors for children's parties. Table coverings come in all colors of the rainbow and are available in all shapes and sizes.
Additional Locations: Whittier (213/944-8044)

PET STORES & ANIMAL SUPPLIES

ALLAN'S AQUARIUM AND PET SHOP
845 Lincoln Blvd.
Venice, CA 90291
213/399-5464
HOURS: MON-FRI: 11-8 SAT-SUN: 11-6
CREDIT CARDS: AE, DISC, MC, V

Allan's Aquarium and Pet Shop has two complete floors of merchandise filled with plexi and glass aquariums, goldfish, tropical fish, salt water fish, live crickets, tarantulas, chameleons, birds of all kinds, guinea pigs, chicks and ducks. Rodents are bought and sold. They also carry dog and cat foods (Kal Kan, Nutro, Iams, Science Diet, Wayne, Breeders Choice), animal traps, cages, dog houses, and cat scratching posts. Your pets will love their toys, too. They also stock aquarium plants.

B & A HAY CO.
7360 Sumner Ave.
Corona, CA 91720
714/272-9050
HOURS: MON-FRI: 6-2
CREDIT CARDS: CASH OR CHECKS ONLY

Selling their products wholesale, this place is for the rancher or horse breeder that buys hay by the trailer load, B & A's minimum order. A trailer load weighs approximately 12–13 tons! They sell varieties of hay/alfalfa and oat hay in various grades. Expect to save $1–2 per bail depending on the variety and grade. Remember, they deal by the trailer load only, so get together with your neighbors to get in on this great deal. Make hay while the sun shines!

BIRDS PLUS
13653 Victory Blvd.
Van Nuys, CA 91401
818/901-1187
HOURS: MON-FRI: 10-7   SAT-SUN: 10-6
CREDIT CARDS: MC, V

Birds Plus specializes in exotic birds, cages and supplies at savings
of 20 to 40% off the prices charged in retail pet stores. They carry
all your favorite name brand pet products. Whether you're feeding a
parakeet or a pelican, they can help you with any of your bird needs
or problems. They offer boarding and consulting on breeding, and
groom for free. Call to find out about their special sales held during
the year.

BRACKEN BIRD FARM
10797 New Jersey St.
Redlands, CA 92373
714/792-5735
HOURS: WED-SUN: 9-5
CREDIT CARDS: MC, V
 (CHECKS ACCEPTED ONLY FOR $100 OR LESS ON WEEKENDS.)

For all of you bird lovers out there, we have found a place where
many pet store owners buy their stock. The Bracken Bird Farm is
an acre filled with hundreds of birds from which to choose. You'll
find macaws, cockatoos, finches, and parakeets. Love birds run
$25 to $70 ($45 to $200 in pet stores), cockatiels are $30 to $50
($48 to $100), and gray cheek parrots are $135 ($249). They have
hand fed baby parrots, and they even have toucans! If you are
looking for a bird for one of your children, it would be well worth
the drive. The beautiful grounds in this pastoral setting feature a
walk-thru aviary, a Texas long horn steer, turtles, and a duck pond.
Also residing in the pond is the Bracken Bird Farm mascot, a yellow
albino frog. While the frog is not for sale, you can save 25 to 50%
below retail on your bird selection.

THE BUZZARD HOUSE
11052 Limonite Ave.
Mira Loma, CA 91752
714/736-0197
HOURS: MON-FRI: 10-7:30   SAT: 10-6   SUN: 10-5
CREDIT CARDS: MC, V

Don't you love the name of this place? Open 7 days a week, The
Buzzard House has a complete selection of pet supplies at discount
prices; you can save 10–25% off the retail prices of other pet stores.
They buy in large quantities and pass on the savings. If you're in
need of dog food, bird food, bird supplies or nonprescription
medicinal items, this is the place to go. You'll also appreciate the
devoted animal lovers working at The Buzzard House.

DISCOUNT TROPICAL FISH
561 W. La Habra
La Habra, CA 90631
213/691-2037
HOURS: MON-FRI: 10-9   SAT-SUN: 10-8
CREDIT CARDS: DISC, MC, V

If it's fresh water or salt water fish you're wanting for your tank or
outdoor pond, make sure to stop at Discount Tropical Fish. They
carry all kinds of fish, and carry both dry and living foods. You
will find basic tropical fish like guppies, neons and black mollies, to
fancy gold fish, koi (Japanese carp), African chiclid, live coral, sea
anemone and invertebrates. Their tanks run 10% over their cost,
fish are discounted 10 to 15%, and all dry goods are discounted
25%. If you have been longing for a koi pond in your backyard,
Discount Tropical Fish can make recommendations for having one
built.

ELLIOT'S PET EMPORIUM
6370 Brockton
Riverside, CA 92506
714/787-0241
HOURS: MON-FRI: 9-9 SAT: 9-7 SUN: 10-7
CREDIT CARDS: V, MC

This is one of the world's largest pet stores with over 25,000 pet items at discount prices. Because they buy in huge volume they pass the savings on to their customers. Every Wednesday they offer an additional 10% discount on everything in the store including items already on sale. Among the brands they carry are: Science Diet, Iams, Nutro, Abo-Derm and Pro Plan. Senior citizens always receive an additional 10% discount on their purchases.
Additional Locations: 6 other stores in the Inland Empire

NORM'S FEED STORE
11708 South East End Ave.
Chino, CA 91710
714/628-7016
HOURS: MON-SAT: 8-6 SUN: 8:30-12
CREDIT CARDS: CASH OR CHECKS ONLY

When was the last time you walked into a store and really felt that the management was there to help you? Norm's Feed Store is that kind of place. You will find very friendly salespeople, knowledgeable about the food your dog and cat eat. They have pet and vet supplies, and you can even pick up hay, straw and alfalfa cubes. Delivery is available for large orders.

PEDLEY VETERINARY SUPPLY INC.
8978 Limonite Ave.
Riverside, CA 92509
714/685-3511
HOURS: MON-FRI: 10-6 SAT: 10-5
CREDIT CARDS: MC, V

Do-it-yourself vaccinations for your dogs, cats, horses and even some available for your goat! Purchasing a dog's vaccination, for example, can save you quite a bit of money. A parvo vaccination for your dog can run from $15 to $25 when administered by your vet. Do it yourself and it costs only $2.50. Most of the vaccinations are ready to go in a syringe, and antibiotics are also available. While not vets, the animal lovers employed at Pedley's are very knowledgeable about your pet's needs. They also carry medical supplies, vitamins, plus most pet supplies.

PET PREVENT-A-CARE
14692-1/2 Parthenia St.
Panorama City, CA 91343
818/892-8683
HOURS: MON-FRI: 9-5
CREDIT CARDS: CASH OR CHECKS ONLY

If you have pets and want to make sure they don't have little ones, Pet Prevent-A-Care is the place for you. They will spay or neuter your pet at 20 to 50% of what a trip to the vet would cost. These folks treat your animal with love and care so you don't have to worry that low cost means poor care for your animal. They are affiliated with Mercy Crusade and Actors and Other Animals, so they do a good job with lots of heart.

RED BARN FEED & SADDLERY INC.**
18601 Oxnard St.
Tarzana, CA 91356
818/345-2510
HOURS: MON-FRI: 9-6 SAT: 9-5 SUN: 11-4
CREDIT CARDS: MC, V

This store has one of the largest inventories of pet products in the Los Angeles area. They carry Kal Kan, Purina, Friskie, Carnation, Breeder's Choice, Quaker, Iams, Science Diet, and many other brand names. You can save 20 to 40% off retail prices. They also carry foods and supplies for your pet chicken, rabbit, or horse. If you need firewood, hay, tack, cages or nursery supplies, Red Barn

PET STORES & ANIMAL SUPPLIES

Feed and Saddlery has it all. You'll save an additional 5% by using your BUYING RETAIL IS STUPID coupon.

TAGS
10144 Balboa Blvd.
Granada Hills, CA 91344
818/366-5004
HOURS: MON-FRI: 10-7   SAT: 10-6   SUN: 11-5
CREDIT CARDS: MC, V

Dog, cat, and bird food, and small animal supplies, can all be found at Tags. You can even get your pet's rabies vaccination here for only $3.99. They keep records and will send you a reminder when your pet is next due for a shot. Tags will also special order any kind of dog or cat food for your favorite pet.
Additional Locations: Santa Clarita (805/251-6625), Van Nuys (818/944-2278)

PHOTOGRAPHY

ABC CAMERA-PHOTO-VIDEO
10224 Mason St.
Chatsworth, CA 91311
818/709-1931
HOURS: MON-FRI: 10-6:30   SAT: 10-4:30
CREDIT CARDS: AE, DISC, MC, V

ABC Camera-Photo-Video is truly your one-stop shop for any type of photography. Whether you are a beginner, amateur or professional, all your needs will be met. They sell, buy, take trade-ins, rent and repair (on the premises) all equipment and are an authorized dealer for major brands such as Nikon, Minolta, Canon, Pentax, Ricoh. You can have your passport pictures done as well as rush custom film developing in color or in black and white. ABC averages 10% over cost on their prices and they have once-a-month special sales. For photographic needs, it's as simple as A–B–C.

ADRAY'S
6609 Van Nuys Blvd.
Van Nuys, CA 91405
818/908-1500
HOURS: MON-FRI: 10-7   SAT-SUN: 10-6
CREDIT CARDS: MC, V

You will save about 40% on almost everything at Adray's. They are the discount headquarters for major brands of televisions, VCR's, camera equipment, answering machines, stereo systems, computers and computer equipment, small and major appliances, jewelry, cosmetics, perfumes and colognes, china and crystal, pots and pans, sporting goods, exercise equipment, furniture, linens and just about anything else that comes to mind. You will find the salespeople courteous and knowledgeable, but they are usually very busy. If you are looking to make a major purchase, we suggest that you do your homework about the product you are interested in before going

to Adray's. Shopping here is much different than shopping in a retail department store, but once you see their prices, adapting won't be a problem.
Additional Locations: Canoga Park (818/348-2600), Los Angeles (213/935-8191), W. Los Angeles (213/479-0797), Torrance (213/378-6777), Ventura (805/644-1111)

AMARS CAMERA
8519 Sunset Blvd.
West Hollywood, CA 90069
213/657-6630
HOURS: MON-FRI: 9:30-5:30 SAT: 10-3
CREDIT CARDS: MC, V

Amars Camera has been in business since the early 1960's offering a complete selection of cameras (Canon, Nikon, Olympus, and Pentax), equipment, supplies and film. You can always save 20% on your film. Savings on camera equipment will vary according to the brand or model you are buying. Custom lab work is also available. For even better prices, call Amars Camera to find out when their twice-a-year sale on used equipment takes place.

BEL AIR CAMERA, AUDIO & VIDEO
1025 Westwood Blvd.
Los Angeles, CA 90024
213/208-5150
HOURS: MON-FRI: 9-6 SAT: 9:30-6
CREDIT CARDS: MC, V

Bel Air is one of the largest camera, audio, and video stores on the West Coast. They offer cameras and camera accessories, video cameras and recorders, audio components, tape recorders, televisions, enlargers and more. Two or three times a year, they have a large Expo & Sale where they invite representatives from over 40 companies to show their products. Shows are usually in May or December, but you can get the above items daily at 10% above their cost and sometimes at cost. They have Nikon, Minolta, Pentax, Vivitar, Olympus, Panasonic, Sony, Speedotron, Hasselblad and others. Feel free to write a check or charge your purchases at Bel Air, but these people give special discounts if you pay in cash.

CAMERA CITY
12236 W. Pico Blvd.
Los Angeles, CA 90064
213/477-8833
HOURS: MON-FRI: 9:30-6 SAT: 9:30-5
CREDIT CARDS: AE, DISC, MC, V

Camera City has been at their present location since 1969 with prices discounted at 20 to 50% below what you'd pay at other camera stores. In photo equipment, they carry camera lenses, flashes, cases and tripods. Their video equipment includes cameras, recorders and lenses. Both departments offer rentals and repairs on Canon, Nikon, Ricoh, Sharp, Vivitar, Kiron, Kodak and Polaroid. Camera City is happy to say that they service what they sell.

FRANK'S HIGHLAND PARK CAMERA
5715 N. Figueroa St.
Los Angeles, CA 90042
213/255-0123
HOURS: MON-THUR, SAT: 9:30-6 FRI: 9:30-8
CREDIT CARDS: MC, V

The Vacek family has been selling all types of cameras in their 10,000 square foot store since 1969. Their bargain tables offer even greater savings than their standard 6% over wholesale pricing. You can also find everything you need for your darkroom including paper, chemicals and equipment. If you would like to trade in your camera or pick up a used one, see Frank's Highland Park Camera.

HOOPER CAMERA AND VIDEO CENTERS**
5059 Lankershim Blvd.
N. Hollywood, CA 91601
818/762-2846
HOURS: MON-SAT: 9-6
CREDIT CARDS: MC, V

If it takes a picture, you can buy it at cost plus 5 to 10% at Hooper Camera and Video Centers. Merchandise other than cameras are sold at 10 to 35% off retail prices. This is the largest chain of photographic stores in the combined areas of San Fernando Valley and Conejo Valley. They carry everything you need in photographic equipment and supplies, at prices you can't beat. They carry all the major brands, and have special sales during the year. Six of their stores have in-house labs for custom, economy, and one hour photo finishing. You'll find helpful, knowledgeable salespeople to assist you. Take your BUYING RETAIL IS STUPID coupon with you for an additional 5% off on your purchase.
Additional Locations: 8 other stores throughout S. CA

LLOYD'S CAMERA SURPLUS
1612 N. Cahuenga Blvd.
Hollywood, CA 90028
213/467-7956
HOURS: MON-FRI: 9-5
CREDIT CARDS: MC, V

Owner Lloyd Berman says, "We may be the largest dealer in the U.S. on 8mm and 16mm movie cameras." In business since 1954, LLoyd's carries a large supply of cameras, tape recorders, and film. You'll find top name brands at savings of about 25% off retail. Rentals are available, and the people are super nice and helpful.

MIKO PHOTO-AUDIO-VIDEO CENTER
1259 3rd Street Promenade
Santa Monica, CA 90401
213/393-9371
HOURS: MON-THUR: 9-6 FRI: 9-7 SAT: 9-6 SUN: 12-4
CREDIT CARDS: AE, DISC, MC, V

Miko Photo-Audio-Video Center prides itself in its high repeat customer business, so you know they are doing something right. They
have everything for your home entertainment center, video cameras,
portable audio systems, stereos, electric games and more. In addition to their camera equipment and supplies, you can have your film
processed there, too. Cordless telephones, answering machines,
and video editing equipment can also be found at Miko's.
*Additional Locations: Manhattan Beach (213/546-5491), Santa
Monica Place (213/395-8185)*

SIMON'S DISCOUNT CAMERA STORE
720 N. Vermont Ave.
Los Angeles, CA 90029
213/665-8825
HOURS: MON-SAT: 9-6
CREDIT CARDS: MC, V

Simon says, "See us first." He'll sell you top-brand cameras like
Nikon and Canon at the best discount prices around. In fact, their
cameras and supplies are usually marked at only 5 to 10% above
cost, so you know you'll be finding good bargains here. Simon's
also rents and services cameras. Now take a minute to focus on
these bargains at Simon's. One hour photo enlargement service is
also available. Their low pricing is based on cash and carry, so
your purchase will be 3% higher if you use your credit card.

VALLEY 1-HOUR PHOTO
7576 Winnetka Ave.
Canoga Park, CA 91306
818/998-6572
HOURS: MON-FRI: 9:30-7 SAT: 10-5
CREDIT CARDS: MC, V

No kidding! If you need a passport picture immediately and you can't possibly wait, this is the place to go. In addition to processing your film right on the premises, you can actually get your keys made or duplicated while you wait. You'll find that Valley 1-Hour Photo beats retail prices by at least 15%.

PLANTS, LAWN & GARDEN

∞ LAWNMOWERS ∞

LEE LAWNMOWER**
1345 S. Bristol
Santa Ana, CA 92704
714/546-6334
HOURS: MON-SAT: 8-7 SUN: 8-3
CREDIT CARDS: MC, V

If you are looking for great service and buys, find your way to Lee Lawnmower, in business since 1960. You can usually get same day service if something goes wrong with your gas, electric or diesel lawnmower. Lee Lawnmower guarantees that nobody can beat their prices or especially their service. In addition to lawnmowers, you can also find blowers, edgers, hedge trimmers, weed-eaters and of course most parts and supplies. They carry Astron, Briggs & Stratton, Echo, Homelite, Snapper, Toro and Power Trim to name just a few of their brand names. If you can't find what you are looking for, just ask. Should you find something you absolutely have to have and can't afford to pay cash, ask about their own credit financing with no interest. Take your BUYING RETAIL IS STUPID coupon with you for an additional discount of 10%.

∞ NURSERIES ∞

AMERICAN WHOLESALE NURSERIES
12940 Balboa Blvd.
Granada Hills, CA 91344
818/368-8591
HOURS: MON-FRI: 6-5 SAT-SUN: 8-5
CREDIT CARDS: MC, V

Wow! They have approximately 30 acres filled with 500,000 plants. If that isn't enough to wow you, you also have 500 varieties from which to choose. They are the largest Snapper lawn equipment supplier in the San Fernando Valley. Discounts are at 50% off retail. Many other name brands are available. Also, come with your truck and fill up on bulk soil blends. They buy their plants direct from growers, so they pass the savings on to you. Any flowering plants you see are grown by American Wholesale Nurseries. You may want to enroll in the Golden Eagle Garden Club that offers bimonthly newsletters, seminars, and additional discounts to members on top of the regular discounts. Membership is free; it's just part of the service offered by American Wholesale Nurseries.

BEVERLY GARDEN CENTER
316 N. La Cienega Blvd.
Los Angeles, CA 90048
213/652-2583
HOURS: 7 DAYS A WEEK: 9-6
CREDIT CARDS: MC, V

You are in for a big surprise at the Beverly Garden Center. As you enter, you'll discover a greenhouse behind the storefront filled with a terrific selection of indoor plants. As these plants are purchased direct from the growers, you can save 20 to 50% of regular nursery prices. The savings are the same on the great selection of baskets, hampers and accessories. Call to find out about their special sales held during the year

DIRT CHEAP PLANT CO.
488 E. 17th. St.
Costa Mesa, CA 92677
714/645-4553
HOURS: 7 DAYS A WEEK: 9-7
CREDIT CARDS: MC, V

Dirt Cheap Plant Company is just that. Assorted house plants from 4" pots to giant jungle monsters in the 4 to 9 foot range are for sale at dirt cheap prices. Check out their outrageous selection of baskets and other plant related items too. All products and plants are first quality, greenhouse fresh and at savings of 40 to 60% off retail. They are always running specials of some sort, so give them a call to see what's happening. Well what are you waiting for? Get those green thumbs moving!

GREENLAND NURSERY
758 S. Maple Ave.
Los Angeles, CA 90014
213/622-4429

HOURS: MON: 4-2 TUES, THUR, SAT: 6-2 WED, FRI: 3-2
CREDIT CARDS: CASH OR CHECKS ONLY

If you would like to save 50% off what you might pay at a retail florist, take a trip down to the Greenland Nursery. If you don't mind getting up before the crack of dawn, you can take advantage of some fabulous bargains and they guarantee the plants they sell are fresh and healthy. Why not give them a shot, the florists do.

NURSERY LIQUIDATORS
1500 S. State College Blvd.
Anaheim, CA 92806
714/533-4065

HOURS: SUN-TUES: 10-4:30 THUR-SAT: 10-4:30
CREDIT CARDS: MC, V ($20 MINIMUM PURCHASE)

Nursery Liquidators has been around for 26 years selling plants and trees at prices you wouldn't believe. Save as much as 50% off the prices of other nurseries. They have over two million plants and trees for your selection. They grow about 70% of their own inventory, so they are able to pass on significant savings to you. They carry very few house plants. If you're doing some landscaping, this is the place to shop.

PANCHO'S PLANTS
27112 5th St.
Highland, CA 92346
714/862-0908

HOURS: MON-SAT: 8-4:30 SUN: 9-3
CREDIT CARDS: MC, V

How elegant to think that you can have your very own pond floating with water lilies in your backyard. You'll find all of the supplies needed to build your own water lily pond, including the water lilies. This wholesale to the public nursery will save you at least 50% off what you'd pay at one of the chain nurseries. You'll find everything from shrubs, palm trees, and fruit trees to cactus, bedding plants or fertilizer. Don't forget to explore Pancho's greenhouse. It covers nearly an acre and is filled with healthy indoor plants like you see in floral shops. The best thing about Pancho's Plants is the very friendly Pancho himself. He has been in the business for over 15 years and is more than willing to share his expertise.

VALLEY SOD FARMS
16405 Chase St.
Sepulveda, CA 91343
818/892-7258
HOURS: MON-SAT: 7:30-5
CREDIT CARDS: MC, V

Blue grass, blue rye, fescue, dichondra, hybrid Bermuda and St. Augustine—no, we're not talking about race horses. These are all the different types of grass sod you can buy at the only sod farm in the San Fernando Valley. They will deliver anywhere in the area, and if you are out of the area, they can make delivery arrangements with some of their affiliates. So, if you're looking for grass sod or even some ground cover, check them out. Savings for the average yard will run 40 to 60% below most nursery prices.

WORLD OF PLANTS AND GIFTS**
3716 Motor Ave.
Los Angeles, CA 90034
213/838-4100
HOURS: MON-FRI: 9-7   SAT-SUN: 9-6
CREDIT CARDS: MC, V

Beautiful fresh cut flowers, indoor plants, trees, baskets, pottery, macrame, flowering plants, plant stands and framed prints, are all available at World of Plants and Gifts for discount prices. Their plants are purchased directly from growers in San Diego, so they can offer their customers the best prices around. If you use your BUYING RETAIL IS STUPID coupon your discount blossoms an additional 10%!

∞ POTS, PLANTERS & FOUNTAINS ∞

FOUNTAINS BY SANTI
1888 Van Buren Blvd.
Riverside, CA 92504
714/780-0622
HOURS: TUES-WED: 9-4 SAT-SUN: 9-5
CREDIT CARDS: MC, V

This is definitely not your run of the mill operation. Descendents of one of the most influential painters from the Italian Renaissance, Raphael, the Santi family has quite a few generations behind them of knowledge and expertise in handcrafted artworks. You will at last be able to find the perfect fountain for your courtyard or patio. In addition, they have Spanish, Italian and Oriental pottery, bird baths and bench sets. Because the manufacturing is done on right on the premises, they have more of selection than most. Look to save 15% on your purchases here.

GLOBE DRUM CO., INC.
1149 S. Eastern Ave.
Los Angeles, CA 90022
213/263-2132
HOURS: MON-FRI: 7-3:30
CREDIT CARDS: CASH ONLY

These are not the kind of drums you beat in a band. Globe Drum is a wholesale factory outlet for empty barrels, drums and trash cans. What would you do with one? They make great packing barrels, water barrels, planters for plants or water lillies, furniture, displays, and whatever else your imagination can come up with.

MAINLY SECONDS–POTTERY, PLANTS & THINGS
12144 Magnolia Blvd.
N. Hollywood, CA 91607
818/985-4499
HOURS: MON-FRI: 9-9 SAT: 9-6 SUN: 10-6
CREDIT CARDS: MC, V

If you're looking for those room accessories that make your house a home, that displays your personality, then this is where you need to

- 319 -

shop. They carry pottery baskets, plants, plant foods, potting soils, cacti, silk flowers, vases, dried flowers, macrame, and wrought iron at 40 to 60% below retail. Each of their locations has over 6,000 square feet always stuffed with goodies.
Additional Locations: Buena Park (714/994-0540), Costa Mesa (714/548-7710)

POTTERY AND FLORAL WORLD**
3352 San Fernando Rd.
Los Angeles, CA 90065
213/254-5281
HOURS: 7 DAYS A WEEK: 8-7
CREDIT CARDS: MC, V

Pottery and Floral World has one of the West Coast's largest selections of pots, pottery, dried and silk flowers, and all the accessories that go along with them. They have macrame supplies, gourmet ware, baskets and wrought iron. Being both a factory outlet and a direct importer, you can expect discounts of 20 to 50% off retail prices found elsewhere. Close-outs occur weekly, so shoppers can always count on seeing different items from visit to visit. If you are into Christmas decorations, they carry a complete line. You will receive an additional 10% off your purchase amount when you use your BUYING RETAIL IS STUPID coupon.

POTTERY MANUFACTURING & DISTRIBUTING
18881 S. Hoover St.
Gardena, CA 90248
213/323-7754
HOURS: MON-SAT: 9-4
CREDIT CARDS: CASH OR CHECKS ONLY

Pottery Manufacturing & Distributing is a wholesale outlet with over an acre of red clay pots. They are also a factory outlet for their manufacturing plant located in Gardena. You can save 50% off retail on factory seconds. They carry pots ranging from 4 inches up to 180 pounds. You'll also find imported Italian stoneware, "poly-planters," and cactus potting soil.

POOL & PATIO

∞ BARBECUES ∞

BARBECUES GALORE
18922 Ventura Blvd.
Tarzana, CA 91356
818/345-7314
HOURS: MON-SAT: 9-6 SUN: 11-5
CREDIT CARDS: AE, MC, V

Just thinking about a Saturday afternoon barbecue makes my mouth water. Barbecues Galore has approximately 200 barbecues on display (gas, electric and charcoal), along with smokers, accessories, fireplaces and fireplace accessories. Some brand names carried include Ducane, Charbroil, Arkla, Amberlight, and Weber. For those chefs that enjoy experimenting, they stock the unusual, as well as products from other countries. Their knowledgeable staff will be able to answer all of your questions regarding your particular needs. In addition to offering assembly and delivery on all of their products, Barbecues Galore discounts everything in the store 20 to 50% off retail. For even higher savings, watch for their special sales held each week.
Additional Locations: 8 other stores throughout S. CA

HALF PRICE STORES INC.
6367 Van Nuys Blvd.
Van Nuys, CA 91401
818/780-6844
HOURS: MON-FRI: 10-6:30 SAT: 10-6
CREDIT CARDS: MC, V

Local consumers have known about exploratory shopping at the Half Price Stores since 1967. Depending on the items purchased, you can save from 10 to 70% shopping here. There are watches, jewelry, toothpaste, paper products, Christmas goods, socks, underwear, cleaning aids, towels, and much more. We could go on and on trying to list the thousands of things on the shelves. In back of the store you'll discover gas and electric barbecues. There are at least 10 units on display representing brand names such as Ameri-light, Broilmaster, Char-Broil and Patio. Barbecue accessories and replacement parts are also stocked.

∞ PATIO FURNITURE ∞

ABC POOL & PATIO**
24449 Hawthorne Blvd.
Torrance, CA 90505
213/373-0935
HOURS: MON-SUN: 10-6
CREDIT CARDS: MC, V

Established in 1958, ABC now has 10,000 square feet of furniture for patios, barbecues, fireplace accessories, pool and spa supplies and gifts. Trapitone furniture and Ducane barbecues are among the various brand names represented. You can expect to save 35% off retail prices on patio furniture. You'll save 10–15% on barbecues and other items. Don't miss their bargain room located upstairs, and special sales on the Fourth of July and Labor Day. Be sure to use your BUYING RETAIL IS STUPID coupon to save an additional 5%!

BERKS
2520 Santa Monica Blvd.
Santa Monica, CA 90404
213/828-7447
HOURS: MON-SAT: 9-6 FRI: 9-9 SUN: 10-5
CREDIT CARDS: MC, V

If you are looking for a complete selection of outdoor and casual indoor furniture, and you'd like to pocket savings of 20 to 60%, then shop at Berks. They've been selling everything you need to furnish your patio or porch since the 1950's. You can purchase things like tables, chaise lounges, and umbrellas by makers such as Brown Jordan, Samsonite, Kenneth James and others. Their customers always find variety of styles and colors, and Berks offers immediate, free delivery. If you find it advertised cheaper anywhere else, show it to them; if they have it in stock they'll meet it or beat it. Check out their special sales during the year for extra big savings.

CHARLIE'S WAREHOUSE
7742 Edinger Ave.
Huntington Beach, CA 92647
714/848-0682
HOURS: WED-THUR: 10-6   FRI: 10-8   SAT: 10-5:30   SUN: 11-5
CREDIT CARDS: MC, V

Are you ready for new patio furniture? At Charlie's Warehouse you'll find 50–60 different patio sets on display and in stock at 25% off retail. The patio furniture is available in redwood, aluminum, resin and wrought iron. You will also find a selection of replacement cushions, acrylic glassware and lots of other outdoor accessories. Some name brands they carry include Grosfillex, Winston, Alumont, Little Lake, Five Star, California Umbrella, Pacific Sun, Samsonite and many others from both American and European manufacturers. Owners Leonard and Judy Small (a.k.a. Mr. & Mrs. Charlie) started this wonderful enterprise after they "retired." They encourage comparison shopping and have writing pads spread all over the store for their customers. This 20,000 square foot store also carries a complete line of baby furniture and accessories, along with juvenile furniture. Delivery service is extra.

COTTAGE SHOPS
7922 W. 3rd St.
Los Angeles, CA 90046
213/658-6066
HOURS: MON-SAT: 9:30-6   SUN: 11-5
CREDIT CARDS: AE, MC, V

This discount store, in business since the late 1940's, has a complete selection of chairs, tables, lamps, pool and patio furniture, lounges, umbrellas, and so much more. A division of Scotty's Casual Furniture, the Cottage Shops will save you about 20% and more off retail on most items and they really stand behind what they sell. Brand names include Tropitone, Allibert, Ducane, and Barlow Tyrie Teak. Delivery and layaway services are available, and they can refurbish your old pool and patio furniture. You'll find free parking in back of the store and a free catalogue is available.

ENCINO DISCOUNT PATIO & BABY FURNITURE**
17563 Ventura Blvd.
Encino, CA 91316
818/986-1074
HOURS: MON-FRI: 9-6 SAT: 9-5 SUN: 11-4
CREDIT CARDS: MC, V

Looking for that perfect outdoor swing for your baby while you're entertaining guests at your backyard garden party? Encino Discount Patio and Baby Furniture has it all. Patio and baby furniture and accessories. They carry Innova, California Umbrella, Homecrest, Pacific Sun, O.W. Lee, Kettler in patio furniture and Childcraft, Century, No-Jo, Lambs and Ivy, and Creative Playthings for baby furniture. Owner Mackie Singer says her customers tell them that they have the best selection and prices (30 to 50% off retail) and have been coming back to the store since 1939. They'll also extend an additional 5% discount when you use your BUYING RETAIL IS STUPID coupon, except on already marked sale items.

MANUFACTURER'S CLEARANCE WAREHOUSE
4601 So. Soto St.
Los Angeles, CA 90058
800/321-0502, 213/583-1836
HOURS: MON-FRI: 9-5
CREDIT CARDS: MC, V

If you are looking for furniture for your dining needs, then look no further! This store has thousands of square feet of low priced merchandise from which to choose. They claim the largest assortment of dining chairs, tables, barstools, and outdoor furniture anywhere in Los Angeles.

WOODLAND CASUAL
19855 Ventura Blvd.
Woodland Hills, CA 91364
818/348-6000
HOURS: MON-SAT: 10-6   SUN: 11-5
CREDIT CARDS: MC, V

Well here it is, the largest selection of patio furniture in the San
Fernando Valley. There are four entire floors of wicker, rattan,
dinette sets, sofa sets, bedroom furniture and entertainment centers
to choose from. You can expect to find such brands as Tropitone,
Grosfillex, Pacific Rattan and Thypon Wicker to name a few. With
a purchase of $500 or more they'll even deliver. You can look for-
ward to saving 30% off retail on most items.

∞ POOL SUPPLIES & SPAS ∞

J. B. SEBRELL CO.
301 S. San Pedro St.
Los Angeles, CA 90013
213/625-2648
HOURS: MON-FRI: 9-5:30   SAT: 9-5   SUN: 10-3
CREDIT CARDS: MC, V

Swimming pool equipment and supplies, all marked at savings of 20
to 50% below list price, are available for you at J. B. Sebrell. They
have everything—heaters, pumps, ladders, chemicals, skimmers,
diving boards, redwood tubs, spas, toy accessories—plus equipment for spas, fish ponds, fountains, even above ground pools.
They accept trade-ins, buy and sell used equipment, and do repairs.
Ask for their free catalog and shop by phone. They've been in
business since 1938 and you'll save money on everything you see in
their huge inventory.

SPA BROKER
6633 Van Nuys Blvd.
Van Nuys, CA 91406
818/782-9000 800/272-3577
HOURS: 7 DAYS A WEEK: 9-7
CREDIT CARDS: MC, V

Woody Woodard has been selling spas before they were the "in" thing. You can view 60 spas and gazebos on display at their 10,000 square foot store in Van Nuys where you'll find brand names including Pageant, Hydro-Swirl, Swim Spas and more. Shopping here will result in savings of $300 to $700 per spa. Keep in touch with Spa Broker to find out when they are offering even greater savings with their special sales. Financing is available.

SECURITY, SAFES & VAULTS

∞ SAFES & VAULTS ∞

1ST SECURITY SAFE CO.
900 S. Hill St.
Los Angeles, CA 90015
213/627-0422
HOURS: MON-FRI: 10-5 SAT: 10-4
CREDIT CARDS: CASH OR CHECKS ONLY

You'll save so much money using this book, you're going to need a safe to keep it in. 1st Security Safe Company specializes in jewelry safes, floor safes, and wall safes at 10–30% below retail. Not only do they sell safes, they install and service their products as well. Arrangements can be made if you'd like to finance your purchase.

IN-A-FLOOR SAFE COMPANY**
1416 S. Los Angeles St.
Los Angeles, CA 90015
213/749-2448
HOURS: MON-FRI: 9-5
CREDIT CARDS: CASH OR CHECKS ONLY

In business since 1925, In-A-Floor Safe Company is the originator of in-floor safes, receiving a patent in 1932. Because the company is family owned and operated, you can expect to receive service not always available in today's world. You pick the combination yourself and if you ever need to have it changed, In-A-Floor Safe will do it for free. In addition to the in-floor safes, you can also get fire safes and media/data safes. Low cost installation is available, and they also service all brands of safes. In-A-Floor Safe will take 10% off your purchase with your BUYING RETAIL IS STUPID coupon.

RAP DISCOUNT SAFE CO.
21407 Vanowen St.
Canoga Park, CA 91303
818/884-3370
HOURS: MON-FRI: 8-10 SAT: 8-5 SUN: 9-5

CREDIT CARDS: MC, V

If you need to lock things up and keep them safe, Rap Discount Safe Company is the place for you. Whether it's commercial or residential, wall or floor, sunken or free standing, you'll find safes at 20 to 50% off retail at Rap. Their safes range from small ones to hold your prize pistol to large, fireproof safes for all your important documents and valuables. With over 50 varieties in stock, they have one of the largest inventories of safes in the San Fernando Valley.

∞ SECURITY SYSTEMS ∞

SECURITY WAREHOUSE**
18345 Ventura Blvd.
Tarzana, CA 91356
800/CRIME-29
HOURS: MON-FRI: 9-5:30 & 24 HOUR PHONE
CREDIT CARDS: MC, V

No frills, just good service here and saving of 10 to 15%. With the increase in robberies these days, you will want to check out Security Warehouse's security systems. They offer a free demonstration of the AT&T emergency response system and a security evaluation. In addition to burglary, they handle medical and fire systems. Count on saving 5% more with your BUYING RETAIL IS STUPID coupon.

UNIQUE SECURITY ALARM ASSOCIATION**
10061 San Fernando Rd.
Pacoima, CA 91331
818/848-0848
HOURS: 24 HOURS A DAY–7 DAYS A WEEK
CREDIT CARDS: CASH OR CHECKS ONLY

These people install and service alarm systems, closed circuit TV and offer monitoring security systems. They provide free estimates at your convenience with no obligation and have their own in-house financing available. Give them a call if you want to save at least 25% below most places and they claim they'll beat any legitimate bid. The areas they cover are Los Angeles and Orange Counties, Thousand Oaks, Camarillo and West Lake. Save an additional 15% using your BUYING RETAIL IS STUPID coupon!

SERVICES

∞ FLORISTS ∞

KIM-E'S FLOWERS**
818/885-6957
HOURS: BY APPOINTMENT ONLY
CREDIT CARDS: CASH OR CHECKS ONLY

With 15 years experience in the floral industry, Michael and Kim Holtzer will definitely put the cherry on the top of your next affair with exceptional floral arrangements at discounted prices. They personally come to your home or office and help select the perfect arrangements to be used for weddings, banquets or parties. When the arrangements are completed, they will then make sure the arrangements are displayed to your satisfaction. Their specialties are preparing arrangements for weddings from bridal bouquet, table centerpieces, and ceremony arrangements, to stands along the aisle. Their prices average about 50% off retail. Don't forget, you can to use your BUYING RETAIL IS STUPID coupon and receive even greater savings of 10%.

SHE'S FLOWERS
712 S. Olive St.
Los Angeles, CA 90014
213/689-1372
HOURS: MON-SAT: 7:30-6
CREDIT CARDS: AE, MC, V

Save up to 50% on flowers and plants for all occasions. She's Flowers grows many of their own flowers and imports others directly; then She's Flowers wholesales them to the public. You can also buy silk flowers, dried flowers, trees, baskets, even balloons for weddings, birthdays, holidays. They deliver, and you can charge your purchase by phone.

∞ LEGAL SERVICES ∞

DIVORCE CENTERS OF CALIFORNIA
6399 Wilshire Blvd., #909
Los Angeles, CA 90048
213/462-3405
HOURS: MON-FRI: 9-5:30
CREDIT CARDS: CASH ONLY

They have offices statewide, but Lois Isenberg at this office can help you in divorce matters and name changes. It's like do-it-yourself with assistance, and prices start as low as $75. You know that's quite a savings if you've ever had to pay an attorney's retainer fee. They've been in business since 1974, and this is a cash operation. In some cases arrangements can be made for payments.
Additional Locations: 6 other offices throughout S. CA

DO-IT-YOURSELF L.A.W.
(LEGAL ACTION WORKSHOP)
4515 Van Nuys Blvd.
Sherman Oaks, CA 91403
818/995-4224
HOURS: MON-FRI: 9-5
CREDIT CARDS: MC, V

Why pay a fortune for standard legal services with complete low cost legal services available? You can get a divorce, file a bankruptcy, change your name, adopt someone, start a corporation, and much more. There is attorney assistance.
Additional Locations: 6 other offices throughout S. CA

WILSON'S DIVORCE CLINIC
3860 Crenshaw Blvd., Suite 201
Los Angeles, CA 90008
213/290-2268
HOURS: MON-FRI: 9-5
CREDIT CARDS: CASH ONLY

If you are a person seeking help in filing for an uncontested divorce, Wilson's Divorce Clinic says they can save you up to 75% of standard legal fees. They provide the typing, filing and serving of papers. Wilson's Divorce Clinic can also provide expert advice and experience in the areas of restraining orders, child support problems, collections and filing bankruptcy.

∞ LOCKSMITH ∞

MARC'S DISCOUNT LOCK & KEY
1503 S. Holt
Los Angeles, CA 90035
213/274-9644
HOURS: 7 DAYS A WEEK, 24 HOURS A DAY
CREDIT CARDS: CASH OR CHECKS ONLY

If you've ever locked yourself out of your house or your car, you'll love this one! Marc handles all jobs, large or small. Allow the phone to ring at least 12 times; someone will always be there. That's good news when you have an emergency, and you save 20% over other locksmiths.

∞ USED MOBILE HOME SALES ∞

MOBILE HOME MANAGEMENT
10712 Sepulveda Blvd.
Mission Hills, CA 91345
818/361-7364
HOURS: MON-SUN: 9-6
CREDIT CARDS: CASH OR CHECKS ONLY

If you've been looking for a mobile home or want to trade up, then this may be the place for you. The team at Mobile Home Management are in-park resale specialists. If you're from out of town, they can put you immediately in a park. Financing and insurance are available. You can save around 20% on brand names such as Home

Systems, National Prebuilt, Baron Homes, and Hallmark. You can save even more on their bank repossessions, and they take trade-ins.

∞ WRITERS ∞

THE WRITE PLACE
213/839-1340, 213/839-6794
HOURS: BY APPOINTMENT ONLY
CREDIT CARDS: CASH OR CHECKS ONLY

Too busy to plan your party? The Write Place will do it all—from addressing your invitations to finding caterers, bands, photographers, even writing your "thank you" notes at savings of 10 to 20%. Calligraphy is their specialty.

THE WRITE RESUME
12444 Ventura Blvd., Suite 201
Studio City, CA 91604
818/763-5459
HOURS: MON-FRI: 9-5   SAT: BY APPOINTMENT ONLY
CREDIT CARDS: CASH OR CHECKS ONLY

This is such an unusual service that we wanted to tell you about the Write Resume because they'll also save you 10% or more when they prepare your "history" for a job search. In addition to resumes, owner Edmund Stone (he used to be a correspondent for the British Broadcasting Corporation) will counsel you on job search ideas, write cover letters, business proposals, biographies, ad copy and prepare proofs. You know your in good hands because they're the official resume company to numerous theatrical agencies. A writer by profession, Stone will personally tailor your resume to suit your needs. Prompt and reasonable service are a trademark.

SPORTS & RECREATION

∞ BICYCLES ∞

BIKECOLOGY–SANTA MONICA
1515 Wilshire Blvd.
Santa Monica, CA 90403
213/451-9977
HOURS: MON-WED: 10-7 THUR-FRI: 10-8 SAT: 9-6 SUN: 9-5
CREDIT CARDS: MC, V

You can save as much as 25% below retail on bicycles, bicycle clothing, parts and accessories here. This big store also has special sales in the fall and after Christmas, where you can save even more. You'll find Centurion, Nishiki, and lots more here, and you can take their bicycles for a test ride. They have bicycles for ages 2 to 102, and clothing from XXS-XL. Ask for a catalogue and make sure you get on their mailing list.

CRITERIUM CYCLE SPORT**
16927 Vanowen St.
Van Nuys, CA 91406
818/344-5444
HOURS: MON-WED, FRI: 10-6 THURS: 10-8 SAT: 9-5 SUN: 11-4
CREDIT CARDS: AE, DISC, MC, V

The folks at Criterium Cycle Sport, specializing in customer service, carry new bicycles and a large selection of cycling accessories. This is not a self-service operation; they have professional salespeople who take the time to make sure you select the right bike for your needs. They carry all major brand bicycles and accessories such as Yakima, Specialized, Nike, Giro Oakley. Mountain bikes are also available by Fisher, Trek, Giant, Univega and Cyclepro. They also provide repairs on all makes and models and offer customers a life-time warranty on all bicycle purchases. You will receive an addi-

tional 10% discount with your BUYING RETAIL IS STUPID coupon
so you can ride away with an even better deal!

I. MARTIN BICYCLES
8330 Beverly Blvd.
Los Angeles, CA 90048
213/653-6900
HOURS: MON: 10-8 TUES-FRI: 10-7 SAT: 9-6 SUN: 11-5
CREDIT CARDS: MC, V

The savings vary according to your selection, but you can be sure to
save money on bicycles and accessories. There are about 900 bicycles on hand. The selection runs from bicycles for children to racing
bicycles. You can also get cycling shoes and have your wheels
serviced and repaired here.

SPOKES 'N STUFF
7494 Santa Monica Blvd.
W. Hollywood, CA 90046
213/650-1076
HOURS: WED-SUN: 10:30-6
CREDIT CARDS: AE, V

Save about 20 to 30% on everything when it comes to bicycles.
Spokes 'N Stuff has bikes by Fuji, Ross, Mongoose, Nitaka, KHS,
Diamond Back, plus tricycles, adult trikes, unicycles, bicycles-for-
two, and the popular Rollerblades, originally invented for hockey
players for use in the off-season. In business since 1972, they do
repairs, ship around the world, and sell clothes and accessories for
the bicycle enthusiast. If on the spur of the moment you want to
cruise the beach on a bicycle or roller skates, you'll find rentals
seven days a week at one of their their beach locations. You can get
more information by calling 213/306-3332.
*Additional Locations: Marina Del Rey (213/306-1763). Venice
(213/306-3332)*

TUAZON'S BIKE SHOP
3375 Iowa St., Suite I
Riverside, CA 92507
714/684-6255
HOURS: MON-SAT: 9:30-6
CREDIT CARDS: MC, V

More and more people are finding alternative ways to get to work, have fun on the weekends and get some exercise at the same time. As a result, the bicycle is a vehicle that is growing in popularity. At Tuazon's you'll find excellent prices (guaranteed best price) on standard, racing, mountain, and folding bicycles. They also carry bikes and scooters for children. If you think that your balance may not be as sharp as it used to be, you can buy a 3 wheeler for adults from Tuazon's, which would definitely make getting around in your community a breeze. Repairs done on all makes.

∞ EXERCISE EQUIPMENT ∞

OLYMPIA HEALTH FITNESS SUPERSTORE**
1660 S. La Cienega Blvd.
Los Angeles, CA 90035
213/285-9944
HOURS: MON-SAT: 9-7   SUN: 11-6
CREDIT CARDS: MC, V

Looking for a great buy on exercise equipment? Olympia Health Fitness Superstore guarantees the best price around. They have a 7,000 square foot showroom loaded with treadmills, home gyms, freeweights, exercise bikes, rowing machines, and boxing supplies. Olympia carries such brand names as Parabody, Maximus, Marcy, Delco, Precor, Trotier, Amerec, Tunturi, and Everlast. They also carry table tennis equipment, offer delivery, service and have rentals too. You get a good price just by walking in, and you'll get an additional 5% discount when you use your BUYING RETAIL IS STUPID coupon.

∞ GAME ROOM "TOYS" ∞

BILLIARDS & BARSTOOLS**
563 N. Central Ave.
Upland, CA 91786
714/946-1366
HOURS: MON-FRI: 10-6 SAT: 10-5 SUN: 11-5
CREDIT CARDS: V, MC

Billiards & Barstools is your one-stop shop for home recreation. Whether you are a dart thrower, poker player or billiard champion, everything you need can be found here in standard or customized form. You'll find at least 30 different styles in billiard tables made by World Leisure and Brunswick. In addition to items found in most billiard stores, you can spice up your game room with a nostalgic juke box, a slot machine, or even a carousel horse or two. If shooting pool makes you thirsty, you can chill your favorite beverages in an old Coke machine found here. How about an antique gas pump converted into a tropical fish aquarium? If you're short on space but still want a pool table, ask out their dining/pool table combination. Being factory direct, you can expect to spend 30–50% below retail and sometimes a lot less! They've been in business since 1967, so they're not behind the eight ball, and neither will you when you use your BUYING RETAIL IS STUPID coupon for an additional 10% discount.
Additional Locations: City of Industry (818/810-1388), San Bernardino (714/885-4669), West Covina (818/332-5099)

GOLDEN WEST BILLIARD MFG.
21260 Deering Court
Canoga Park, CA 91304
818/888-2300
HOURS: MON-SAT: 9:30-5:30
CREDIT CARDS: MC, V

Buy factory direct and save on pool tables at Golden West. They always have at least 12–14 tables of every size and style on display

with prices starting at just over $800. Their prices represent savings of 15 to 20% off retail stores. Golden West has been in business in California since 1962. They have a big selection of lamps, racks, custom cues, oak bars and barstools, and game tables, too. You can give them a call if you have a table in need of repair. When you are in their store, don't overlook their Brunswick antique tables.
Additional Locations: Beverly Hills (213/659-9487)

MURREY AND SONS
14150 S. Figueroa
Los Angeles, CA 90061
213/321-5161
HOURS: MON-FRI: 8:30 SAT: 10-3
CREDIT CARDS: MC, V

Murrey and Sons has been in business since 1938 selling billiard tables, pool tables, and all the supplies that go along with them. Their prices are 25% below retail, and the customer can customize his or her table with over 24 different cloth covers. Murrey and Sons has one of the largest inventories in Los Angeles, so don't miss out on this one.

PINBALL WAREHOUSE
8751 Tampa Ave.
Northridge, CA 91324
818/885-5050
HOURS: MON-SAT: 10-5
CREDIT CARDS: MC, V

If you're a pinball wizard or want to be one, then Pinball Warehouse is a place you must visit. You can buy your own pinball machine at wholesale prices here. Whether for personal or commercial use, Pinball Warehouse is the home for coin-operated entertainment fun. They have 2,500 square feet of showroom and carry brand names such as Williams, Bally, Data East, Nintendo, Merit and Atari. Pinball machines share the showroom with video games, foosball tables, juke boxes, and dart machines. They service what they sell and have a parts department. Don't miss this one!

∞ GOLF ∞

GOLF FAIRE
17635 Vanowen
Van Nuys, CA 91604
818/343-2454
HOURS: MON-FRI: 9:30-7   SAT: 9:30-6   SUN: 10-5
CREDIT CARDS: MC, V

You may be wondering where all the golf fanatics go. Well, stop by the Golf Faire which has one of the largest selections of equipment in the Southland. These people are serious, claiming "absolutely no lower prices on all name brands." For Foot Joy and Dexter Shoes, the PGA tour clothing collection, bags, putters, videos, balls, gloves and all accessories, don't drive past the Golf Faire. They carry Pro-Line clubs and brand names include, Ping, Hogan, Wilson, Lynx, MacGregor, Powerbilt, Titleist and Spaulding too. They also offer one day repair service and regripping while-U-wait.

ROGER DUNN GOLF SUPERMARKETS
4744 Lankershim Blvd.
N. Hollywood, CA 91602
818/763-3622, 800/682-5351
HOURS: MON-FRI: 10-7   SAT: 9-6   SUN: 10-5
CREDIT CARDS: MC, V

Roger Dunn, the world's largest golf supermarket, guarantees they will never be undersold. Their prices average 20 to 60% below retail prices, and even greater savings over pro shops. They have been in business over 20 years and carry every conceivable item related to golf. You can even hit with demo clubs before you make your purchase, and they take trade-ins on your old golf clubs. Be sure to join their club, so you can save an additional 10% with your Roger Dunn membership card.
Additional Locations: 18 other stores in S. CA–Call 800/682-5351

∞ GUNS, AMMO & FISHING GEAR ∞

ARMY-NAVY SURPLUS
11812 E. Garvey
El Monte, CA 91732
213/283-6272
HOURS: MON-SAT: 10-7 SUN: 10-4
CREDIT CARDS: AE, DISC, MC, V

Going hunting? This store has handguns and rifles plus a complete stock of ammunition. Do you need something to wear? Levi's jeans are here, plus shoes, t-shirts, and camouflage pants. They also carry tents, tent poles, boats, tarps in poly and canvas. Everything already mentioned plus car covers and hard-to-get surplus items are all at 20 to 50% above cost.
Additional Locations: Hollywood (213/463-4730), Santa Barbara (805/963-3868), Santa Monica (213/458-4166)

B & B SALES
12521 Oxnard St.
N. Hollywood, CA 91606
818/985-2329
HOURS: OPEN 7 DAYS A WEEK 11-7
CREDIT CARDS: MC, V

With over 12,000 guns in stock, B & B Sales claims to be the largest gun store in the United States. They have every brand of quality firearm known to man, from Colt and Smith & Wesson to Beretta and Walther, plus ammunition, reloading equipment and shooting accessories. In business since 1969, they say you'll save 20–50% off retail prices. They do expert gunsmithing, and buy and trade guns, too.
Additional Locations: Westminster (714/892-8881)

COBURN'S DISCOUNT GUNS
14859 Whittram Ave.
Fontana, CA 92335
714/829-0603
HOURS: MON-SAT: 10-6
CREDIT CARDS: DISC, MC, V

Whether you are a crack shot on the American Olympic Team or need reloading supplies for your coming hunting excursion, this 2,500 square foot store covers all bases. At Coburn's Discount Guns, you'll find discounts of 20 to 35% off retail prices on brand names such as Smith & Wesson, Colt, Ruger, Browning and others. Owner George Coburn is an expert at his trade. You will appreciate shopping in a place where you can count on getting factual anwers to your questions.

TURNER'S OUTDOORSMAN
1932 N. Tustin Ave.
Orange, CA 92667
714/974-0600
HOURS: MON-FRI: 10-9   SAT-SUN: 10-6
CREDIT CARDS: MC, V

This is the largest chain west of the Rockies specializing in hunting and fishing products. Turner's Outdoorsman carries everything you need for hunting and fishing at savings of 20 to 30% off retail prices. You will find a huge selection of handguns, rifles and shotguns along with necessary supplies. The fisherman will love the various rods, reels, tackle boxes, lures and you name it. They have been in business since 1970.
Additional Locations: 7 other stores in S. CA

TURNER'S OUTDOORSMAN OUTLET
12615 Colony St.
Chino, CA 91710
714/590-7225
HOURS: MON-FRI: 10-9   SAT-SUN: 10-6
CREDIT CARDS: MC, V

The Turner's Outdoorsman chain sells equipment and supplies for hunting and fishing at 20 to 30% off retail prices. This is their outlet store. You'll find 2,000 square feet of merchandise with prices at approximately 50% off retail. Overstock and last year's hottest items from their chain stores all end up here. So, anglers, cast your lines, and hunters, set your traps, for a good deal here.

∞ SPORTING GOODS ∞

SANDY'S SKI & SPORT
19905 Ventura Blvd.
Woodland Hills, CA 91364
818/346-1801
HOURS: MON-SAT: 10-8 SUN: 10-6
CREDIT CARDS: AE, DISC, MC, V

Save time and money at Sandy's: the prices are competitive, and the expert staff will steer you to what you need. They have a complete selection, so you don't waste time or money running around to different stores trying to find something you need or possibly ending up settling for equipment you wouldn't normally buy. They are specialists, so check out their stock.

SAWYERS & SAWYERS
5263 Lankershim Blvd.
N. Hollywood, CA 91604
818/761-5781
HOURS: MON-SAT: 10-6
CREDIT CARDS: CASH ONLY

At Sawyers & Sawyers you'll find a rather strange combination of sporting goods and musical instruments. Joe used to sell wholesale only to the studios, but he now sells to the public out of a 2,500 square foot store located in North Hollywood. The brand name merchandise is sold at 50% below name store sale prices. If you know the merchandise you want and have the model number, call

Joe and he can order it for you. He can't accept coupons or credit cards because his discounts are so high!

SUNSHINE SPORTS FACTORY OUTLET
8941 De Soto Ave.
Canoga Park, CA 91304
818/341-5805
HOURS: TUES-FRI: 11-6   SAT: 10-4   SUN: 12-4
CREDIT CARDS: CASH OR CHECKS ONLY

Skiers, campers and backpackers are going to love us for finding the Sunshine Sports Factory Outlet. Skiers will find everything they need in clothing for the slopes, along with some ski accessories. Campers, backpackers and bicyclists will find clothing and accessories, along with many other related items. They feature tents (more than 40 different models to choose from), both new and factory seconds, and a large selection of sleeping bags (over 50 different styles). Sunshine is the only store in Southern California that specializes in replacement tent poles. They can usually supply a pole (a single section or a complete set) for most styles of tents. They offer low prices all year round of 10 to 60% off retail.

SURPLUS

AMERICAN SURPLUS TRADERS**
18643 Parthenia St.
Northridge, CA 91324
818/993-5355
HOURS: MON-FRI: 8:30-5:30 SAT: 10:30-3:30
CREDIT CARDS: MC, V

They specialize in Holga office furniture and have 6,000 square feet of desks, secretarial chairs, executive chairs, file cabinets, lateral files, storage cabinets, shelf files, bookcases, and computer furniture. You will find new furniture, which are factory seconds, used furniture, and industrial shelving. If you're starting a new business on a low budget, this is a good place to start. You can anticipate saving 15 to 60% off retail, but if you use your BUYING RETAIL IS STUPID coupon, you'll save an additional 10%!

ARMY-NAVY SURPLUS
11812 E. Garvey
El Monte, CA 91732
213/283-6272
HOURS: MON-SAT: 10-7 SUN: 10-4
CREDIT CARDS: AE, DISC, MC, V

Going hunting? This store has handguns and rifles plus a complete stock of ammunition. Do you need something to wear? Levi's jeans are here, plus shoes, t-shirts, and camouflage pants. They also carry tents, tent poles, boats, tarps in poly and canvas. Everything already mentioned plus car covers and hard-to-get surplus items are all at 20 to 50% above cost.
Additional Locations: Hollywood (213/463-4730), Santa Barbara (805/963-3868), Santa Monica (213/458-4166)

FRANCO SURPLUS
8652 Amigo Ave.
Northridge, CA 91324
818/349-7631
HOURS: MON-FRI: 9-5:30
CREDIT CARDS: MC, V

You never can tell what you're likely to find at Franco Surplus. Save about 20% on a kaleidoscope of things in Rich Franco's place and even more on used office furniture. They have file cabinets, desks, computer furniture, floor mats for shops, chairs, safes, clocks, tables, folding tables, fans and more. You should definitely check them out for file cabinets since they say they have the largest selection in the Valley. Delivery is available at an extra charge.

KAGAN SURPLUS SALES**
8050 Webb Ave.
N. Hollywood, CA 91605
818/768-1422
HOURS: MON-THUR: 8:45-5:45 FRI: 8:30-5:15 SAT: 10-4:30
CREDIT CARDS: CASH OR CHECKS ONLY

Kagan Surplus Sales specializes in used office furniture, hospital furniture, home care items, and material handling equipment. This 4,000 square foot warehouse offers items that have been completely refurbished (repaired, painted and recovered if necessary). Savings range from 50 to 90% off what you would pay normally if these items were brand new. The price is the only way to tell that the wheelchairs (always a large selection) and Geri-chairs are used. In addition, Kagan Surplus Sales carries desks, credenzas, chairs, file cabinets, shelving, casters, carts, lockers, storage cabinets, medical, lab and x-ray equipment. Don't forget to use your BUYING RETAIL IS STUPID coupon for additional savings. You'll save 5% if your purchase is under $100, and 10% if your purchase is over $100.

SURPLUS CITY RETAIL CO.**
11796 Sheldon St.
Sun Valley, CA 91352
818/768-2888
HOURS: MON-SAT: 9-6
CREDIT CARDS: MC, V

Surplus City Retail Company has the largest supply of surplus clothing in Los Angeles with the best prices. You will discover camping supplies, maps, knives, and camouflage uniforms, new and used, from all over the world for 10 to 30% below list. Call to find out about the sales they have every month on 501 jeans featuring the lowest prices around. If you buy a pair of boots at Surplus City, use your BUYING RETAIL IS STUPID coupon for an additional 25% discount. The coupon is good only on boots not already on sale. Surplus isn't the only thing at Surplus City. You will see 105mm cannons and messenger bikes from WWII, a Nike missile, tanks, trailers and even an old astronaut's uniform. Unfortunately, only surplus goods are for sale.

VAN NUYS ARMY & NAVY STORE
6179 Van Nuys Blvd.
Van Nuys, CA 91401
818/781-3500
HOURS: MON-SAT: 8:30-9 SUN: 9-6
CREDIT CARDS: MC, V

You will find this to be one of the best stocked surplus stores in the area. Van Nuys Army & Navy Store is filled to the rafters with Levis, jackets, belts, caps, camping gear, sleeping bags, pea coats, sweats, thermal pants, boots, and a million other items for both men and women. You can find Coleman coolers here and motorcycle boots, Swiss army and Buck knives, Schott leather jackets, outdoor products, MA-1 and M65 field jackets come in both nylon and leather, soft packs, and duffels. Their complete military department stocks camouflage from at least six different companies. In business since 1950, Carol and Joe head the Van Nuys store and Dave oversees the one in Reseda. Both stores will meet or beat their competitors' prices. Check out the Air Force sunglasses and Halloween costumes too.

Additional Locations: Reseda (818/344-0237)

TOYS, DOLLS & GAMES

∞ TOYS & STUFFED ANIMALS ∞

D 'N J BEARS & DOLLS**
18583 Main St.
Huntington Beach, CA 92648
714/847-6266
HOURS: MON-THUR: 10-5:30   FRI: 10-6   SAT: 10-5   SUN: 12-4
CREDIT CARDS: AE, DISC, MC, V

A children's paradise can be found at D 'n J Bears & Dolls with their hundreds of stuffed animals and dolls. You can expect savings of 10 to 25% on brand names such as Applause, Aventi, Madame Alexander, Oakin, Russ Berrie, Steiff, Merrythought, Eden, North American Bear Co, Robin Woods and many more. You can even taste some of their fudge made on the premises while browsing in this 2,000 square foot shop. Gift wrapping and deliveries are available. They won't "fudge" on an additional 10% discount, if you use one of your BUYING RETAIL IS STUPID coupons!

TOYS R US
16040 Sherman Way
Van Nuys, CA 91411
818/780-5115
HOURS: MON-SAT: 9:30-9:30   SUN: 10-7
CREDIT CARDS: AE, DISC, MC, V

These stores are huge toy warehouses filled with discounted and low priced toys for youngsters of every age, plus goods and furniture for infants, children's books, games, bikes and tricycles, and much more. When a toy is "Hot" they're sure to have it here and at great prices save you money. Toys R Us also stocks quite a bit of merchandise for babies. By the way, this place isn't just for

youngsters. They have things like games, puzzles and other items for adults. Frequent sales and specials are held all year round.
Additional Locations: 50 other stores throughout S. CA

∞ TOYS & GAMES FOR ADULTS ∞

BILLIARDS & BARSTOOLS**
563 N. Central Ave.
Upland, CA 91786
714/946-1366
HOURS: MON-FRI: 10-6 SAT: 10-5 SUN: 11-5
CREDIT CARDS: V, MC

Billiards & Barstools is your one-stop shop for home recreation. Whether you are a dart thrower, poker player or billiard champion, everything you need can be found here in standard or customized form. You'll find at least 30 different styles in billiard tables made by World Leisure and Brunswick. In addition to items found in most billiard stores, you can spice up your game room with a nostalgic juke box, a slot machine, or even a carousel horse or two. If shooting pool makes you thirsty, you can chill your favorite beverages in an old Coke machine found here. How about an antique gas pump converted into a tropical fish aquarium? If you're short on space but still want a pool table, ask out their dining/pool table combination. Being factory direct, you can expect to spend 30–50% below retail and sometimes a lot less! They've been in business since 1967, so they're not behind the eight ball, and neither will you when you use your BUYING RETAIL IS STUPID coupon for an additional 10% discount.
Additional Locations: City of Industry (818/810-1388), San Bernadino (714/885-4669), West Covina (818/332-5099)

GOLDEN WEST BILLIARD MFG.
21260 Deering Court
Canoga Park, CA   91304
818/888-2300
HOURS: MON-SAT: 9:30-5:30
CREDIT CARDS: MC, V

Buy factory direct and save on pool tables at Golden West. They always have at least 12–14 tables of every size and style on display with prices starting at just over $800. Their prices represent savings of 15 to 20% off retail stores. Golden West has been in business in California since 1962. They have a big selection of lamps, racks, custom cues, oak bars and barstools, and game tables, too. You can give them a call if you have a table in need of repair. When you are in their store, don't overlook their Brunswick antique tables.
Additional Locations: Beverly Hills (213/659-9487)

MURREY AND SONS
14150 S. Figueroa
Los Angeles, CA 90061
213/321-5161
HOURS: MON-FRI: 8:30   SAT: 10-3
CREDIT CARDS: MC, V

Murrey and Sons has been in business since 1938 selling billiard tables, pool tables, and all the supplies that go along with them. Their prices are 25% below retail, and the customer can customize his or her table with over 24 different cloth covers. Murrey and Sons has one of the largest inventories in Los Angeles, so don't miss out on this one.

PINBALL WAREHOUSE
8751 Tampa Ave.
Northridge, CA 91324
818/885-5050
HOURS: MON-SAT: 10-5
CREDIT CARDS: MC, V

If you're a pinball wizard or want to be one, then Pinball Warehouse is a place you must visit. You can buy your own pinball machine at wholesale prices here. Whether for personal or commercial use, Pinball Warehouse is the home for coin-operated entertainment fun. They have 2,500 square feet of showroom and carry brand names such as Williams, Bally, Data East, Nintendo, Merit and Atari. Pinball machines share the showroom with video games, foosball tables, juke boxes, and dart machines. They service what they sell and have a parts department. Don't miss this one!

TRAVEL & VACATION NEEDS

∞ LUGGAGE & TRAVEL ACCESSORIES ∞

H. SAVINAR LUGGAGE
4625 W. Washington Blvd.
Los Angeles, CA 90016
213/938-2501
HOURS: MON-SAT: 8-5:30
CREDIT CARDS: MC, V

This is a good example of why "BUYING RETAIL IS STUPID!" was written. Why pay retail prices when you can go to stores like H. Savinar, enjoy big savings, have a more complete selection than any department store offers, and be waited on by helpful and knowledgeable salespeople? With a selection that is incomparable, this 14,000 square foot warehouse is stocked with luggage representing every major brand. The savings range from 20 to 60% on luggage, briefcases and wallets. The Savinar family has been in business since 1917, and at this location since 1958. Most of their salespeople have been working there for 10 years. Look for their special sales during the year. If you want to buy the best for less, be sure to visit H. Savinar luggage.
Additional Locations: Canoga Park (818/703-1313)

HANDBAG HANGUP
8580 Washington Blvd.
Culver City, CA 90232
213/559-4705
HOURS: MON-SAT: 10-5:30
CREDIT CARDS: MC, V

Someone definitely gave this store the right name. It's hard to visualize, but on the average, Handbag Hangup carries 20,000 to

30,000 handbags! Prices range from $1 to $300. In addition to all of those handbags, they also carry a small selection of luggage, small leather goods, and purse and travel accessories. All merchandise is 25% off retail prices set by manufacturers.

LAX LUGGAGE
18711 Ventura Blvd.
Tarzana, CA 91356
818/343-4422
HOURS: MON-SAT: 10-6   SUN: 11-5
CREDIT CARDS: MC, V

Find name brand luggage here at discounted prices. At LAX Luggage you'll see sets made by Ricardo, Samsonite, Skyway, Lucas, Members Only, Adolfo, Andiaro, Turi and Lark just to name a few. They also carry attaches, briefcases, agendas, travel items and Seiko clocks. If your luggage is in need of repair, they do authorized airline luggage repair as well.
Additional Locations: Inglewood (213/417-2307), West Los Angeles (213/478-2661)

LUGGAGE OUTLET
21223 Hawthorne Blvd.
Torrance, CA 90503
213/316-2323
HOURS: MON-SAT: 10-6
CREDIT CARDS: AE, MC, V

Whether you're traveling overnight to San Francisco or touring Europe for a month, Luggage Outlet will help you choose the perfect luggage for your journey. They have discounted prices (20 to 35% off retail) on all name brand luggage such as Samsonite, Andiamo, Tumi, Hartman, Boyt, Lark, Skyway, Ventura, Delsey and more. And while you're at it, why not get your initials monogrammed on

your new set, free of charge? The Luggage Outlet also has business cases and does luggage repair.
Additional Locations: Brea (714/671-6911), Irvine (714/250-0774)

∞ TRAVEL ARRANGEMENTS ∞

ALL REASONS TRAVEL**
18902 Ventura Blvd.
Tarzana, CA 91356
818/705-2810
HOURS: MON-FRI: 9-5:30   SAT: BY APPOINTMENT ONLY
CREDIT CARDS: AE, DC, DISC, MC, V

We all have a good reason to travel and that's to get away so we can relax! These folks specialize in trips to Hawaii, South America and Mexico. Give them a call and see if you can arrange for that fantastic, well deserved get-away. Don't forget to ask about extra savings on flights outside the United States. With your Buying Retail is Stupid Coupon you can get an additional 10% discount on a cruise, so how can you resist?

THE CRUISE COMPANY
416 N. Brand Blvd.
Glendale, CA 91203
818/247-2600
HOURS: MON-FRI: 9-5:30
CREDIT CARDS: ALL MAJOR CREDIT CARDS

Save money (20–50%) and relax while traveling on one of their many cruises on Holland America, Princess, Cunard or Carnival. Your savings can be used to increase the amount you've budgeted for shopping. Get on their mailing list to be notified about specials on upcoming cruises. This is a "no frills" operation, so you can have your "frills" on the cruise of your choice.

FLIGHT COORDINATORS
1150 Yale St.
Santa Monica, CA 90403
213/453-1396 800/366-3544
HOURS: MON-FRI: 9-5:30 SAT: 10-4
CREDIT CARDS: AE, MC, V

Offering more than 30 years experience in low cost air fare, Flight Coordinators say they can save you plenty on your overseas flights, especially if you need to fly on one day's notice. They deal mostly with overseas flights, but they do handle some domestic flights at a discount. Depending on where you're off to, you can expect to save from 5 to 50% on your airline tickets.

VARIETY STORES

∞ GENERAL MERCHANDISE ∞

99¢ ONLY STORE
18222 Sherman Way
Reseda, CA 91335
213/LUCKY-99
HOURS: 7 DAYS A WEEK: 9-9
CREDIT CARDS: MC, V

If your lucky number is 99, then this is the store for you! Absolutely everything in the store is sold for 99¢. You can really get great bargains on things like sundries, food, glassware, paper goods, small gift items, plus much more. New merchandise arrives daily and there is never any limit on quantities purchased. Call 213/LUCKY-99 for information.
Additional Locations: 21 other stores in S. CA

BARGAIN SAVER
5500 Hollywood Blvd.
Los Angeles, CA 90028
213/466-5383
HOURS: MON-SAT: 10:30-7 SUN: 12-6
CREDIT CARDS: MC, V

With just about absolutely everything you can imagine in this catch-all store, you've got to see it to believe it! Bargain Saver has household items, clothing, cookware, drinking glasses, jogging shoes, pillows, comforters, blankets, mattress pads, towels, toys, soap, rugs, statues, and a lot of odds and ends. Yes, we said odds and ends. Nonetheless, you can get Toastmaster and Hamilton Beach products for 20 to 50% above their cost.

HALF PRICE STORES INC.
6367 Van Nuys Blvd.
Van Nuys, CA 91401
818/780-6844
HOURS: MON-FRI: 10-6:30 SAT: 10-6
CREDIT CARDS: MC, V

Local consumers have known about exploratory shopping at the Half Price Stores since 1967. Depending on the items purchased, you can save from 10 to 70% shopping here. There are watches, jewelry, toothpaste, paper products, Christmas goods, socks, underwear, cleaning aids, towels, and much more. We could go on and on trying to list the thousands of things on the shelves. In the back room you'll discover gas and electric barbecues. There are at least ten units on display representing brand names such as Amerilight, Broilmaster, Char-Broil and Patio. Barbecue accessories and replacement parts are also stocked.

LA BREA BARGAIN CIRCUS
852 N. La Brea
Los Angeles, CA 90038
213/466-7231
HOURS: MON-SAT: 9:30-8:30 SUN: 10-8
CREDIT CARDS: MC, V

A grocery store and so much more! In addition to food products, La Brea Bargain Circus features knives, silver, beer and an assortment of ceramic planters and dishes. The stock changes weekly, so it's like going to a new store every week. They buy inventory close-outs and job lots, so the prices are terrific; the people are nice and friendly, too. With this store having over 80,000 square feet, not only do you have a large assorted selection, you have lots of area to cover. Watch for their newspaper ads for their latest specials.

VARDAK DISCOUNT STORE
5211 Lankershim Blvd.
N. Hollywood, CA 91601
818/509-1211
HOURS: MON-SAT: 10-8 SUN: 10-6
CREDIT CARDS: CASH OR CHECKS ONLY

Need a good price on telephones, radios, stereos, toys, clothing or a variety of merchandise at 50% off retail? In addition to a constantly changing inventory, you'll find 1,600 square feet of good values here. You never know what you're bound to find at Vardak's.

∞ NEW & USED MERCHANDISE ∞

CINEMA GLAMOUR SHOP
343 No. La Brea
Los Angeles, CA 90036
213/933-5289
HOURS: WED: 1-4 MON-FRI: 10-4
CREDIT CARDS: CASH ONLY

Now you can wear or use things from movie stars. Cinema Glamour Shop's entire stock of merchandise is from donations made by the movie industry. Anything and everything donated to them by the industry is for sale here, so you never know what you are going to find. If you go down to the Cinema Glamour Shop to do some exploring, leave your checkbook and credit cards at home. This thrift shop operates strictly on a cash basis.

COLLATERAL LOANS, INC.
18520 Sherman Way
Reseda, CA 91335
818/345-9600
HOURS: MON, WED-SAT: 9-5
CREDIT CARDS: CASH OR CHECKS ONLY

This is really a loan corporation store where all of the merchandise has been preowned but not necessarily used. You can save as much as 80% on video equipment, typewriters, jewelry, crystal, collectibles, bicycles, stereos, household appliances, and more. Some personal property was collateral on loans; other items have been bought outright from individuals and estates. You'll see some items still in factory-sealed cartons from Remington, IBM, Nikon, Singer, Pioneer, Martin, Gibson, Waterford, Zeiss, Kodak, Rolex and Sony. Ask for Sam or Scott, and be sure to inquire about their twice-yearly sales. Parking is free.

LOAN MART, INC.
6426 Van Nuys Blvd.
Van Nuys, CA 91401
818/787-3502
HOURS: MON-SAT: 9-5
CREDIT CARDS: MC, V

Don't judge this store by its name! They don't sell loans; they sell out-of-pawn merchandise. You can get great buys on fine jewelry, cameras, lens, binoculars, guns, and art objects sold at 20 to 50% above cost. They are the largest pawn shop in the San Fernando Valley. If you have never been in a pawn shop, Loan Mart is a good place to start. You'll find them to be a unique store with some really terrific buys!

CATALOGS

Buying from catalogs is a huge part of the consumer scene. Mail-order purchasing has become significant to consumers who want to buy conveniently (from your home), locate articles that may not be readily available in stores, and save money (through discounts and low prices offered due to low overhead—no sales people or fancy facilities are needed). We have included here, for the most part, only mail-order houses that sell at a discount and government and other booklets which offer advice to the consumer on how to shop effectively and economically. A few catalogs have been included because they offer unique, special merchandise and/or low prices. So send for the ones that interest you and start your collection today. You will have a lot of fun going through these interesting, informative, colorful materials. And, when your purchases start arriving in the mail, it will seem like Christmas every day.

∞ ARTS, CRAFTS, & HOBBIES ∞

– ART SUPPLIES –

CARTOON COLOUR COMPANY, INC.
9024 Lindblade St.
Culver City, CA 90230
213/838-8467
COST: FREE

Since 1947, Cartoon Colour Company has manufactured superior artists' paints for the animation industry, as well as for other fields of commercial art. You'll appreciate the low prices.

CATALOGS

CO-OP ARTISTS' MATERIALS ATLANTA AIRBRUSH
P.O. Box 53097
Atlanta, GA 30355
800/877-1228
COST: FREE

Featured in this catalog is everything an artist needs—brushes, easels, pens, markers, portfolios, paper and much more. They rate high in customer service too.

COS-TOM PICTURE FRAMES
1031 Bay Blvd.
Chula Vista, CA 92011
800/854-6606
COST: FREE

Cos-Tom Picture Frames is your connection to hundreds of frames of all types and styles at factory direct prices. Their selection includes the popular look of the Southwest, furniture finish wood tones, contemporary metal, embossed European designs, rustics and formica frames in every color of the rainbow.

DANIEL SMITH ARTISTS MATERIALS
4130 First Ave. South
Seattle, WA 98134
800/426-6740
COST: FREE

Daniel Smith Artists Materials has a beautiful catalog and offers savings for the artistic minded. They have a wide selection of brushes, paint, paper, and equipment. You'll also find that ordering from them is a pleasure. They are very customer service oriented.

– CRAFT SUPPLIES –

OLMSTED WOOD PRODUCTS, INC.
8153 Orchard St.
Olmsted Falls, OH 44138
216/235-4020
COST: FREE

For those of you who are good with your hands and enjoy building things, Olmsted Wood Products guarantees you'll be satisfied with their quartz clock movements and clock making supplies. It's nice to know there is still a company around that offers do-it-yourself clock making supplies.

ROUSSEL
1013 Mass Ave.
Arlington, MA 02174
617/643-3388
COST: FREE

Roussel offers terrific buys on supplies and equipment for making your own costume jewelry. In addition to jewelry kits and findings, you never know what you'll find in Roussel's special deals and closeouts. Most items are sold by the dozen, but the prices can't be beat.

– FABRIC –

THAI SILKS
252 State St.
Los Altos, CA 94022
800/221-SILK, 415/948-8611
COST: FREE

Lustrous, exotic silks in over 400 designs makes Thai Silks one of the leaders in supplying silk fabrics to the public. You can get an entire sample collection of all their styles and various types of silks for only $20.00 which is refunded if returned in 30 days. They also carry a selection of silk clothing. All this at 30–50% savings.

– STAMPS –

JAMESTOWN STAMP COMPANY
341–3 E. Third St.
Jamestown, NY 14701-0019
716/488-0763
COST: FREE

This catalog offers stamps from all over the world, plus all related supplies and accessories. You'll get the best prices buying stamps in bulk, which is perfect for someone just starting a collection. Collectors of baseball cards, postcards and bank notes will also find this catalog interesting.

∞ APPLIANCES ∞

AAA-ALL FACTORY, INC.
241 Cedar
Abilene, TX 79601
915/688-1311
COST: $2.00

AAA-All Factory provides brand name vacuum cleaners such as Hoover, Panasonic, Royal, Eureka and more at substantial savings.

ABC VACUUM CLEANER WAREHOUSE
6720 Burnet Rd.
Austin, TX 78757
512/459-7643
COST: FREE

ABC Vacuum Cleaner Warehouse is known for their inventory of leading brand name vacuum cleaners with savings up to 35%. They also carry liquidated merchandise at up to 75% off retail.

SEWIN' IN VERMONT
84 Concord Ave.
St. Johnsbury, VT 05819
800/451-5124
COST: FREE

If you do your own sewing, check out Sewin' in Vermont. They carry brand name sewing machines at unbelievable prices.

∞ AUTOMOTIVE PARTS & ACCESSORIES ∞

J.C. WHITNEY & CO.
P.O. Box 8410
Chicago, IL 60680
312/431-6102
COST: FREE

Save up to 50% by shopping from J.C. Whitney's catalog featuring a huge selection of parts and accessories for all American and imported cars, vans, pickups, RV's, off-road vehicles and motorcycles.

∞ BOOKS, MOVIES & MUSIC ∞

BARNES & NOBLE
126 Fifth Ave.
New York, NY 10011
800/242-6657
COST: FREE

Claiming to be the world's largest bookstore, Barnes & Noble has been selling books since 1873. Their catalog offers a tremendous selection of books at up to 75% off retail. They have hard and soft cover books on just about every subject. You'll even find a few "coffee table" art books. Audio book fans will enjoy the selection of best sellers and classics on cassettes. They also have videos featuring movie classics, foreign films and documentaries. Culture vultures will appreciate videos on subjects such as opera, ballet, classical music and theater featuring the greatest artists of our time. Cassettes, CD's and LP's are also available.

CABLE FILMS
P.O. Box 7171
Kansas City, MO 64113
913/362-2804
COST: FREE

Established in 1976, Cable Films features film classics. You'll find films from the 30's and 40's, silents, Chaplin short features, Hitchcock and Sherlock Holmes mysteries, Bela Lugoisi and more.

PUBLISHERS CENTRAL BUREAU
One Champion Ave., Dept. 491
Avenel, NJ 07001-2301
800/722-9800, Ext. 491
COST: FREE

This catalog is chocked full of books, videos, cassettes and compact discs. You'll find savings of up to 87% off retail on their enormous selection of books and audio/visual products.

SPECIAL INTEREST VIDEO
475 Oberlin Ave. South, CN2112
Lakewood, NJ 08701
800/522-0502
COST: FREE

Special Interest Video is just what they say. Offering videos you can't buy in your local video shop, you'll find titles on the Civil War, modern military aircraft, World War II and even an exclusive volume of Arthur Murray Dance Steps. Other exciting titles are Play Bridge with Omar Sharif, The Smothers Brothers Show, How to Gamble and Win, Hummingbirds Up Close and many more.

U.S. GOVERNMENT BOOKS
Superintendent of Documents
U.S. Government Printing Office
Washington, DC 20402-9325
COST: FREE

Government publications for people of all ages are available through this catalog. This is an unbelievable source for government books on all subjects. Covering everything from agriculture, military equipment and foreign policy to travel, exercise and nutritional needs, there are over 21,000 different publications available. Some items such as informational booklets are $1, and historical documents reproduced on parchment paper run $2 (great for student projects). Also listed are the locations of Government Bookstores in various states where you can browse to your heart's content.

∞ CIGARS, PIPES & TOBACCO ∞

WALLY FRANK, LTD.
63-25 69th St.
Middle Village, NY 11379
718/326-2233
COST: FREE

Save up to 50% on a wide selection of domestic and imported cigars, pipes and tobacco. They even have a 8 3/4" long 60 ring gauge cigar that comes in a cedar wood hinged case. You can buy both name brand products and generic brands from Wally Frank. Also in their catalog are gift items such as various flasks, walking sticks and a selection of scrimshaw collectibles.

∞ CLOTHING ∞

CHADWICK'S OF BOSTON
One Chadwick Place, Box 1600
Brockton, MA 0240-1600
508/583-6600
COST: FREE

Chadwick's of Boston is known as the original off-price catalog. They feature the latest in fashion and yet carry classic clothing as well. For the busy career woman or the equally busy woman at home, Chadwick's has a marvelous selection at affordable prices.

THE DEERSKIN PLACE
283 Akron Rd.
Ephrata, PA 17522
717/733-7624
COST: FREE

Choose from a wide selection of jackets, handbags, shoes, moccasins, gloves and wallets for men and women made from cowhide, sheepskin and deerskin. You can even order a coonskin cap.

DESIGNER DIRECT
Designer Circle
Salem, VA 24156-0501
800/848-2929
COST: FREE

Designer Direct brings you exclusive women's fashions you won't find elsewhere, plus A.J. Valenci footwear and elegant accessories at up to 60% below retail. Make a positive impact with their up-to-date women's fashions.

WINTER SILKS
2700 Laura Lane
Middleton, WI 53562
800/648-7455
COST: FREE

This catalog features all kinds of clothing and accessories made of silk. You'll find silk turtlenecks, pajamas, gloves, sweaters, blouses, lingerie and even long johns at substantially lower prices than found in retail stores. Snow skiers that wear only long underwear made of silk will be amazed at the money they can save ordering from Winter Silks.

∞ CONSUMER INFORMATION ∞

AUTOMOBILE CLUB SOUTHERN CALIFORNIA
AUTOMOTIVE INFORMATION CENTER (AIC)
P.O. Box 2890, Terminal Annex
Los Angeles, CA 90051-0890
213/741-4487
COST: FREE

If you're in the market for a new car or you want to sell one, you can order informational brochures from the Auto Club. Choose from "Buying a New Car," "Buying a Used Car," "Financing a Car," "Leasing vs. Buying," and "Selling Your Vehicle." The brochures are well-written, contain much useful information, and can save you time and money. Auto Club members need only call and they will send you any of these easy-to-understand brochures.

CONSUMER ACTION
116 New Montgomery St.
San Francisco, CA 94105
COST: $1.00

The Consumer Services Guide is a must! It includes the addresses and telephone numbers of regulatory and law enforcement government agencies, business sponsored complaint resolution offices, nonprofit information and referral organizations and agencies that offer free, or low cost legal assistance.

CONSUMER INFORMATION CENTER
Pueblo, CO 81009
COST: FREE

Hundreds of booklets free or low cost featuring information on such topics as small business, careers, cars, children, education, health, nutrition, building, buying and financing a house, exercise and weight control, money management, travel and hobbies and much more.

FREE THINGS FOR KIDS TO WRITE AWAY FOR
Jetco Publications, Dept. TFK
P.O. Box 85
Livingston, NJ 07039-0085
COST: $2.00

Children will be thrilled with this catalog filled with all kinds of free things to send away for. Mini-flashlights, replicas of historical documents, animal iron-ons, vegetable seeds, puppets, coloring books, posters, genuine foreign money are just a few samples of the free offers in this catalog. Young sports fans can send for freebies from several professional football and baseball teams. Also available are many informational and how-to brochures and booklets. Parents will also find items of interest in this catalog.

∞ COSMETICS & WIGS ∞

BEAUTIFUL VISIONS
810 S. Hicksville Rd.
Hicksville, NY 11855
516/349-7180
COST: FREE

Name brand cosmetics and nationally advertised fragrances at remarkable savings of up to 90% off. There are regular sizes as well as samples sizes that are great for traveling.

BEAUTY BOUTIQUE
6836 Engle Rd.
Cleveland, OH 44101-4519
216/826-1712
COST: FREE

Save up to 90% on nationally known cosmetics when you order from Beauty Boutique. You'll find products for your face, hands, feet and the rest of your body in name brands such as Estee Lauder, Loreal, Revlon and Cutex. Fragrances and various personal products are also featured in this catalog.

BEAUTY BY SPECTOR, INC.
Dept. OR
McKeesport, PA 15134
COST: FREE

Exciting designer styles of wigs and hairpieces up to 50% off are available from Beauty by Spector. Also featured is an extensive list of additional catalogs you can order for convenient shopping from your home.

∞ FOOD & BEVERAGE ∞

– BEER & WINE MAKING KITS –

THE CELLAR
14411 Greenwood Ave. N.
Seattle, WA 98133
206/365-7660
COST: FREE

The Cellar has everything you need for brewing beer and making wine and liqueur at the best prices around. Their catalog features free recipes and if you have a problem there's an expert on duty (just a phone call away) to help you Monday through Sunday.

– HEALTH FOODS & VITAMINS –

VITAMIN CO-OP
44-823 Guadalupe Dr.
Indian Wells, CA 92210
619/341-1070
COST: FREE

Save 30% and more on special formulas, vitamins, and health and beauty aids. They also have an extensive list of hard to find items.

VITAMIN POWER, INC.
39 Saint Mary's Pl.
Freeport, NY 11520
800/645-6567
COST: FREE

Vitamin Power is in the business of promoting health. They sell products that help people relax, sleep, control weight, build strength and increase energy. You'll find their healthcare products include exclusive formulations and specialty products that cannot be found in mass merchandise stores or discount chains.

– NUTS & CANDY–

ACE SPECIALTY FOODS
P. O. Box 100
Cordele, GA 31015
800/729-8999
COST: FREE

Ace Specialty Foods offers very fancy nuts at very "un-fancy" prices. Their cashews, pecans, pistachios, macadamia nuts, dried fruit and chocolate candy are all guaranteed to be delivered fresh to your doorstep.

∞ GENERAL MERCHANDISE ∞

DAMARK INTERNATIONAL
6707 Shingle Creek Pky.
Minneapolis, MN 55430
800/729-9000
COST: FREE

This catalog specializes in manufacturer close-outs and some of their prices are out of this world. The Sharp Copier/Fax Machine UX80 has a suggested retail price of $2,295.00, but you can order if from Damark International for only $499.99! They call this the "Great Deal" catalog because you can get famous name products below dealer cost. They carry a wide selection of merchandise such as appliances, sports equipment, electronics, furniture, giftware and luggage. Your first catalog is free, but if you don't order something they won't automatically send you another.

∞ HOME FURNISHINGS ∞

– CHINA, SILVER & TABLEWARE –

BARRONS
22790 Heslip Dr.
Novi, MI 48050
800/538-6340
COST: FREE

Fifteen years in business, Barrons provides you with the finest gift-ware, collectibles, crystal, dinnerware and flatware. They have the largest in-stock selection in the United States. Brand names include Hummel, Royal Doulton, Lenox and many more.

BEVERLY BREMER SILVER SHOP
3164 Peachtree Rd. NE
Atlanta, GA 30305
404/261-4009
COST: FREE

Missing a piece of your sterling silver flatware? Beverly Bremer Silver Shop keeps over a thousand patterns of new and beautiful-as-new sterling in stock so they can help you locate exotic as well as practical flatware items for your collection. They also specialize in new and antique silver gift items. Contact them if you are interested in selling your sterling silver.

BUSCHEMEYER'S SILVER EXCHANGE
515 S. 4th Ave.
Louisville, KY 40202
502/587-7342
COST: FREE

This is a source for approximately 1,400 different active, inactive and obsolete sterling and silverplate patterns. They will be glad to find your pattern and quote prices. Send for brochures listing active sterling silver or silverplate patterns which are available from Buschemeyer's Silver Exchange at discount prices.

THE CHEF'S CATALOG
3215 Commercial Ave.
Northbrook, IL 60062-1900
708/480-8305
COST: FREE

This catalog is filled with products for indoor and outdoor cooking. You'll find items for basic food preparation and specialized equipment for unusual or complicated recipes. This catalog has range and oven cookware in a variety of shapes, sizes and materials, barbecues (indoor, outdoor, large and small) and accessories, cookbooks, ice cream makers and many other culinary necessities. There are also lots of kitchen gadgets chefs won't be able to live without.

COLONIAL GARDEN KITCHENS AND HOME
P. O. Box 66
Hanover, PA 17333-0066
COST: FREE

If you enjoy unique, cleverly designed products that in many cases aren't available in any store, this catalog is full of interesting and unusual products that can make cooking and entertaining easier. Everything from appliances to furniture and lots of great gadgets all at terrific prices!

MIDAS CHINA & SILVER
5050 Nicholson Lane
Rockville, MD 20852
800/368-3153
COST: FREE

Pass on the memories of fine china and sterling flatware from Midas China & Silver. Your children and grandchildren will enjoy receiving items from their elegant selection. Only the finest merchandise is in this catalog at savings up to 60%.

ROSS-SIMONS
136 Lambert Lind Hwy (Rt 5)
Warwick, RI 02886
800/556-7376
COST: FREE

Whether fine jewelry or beautiful things for your home, Ross-Simons offers it priced up to 40% below fair retail. They also carry a line of Christmas collectibles.

– FLOOR COVERINGS –

JOHNSON'S CARPETS
3239 South Dixie Highway
Dalton, GA 30720
800/235-1079, 404/277-2775
COST: FREE

No need to spend days looking for the perfect carpet and the best price because Johnson's Carpets manufactures carpets and sells direct to you with savings as high as 80%. Samples are available for all carpets they manufacture so you can feel the weight and select exactly the right color before placing an order.

WAREHOUSE CARPETS, INC.
Box 3233
Dalton, GA 30721
800/526-2229
COST: FREE

Save as much as 50% on brand name carpets such as Mohawk, Aladdin, Columbus, Galaxy, Masland, World, Salem, Coronet and many more.

– FURNITURE –

BRASS BEDS DIRECT
4866 W. Jefferson Blvd.
Los Angeles, CA 90016
800/727-6865
COST: FREE

Superb workmanship and attention to detail has kept Brass Beds Direct in business for the past 19 years with happy customers from all over the United States. They have excellent prices too.

SHAW FURNITURE GALLERIES
P.O. Box 576
Randelman, NC 27317
800/334-6799
COST: FREE

Shaw Furniture Galleries represents 300 major manufacturers of home furnishings with savings up to 40% off retail. This company is for people who know what they want and are looking for the best buy. They have been serving their customers since 1940.

SOBOL HOUSE OF FURNISHINGS
Richardson Blvd.
Black Mountain, NC 28711
704/669-8031
COST: FREE

Shop around and compare brand names and cost on your next furniture purchase, then call Sobol House of Furnishings. They'll save you 40 to 50% off retail prices on their selection of traditional, 18th century or modern furniture.

– LAMPS & LIGHT FIXTURES –

ALLIED LIGHTING
Drawer E
Trextertown, PA 18087
800/322-4468, Ext. 10
COST: FREE

Elegant crystal chandeliers, Tiffany style lamps, outdoor lighting, floor lamps and more with up to 60% savings. Over 40 manufacturers are represented in their catalog.

– LINENS –

THE COMPANY STORE
500 Company Store Rd.
La Crosse, WI 54601-4477
800/356-9367
COST: FREE

The Company Store has been in business since 1911 keeping people warm and toasty with their plush down products. Their comforters, in a variety of styles and grades, are all covered in downproof fabric with a minimum 232 thread count. You can get high quality merchandise without paying department store prices.

HARRIS LEVY, INC.
278 Grand St.
New York, NY 10002
800/221-7750, 212/226-3102
COST: FREE

Discounted up to 40%, Harris Levy will send you linens for your bed, bath and table. Their motto is, "The very best at the least."

– WALL & WINDOW TREATMENTS–

AMERICAN DISCOUNT WALLCOVERINGS
1411 Fifth Ave.
Pittsburgh, PA 15219
800/777-2737
COST: FREE

You'll find over 100 brands of wallpaper, window treatments and upholstery fabrics at substantial savings of 10–50% off retail. They don't have a catalog, but they'll send you a list covering most of the brand names they carry. After you've shopped around call American Discount Wallcoverings with pattern numbers and book names.

NATIONAL WHOLESALE WALLCOVERINGS
Box 396
Ledgewood, NJ 07852
800/631-9341
COST: FREE

Leading distributor for over 90% of the wallcoverings available in
the United States. Their merchandise is delivered free to your home
and savings run 35–70% off retail.

ROBINSON'S WALLCOVERINGS
222 West Spring St.
Titusville, PA 16354
814/827-1893
COST: 50¢

Walk from room to room with Robinson's catalog in hand and
visualize the beautiful new rooms you can create. Do-it-yourself
decorators have been shopping Robinson's for 70 years

SILVER WALLPAPER, INC.
3001-15 Kensington Ave.
Philadelphia, PA 19134
800/426-6600, 215/426-7600
COST: FREE

Silver Wallpaper has an extensive selection of first quality wallcoverings, borders and fabrics, in virtually every pattern manufactured in the country. Call them with the name of book and pattern
number to receive their discounted prices up to 66% below retail.

WALLPAPER WAREHOUSE, INC.
1434 Ellis Ave
Jackson, MS 30204
800/523-3503
COST: FREE

Wallpaper Warehouse says they'll save you lots of money once you
know exactly what kind of wallpaper you're looking for.

∞ JEWELRY ∞

JAMES KAPLAN JEWELERS
40 Freeway Dr.
Cranston, RI 02920
800/343-0712
COST: FREE

Unusual gift items, elegant jewelry, and brand name china and silver has been offered by James Kaplan Jewelers for the past 35 years. Savings are approximately 20–75% off retail.

ROSS-SIMONS JEWELERS
9 Ross-Simons Dr.
Cranston, RI 02920-9848
800/556-7376
COST: FREE

This catalog features fine jewelry priced at 40% below retail. They have traditional and contemporary styles in gold and sterling silver. Call their toll-free number for their catalog or to place an order.

∞ LUGGAGE ∞

A TO Z LUGGAGE
4627 New Ultrecht Ave.
Brooklyn, NY 11219
800/342-5011
COST: FREE

Famous maker luggage, briefcases and leather accessories up to 50% off. Some brand names to look for are Hartmann, American Tourister, Samsonite and more.

ACE LEATHER PRODUCTS
2211 Avenue U
Brooklyn, NY 11229
800/DIAL ACE
COST: FREE

You'll love their excellent selection on name brand luggage, attache cases, handbags, travel and desk clocks and small leather goods. Ace Leather Products has been in business for 69 years.

∞ MUSICAL INSTRUMENTS ∞

ALAS ACCORDION-O-RAMA
16 W. 19th St.
New York, NY 10011
212/675-9089
COST: FREE

Now you can own a top brand, expertly rebuilt accordion, that has been completely reconditioned and approved by a tuning and service expert to be as good as new. And at a substantial savings.

SAM ASH MUSIC CORPORATION
124 Fulton Ave.
Hempstead, NY 11550
800/4 SAM ASH, 516/485-2151
COST: FREE

For over 60 years the family owned business of Sam Ash Music has been selling musical instruments and equipment at discounted prices. They run monthly specials, deals on closeout items and have one-of-a-kind items in addition their already low prices.

∞ OPTICAL PRODUCTS ∞

– CONTACT LENS SUPPLIES –

EYE SOLUTIONS
Box 262
Galion, OH 44833
419/683-1608
COST: FREE

If you're one of the thousands of people who wear contacts this catalog is a must. Save up to 70% on a wide selection of eyecare products—saline/rinsing solutions, weekly and daily cleaners and travel kits which contain everything you'll need for your next trip.

– *SUNGLASSES* –

SUNGLASSES U.S.A.
469 Sunrise Hwy.
Lynbrook, NY 11563
800/USA-RAYS
COST: $1.00

Now you can buy everyone's favorite sunglasses, Ray-Bans, at genuine wholesale prices. You'll pay the same price as your local optometrist pays when you order from Sunglasses U.S.A. Their catalog offers quite a large selection of shades (75 categories on the price list) from which to choose, and they'll waive the customary $2.00 shipping and handling charge on your first order.

∞ OFFICE SUPPLIES & EQUIPMENT ∞

FIDELITY PRODUCTS
P. O. Box 155
Minneapolis, MN 55440
800/328-3034
COST: FREE

You'll find a quality selection of all office supplies, furniture, machines and equipment all at the lowest prices guaranteed. If you find a current price lower than the prices shown in their catalog, send them a copy of the ad or catalog page within 30 days of purchase and you'll receive a refund of the difference.

VIKING DISCOUNT OFFICE PRODUCTS
P. O. Box 61144
Los Angeles, CA 90061-0144
800/421-1222
COST: FREE

With savings up to 75% off retail on some items, you'll find some really terrific discounts on office supplies in this catalog. Orders over $25 are delivered free anywhere in the continental United States. Most orders arrive within two days.

∞ PARTY & PAPER PRODUCTS ∞

CURRENT
The Current Building
Colorado Springs, CO 80941
COST: FREE

From stationery to wrapping paper, note cards to gifts, Current offers a unique line of fine quality products suitable for every occasion at lower than card shop prices. Their selection of items with nature and animal themes are bound to please children and adults alike. Gift wrapping perfectionists will appreciate the multitude of styles and colors available individually or in sets. Their catalog that comes out in time for Valentines Day is not to be missed. In addition to their already low prices, they have discounts on top of discounts.

∞ PET SUPPLIES ∞

R.C. STEEL
1989 Transit Way
Brockport, NY 14420
800/872-3773
COST: FREE

This catalog offers dog equipment and kennel supplies at wholesale prices! You can order books, grates, cages, grooming supplies, toys, treats, nutritional products, training aids plus anything else found at your local pet store, but at bargain prices.

UNITED PHARMACAL CO., INC.
Box 969
St. Joseph, MO 64502
816/233-8800
COST: FREE

Since 1952 UPCO has cared about serving you and your animal's needs. They offer dependable products at the lowest possible prices backed by guaranteed service. You'll find literally everything for your pet in their 160 page catalog.

∞ PHOTOGRAPHY ∞

BI-RITE PHOTO AND ELECTRONICS
15 E. 30th St.
New York, NY 10016
800/223-1970
COST: FREE

You can save up to 60% on cameras and accessories, typewriters, video equipment, telephone systems and more.

CROWN PRODUCTS
2142 Superior Ave.
Cleveland, OH 44114
800/782-2160
COST: FREE

Everything from photo albums, mounts, and folios and introductory studio kits all competitively priced. Most items need to be ordered in quantities of 25 or more.

PORTER'S CAMERA STORE, INC.
P. O. Box 628
Cedar Falls, IA 50613
800/553-2001
COST: $2.00

Whether you are a professional or an amateur photographer, you'll appreciate the savings (10-88% off retail) found in this catalog. In addition to cameras, lenses, filters, tripods and all other necessary camera accessories, Porter's Camera Store carries everything you need in darkroom equipment and supplies. Backdrops, light meters, slide mounts and various slide viewers, how-to books and videos, film and projectors are just a few more items carried in their extensive inventory.

∞ Plants, Lawn & Garden ∞

BURPEE–W. ATLEE BURPEE & CO.
300 Park Ave.
Warminster, PA 18991-0001
215/674-4915
COST: FREE

Neighborhood horticulturists in all parts of the country have been buying seeds, bulbs, and plants from Burpee for years. You can make your garden more beautiful with flowers, roses, vines, trees, shrubs and hedges. Chefs can create and enhance dishes with vegetables and herbs picked fresh from the backyard. You can also order anything you need in tools, supplies and specialized products for gardening.

HARRIS MORAN SEED COMPANY
1155 Harkins Rd.
Salinas, CA 93901
408/757-3651
COST: FREE

Treat yourself to the finest flower and vegetable seeds and bedding plants from Harris Moran Seed Company. Their reasonable prices will even encourage the part time gardener into growing tomatoes and lettuce in the backyard.

INDOOR GARDENING SUPPLIES
P. O. Box 40567
Detroit, MI 40567
313/668-8384
COST: FREE

Want to have country living in the city, then purchase some of these light fixtures, plant stands and accessories and get your greenhouse started in your apartment or house. Your plants will love you!

VAN BOURGONDIEN
P.O. Box A
Babylon, NY 11702
800/873-9444
COST: FREE

Familiar and unfamiliar varieties of tulips, daffodils, iris, ranunculus, geraniums, crocus (including rare Crocus Sativus, source of the ultra expensive spice, saffron), hyacinths, lilies, ground covers, ferns, and perennials are all available from Van Bourgondien in bulb or plant form. Discerning gardeners will appreciate the unusual specimens most of us have never seen or heard of before.

∞ SPORTING GOODS ∞

CAMPMOR
Box 999
Paramus, NJ 07653
800/525-4784
COST: FREE

You'll find everything needed for backpacking and camping in Campmor's catalog at discounted prices. This catalog is a must for outdoor lovers.

E & B DISCOUNT MARINE
201 Meadow Rd.
Edison, NJ 08818-3138
800/523-2926
COST: $5.00

Boating enthusiasts will find this catalog to be an absolute find. We found a SeaRanger ALN 200 Advanced Loran Navigator that retails for $1,395 priced at $499.99 Whether you're into boats powered by sails or high performance engines, you'll find all that you need from barbecues, fishing reels, water skis and nautical clothing to bilge pumps, anchors.and engines. Helms alee!

HOLABIRD SPORTS DISCOUNTERS
9008 Yellow Brick Rd, Rossville Industrial Park
Baltimore, MD 21237
301/687-6400
COST: FREE

There are hundreds of items to choose from at guaranteed lowest prices on tennis, squash, racquetball, badminton racquets. And don't forget the balls to go with each sport as well as the proper attire from shoes to clothing. You can buy stringing machines, ball machines, tennis nets, ball hoppers, court equipment, grips, vibration dampeners, eyeguards and even sports medical supplies. We found many of their everyday prices to be lower than sale prices at sporting good stores. Brand names include Head, Prince, Wilson, Fila, Slazenger, Ektelon, Adidas, Ellesse, Etonic, Keds, K-Swiss, Tretorn, Nike, New Balance, Estusa and Lobster. Their 48 hour shipping policy can come in handy if you need something fast .

OKUN BROTHERS SHOES
356 E. South St.
Kalamazoo, MI 49007
800/433-6344
COST: FREE

Save up to 35% off retail on shoes for the entire family through this catalog service. Okun Brothers Shoes handles brand name such as New Balance, K-Swiss, Dexter, Rocsports, Allen Edmonds, Reebok, Avia and many more. They can provide nearly every shoe size in widths from AAA to EEEE. They say, "Shop by mail, no traffic, no parking, no babysitters and no fuss!"

OVERTON'S
111 Red Banks Rd, Box 8228
Greenville, NC 27835
800/334-6541
COST: FREE

Overton's catalog is filled with everything, and we mean everything, you can think of related to water sports. Products such as boat seats, skis and accessories, vests, running lights, electronics and navigation equipment are all available at discounted prices.

∞ TELESCOPES & BINOCULARS ∞

MARDIRON OPTICS
37 Holloway St.
Malden, MA 02148
617/322-8733
COST: FREE

See the action explode with a pair of binoculars from Mardiron
Optics, a Steiner brand dealer. Steiner Binoculars have been used
by over 40 military forces worldwide and are rugged, yet
lightweight for concert goers. They also carry telescopes, astro-
nomy equipment and accessories.

Index – Stores

INDEX – CATALOGS

*PAGE NUMBERS FOR DISCOUNT COUPONS ARE IN *ITALICS*.

*Page numbers for Discount Coupons are in *ITALICS*.

*PAGE NUMBERS FOR DISCOUNT COUPONS ARE IN *ITALICS*.

BUYING RETAIL IS STUPID! DISCOUNT COUPON

THE 2NDS SHOP

10%
OFF PURCHASE

MAY NOT BE VALID ON CERTAIN ITEMS. EXPIRES 12-31-92

BUYING RETAIL IS STUPID! DISCOUNT COUPON

AAA EXTERNAL STAINLESS STEEL

10%
OFF PURCHASE

MAY NOT BE VALID ON CERTAIN ITEMS. EXPIRES 12-31-92

BUYING RETAIL IS STUPID! DISCOUNT COUPON

ABC POOL & PATIO

5%
OFF PURCHASE

MAY NOT BE VALID ON CERTAIN ITEMS. EXPIRES 12-31-92

BUYING RETAIL IS STUPID! DISCOUNT COUPON

ACTA FAST FRAME

10%
OFF PURCHASE

MAY NOT BE VALID ON CERTAIN ITEMS. EXPIRES 12-31-92

BUYING RETAIL IS STUPID!

18345 VENTURA BLVD., SUITE 314

TARZANA, CA 91356

BUYING RETAIL IS STUPID!

18345 VENTURA BLVD., SUITE 314

TARZANA, CA 91356

BUYING RETAIL IS STUPID!

18345 VENTURA BLVD., SUITE 314

TARZANA, CA 91356

BUYING RETAIL IS STUPID!

18345 VENTURA BLVD., SUITE 314

TARZANA, CA 91356

BUYING RETAIL IS STUPID! DISCOUNT COUPON

AL'S DISCOUNT FURNITURE

5%
OFF PURCHASE

MAY NOT BE VALID ON CERTAIN ITEMS. EXPIRES 12-31-92

BUYING RETAIL IS STUPID! DISCOUNT COUPON

ALEX LAZAR JEWELERS, INC.

5%
OFF PURCHASE

MAY NOT BE VALID ON CERTAIN ITEMS. EXPIRES 12-31-92

BUYING RETAIL IS STUPID! DISCOUNT COUPON

ALL REASONS TRAVEL

10%
DISCOUNT ON CRUISES ONLY

MAY NOT BE VALID ON CERTAIN ITEMS. EXPIRES 12-31-92

BUYING RETAIL IS STUPID! DISCOUNT COUPON

ALPERT'S BEDROOM CITY

5%
OFF PURCHASE

MAY NOT BE VALID ON SALE ITEMS. EXPIRES 12-31-92

BUYING RETAIL IS STUPID!

18345 VENTURA BLVD., SUITE 314

TARZANA, CA 91356

BUYING RETAIL IS STUPID!

18345 VENTURA BLVD., SUITE 314

TARZANA, CA 91356

BUYING RETAIL IS STUPID!

18345 VENTURA BLVD., SUITE 314

TARZANA, CA 91356

BUYING RETAIL IS STUPID!

18345 VENTURA BLVD., SUITE 314

TARZANA, CA 91356

BUYING RETAIL IS STUPID! DISCOUNT COUPON

AMERICAN SURPLUS TRADERS

10%
OFF PURCHASE

MAY NOT BE VALID ON CERTAIN ITEMS. EXPIRES 12-31-92

BUYING RETAIL IS STUPID! DISCOUNT COUPON

ASSOCIATED AUTO BODY

5%
OFF LABOR ONLY

EXPIRES 12-31-92

BUYING RETAIL IS STUPID! DISCOUNT COUPON

BAG LADY

5%
OFF PURCHASE

MAY NOT BE VALID ON CERTAIN ITEMS. EXPIRES 12-31-92

BUYING RETAIL IS STUPID! DISCOUNT COUPON

BATTERY DEPOT

FREE 40 PIECE SOCKET SET
WITH PURCHASE OF NEW BATTERY

MAY NOT BE VALID ON CERTAIN ITEMS. EXPIRES 12-31-92

BUYING RETAIL IS STUPID!

18345 VENTURA BLVD., SUITE 314

TARZANA, CA 91356

BUYING RETAIL IS STUPID!

18345 VENTURA BLVD., SUITE 314

TARZANA, CA 91356

BUYING RETAIL IS STUPID!

18345 VENTURA BLVD., SUITE 314

TARZANA, CA 91356

BUYING RETAIL IS STUPID!

18345 VENTURA BLVD., SUITE 314

TARZANA, CA 91356

BUYING RETAIL IS STUPID! DISCOUNT COUPON

BED BROKER

5%
OFF PURCHASE

MAY NOT BE VALID ON CERTAIN ITEMS. EXPIRES 12-31-92

BUYING RETAIL IS STUPID! DISCOUNT COUPON

BEDSPREAD CREATIONS

5%
OFF PURCHASE

MAY NOT BE VALID ON CERTAIN ITEMS. EXPIRES 12-31-92

BUYING RETAIL IS STUPID! DISCOUNT COUPON

BILLIARDS & BARSTOOLS

10%
OFF PURCHASE

MAY NOT BE VALID ON CERTAIN ITEMS. EXPIRES 12-31-92

BUYING RETAIL IS STUPID! DISCOUNT COUPON

BLIND FAITH

5%
OFF PURCHASE

MAY NOT BE VALID ON CERTAIN ITEMS. EXPIRES 12-31-92

BUYING RETAIL IS STUPID!

18345 VENTURA BLVD., SUITE 314

TARZANA, CA 91356

BUYING RETAIL IS STUPID!

18345 VENTURA BLVD., SUITE 314

TARZANA, CA 91356

BUYING RETAIL IS STUPID!

18345 VENTURA BLVD., SUITE 314

TARZANA, CA 91356

BUYING RETAIL IS STUPID!

18345 VENTURA BLVD., SUITE 314

TARZANA, CA 91356

BUYING RETAIL IS STUPID! DISCOUNT COUPON

BOOT HILL SQUARE DANCE APPAREL

5%

OFF PURCHASE

MAY NOT BE VALID ON CERTAIN ITEMS. EXPIRES 12-31-92

BUYING RETAIL IS STUPID! DISCOUNT COUPON

BOX CITY

10%

OFF PURCHASE

MAY NOT BE VALID ON CERTAIN ITEMS. EXPIRES 12-31-92

BUYING RETAIL IS STUPID! DISCOUNT COUPON

BRASS BED FACTORY

10%

OFF PURCHASE

MAY NOT BE VALID ON CERTAIN ITEMS. EXPIRES 12-31-92

BUYING RETAIL IS STUPID! DISCOUNT COUPON

BRIDAL DESIGNERS DIRECT

5%

OFF PURCHASE

MAY NOT BE VALID ON CERTAIN ITEMS. EXPIRES 12-31-92

BUYING RETAIL IS STUPID!

18345 VENTURA BLVD., SUITE 314
TARZANA, CA 91356

BUYING RETAIL IS STUPID!

18345 VENTURA BLVD., SUITE 314
TARZANA, CA 91356

BUYING RETAIL IS STUPID!

18345 VENTURA BLVD., SUITE 314
TARZANA, CA 91356

BUYING RETAIL IS STUPID!

18345 VENTURA BLVD., SUITE 314
TARZANA, CA 91356

BUYING RETAIL IS STUPID! DISCOUNT COUPON

BUKY'S

5%
OFF PURCHASE

MAY NOT BE VALID ON CERTAIN ITEMS. EXPIRES 12-31-92

BUYING RETAIL IS STUPID! DISCOUNT COUPON

CANDY STORE

10%
OFF PURCHASE

MAY NOT BE VALID ON CERTAIN ITEMS. EXPIRES 12-31-92

BUYING RETAIL IS STUPID! DISCOUNT COUPON

CARLSON'S T.V. & APPLIANCES

$10
OFF PURCHASE

MAY NOT BE VALID ON CERTAIN ITEMS. EXPIRES 12-31-92

BUYING RETAIL IS STUPID! DISCOUNT COUPON

CARPET COLLECTION

5%
OFF PURCHASE

MAY NOT BE VALID ON CERTAIN ITEMS. EXPIRES 12-31-92

BUYING RETAIL IS STUPID!

18345 VENTURA BLVD., SUITE 314

TARZANA, CA 91356

BUYING RETAIL IS STUPID!

18345 VENTURA BLVD., SUITE 314

TARZANA, CA 91356

BUYING RETAIL IS STUPID!

18345 VENTURA BLVD., SUITE 314

TARZANA, CA 91356

BUYING RETAIL IS STUPID!

18345 VENTURA BLVD., SUITE 314

TARZANA, CA 91356

BUYING RETAIL IS STUPID! DISCOUNT COUPON

CARPET MANOR

5%

OFF PURCHASE

MAY NOT BE VALID ON CERTAIN ITEMS. EXPIRES 12-31-92

BUYING RETAIL IS STUPID! DISCOUNT COUPON

CELLULAR WHOLESALERS

5%

OFF PURCHASE

MAY NOT BE VALID ON CERTAIN ITEMS. EXPIRES 12-31-92

BUYING RETAIL IS STUPID! DISCOUNT COUPON

CHEAP FRILLS

5%

OFF PURCHASE

MAY NOT BE VALID ON CERTAIN ITEMS. EXPIRES 12-31-92

BUYING RETAIL IS STUPID! DISCOUNT COUPON

COPIER LAND

10%

OFF PURCHASE

MAY NOT BE VALID ON CERTAIN ITEMS. EXPIRES 12-31-92

BUYING RETAIL IS STUPID!

18345 VENTURA BLVD., SUITE 314
TARZANA, CA 91356

BUYING RETAIL IS STUPID!

18345 VENTURA BLVD., SUITE 314
TARZANA, CA 91356

BUYING RETAIL IS STUPID!

18345 VENTURA BLVD., SUITE 314
TARZANA, CA 91356

BUYING RETAIL IS STUPID!

18345 VENTURA BLVD., SUITE 314
TARZANA, CA 91356

BUYING RETAIL IS STUPID! DISCOUNT COUPON

COUNTRY LINENS

10%
OFF PURCHASE

MAY NOT BE VALID ON CERTAIN ITEMS. EXPIRES 12-31-92

BUYING RETAIL IS STUPID! DISCOUNT COUPON

CRITERIUM CYCLE SPORT

10%
OFF PURCHASE

MAY NOT BE VALID ON CERTAIN ITEMS. EXPIRES 12-31-92

BUYING RETAIL IS STUPID! DISCOUNT COUPON

CROWN DISCOUNT BEAUTY SUPPLY

10%
OFF PURCHASE

MAY NOT BE VALID ON CERTAIN ITEMS. EXPIRES 12-31-92

BUYING RETAIL IS STUPID! DISCOUNT COUPON

CS x 2

5%
OFF PURCHASE

MAY NOT BE VALID ON CERTAIN ITEMS. EXPIRES 12-31-92

BUYING RETAIL IS STUPID!

18345 VENTURA BLVD., SUITE 314

TARZANA, CA 91356

BUYING RETAIL IS STUPID!

18345 VENTURA BLVD., SUITE 314

TARZANA, CA 91356

BUYING RETAIL IS STUPID!

18345 VENTURA BLVD., SUITE 314

TARZANA, CA 91356

BUYING RETAIL IS STUPID!

18345 VENTURA BLVD., SUITE 314

TARZANA, CA 91356

BUYING RETAIL IS STUPID! DISCOUNT COUPON

D 'N J BEARS & DOLLS

10%
OFF PURCHASE

MAY NOT BE VALID ON CERTAIN ITEMS. EXPIRES 12-31-92

BUYING RETAIL IS STUPID! DISCOUNT COUPON

DISCOUNT TRAIN WAREHOUSE

5%
OFF PURCHASE

MAY NOT BE VALID ON CERTAIN ITEMS. EXPIRES 12-31-92

BUYING RETAIL IS STUPID! DISCOUNT COUPON

DONNA'S PLACE

10%
OFF PURCHASE

MAY NOT BE VALID ON CERTAIN ITEMS. EXPIRES 12-31-92

BUYING RETAIL IS STUPID! DISCOUNT COUPON

DR. M. FRIEDMAN AND ASSOCIATES

$19
EYE EXAM

EXPIRES 12-31-92

BUYING RETAIL IS STUPID!

18345 VENTURA BLVD., SUITE 314

TARZANA, CA 91356

BUYING RETAIL IS STUPID!

18345 VENTURA BLVD., SUITE 314

TARZANA, CA 91356

BUYING RETAIL IS STUPID!

18345 VENTURA BLVD., SUITE 314

TARZANA, CA 91356

BUYING RETAIL IS STUPID!

18345 VENTURA BLVD., SUITE 314

TARZANA, CA 91356

BUYING RETAIL IS STUPID! DISCOUNT COUPON

DR. THOMAS KUTROSKY

5%

OFF PURCHASE OF LENSES, FRAMES & CONTACTS

EXPIRES 12-31-92

BUYING RETAIL IS STUPID! DISCOUNT COUPON

ENCINO DISCOUNT PATIO AND BABY FURNITURE.

5%

OFF PURCHASE

MAY NOT BE VALID ON CERTAIN ITEMS. EXPIRES 12-31-92

BUYING RETAIL IS STUPID! DISCOUNT COUPON

ESPANORE LTD.

5%

OFF PURCHASE

MAY NOT BE VALID ON CERTAIN ITEMS. EXPIRES 12-31-92

BUYING RETAIL IS STUPID! DISCOUNT COUPON

EVER-RICH BEDDING

10%

OFF PURCHASE OF $100 OR MORE ONLY

MAY NOT BE VALID ON CERTAIN ITEMS. EXPIRES 12-31-92

BUYING RETAIL IS STUPID!

18345 VENTURA BLVD., SUITE 314
TARZANA, CA 91356

BUYING RETAIL IS STUPID!

18345 VENTURA BLVD., SUITE 314
TARZANA, CA 91356

BUYING RETAIL IS STUPID!

18345 VENTURA BLVD., SUITE 314
TARZANA, CA 91356

BUYING RETAIL IS STUPID!

18345 VENTURA BLVD., SUITE 314
TARZANA, CA 91356

BUYING RETAIL IS STUPID! DISCOUNT COUPON

FRAMING OUTLET

10%
OFF PURCHASE

MAY NOT BE VALID ON CERTAIN ITEMS. EXPIRES 12-31-92

BUYING RETAIL IS STUPID! DISCOUNT COUPON

GLAMOUR UNIFORM SHOP

10%
OFF PURCHASE

MAY NOT BE VALID ON CERTAIN ITEMS. EXPIRES 12-31-92

BUYING RETAIL IS STUPID! DISCOUNT COUPON

GOLDEN FLEECE DESIGNS INC.

10%
OFF PURCHASE

MAY NOT BE VALID ON CERTAIN ITEMS. EXPIRES 12-31-92

BUYING RETAIL IS STUPID! DISCOUNT COUPON

THE GREAT GATSBY

10%
OFF PURCHASE

MAY NOT BE VALID ON CERTAIN ITEMS. EXPIRES 12-31-92

BUYING RETAIL IS STUPID!

18345 VENTURA BLVD., SUITE 314

TARZANA, CA 91356

BUYING RETAIL IS STUPID!

18345 VENTURA BLVD., SUITE 314

TARZANA, CA 91356

BUYING RETAIL IS STUPID!

18345 VENTURA BLVD., SUITE 314

TARZANA, CA 91356

BUYING RETAIL IS STUPID!

18345 VENTURA BLVD., SUITE 314

TARZANA, CA 91356

BUYING RETAIL IS STUPID! DISCOUNT COUPON

H. LEWIS REX FINE ART

10%
OFF PURCHASE

MAY NOT BE VALID ON CERTAIN ITEMS. EXPIRES 12-31-92

BUYING RETAIL IS STUPID! DISCOUNT COUPON

HANSEN WHOLESALE FAN CO.

5%
OFF PURCHASE

MAY NOT BE VALID ON CERTAIN ITEMS. EXPIRES 12-31-92

BUYING RETAIL IS STUPID! DISCOUNT COUPON

HARTMAN JEWELRY & GIFTS

10%
OFF PURCHASE

MAY NOT BE VALID ON CERTAIN ITEMS. EXPIRES 12-31-92

BUYING RETAIL IS STUPID! DISCOUNT COUPON

HIAWATHA HOMES

10%
OFF PURCHASE

MAY NOT BE VALID ON CERTAIN ITEMS. EXPIRES 12-31-92

BUYING RETAIL IS STUPID!

18345 VENTURA BLVD., SUITE 314

TARZANA, CA 91356

BUYING RETAIL IS STUPID!

18345 VENTURA BLVD., SUITE 314

TARZANA, CA 91356

BUYING RETAIL IS STUPID!

18345 VENTURA BLVD., SUITE 314

TARZANA, CA 91356

BUYING RETAIL IS STUPID!

18345 VENTURA BLVD., SUITE 314

TARZANA, CA 91356

BUYING RETAIL IS STUPID! DISCOUNT COUPON

HOME COMFORT CENTER

10%
OFF PURCHASE

MAY NOT BE VALID ON CERTAIN ITEMS. EXPIRES 12-31-92

BUYING RETAIL IS STUPID! DISCOUNT COUPON

HOOPER CAMERA AND VIDEO CENTERS

5%
OFF PURCHASE

MAY NOT BE VALID ON CERTAIN ITEMS. EXPIRES 12-31-92

BUYING RETAIL IS STUPID! DISCOUNT COUPON

IN-A-FLOOR SAFE COMPANY

10%
OFF PURCHASE

MAY NOT BE VALID ON CERTAIN ITEMS. EXPIRES 12-31-92

BUYING RETAIL IS STUPID! DISCOUNT COUPON

ITC ELECTRONICS

5%
OFF PURCHASE

MAY NOT BE VALID ON CERTAIN ITEMS. EXPIRES 12-31-92

BUYING RETAIL IS STUPID!

18345 VENTURA BLVD., SUITE 314
TARZANA, CA 91356

BUYING RETAIL IS STUPID!

18345 VENTURA BLVD., SUITE 314
TARZANA, CA 91356

BUYING RETAIL IS STUPID!

18345 VENTURA BLVD., SUITE 314
TARZANA, CA 91356

BUYING RETAIL IS STUPID!

18345 VENTURA BLVD., SUITE 314
TARZANA, CA 91356

BUYING RETAIL IS STUPID! DISCOUNT COUPON

JACK SPERLING BEAUTY SUPPLY

10%

OFF PURCHASE

MAY NOT BE VALID ON CERTAIN ITEMS. EXPIRES 12-31-92

BUYING RETAIL IS STUPID! DISCOUNT COUPON

KAGAN SURPLUS SALES

5% OR 10%

5% OFF PURCHASE UNDER $100, 10% IF OVER $100

MAY NOT BE VALID ON CERTAIN ITEMS. EXPIRES 12-31-92

BUYING RETAIL IS STUPID! DISCOUNT COUPON

KIM-E'S FLOWERS

10%

OFF PURCHASE

EXPIRES 12-31-92

BUYING RETAIL IS STUPID! DISCOUNT COUPON

KITCHEN & BATH CENTER

5%

OFF PURCHASE

MAY NOT BE VALID ON CERTAIN ITEMS. EXPIRES 12-31-92

BUYING RETAIL IS STUPID!

18345 VENTURA BLVD., SUITE 314

TARZANA, CA 91356

BUYING RETAIL IS STUPID!

18345 VENTURA BLVD., SUITE 314

TARZANA, CA 91356

BUYING RETAIL IS STUPID!

18345 VENTURA BLVD., SUITE 314

TARZANA, CA 91356

BUYING RETAIL IS STUPID!

18345 VENTURA BLVD., SUITE 314

TARZANA, CA 91356

BUYING RETAIL IS STUPID! DISCOUNT COUPON

THE KITCHEN & BATH WAREHOUSE

5%
OFF PURCHASE

MAY NOT BE VALID ON CERTAIN ITEMS. EXPIRES 12-31-92

BUYING RETAIL IS STUPID! DISCOUNT COUPON

KLEIN'S BEAD BOX

5%
OFF PURCHASE

MAY NOT BE VALID ON CERTAIN ITEMS. EXPIRES 12-31-92

BUYING RETAIL IS STUPID! DISCOUNT COUPON

LEE LAWNMOWER

10%
OFF PURCHASE

MAY NOT BE VALID ON CERTAIN ITEMS. EXPIRES 12-31-92

BUYING RETAIL IS STUPID! DISCOUNT COUPON

LEONARDO'S ITALIAN FASHION

10%
OFF PURCHASE

MAY NOT BE VALID ON CERTAIN ITEMS. EXPIRES 12-31-92

BUYING RETAIL IS STUPID!

18345 VENTURA BLVD., SUITE 314

TARZANA, CA 91356

BUYING RETAIL IS STUPID!

18345 VENTURA BLVD., SUITE 314

TARZANA, CA 91356

BUYING RETAIL IS STUPID!

18345 VENTURA BLVD., SUITE 314

TARZANA, CA 91356

BUYING RETAIL IS STUPID!

18345 VENTURA BLVD., SUITE 314

TARZANA, CA 91356

BUYING RETAIL IS STUPID! DISCOUNT COUPON

LEONORE'S FUR OUTLET

10%
OFF PURCHASE

MAY NOT BE VALID ON CERTAIN ITEMS. EXPIRES 12-31-92

BUYING RETAIL IS STUPID! DISCOUNT COUPON

THE LIQUIDATION CLUB

10% OFF PURCHASE PLUS
FREE MEMBERSHIP
MAY NOT BE VALID ON CERTAIN ITEMS. EXPIRES 12-31-92

BUYING RETAIL IS STUPID! DISCOUNT COUPON

LORD OF THE RINGS

5%
OFF PURCHASE

MAY NOT BE VALID ON CERTAIN ITEMS. EXPIRES 12-31-92

BUYING RETAIL IS STUPID! DISCOUNT COUPON

MARBLE PRODUCTS OF FULLERTON

5%
OFF PURCHASE

MAY NOT BE VALID ON CERTAIN ITEMS. EXPIRES 12-31-92

BUYING RETAIL IS STUPID!

18345 VENTURA BLVD., SUITE 314

TARZANA, CA 91356

BUYING RETAIL IS STUPID!

18345 VENTURA BLVD., SUITE 314

TARZANA, CA 91356

BUYING RETAIL IS STUPID!

18345 VENTURA BLVD., SUITE 314

TARZANA, CA 91356

BUYING RETAIL IS STUPID!

18345 VENTURA BLVD., SUITE 314

TARZANA, CA 91356

BUYING RETAIL IS STUPID! DISCOUNT COUPON

MEDCHOICE WAREHOUSE CLUB

1 DAY PASS

MAY NOT BE VALID ON CERTAIN ITEMS. EXPIRES 12-31-92

BUYING RETAIL IS STUPID! DISCOUNT COUPON

MIJANOU'S SILK DESIGNS

5%
OFF PURCHASE

MAY NOT BE VALID ON CERTAIN ITEMS. EXPIRES 12-31-92

BUYING RETAIL IS STUPID! DISCOUNT COUPON

MY FAIR LADY

10%
OFF PURCHASE
NOT VALID FOR PARKING LOT SALES OR BLOW-OUT ROOM ITEMS.
EXPIRES 12-31-92

BUYING RETAIL IS STUPID! DISCOUNT COUPON

NAT DIAMOND EMPIRE FURNITURE

10%
OFF PURCHASE

MAY NOT BE VALID ON CERTAIN ITEMS. EXPIRES 12-31-92

BUYING RETAIL IS STUPID!

18345 VENTURA BLVD., SUITE 314

TARZANA, CA 91356

BUYING RETAIL IS STUPID!

18345 VENTURA BLVD., SUITE 314

TARZANA, CA 91356

BUYING RETAIL IS STUPID!

18345 VENTURA BLVD., SUITE 314

TARZANA, CA 91356

BUYING RETAIL IS STUPID!

18345 VENTURA BLVD., SUITE 314

TARZANA, CA 91356

BUYING RETAIL IS STUPID! DISCOUNT COUPON

OLYMPIA HEALTH FITNESS SUPERSTORE

5%
OFF PURCHASE

MAY NOT BE VALID ON CERTAIN ITEMS. EXPIRES 12-31-92

BUYING RETAIL IS STUPID! DISCOUNT COUPON

ORIENTAL RUG EXCHANGE

5%
OFF PURCHASE

MAY NOT BE VALID ON CERTAIN ITEMS. EXPIRES 12-31-92

BUYING RETAIL IS STUPID! DISCOUNT COUPON

P X DRUGS NO. 2
10%
OFF PURCHASE–PERSCRIPTIONS NOT INCLUDED

EXPIRES 12-31-92

BUYING RETAIL IS STUPID! DISCOUNT COUPON

PAR PAINT COMPANY INC.

5%
OFF PURCHASE

MAY NOT BE VALID ON CERTAIN ITEMS. EXPIRES 12-31-92

BUYING RETAIL IS STUPID!

18345 VENTURA BLVD., SUITE 314

TARZANA, CA 91356

BUYING RETAIL IS STUPID!

18345 VENTURA BLVD., SUITE 314

TARZANA, CA 91356

BUYING RETAIL IS STUPID!

18345 VENTURA BLVD., SUITE 314

TARZANA, CA 91356

BUYING RETAIL IS STUPID!

18345 VENTURA BLVD., SUITE 314

TARZANA, CA 91356

BUYING RETAIL IS STUPID! DISCOUNT COUPON

PARTY CORNER DISCOUNT CENTER

10%
OFF PURCHASE

MAY NOT BE VALID ON CERTAIN ITEMS. EXPIRES 12-31-92

BUYING RETAIL IS STUPID! DISCOUNT COUPON

POTTERY & FLORAL WORLD

10%
OFF PURCHASE

MAY NOT BE VALID ON CERTAIN ITEMS. EXPIRES 12-31-92

BUYING RETAIL IS STUPID! DISCOUNT COUPON

RAY'S TAILORING & EUROPEAN FASHION CENTER

10%
OFF PURCHASE

MAY NOT BE VALID ON CERTAIN ITEMS. EXPIRES 12-31-92

BUYING RETAIL IS STUPID! DISCOUNT COUPON

RED BARN FEED & SADDLERY INC.

5%
OFF PURCHASE

MAY NOT BE VALID ON CERTAIN ITEMS. EXPIRES 12-31-92

BUYING RETAIL IS STUPID!

18345 VENTURA BLVD., SUITE 314
TARZANA, CA 91356

BUYING RETAIL IS STUPID!

18345 VENTURA BLVD., SUITE 314
TARZANA, CA 91356

BUYING RETAIL IS STUPID!

18345 VENTURA BLVD., SUITE 314
TARZANA, CA 91356

BUYING RETAIL IS STUPID!

18345 VENTURA BLVD., SUITE 314
TARZANA, CA 91356

BUYING RETAIL IS STUPID! DISCOUNT COUPON

ROSCOE FURNITURE LIQUIDATORS

5%
OFF PURCHASE

MAY NOT BE VALID ON CERTAIN ITEMS. EXPIRES 12-31-92

BUYING RETAIL IS STUPID! DISCOUNT COUPON

THE ROUNDHOUSE TRAIN STORE

10%
OFF PURCHASE

MAY NOT BE VALID ON CERTAIN ITEMS. EXPIRES 12-31-92

BUYING RETAIL IS STUPID! DISCOUNT COUPON

SANDLER OF THE VALLEY

10%
OFF PURCHASE

MAY NOT BE VALID ON CERTAIN ITEMS. EXPIRES 12-31-92

BUYING RETAIL IS STUPID! DISCOUNT COUPON

SECOND TIME AROUND RECORDS

5%
OFF PURCHASE

MAY NOT BE VALID ON CERTAIN ITEMS. EXPIRES 12-31-92

BUYING RETAIL IS STUPID!

18345 VENTURA BLVD., SUITE 314

TARZANA, CA 91356

BUYING RETAIL IS STUPID!

18345 VENTURA BLVD., SUITE 314

TARZANA, CA 91356

BUYING RETAIL IS STUPID!

18345 VENTURA BLVD., SUITE 314

TARZANA, CA 91356

BUYING RETAIL IS STUPID!

18345 VENTURA BLVD., SUITE 314

TARZANA, CA 91356

BUYING RETAIL IS STUPID! DISCOUNT COUPON

SECURITY WAREHOUSE

5%
OFF PURCHASE

MAY NOT BE VALID ON CERTAIN ITEMS. EXPIRES 12-31-92

BUYING RETAIL IS STUPID! DISCOUNT COUPON

SHIRLEY'S DISCOUNT SHOES

10%
OFF PURCHASE

MAY NOT BE VALID ON CERTAIN ITEMS. EXPIRES 12-31-92

BUYING RETAIL IS STUPID! DISCOUNT COUPON

SUPERIOR WINDOW COVERING, INC.

10%
OFF PURCHASE

MAY NOT BE VALID ON CERTAIN ITEMS. EXPIRES 12-31-92

BUYING RETAIL IS STUPID! DISCOUNT COUPON

SURPLUS CITY RETAIL CO.

25%
OFF PURCHASE OF ANY NEW BOOTS

NOT VALID FOR BOOTS ON SALE. EXPIRES 12-31-92

BUYING RETAIL IS STUPID!

18345 VENTURA BLVD., SUITE 314

TARZANA, CA 91356

BUYING RETAIL IS STUPID!

18345 VENTURA BLVD., SUITE 314

TARZANA, CA 91356

BUYING RETAIL IS STUPID!

18345 VENTURA BLVD., SUITE 314

TARZANA, CA 91356

BUYING RETAIL IS STUPID!

18345 VENTURA BLVD., SUITE 314

TARZANA, CA 91356

BUYING RETAIL IS STUPID! DISCOUNT COUPON

T.V.WORLD DISCOUNT SALES & SERV.

10%
OFF PURCHASE

MAY NOT BE VALID ON CERTAIN ITEMS. EXPIRES 12-31-92

BUYING RETAIL IS STUPID! DISCOUNT COUPON

THEL'S CLOTHES

5%
OFF PURCHASE

MAY NOT BE VALID ON CERTAIN ITEMS. EXPIRES 12-31-92

BUYING RETAIL IS STUPID! DISCOUNT COUPON

TILE, MARBLE & GRANITE WAREHOUSE

10%
OFF PURCHASE

MAY NOT BE VALID ON CERTAIN ITEMS. EXPIRES 12-31-92

BUYING RETAIL IS STUPID! DISCOUNT COUPON

TILECLUB

10%
OFF PURCHASE

MAY NOT BE VALID ON CERTAIN ITEMS. EXPIRES 12-31-92

BUYING RETAIL IS STUPID!

18345 VENTURA BLVD., SUITE 314

TARZANA, CA 91356

BUYING RETAIL IS STUPID!

18345 VENTURA BLVD., SUITE 314

TARZANA, CA 91356

BUYING RETAIL IS STUPID!

18345 VENTURA BLVD., SUITE 314

TARZANA, CA 91356

BUYING RETAIL IS STUPID!

18345 VENTURA BLVD., SUITE 314

TARZANA, CA 91356

BUYING RETAIL IS STUPID! DISCOUNT COUPON

UNIQUE SECURITY ALARM ASSOC.

15%
OFF PURCHASE

MAY NOT BE VALID ON CERTAIN ITEMS. EXPIRES 12-31-92

BUYING RETAIL IS STUPID! DISCOUNT COUPON

VALLEY INDOOR SWAPMEET

FREE ADMISSION
POMONA, VAN NUYS OR WOODLAND HILLS

MAY NOT BE VALID ON CERTAIN ITEMS. EXPIRES 12-31-92

BUYING RETAIL IS STUPID! DISCOUNT COUPON

VALLEY MATTRESS & BUNK BED CTR.

5%
OFF PURCHASE

MAY NOT BE VALID ON CERTAIN ITEMS. EXPIRES 12-31-92

BUYING RETAIL IS STUPID! DISCOUNT COUPON

VAN DE CAMPER

5% OR 10%
5% OFF VAN SUPPLIES OR 10% OFF CATALOG ORDERS

MAY NOT BE VALID ON CERTAIN ITEMS. EXPIRES 12-31-92

BUYING RETAIL IS STUPID!

18345 VENTURA BLVD., SUITE 314
TARZANA, CA 91356

BUYING RETAIL IS STUPID!

18345 VENTURA BLVD., SUITE 314
TARZANA, CA 91356

BUYING RETAIL IS STUPID!

18345 VENTURA BLVD., SUITE 314
TARZANA, CA 91356

BUYING RETAIL IS STUPID!

18345 VENTURA BLVD., SUITE 314
TARZANA, CA 91356

BUYING RETAIL IS STUPID! DISCOUNT COUPON

WEAR ART THOU
10%
OFF PURCHASE

MAY NOT BE VALID ON CERTAIN ITEMS. EXPIRES 12-31-92

BUYING RETAIL IS STUPID! DISCOUNT COUPON

WEBSTER'S ANTIQUE IMPORTERS
10%
OFF PURCHASE

MAY NOT BE VALID ON CERTAIN ITEMS. EXPIRES 12-31-92

BUYING RETAIL IS STUPID! DISCOUNT COUPON

WHOLESALE PRINTING FACTORY 1
5%
OFF PURCHASE

MAY NOT BE VALID ON CERTAIN ITEMS. EXPIRES 12-31-92

BUYING RETAIL IS STUPID! DISCOUNT COUPON

WORLD OF PLANTS AND GIFTS
10%
OFF PURCHASE

MAY NOT BE VALID ON CERTAIN ITEMS. EXPIRES 12-31-92

BUYING RETAIL IS STUPID!

18345 VENTURA BLVD., SUITE 314
TARZANA, CA 91356

BUYING RETAIL IS STUPID!

18345 VENTURA BLVD., SUITE 314
TARZANA, CA 91356

BUYING RETAIL IS STUPID!

18345 VENTURA BLVD., SUITE 314
TARZANA, CA 91356

BUYING RETAIL IS STUPID!

18345 VENTURA BLVD., SUITE 314
TARZANA, CA 91356

TO ORDER

BUYING RETAIL IS STUPID!

Please enclose a check or money order for $19.95* per book (shipping and handling already included). Checks or money orders should be made payable to BUYING RETAIL IS STUPID!

B

_____
NAME

_____ _____
ADDRESS   APT. #

_____ _____ _____
CITY   STATE   ZIP CODE

_____
PHONE NUMBER (PLEASE INCLUDE AREA CODE)

Please send _____ copies of **BUYING RETAIL IS STUPID!**
Enclosed is my check or money order for $ _____

MAIL TO:

BUYING RETAIL IS STUPID!
18345 VENTURA BOULEVARD, SUITE 314B
TARZANA, CA 91356

THANK YOU FOR YOUR ORDER.

* For special pricing on orders of 12 or more books please call 818/708-1245. Case pricing (48 books) is also available.

TO ORDER

BUYING RETAIL IS STUPID!

Please enclose a check or money order for $19.95* per book (shipping and handling already included). Checks or money orders should be made payable to BUYING RETAIL IS STUPID!

B

_____

NAME

_____

ADDRESS   APT. #

_____

CITY   STATE   ZIP CODE

_____

PHONE NUMBER (PLEASE INCLUDE AREA CODE)

Please send _____ copies of **BUYING RETAIL IS STUPID!**

Enclosed is my check or money order for $ _____

MAIL TO:

BUYING RETAIL IS STUPID!
18345 VENTURA BOULEVARD, SUITE 314B
TARZANA, CA 91356

THANK YOU FOR YOUR ORDER.

* For special pricing on orders of 12 or more books please call 818/708-1245. Case pricing (48 books) is also available.

TO ORDER
BUYING RETAIL IS STUPID!

Please enclose a check or money order for $19.95* per book (shipping and handling already included). Checks or money orders should be made payable to BUYING RETAIL IS STUPID!

B

_____

NAME

_____

ADDRESS   APT. #

_____

CITY   STATE   ZIP CODE

_____

PHONE NUMBER (PLEASE INCLUDE AREA CODE)

Please send _____ copies of **BUYING RETAIL IS STUPID!**

Enclosed is my check or money order for $ _____

MAIL TO:
BUYING RETAIL IS STUPID!
18345 VENTURA BOULEVARD, SUITE 314B
TARZANA, CA 91356

THANK YOU FOR YOUR ORDER.

* For special pricing on orders of 12 or more books please call 818/708-1245. Case pricing (48 books) is also available.

REVERSE SIDE OF ORDER BLANK

∞ Notes & Favorite Stores ∞

∞ NOTES & FAVORITE STORES ∞

∞ NOTES & FAVORITE STORES ∞